Violence in Colombia

The Contemporary Crisis in Historical Perspective

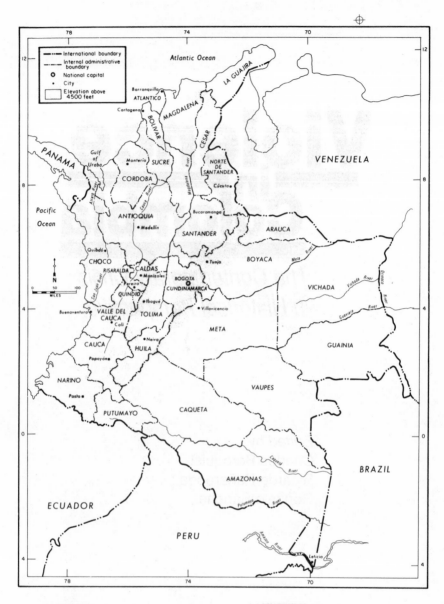

Map of Colombia, from Howard I. Blutstein and Thomas E. Weil, *Area Handbook of Colombia*, 3d ed. (Washington, DC: Government Printing Office, 1977).

Violence in Colombia

The Contemporary Crisis in Historical Perspective

Edited by
Charles Bergquist
Ricardo Peñaranda
Gonzalo Sánchez

A Scholarly Resources Inc. Imprint
Wilmington, Delaware

The paper used in this publication meets the minimum requirements of the American National Standard for permanence of paper for printed library materials, Z39.48, 1984.

Scholarly Resources Inc.
104 Greenhill Avenue
Wilmington, DE 19805-1897

Library of Congress Cataloging-in-Publication Data

Violence in Colombia : the contemporary crisis in historical
   perspective / edited by Charles Bergquist, Ricardo Peñaranda,
   Gonzalo Sánchez .
       p. cm. — (Latin American silhouettes)
       Includes index.
       ISBN 0-8420-2369-0 (cloth). — ISBN 0-8420-2376-3 (pbk.)
       1. Violence—Colombia—History—20th century. 2. Colombia—
   Politics and government—20th century. I. Bergquist, Charles W.
   II. Peñaranda, Ricardo. III. Sánchez G., Gonzalo. IV. Series.
   HN310.29V579   1992
   303.6'09861—dc20
                                                        91-22992
                                                        CIP

Contents

Part III The Contemporary Crisis

Preface

This book had its origins in Bogotá in 1985 at the first international symposium on the Violence in Colombia where some of its essays were presented in preliminary form. Funded by the Department of History of the National University and the Centro Gaitán in Bogotá, the symposium brought together specialists from Colombia, North America, and Europe to explore the relationship between the phenomenon known as the Violence (1946–1966) and the violent contemporary crisis enveloping the country. Some of the essays were published later in Spanish in *Pasado y presente de la Violencia en Colombia* (Bogotá, 1986), edited by Gonzalo Sánchez and Ricardo Peñaranda. *Pasado y presente* sought to broaden readers' understanding of the crisis facing Colombia through an exploration of its historical antecedents.

In this volume, we have developed the historical perspective of *Pasado y presente* further and expanded and updated its analysis of the current crisis for English readers. *Violence in Colombia* incorporates, in revised form, some of the work previously published in *Pasado y presente* (Chapters 3, 4, 6, and 8), but primarily, it is composed of new material. Some of the new essays were published in Spanish after 1986 (Chapters 7, 9, and 12), and some were prepared especially for this volume (Chapters 1, 2, 5, 10, 11, 13, and 14). Chapters 5 through 14 were translated into English for this book. Their translation was, as translation always is, a creative, challenging, and arduous process. With two exceptions, these chapters were translated from the Spanish by Elizabeth Glick. The translator for Chapter 6 was Richard Stoller, and Susan Brooks translated Chapter 10 from the French.

Charles Bergquist revised the translations, put together the chronology and glossary, and wrote the introductions to each essay. Throughout this process the editorial staff at Scholarly Resources, particularly Richard Hopper, and the editors of this series, William Beezley and Judith Ewell, provided much-needed guidance and assistance. We wish to thank all of the institutions and people who made this volume possible; we ourselves are responsible for its final content.

CB, RP, GS
July 1991

Chronology*

1810–24   —Colombia's war for independence. Present-day Colombia emerged from Spanish colonialism as part of the Republic of New Granada, which included the modern nations of Venezuela, Ecuador, and Panama. Venezuela and Ecuador separated in 1830; Panama in 1903.

ca. 1850   —Liberal and Conservative parties crystalize following intermittent civil wars, fought over, among other issues, the pace and degree of liberal reform.

1863   —Constitution of Rionegro promulgated following victory of Liberals in the civil war of 1860–1863. Under this ultraliberal document, the Liberal party dominates national government until 1885.

1886   —Promulgation of the conservative constitution that is still in effect today. Follows victory of an alliance of dissident Liberals and Conservatives in the civil war of 1885 and ushers in period of Conservative hegemony that lasts until 1930.

1886–1900   —Period of Conservative governments known as the Regeneration, in which Liberal participation in government is severely limited. Pursuit of economic policies (particularly a regime of unbacked paper currency) that were anathema to orthodox Liberals. Beginning of ascent of coffee economy.

*This chronology focuses on twentieth-century political history, although it notes as well some of the economic and social developments emphasized in the text. Acronyms are explained in the Glossary at the end of the volume.

1899–1902   —War of the Thousand Days, the greatest of Latin America's nineteenth-century civil wars. Colombia's most intense period of violence: 100,000 estimated deaths in a total population of 4 million. Liberals revolt within context of sharp decline in world coffee prices. Struggle degenerates into guerrilla warfare, presaging forms of violence in later twentieth century. War intensifies partisan loyalties.

1903   —Separation of Panama. A consequence of the War of the Thousand Days, it is assured by U.S. intervention.

1904–09   —Quinquennium of dictator Rafael Reyes. A pragmatic Conservative, Reyes integrates Liberals into his government and begins economic reconstruction following principles of liberal economic orthodoxy.

1910   —Constitutional reform. Paper money banned, and minority party representation in government guaranteed.

1910–30   —Period of bipartisan consensus regimes dominated by Conservatives. Orthodox liberal economic policy and dramatic rise in coffee production and prices bring unprecedented economic growth.

1922–28   —"Dance of the Millions." Coffee expansion, U.S. indemnification for its role in Panama's separation, and sharp increase in U.S. investment in and public loans to Colombia help fuel rapid economic growth. Tight labor markets favor worker mobilization. In parts of coffee zone, agrarian struggle begins that will continue into 1930s.

1928   —Government massacre of striking banana workers in United Fruit enclave near Santa Marta leaves estimated one thousand dead and helps discredit Conservative regime.

1930   —Communist party founded. Radical organizing drive begins in cities and countryside.

1930–46   —Liberal Republic. Conservative split in election of 1930 brings the Liberal party to power, initiating period of social reform, economic development (especially in industry), and growing tension between the parties.

1930–34 —Government of moderate Liberal Enrique Olaya Herrera. Partisan violence breaks out in parts of countryside as Liberals remove Conservatives from political sinecures. Labor legislation grants workers fundamental organizational rights and begins process of incorporating labor into the state under auspices of the Liberal party.

1933 —Liberal dissident Jorge Eliécer Gaitán forms a third party, the Unión Nacional Izquierdista Revolucionaria (UNIR), and begins to champion the cause of urban and rural workers.

1934–38 —Reformist government of Alfonso López Pumarejo. Gaitán and Communist party ally themselves with the regime. Constitutional reform of 1936 defines social responsibilities of property owners and paves way for agrarian reform, which diffuses rural unrest by legalizing status quo and threatening fundamental reform within ten years. Conservatives, led by Laureano Gómez, abstain from elections and vociferously denounce reforms as partisan, anti-Catholic, and socialistic.

1938–42 —Government of Liberal moderate Eduardo Santos under which pace of reforms slows. Regime cooperates closely in Allied war effort.

1942–45 —Second administration of Alfonso López Pumarejo. Social reforms halted or reversed. Agrarian legislation favored big landowners and labor laws sought greater state control over unions. Military coup attempted against government.

1945–46 —Transitional government of Liberal moderate Alberto Lleras Camargo, which follows renunciation of López Pumarejo. Repression of Communist-led Magdalena River workers' union shatters strength of organized labor. Liberal party splits in presidential election of 1946 when Gaitán runs against official candidate, and

Conservative moderate Mariano Ospina Pérez wins
with a plurality.

1946–66   —Period conventionally defined as the Violence.

1946–53   —Conservative party controls government. The Violence
begins during presidency of Ospina Pérez (1946–1950)
as Conservatives replace and persecute Liberals in many
locales. Virtual civil war ensues following assassination
of Gaitán on April 9, 1948. Crowds attack Presidential
Palace and devastate downtown Bogotá. Liberal
insurrection then spreads to provincial capitals and
countryside. Liberals withdraw from government and
abstain from presidential election of 1950, which brings
to power ultraconservative Laureano Gómez. Gómez's
government (1950–1953) unleashes terror to quell
Liberal insurgency/resistance. Government falls from
power in military coup in 1953.
    Whole period one of economic growth paced by
high coffee prices. Restrictive legislation further limits
power of organized labor. Repression of communism
at home coupled with sending of troops to Korea.

1953–57   —Military government of Gustavo Rojas Pinilla, who
seeks pacification of and promulgates amnesty for
Liberal guerrillas. He also fosters major public works
projects and attempts to build a political force loyal to
his person. Initial success at pacification turns sour by
1955. Coffee prices decline that same year. Violent
repression of public protests against regime. Traditional
party elites sign power-sharing agreements abroad and
support military coup that topples government in May
1957.

1957–58   —Caretaker government by military junta. Oversees
plebiscite that establishes National Front.

1958–74   —National Front. Liberal and Conservative parties
alternate presidency and share power and government
posts at all levels. Governments of Liberal Alberto
Lleras Camargo (1958–1962), Conservative Guillermo
León Valencia (1962–1966), Liberal Carlos Lleras

Restrepo (1966–1970), and Conservative Misael Pastrana Borrero (1970–1974).

With advent of National Front traditional political violence ends. Its sequel of political banditry is repressed by 1966. After 1960, Cuban-inspired guerrilla groups (FARC, ELN, EPL), with some linked to previous Liberal resistance, proliferate. Governments continually resort to state-of-siege powers to contain internal dissent and social unrest. Under orthodox liberal policies and adequate coffee prices, economy continues to grow and diversify, and multinational corporations enter Colombia in force. Social reform, encouraged under U.S.-backed Alliance for Progress, is limited; however, in 1961 modest, ongoing, agrarian reform was begun. Efforts to stem growing migration to cities in late 1960s leads to government support of agrarian organizations; by early 1970s rural mobilization repressed by government. Opposition party of Rojas Pinilla (ANAPO) claims presidential election of April 19, 1970, "stolen" from it; M-19 guerrilla group founded in 1972.

1974   —National Front officially ends. Although mandatory alternation of presidency over, most of National Front power-sharing agreement remains in force.

1974–78   —Government of Liberal Alfonso López Michelsen. Reformist expectations for government of this former Liberal dissident (and son of López Pumarejo) are not realized. Regime's neoliberal economic policies generate powerful urban protest of 1977. "Green Revolution" in coffee production and bonanza from high coffee prices pace continued growth of economy.

1978–82   —Government of Liberal Julio Cesar Turbay Ayala. Attempts made to deal with expanding power of guerrillas through extreme repression; nevertheless, guerrilla movement continues to grow and disrupt national life. Drug trade (first in marijuana, then cocaine) emerges as important factor in economy, society, and politics. Charges of clientelism and corruption plague administration.

1982–86   —Government of populist Conservative Belisario Betancur. Temporary economic downturn limits plans for social measures; government concentrates on peace negotiations and cease-fire with guerrillas. M-19 takeover of Palace of Justice in Bogotá in 1985 and massacre of guerrillas by army that follows doom peace initiative and undercut effectiveness of government.

1986–90   —Government of Liberal Virgilio Barco. Barco presides over continued growth and liberalization of economy, implements modest social welfare measures and large-scale development projects, pursues negotiations with guerrillas, and, beginning in 1988, engages in bloody war against drug mafia. Government successfully negotiates peace with M-19. Breakdown of international coffee agreement threatens price of Colombia's main legal export. Organized labor, divided since mid-1940s, achieves greater unity, paced by powerful leftist-led unions in oil and banana production.

1990   —Election and inauguration of Liberal president César Gaviria Trujillo following bloody campaign that witnessed assassination of three presidential candidates representing reformist Liberal forces and the left. Approval by Colombian voters of constituent assembly to consider constitutional reform.

1

Introduction: Colombian Violence in Historical Perspective

Charles Bergquist

To the extent that they think about it, most people in the United States probably view the violence in contemporary Colombia as a simple product of the drug trade. This view is promoted in the U.S. media and informs U.S. government policy. It is accepted by numerous Latin American specialists. And it has considerable basis in fact. For example, the trade in cocaine, most of it destined for the U.S. market, is widely held responsible for the astronomical homicide rate of the city of Medellín. The headquarters of the largest organizations involved in the trade, Medellín had a homicide rate by 1988 twice that of Detroit, making it one of the most violent cities in the world. The link between homicide and cocaine is clearest in the institution of the *sicario* (an assassin who can be hired for U.S. $100 or less).* The drug mafia runs schools for the training of *sicarios,* and it uses these killers to "settle accounts" and to punish attempts to subvert established trade monopolies and hierarchies.

Several of Colombia's numerous leftist guerrilla groups, to take another example, are believed to be involved in the cultivation of coca and the processing and commercialization of cocaine. In recent years, their violent activities, bankrolled in some cases by drug profits, have included the systematic—and highly effective—sabotage of major oil pipelines (after coffee, oil is Colombia's most important legal export); the kidnapping for ransom or the murder of scores of high-level public

*Throughout this volume, Colombian terms and acronyms are defined in the text where they first appear. Important terms found in more than one chapter are defined either in the glossary following Chapter 14 or in the political chronology at the beginning of the volume.

officials and political leaders, as well as of hundreds of private citizens, Colombian and foreign alike; and thousands of confrontations, ranging from minor skirmishes to major battles, with the Colombian armed forces.

Finally, and most ominously, drug money and organizations are linked closely to the recent proliferation in Colombia of right-wing, paramilitary organizations. Some of these groups allegedly have direct ties to the state, especially to elements of the police and army. About one hundred forty such groups exist in the country, according to official sources. These groups were formed ostensibly to combat leftist guerrillas and protect rural and urban neighborhoods and communities, but their main targets in fact have been elements of the democratic left—labor leaders, candidates and elected officials belonging to the political party Unión Patriótica, professionals, and student activists. In recent years, hundreds have lost their lives at the hands of right-wing death squads, often in massacres, and hundreds more, victims of anonymous death threats, have been silenced or hounded into exile.

Readers of the essays in this volume will find evidence of these and other links between the drug trade and the escalating violence that permeates contemporary Colombian society. They also will learn just how complex and intractable these relationships are. The vertiginous homicide rate, for example, is not a result simply of the activities of the drug mafia's *sicarios*. In the first place, the use of *sicarios*, pioneered by the *capos* (kingpins) of the drug trade, now has entered spheres of social life totally unrelated to drugs. *Sicarios* are employed for purposes as diverse as political assassination and the settling of personal grudges and intimate family affairs. In the second place, addiction to cocaine, primarily in the form of cheap cracklike *bazuco* cigarettes, has become widespread among the poorest, most marginal inhabitants of Colombia's larger cities. Until recently, cocaine consumption was not a serious problem in Colombia; but the violent crime and social disintegration that are its sequel, long familiar to North Americans, are now a feature of the Colombian scene as well. Alvaro Camacho's examination (Chapter 11) of homicides in Cali (after Medellín, Colombia's most violent city and, like Medellín, the site of major drug operations) indicates an even more complicated picture. Camacho distinguishes between "public" homicide and "private" homicide and argues that the former is more common, proportionally, in Cali and that the latter is more typical of Medellín. His data show that the rate of homicide in Medellín (in the mid-1980s already more than double that of Cali) is rising, whereas the rate in Cali in the late 1980s appears to have fallen. The difference, he argues, is in part the result of Cali's peculiar forms of elite cultural and political hegemony.

The full implications of guerrilla involvement with the drug trade are equally complex. As the essays by Eduardo Pizarro (Chapter 8) and Alfredo Molano (Chapter 9) demonstrate, the growing strength and appeal of revolutionary groups are not merely the result of these groups' access to drug profits. It is true that the guerrillas' drug money and connections have facilitated their acquisition of increasingly sophisticated weaponry and have allowed some groups to offer monetary incentives to young recruits from among the urban poor and unemployed. But guerrilla organization of social life in isolated regions of coca production—often areas of recent smallholder settlement far from the effective reach of government agencies and services—has also created viable new communities. In these communities, in contrast to many other parts of rural Colombia affected by the violence, justice actually functions and adequate protection from other sources of violence exists. The prestige and popular support enjoyed by some guerrilla groups thus may owe more than generally is realized to effective local administration than it does to popular endorsement of the guerrillas' Marxist-inspired ideology. Nevertheless, the decision by some guerrilla groups to establish links with the drug trade was a fateful one, which generated intense internal debate. And well it should have, for if the political and ideological costs so far seem ambiguous, the physical costs, for some groups, have been fatal as the guerrillas sometimes have found themselves on the losing side in armed confrontations with their erstwhile drug mafia partners.

Several of the essays in this book document the activities of right-wing paramilitary groups, but the measured conclusions of the Commission for the Study of the Violence (Chapter 12) offer the most comprehensive analysis of this topic. The origins and activities of some paramilitary groups and death squads can be connected to drug money and criminal organizations. Their self-appointed mission to preserve Christian values and capitalist property rights as well as rid society of undesirable leftists has led them into activities that go beyond terrorizing the left. Their victims include prostitutes, homosexuals, and the indigent and, paradoxically, drug addicts and pushers as well.

The essay by Luís Alberto Restrepo (Chapter 13) analyzes these drug-related processes, but perhaps its most important contribution is to explore the links, generally poorly understood outside Colombia, between the drug traffic and the Colombian Establishment. These connections go far beyond the involvement of high Colombian officials in the trade or the suborning of judges. The drug trade confronts the Colombian elite with a major ideological and political dilemma. On the one hand, the infusion of cocaine-generated hard currency into the Colombian economy (more evident in real estate, construction, and luxury consumption than in manufacturing industry or agriculture) has enabled the country, in large part, to avoid the terrible economic and fiscal crisis that has affected most other Latin American nations during the last decade. On the other hand, Colombia's legal economy remains highly dependent on the United States, which has demanded that Colombia vigorously pursue an end to the drug trade. The tortuous course of Colombian public policy on the drug question, which revolves around the explosive issue of extradition, reflects this dilemma. The drug trade guarantees the health of Colombia's dependent capitalist economy, which preserves the elite's privileged social position as the dominant class. But pressure from the U.S. government, a government perceived to be the ultimate guarantor of a social order that is being challenged by popular democratic mobilization and violent revolutionary activity, demands that Colombia take vigorous, albeit risky, action against drug trafficking.

In these ways, and in many others detailed in the essays in this volume devoted to the contemporary crisis (Part III), the narcotics trade contributes to the violence of contemporary Colombian society. Yet however potent its influence, however varied and paradoxical its effects, the drug trade, by itself, cannot explain the full dimensions of this violence. Contrary to what most informed U.S. citizens and policymakers might believe, the roots and dynamics of contemporary violence reach far into Colombia's past. Between 1946 and 1966, long before the drug trade constituted a significant factor, Colombia experienced a period of violence that by comparison dwarfs the current state of affairs. Known as *la Violencia* (the Violence), the civil commotion of those years featured gruesome analogues to the violent processes subsumed under the effects of the drug trade and sketched in the preceding paragraphs. Homicide rates, highest during this period in rural rather than in urban areas, reached extraordinary levels, particularly in the early 1950s. Revolutionary groups operating during this period, initially, at least, under the banner of the traditional Liberal party, not the Marxist left, occupied extensive areas of the country's coffee-producing heartland in contrast to the largely peripheral areas controlled by Colombian guerrillas today. Counterrevolutionary paramilitary groups linked to the Conservative government and party sought to destroy the revolutionaries and cleanse the country of non-Catholic and "communistic" elements. In the process some two hundred thousand mostly rural Colombians lost their lives, many of them innocent victims of political partisanship gone wildly out of control.

The period of the Violence, the subject of Part II, thus prefigures the current situation in obvious ways. But as the essays by Gonzalo Sánchez (Chapter 5), Carlos Miguel Ortiz Sarmiento (Chapter 6), and

Medófilo Medina (Chapter 7) reveal, the relationship between the two phenomena—the "classical" Violence of midcentury and the violence of the 1980s—is far more complicated than these simple analogies imply. That complexity is captured best by emphasizing the continuities that connect these historically particular periods to each other and to the larger history of Colombia in the nineteenth and twentieth centuries. These continuities, introduced in Part I, are of two types. First, there are underlying social issues, particularly an ongoing struggle for land. Second, there is the influence of Colombia's peculiar and destructive political system. The analysis of these continuities links all of the essays in this volume and binds together its three parts.

The effort to unravel the effects of these two contributing factors—the socioeconomic and the political—and, conversely, to chart their intricate interaction over time, has presented students of the Violence with a formidable theoretical and interpretative challenge. On the surface a traditional partisan struggle between Colombia's Liberal and Conservative parties,* the Violence seems to resemble more closely the civil wars of the nineteenth century (when those parties were formed) than it does the social revolution that many early analysts on the left hoped to find in it. Yet virtually all of the essays in Parts I and II reveal that the struggle for land and the emerging class dimensions of the Violence were never far below the surface; and, as the essays in Part III indicate, these land and class issues became even more salient in the 1960s, 1970s, and 1980s. Nevertheless, as nearly all of the essays also demonstrate, class struggle in the Violence (as before and as after it) continually was obscured, distorted, and channeled by a political system that however dysfunctional in its capacity to contain civil violence was supremely functional in shielding the elite from the full social consequences of political conflict.

Violence and the Struggle for Land

The immediate historical origins of the struggle for land lay in the massive alienation of territory in the public domain that occurred in the late nineteenth and early twentieth centuries. As Catherine LeGrand shows in Chapter 3, Colombian land policy, ostensibly designed to stimulate the growth of productive small- and medium-size farms, generally resulted in the consolidation of great estates and the proletarianization of would-be smallholders. I argue in Chapter 4 that

*Throughout this volume, capitalization is used to designate the Colombian Liberal and Conservative parties, their partisans, and programs; lowercase indicates the more general meaning of these terms.

this process was reversed in the 1920s, 1930s, and 1940s in the all-important coffee sector and that the social, ideological, and political implications of this fact all led directly to the Violence of the post-1946 era.

The struggle for land, especially in the coffee zone, is a central feature of the Violence, as both Sánchez and Ortiz Sarmiento make clear. Sánchez, however, is more concerned with urban expressions of class struggle. In particular, he looks at the meaning of the politics of Jorge Eliécer Gaitán, whose assassination on April 9, 1948, precipitated the *Bogotazo*, a bloody popular explosion in which Gaitán's partisans destroyed much of downtown Bogotá. Gaitán's death also triggered revolutionary Liberal resistance in much of the Colombian countryside. Ortiz Sarmiento, on the other hand, revises earlier notions, propagated in much leftist scholarship, that the Violence witnessed a uniform and successful offensive by large landowners against smallholders. Although that process occurred in some areas, the reordering of land tenure patterns in the coffee zone seems to have favored primarily new groups, especially small merchants.

Since the 1940s the relationship of land colonization and violence, especially in newly settled areas outside the coffee zone, has continued to prove explosive. As Pizarro and, especially, Molano show, these are precisely the areas where, beginning in the 1960s, revolutionary guerrilla groups have been able to establish secure bases of operation.

Violence and the Political System

In Chapter 2, David Bushnell surveys the nineteenth-century origins of the Liberal and Conservative parties and the genesis of Colombia's bipartisan political system, which, in contrast to the experience of virtually every other Latin American nation, has preserved its monopoly on political power throughout the present century. Bushnell argues that the basic cleavage between the parties—the primary cause of the violent conflict between them—was the issue of the power and privileges to be accorded the Catholic Church. Persuasive as his argument is for the early and midnineteenth century, some historians (including myself) would argue that, by the late nineteenth century, economic differences between and within the elite leaderships of the parties had become more salient.

Be that as it may, what is certain is that, throughout the twentieth century, the two traditional parties have dominated politics, their major alternations in power marked by violent contention, especially in rural areas. I argue in Chapter 4 that these crucial alternations—in 1930, when the Liberal party acceded to power after a half century of Conservative control, and in 1946, when the Liberals lost control of the government to the Conservatives—are best understood in terms of class conflict and the changing imperatives of the capitalist world order. In Chapter 5, Sánchez analyzes the emerging class content of the rise of Gaitanismo in the postwar period and of the forms of the Violence that ensued. By 1958 the elites of the two traditional parties, chastened by the nightmare of the Violence and alarmed by the emergence of a third force, the populist military government of Gustavo Rojas Pinilla (a government that they themselves had helped bring to power in an effort to end the Violence in 1953), had entered into the National Front, a pact wherein they agreed to share political power equally.

As Daniel Pecaut (Chapter 10) and Restrepo both demonstrate, although legally the National Front was ended in 1974, it still structures the political life of the nation. Pecaut reveals the myriad ways in which the formal, limited democracy of the National Front in fact engendered political violence, particularly by encouraging the rise and consolidation of guerrilla groups since the 1960s. Restrepo surveys this same post-1958 history and comes to similar conclusions. For him the most probable scenario for the future, barring an extraordinary democratic mobilization able to break out of the confines of traditional politics, is more, escalating violence.

This sketch of the socioeconomic and political continuities that bind together the study of violence in both its past and present forms supports Ricardo Peñaranda's contention (Chapter 14) that the subject has become the central problem in modern Colombian historiography. His survey of the now-voluminous literature on the Violence, which concludes this volume, reveals that as these studies have grown in quantity, empirical richness, and analytical sophistication, they also have extended themselves forward and backward in time to cover crucial aspects of the whole of the nation's nineteenth- and twentieth-century history.

The essays selected here constitute a representative sample of this recent work. In grouping the studies in three parts—"Antecedents," "The Violence," and "The Contemporary Crisis"—we have sought to convey a sense of the current state of the literature and to emphasize our conviction that an understanding of and solution to the terrible contemporary crisis facing Colombia must include an appreciation of its historical roots.

It would be nice to believe that the current violence in Colombia could be resolved by elimination of the drug trade, remote as that possibility may be. The authors of these essays argue, however, that no such quick fix, even were it possible, would address the heart of the problem. Only a basic democratization of Colombian society—informed by an understanding of past conflicts and aimed at fundamental social and political reform—will create the conditions for future peace.

In presenting these essays to an English-reading public, we recognize that the achievement of such reform depends not only on the informed political action of democratic-minded Colombians but also, in part, on that of their counterparts abroad, particularly in the United States. We hope that U.S. citizens and policymakers will find in this book much more than a detailed description and analysis of the violent consequences of the drug trade in Colombian society. We hope that they will gain a deeper appreciation of the depth and complexities of the democratic struggle of the majority of Colombians for a freer and more just social order.

Part I

ANTECEDENTS

2

Politics and Violence in Nineteenth-Century Colombia

David Bushnell

In this measured synthesis, historian David Bushnell explores the nineteenth-century antecedents of Colombia's violent twentieth-century politics. He begins with a warning against facile comparisons between the politics and violence in the nineteenth century and developments since the 1940s. He then critically surveys explanations for the origins of Colombia's two traditional political parties, the Liberal and the Conservative, in the midnineteenth century. Bushnell concludes that their primary differences revolved around the role and prerogatives of the Catholic Church. Finally, he attempts to explain the nineteenth-century roots of the two features that in the twentieth century most sharply differentiate Colombia's politics from those of the other Latin American nations: first, the longevity of the traditional parties, whose monopoly on power persists today, effectively unchallenged by parties of the left or of the right; and second, the sources of the intermittent, violent contention between these two parties in this century.

The dean of Colombian historians in the United States, Bushnell has spent most of his professional life studying the origins and nature of Colombian liberalism. His classic monograph *The Santander Regime in Gran Colombia* (Newark, DE, 1954) remains unsurpassed as an account of the government of the father of Colombian liberalism, Francisco de Paula Santander. A subsequent book, *Eduardo Santos and the Good Neighbor, 1938–42* (Gainesville, 1967), is a study of the government of another important Colombian Liberal, Eduardo Santos, whose influence, through his editorship of the country's major news-paper, *El Tiempo*, stretched across much of the twentieth century. Most recently, Bushnell has published, with Neil Macaulay, *The Emergence of Latin America in the Nineteenth Century* (New York, 1988), an examination of the struggle for liberalism in the region as a whole. This book, an excellent synthesis of nineteenth-century Latin American political history, places the Colombian themes Bushnell analyzes in his chapter here in a comparative Latin American perspective.

David Bushnell teaches Latin American history at the University of Florida and is currently the editor of the *Hispanic American Historical Review*, the most important journal in the field of Latin American history.

All history is written from a present-oriented perspective. It is thus hardly surprising and wholly appropriate that historians of nineteenth-century Colombia, in examining that century's many and dreary civil disturbances, should bear in mind the tragedy of the Violence of this century and seek to detect in earlier conflicts a key to better understanding of those more recent. There is certainly no scarcity of concrete cases to study, from the abortive series of uprisings against the dictatorship of Simón Bolívar in 1828 to the War of the Thousand Days that closed out the century. In addition to national-level "revolutions," there were all the outbreaks whose aim was to overthrow only state governments during the years when a federal form of constitutional organization was in effect, especially from 1863 to 1885. What is inescapable is the sheer frequency with which political factions in this land, which paradoxically always has prided itself on its adherence to civil government and strict legalism, made use of force, or the implied threat of force, in the hope of effecting a change of rulers.

The precise significance of the political use of violence in the last century as a precedent for the violence of the present century, and especially of the period since 1946, is nevertheless far from clear. Malcolm Deas, for one, has stressed the numerous differences between nineteenth-century civil wars and the later Violence, such as the direct participation of "elite" political figures in the former and not in the latter as well as the shorter duration of the former and its lesser degree of ferocity. He therefore warns against seeing artificial continuities from one period to the other.[1] Gonzalo Sánchez, on the other hand, while noting some of the same differences, underscores what he considers a critically important continuity: the mere fact that "Colombia has been a country of *permanent and endemic warfare*."[2] From this conclusion one might draw the inference that a violent past, at the very least, has created in the Colombian body politic a predisposition to violence that may express itself in different ways at different times but never has been far beneath the surface.

Even so, to say that violence was always close to the surface and that it burst into the open with some frequency is only a first step toward the characterization of political violence in nineteenth-century Colombia. In view of the current vogue of quantitative methods in history and social science, a logical next step would be to draw up a statistical tabulation of civil wars and their consequences; but any such tabulation must be approximate at best. Indeed, what was a civil war?

At what point does a series of illegal protest actions become incipient civil warfare, or a riot deserve to be counted as at least an attempted revolution? The answers to these questions are often less obvious than one would assume. And should one—could one—count all the outbreaks whose immediate aim was to overthrow only regional authorities? For purposes of discussion it nevertheless may be useful to present a list of rebellions directed against the national authorities, rebellions whose seriousness varied widely but ones that, presumably, most scholars still would accept as having taken place although not necessarily as having succeeded. The uprising of 1826, launched by José Antonio Páez against the government of Gran Colombia, is excluded from the list, although it began the process of dissolution of the larger union, because the provinces of New Granada, which became the nucleus of present-day Colombia, were largely unaffected.

National-level Rebellions in Nineteenth-Century Colombia

1828	—José María Obando and José Hilario López vs. dictatorship of Simón Bolívar
1829	—José María Córdova vs. the same
1830	—Florencio Jiménez vs. government of Joaquín Mosquera
1831	—Obando, López, and others vs. dictatorship of Rafael Urdaneta that resulted from the preceding movement
1839–41	—War of the Supremes, Obando and other Liberals vs. government of José Ignacio Márquez (Ministerial)
1851	—Conservative uprising vs. government of López (Liberal)
1854	—Coup of José María Melo vs. Obando (Liberal vs. Liberal)
1859–62	—Revolution led by Tomás C. Mosquera (Liberal) vs. government of Mariano Ospina Rodríguez (Conservative)
1867	—Coup of Radical Liberals vs. Tomás C. Mosquera
1876–77	—Conservative uprising against government of Aquileo Parra (Liberal)
1885	—Radical Liberal uprising vs. government of Rafael Núñez (independent Liberal)
1895	—Liberal uprising vs. government of Miguel Antonio Caro (Conservative)
1899–1902	—War of the Thousand Days, Liberal uprising vs. government of Manuel Antonio Sanclemente (Conservative)

1900   —Coup of José Manuel Marroquín vs. Sanclemente (His-
             torical Conservatives vs. Nationalist Conservatives)

This list includes three coups that were essentially instantaneous. However, the coup by José Mariá Melo, although executed with minimal violence on April 17, 1854, gave rise to a hard-fought military conflict later that year as constitutionalist forces of both the Liberal and the Conservative parties joined to remove the intrusive Melo regime. The list does not include abortive coup attempts, such as the unsuccessful effort to overthrow and assassinate Bolívar in September 1828, although the uprising of José María Obando and José Hilario López, which was part of the same broad movement against the Bolivarian dictatorship, heads the list. Neither does it include conspiracies that were discovered and repressed before they had a chance to go into effect, for example, the 1833 plot of José Sardá against the administration of Francisco de Paula Santander. Nor does the list take note of the coups and rebellions directed against state governments during the federal era, whether successful or unsuccessful, although some states (for example, Panama) during the lifetime of the ultrafederalist 1863 constitution experienced more attempted and successful overthrows of their own governments than did the nation as a whole from the 1820s to the end of the century.

Even if greater mathematical precision were possible, the mere number of coups and rebellions would not tell us much about the level of violence. Not only was violence often associated with urban rioting and with protests concerned only with specific grievances but also the amount of violence displayed, even in efforts to overturn the national government, varied widely. The three listed coups did not involve bloodshed, although the overthrow of President Manuel Antonio Sanclemente took place in the very midst of the War of the Thousand Days, and the Melo coup, as already mentioned, proved to be the first episode in a brief civil war.

At the other extreme stands the War of the Thousand Days, in which, according to the long-standard text of Colombian history by Jesús María Henao and Gerardo Arrubla, "one hundred thousand or more men lost their lives on the fields of battle."[3] If true, this figure would be roughly the same as the lower estimates for loss of life during the Violence of 1946–1966—and with a national population then one fourth as large. The notion of one hundred thousand deaths during the War of the Thousand Days, which would mean slightly over 2 percent of the Colombian population at the turn of the century, has found a secure niche in historical writings, fortunately in most cases without the mention that so many lives were actually lost in battle. In Charles Bergquist's *Coffee and Conflict in Colombia*, which contains the most recent scholarly examination of the war, the figure is introduced with a cautious "perhaps."[4] Indeed, there is simply no reliable information on total casualties, least of all those resulting from the guerrilla phase of the struggle, and continuing skepticism is certainly warranted. The wide disparity in estimates of deaths even for the more recent violence underscores the need for extreme care in assessing the effects of earlier conflicts.

Whatever may have been the actual losses in the War of the Thousand Days, the toll from all the other nineteenth-century civil wars combined can only have been much less, although few authors have been bold enough to offer even a rough guess as to the losses in those other conflicts. Alvaro Tirado Mejía, one of the few contemporary historians to have attempted a serious examination of the social consequences of Colombian civil wars, avoids giving an estimate of his own,[5] but he does reproduce the statistical table prepared by William Paul McGreevey, who gives a total of 33,300 "estimated deaths in hostilities" for the entire period from 1830 to 1899.[6] The period in question would include the first weeks of the Thousand Days, and the total makes it quite obvious that no other outbreak of political violence could have come close to equaling the toll of the turn-of-the-century struggle. Even if we were to take at face value the estimate of 100,000 deaths in the War of the Thousand Days, the Colombian total of deaths in civil conflict falls short (in proportionate terms) of losses in the U.S. Civil War (1861–1865), which caused the death of nearly 600,000 men in a population of somewhere between seventeen and eighteen million, or about 3 percent. That was the one civil war fought by the United States during the nineteenth century, although not the only outbreak of political violence. The intermittent fighting with Indian groups along the western frontier throughout the century, whether classified as "international" or "civil" war or as a series of police actions, shared at least some of the characteristics of Latin American civil conflicts.

McGreevey calculates the economic cost of the loss of life in civil conflict by assuming that the victims usually were males in their early twenties who might be expected to earn $300 per year for another thirty years. Having made some further adjustments, he concludes that "The total of losses due to death by violence can be put at $822 million."[7] This figure itself conveniently escapes any possibility of verification, but it serves as a useful reminder that human life has material as well as moral value. The destruction of property, including various parts of the infrastructure, had an even more obvious economic impact, although not even McGreevey tries to estimate it. Colombian authors have offered only illustrative partial estimates. Several of these are gathered together in Tirado Mejía's *Aspectos sociales de las guerras civiles en*

Colombia, for example, the 50,000 pesos worth of canoes destroyed by rebels in 1860 to prevent government forces from crossing the Magdalena River, as noted by Miguel Samper. Tirado Mejía likewise reproduces Jorge Holguín's estimate of 37.9 million pesos in costs to the national treasury resulting from civil warfare between 1830 and 1902.[8] But this still is not the whole story, for the loss to the economy must include a wide array of lost or diminished opportunities for productive activity. In this last respect, especially, it is safe to assume that the greater bloodletting experienced by the United States in the nineteenth century was less disruptive than that experienced by Colombia and, therefore, less economically damaging in the long term. In the United States most of the violence was compressed into a single five-year period, and much of the rest was isolated on the Indian frontier. In Colombia, despite the particular fury of the Thousand Days, violence was distributed more evenly both chronologically and geographically thereby giving less time and space for recuperation as well as creating a general climate of uncertainty that, at the very least, inhibited investment.

Whatever their economic impact, nineteenth-century rebellions had as their immediate objective the production not of goods but of changes of government. From this standpoint too they left much to be desired. Of the listed national-level movements, at most five could be considered in some sense successful, and even that figure is misleading. Both of the two rebellions noted against the dictatorship of Bolívar (Obando and López in 1828 and Córdova in 1829) were defeated. The uprising led by Colonel Florencio Jiménez against the government of Joaquín Mosquera was successful in the short run, but the dictatorship of Rafael Urdaneta that resulted from it was overthrown in its turn by a counterrebellion the very next year, so that the two "successful" uprisings in effect canceled out each other. The next three uprisings—the War of the Supremes, the Conservative revolution of 1851, and the Melo coup—all ended in failure. Not until the civil war of 1859–1862, which brought Tomás C. Mosquera to power as a Liberal, do we come to an unqualifiedly successful revolution; indeed, it is the singular instance in all Colombian history in which a government has been overthrown by all-out civil warfare. The overthrow of the same Mosquera in 1867 was successful, but it was a quick and bloodless coup and not a full-scale revolution. It was followed in turn by a single unsuccessful Conservative uprising (1876) and three equally futile Liberal efforts (1885, 1895, and 1899–1902). Only with the ejection from office in 1900 of Manuel Antonio Sanclemente in favor of his own vice president, José Manuel Marroquín, does illegal force score another victory, and this is one more bloodless coup.

Among the last group of failed revolutions, there is one that is a truly classic case of the use of violence being not only unsuccessful but also glaringly counterproductive, namely, the Radical Liberal rebellion against President Rafael Núñez in 1885. In trying to forestall Núñez from carrying out a reform of the 1863 constitution by unconstitutional means, his opponents in effect played into his hands, giving him the pretext and opportunity he needed to announce (once he had suppressed the rebellion with massive Conservative help) that "the Constitution of 1863 has ceased to exist." A possibly less clear-cut but analogous case of counterproductivity would be the Melo coup, which also began as a blow struck by one faction of Liberals against another—that is, by the Draconianos who supported Melo against the so-called Gólgotas, or Radical Liberals, whose influence in government they regarded as the source of most of the country's problems. In practice what came about was a return to power of the Conservatives, who had come to the aid of Melo's Liberal enemies and emerged as the dominant partners in the coalition government established after the suppression of the coup.

At state level during the federal era (roughly 1858 to 1886), a higher proportion of successful appeals to arms sometimes could be found. It was possible even to overthrow a state government whose political affiliation was the same as that of the national authorities in Bogotá, as when the Conservatives under Pedro Justo Berrío seized control of Antioquia from the Liberals in 1864, and the Liberal federal government of President Manuel Murillo Toro let them do it. Still, the general ineffectiveness of resorting to violent means to gain power in the Colombian case is striking, particularly when compared with the simultaneous experience of so many other Spanish American countries. In Mexico, there was not one instance of a normal, peaceful transfer of authority from one president to another until 1850. Venezuela, once it had separated from Gran Colombia and organized itself into an independent republic, did maintain a perfect record for peaceful, constitutional, presidential succession until midcentury (unless one were to view the 1835 resignation of Venezuela's first, and for many years its only, civilian president, José María Vargas, to be the result of at least indirect military pressure). But after 1850 even a conservative definition of what constitutes the overthrow by force of a chief executive would yield a list of seven victims: José Tadeo Monagas (1858), José Antonio Páez (1863), Juan C. Falcón (1868), Esteban Palacios (1870), José Gregorio Valera (1879), Raimundo Andueza Palacio (1892), and Ignacio Andrade (1899). Although Chile and a few other Latin American countries either matched or exceeded the Colombian record with respect to nonviolent presidential transitions, there were far more countries that matched or exceeded the Mexican and Venezuelan patterns.

The relative immunity of Colombian presidents to violent over-throw, despite a political culture marked by a fairly high level of violence, is often overlooked amid the emphasis placed on the violence itself. However, it caught the attention of the political scientist James Payne, whose study, *Patterns of Conflict in Colombia*, generally has not been given the attention it deserves (no doubt because of its somewhat condescending tone and his heretical denial of the existence of an "oligarchy"). Payne attributes the phenomenon to the particular dynamics of the Colombian party system, which has been distinctive in Latin America by virtue of its being built around two parties that have been in existence continually since the first half of the nineteenth century. Only Uruguay has had a comparable system, and there the cases of violent overthrow of a president have been comparably rare. The reason, he argues, is that in a two-party system, in which the parties have existed long enough for their followers to develop strong attach-ments to them, the strength of party loyalties when added to the natural advantages of incumbency makes a government almost impossible to dislodge unless the ruling party itself becomes irrevocably divided. If a president is merely incompetent or unpopular, there still will be enough of the faithful who will rally to his support out of loyalty to the party label to enable him to beat back a challenge from the opposite party. Only a succession of arbitrary actions or political errors by the incum-bent so grievous as to ignite a general revulsion against him might erode his support within his own party to the point that he can be overthrown. In enunciating the latter principle, Payne had in mind something similar to the overthrow of Laureano Gómez in 1953, which became possible once Gómez had alienated the Ospinista wing of his own Conservative party almost as thoroughly as the opposition Liber-als.[9] The circumstances that led to the successful revolution against the government of Mariano Ospina Rodríguez or to the coups that removed from office Mosquera and Sanclemente were not exactly similar, but in each case there was serious strife within the governing party whereas under normal circumstances the instinctive party loyalties would have provided a government under fire with the needed margin of safety.

The instinctive tendency of party members to close ranks in times of political danger also made it more difficult to dislodge a ruling party by electoral means. However, a party was more likely to field rival slates of candidates in an election than it was competing armies in a civil war, with the result that to lose a disputed election was more common than to lose an armed struggle. The most striking case no doubt is the election of 1849, won by the Liberal José Hilario López against the two candidates put up by rival factions of the governing Conservative party; it was this opposition victory that ushered in the frenzy of doctrinaire liberal reform measures that reached its climax in the constitution of 1863. A somewhat similar case, again involving a split in the ruling party, had occurred in 1836, when the protoconservative candidacy of José Ignacio Márquez scored an electoral victory against the preferred candidate of outgoing President Santander, namely, General Obando and also against the candidate of the more doctrinaire liberal wing of Santander's followers, Vicente Azuero. These are the only two instances in the nineteenth century in which elections directly caused a change of party in power, but that is still twice as many changes as occurred by civil warfare.

Although the Liberals maintained unbroken control of the national administration during the lifetime of the 1863 constitution—that is, until 1885—there were a number of instances in which one or another Liberal faction alternated in power by means of elections. Also, the election of the independent Liberal Núñez led indirectly to a return to power of the Conservatives, due to the Radicals' launching of the 1885 civil war that hastened Núñez's rapprochement with the Conservative party and strengthened its position until it became the real political heir of Nuñismo. Needless to say, all of these changes carried out by electoral means were in addition to the use of elections for the routine rotation of government officials, who were drawn from the very same political faction in the absence of effective challenges from either the opposition party or rival elements of the ruling party. In any event, the greater political payoff from the election process compared with recourse to violence is scarcely open to question in the Colombian case, despite the frequency with which violence was used.

It must be recognized, though, that election campaigns were often marked by violent incidents and that either force or the perceived threat of force often dissuaded members of an opposition party, at the local or national level, from participating fully. If according to Karl von Clausewitz war is the continuation of diplomacy by other means, then it might be said that in nineteenth-century Colombia there was not always a clear distinction between election campaigns and revolutionary violence. Even so, the casualty rate was normally a good bit lower in elections. What both types of political conflict had in common was the role of the two traditional parties, at least from the time those parties came into existence.

Curiously, however, Colombian scholars still cannot agree on either when the parties were created or what sectors of the population they represented and indeed if there were significant differences between them in that regard. The party names did not come into regular use until midcentury, and permanent nationwide party organizations appeared even later, 1880 according to Helen Delpar in her study

Red against Blue: The Liberal Party in Colombian Politics.[10] Yet embryonic parties, in the sense of distinct and recognizable currents of political thought and action, are in evidence even before the middle of the century, possibly from almost the time of independence.

A once-hallowed tradition in Colombian historical writing, echoed in and echoing the claims made by many of the party leaders themselves, traced the two parties back to the period of the Gran Colombian union in the 1820s, and associated the Conservative party (in embryo) with forces loyal to the Liberator Bolívar and the Liberal party (also in embryo) with the immediate followers of Santander, who was Bolívar's vice president and eventually his bitter political rival. This view has been subject to strong revisionist attack in recent years, but it does contain some truth. As acting chief of Gran Colombia while Bolívar was away fighting the royalists in southern New Granada, Ecuador, and Peru, Santander became the immediate target of all persons who were in any way displeased with the new government. Those expressing displeasure included Venezuelan separatists, who were not prepared to accept any government that presumed to rule them from far-off and chilly Bogotá, as well as individuals who felt themselves offended or adversely affected by the liberal reforms that Santander and his collaborators were trying to implement (including those reforms decreed by the Gran Colombian constituent congress of 1821). The motives of these individuals for complaint were many and varied: for devout Catholics, the suppression of the smaller convents (with their assets to be used for secondary education) and the presence of works by Jeremy Bentham and other heterodox authors in the approved school curriculum; for slave owners, the law of free birth, which had begun the gradual elimination of slavery; for manufacturers, the failure to grant tariff protection; and for still others, the attempt to introduce a form of direct taxation in place of the colonial *alcabala* (sales tax).

Bolívar, who had been hearing a rising tide of complaints against the administration of Santander, came to accept many of them as valid, particularly when Santander showed a lack of enthusiasm for the Liberator's proposed remedy. Bolívar's solution was to reorganize the government of Gran Colombia along quasi-monarchical lines under a constitution similar to the one he had drafted for the new nation of Bolivia, its centerpiece a president with strictly limited powers but serving for life. Bolívar did not seriously differ with Santander in long-term objectives, but he tended to believe that liberal innovations, apart from the abolition of slavery, were being pushed too far too fast and, also, that Gran Colombia's political institutions were somehow too liberal. The result was an open split between the two men, which became increasingly bitter after Bolívar returned to Bogotá. When

Bolívar established a personal dictatorship, Santander countenanced efforts by his own supporters to overthrow him and, it was alleged, even to assassinate him, although Santander's direct complicity in the assassination plans was never proven and, in fact, seems unlikely.

At least in New Granada—that is, the territory that became the later Colombian republic—the groups that were unhappy with the policies of Santander and therefore aligned themselves with Bolívar to some extent foreshadowed the makeup of the Conservative party without yet using that label. Indeed, at that time everyone still was calling himself a liberal, in the independence era the equivalent of saying he was patriotic, republican, and right thinking. Some liberals naturally were more liberal than others, and the more moderate liberals might be considered protoconservatives. They included, among others, the majority of the clergy and the upper crust of the Bogotá aristocracy, which looked down just a bit on Santander, who was from Cúcuta, as a provincial upstart. They also included the aristocrats of Popayán in the southwest, even though illustrious families of Popayán, such as the Mosqueras and the Arboledas, were never unconditional supporters of Bolívar. They were unconditional in support only of their own interests.

The faction of Santander had as its most prominent members professional men who, like Santander, were native to the eastern provinces, but it also included a handful of businessmen from Antioquia to the west. Other faction members undoubtedly were more interested in possible favors from the state than in matters of policy and doctrine. In the interpretation of Indalecio Liévano Aguirre, which has won remarkably wide acceptance in Colombia in recent years, these Santanderistas were the true "oligarchy" of New Granada and not, apparently, the large Bolivarian upper class of Bogotá or the first families of Popayán.[11] A more reasonable interpretation would be that the Santanderistas were a sort of second-class or emerging oligarchy in that its centers of regional strength had been less influential during the colonial period whereas in the republic regime its members could figure on the political scene in ways that had been simply impossible before.[12] It is often said that the republican political class was a small minority of the population, but it was a larger minority than its colonial equivalent had been. In effect, there had been an appreciable increase in the number of political actors as a result of the types of institutions adopted following independence, with the creation of separate executive, legislative, and judicial branches, and even diplomatic corps abroad as well as military forces that were also larger than their predecessors. The chances to rise in society by climbing the bureaucratic, legislative, or military ladders had multiplied, and the appearance on the public stage of new faces could only have been a source of annoyance to the people who before

independence had monopolized informal political influence as well as great social prestige.

Friction had to arise, and it had something to do with the initial division between Santanderistas and Bolivarianos, although there were also some obvious exceptions. Indeed, there were people on both sides who were neither emerging nor already-emerged oligarchs and who had no clear social rank. For that matter, it was not only the "political class" in a strict sense that had grown in size. Even under a regime of limited suffrage (such as Gran Colombia and virtually all the American nations had adopted), many people who would have played almost no role in colonial political life, save perhaps when a sudden riot broke out, at least were taking part as voters. And the possibility of taking part in riots was present still under the republic, not to mention the chance to fight in a civil war.

It is difficult to determine to what extent the participation of the popular sectors in national politics, whether as voters on election day or as cannon fodder in civil war or as something in between, was undertaken by them voluntarily and with a clear consciousness of the issues. Undoubtedly, there was from the start a great deal of crass clientelism, not to mention outright coercion. Whatever the case, however, it appears that the figures with a more popular, even populist, style of leadership tended to align themselves with the faction of Santander and not with that of Bolívar. Two obvious examples are Obando, the former royalist guerrilla leader who was now the most popular *caudillo* of the southwestern provinces, and Admiral José Padilla, a man of triethnic racial background and relatively humble social origins who had a strong following among the lower class of Cartagena. In the end, Padilla was executed for political crimes by Bolívar's dictatorship. The presence of such men among the ranks of the Santanderistas seems to prefigure a relatively greater openness to rising social groups by the later Liberal party than by the Conservative.

The parties, however, were still not quite ready to be born. The conflict between Santanderistas and Bolivarianos persisted even after the dissolution of Gran Colombia (due less to that quarrel than to the constant disaffection of Venezuela) until the abortive Urdaneta dictatorship of 1830–31, which was really the Bolivarianos' last stand. The defeat of Urdaneta led to the eclipse of the Bolivarian faction and to the triumphant return to power of Santander, now as president of the Republic of New Granada. He was prepared to take a more moderate stand than he had while he was acting chief executive of Gran Colombia on a number of policy issues, and in tariff policy he had even turned protectionist. But Santander had neither forgotten nor forgiven the acts of repression inflicted on him and his followers by Bolívar's dictatorship, and his political style was clearly what came to be known in Colombia as "sectarian," or highly partisan behavior.

Faithful to his own legalistic bent, Santander was careful not to violate directly the political rights of his opponents—he shot only genuine subversives—but he was not much interested in conciliating those individuals who had backed the dictatorship. He expressed his sectarianism more in words, including the quasi-anonymous articles that he liked to write against his adversaries in the progovernment press, and in his associations than he did in violent actions. Even so, Santander's style contributed to a growing rift among elements that previously either had supported or had actively collaborated with him. Those persons who felt more conciliatory toward their former opponents, and who, in general, had been moderating their stands on the issues even more than had Santander, backed one of their own, José Ignacio de Márquez, for the presidential succession of 1837. Márquez also had the support of what remained of the Bolivarianos, and when he won the election he brought some of them into his administration. This conciliatory approach stood Márquez in good stead when a number of the former president's ardent supporters (although not Santander) embarked on the so-called War of the Supremes against his government. With the help of the Bolivarianos, who, in fact, provided the leading military commanders on the government's side, Márquez was able to suppress the revolt. This civil conflict thus represented a further, many would say the definitive, step in the emergence of the two parties, as the more zealous Santanderistas lined up on one side in opposition to the alliance of moderates and Bolivarianos. That alliance was to become the Conservative party, although for a time its members continued to be known simply as "Ministerials." Their opponents were left in exclusive possession of the Liberal label, although for a while they were called also "Progressives."

The best-known Conservatives of Bolivarian origin were military men, above all Generals Pedro Alcántara Herrán and Tomás C. Mosquera, both future Conservative presidents (and Mosquera a future Liberal president too). Most of the clergy was also to be found in the Conservative camp, as were such civilian former Bolivarianos as José Manuel Restrepo and Rufino Cuervo, both of whom had been actually rather lukewarm supporters of Bolívar's final dictatorship. The founding fathers of Colombian conservatism included still other individuals who had been associated with Santander even after his break with Bolívar, such as Márquez and Mariano Ospina Rodríguez. Although he too eventually would become a Conservative president, Ospina Rodríguez, in earlier years, had been one of the most fanatical and Bolívar-hating of Santanderistas even to the extent of taking part in the

September 1828 conspiracy to assassinate Bolívar. He had evolved from radical hothead to moderate liberal to Ministerial/Conservative, whereas those Santanderistas who either had not evolved or had not evolved as far remained to become the charter members of the Liberal party.

Like the original Bolivarian faction vis-à-vis that of Santander in Gran Colombia, Conservative party activists were on average a shade more distinguished socially than their Liberal counterparts. This was, however, only a matter of degree, since the leaders of both parties were predominantly members of the upper and upper-middle sectors. The urban and rural masses became identified with both of the parties also but only exceptionally in leadership roles and in most cases presumably in a dependent/clientelistic relationship. This relationship was especially true of rural areas, as suggested by the frequency, during the years when universal male suffrage was in effect (1853–1863), of unanimous or near-unanimous voting for a given party's slate.[13] Such unanimity was much less common at urban polling places, where the electorate was harder to manipulate. Indeed, the urban artisans, who were the elite of city workers, displayed a generally high level of political awareness of their own interests. A majority of them supported José Hilario López in 1849 but were soon alienated because the Liberal administration did not heed their calls for tariff protectionism. They therefore backed the abortive Melo coup of 1854, and most of them may well have supported Miguel Antonio Caro and the Nationalist Conservatives at the very end of the century, in the 1890s.[14]

It is obvious that the artisans in terms of their own interests had no reason to support blindly either one party or the other. If we analyze the programs and ideology of the parties, only one element of society had a decisive reason to affiliate with just one of the two. That element is the clergy because a difference between Liberals and Conservatives in religious policy became steadily more clear. This difference already was foreshadowed in the political quarrels of Gran Colombia, but religious conflict broke out in its definitive form only at midcentury. At that point in time the Liberals at last felt strong enough for a direct attack on all those ecclesiastical structures and privileges that in their view stood in the way of progress, and the Church and lay Catholic spokesmen, for their parts, redoubled their support of Roman Catholic tradition for a combination of reasons. The principal external influence was the increasingly reactionary stance of the papacy, while within Colombia itself, worried defenders of "good customs" and of the social order were ever more convinced that only the common bond of Catholic religion could halt the social and political disintegration that they claimed to see on every hand.

Elsewhere, however, one often needs a magnifying glass and an aptitude for refined hair-splitting to distinguish between the programs of the Liberal and Conservative parties. The former raised a hue and cry over the supposedly authoritarian tendencies of the constitutional reform carried out in 1843 by the Conservatives (or, as they still were called, Ministerials). When looked at with some historical perspective, however, the constitution of 1843 seems not very different from that of 1832, written by the Santanderistas after their defeat of the Urdaneta dictatorship, which, in turn, had much in common with the Gran Colombian constitution of 1821 that Bolívar had criticized as too liberal. Even those of Bolívar's followers who had supported his final dictatorship warmly were now closer in their political thinking to Santander and his followers. It did not occur to anyone to revive Bolívar's pet project for a Bolivian-style life-term presidency or anything like it. Nor did the question of federalism pose a fundamental division between the parties, at least before the 1880s. There may have been a slightly greater tendency for Liberals to favor a federalist and Conservatives to support a centralist type of constitutional organization, but there were also Liberal centralists and Conservative federalists. The only generalization that admits no exception is that professed federalists once they had attained power at the national level tended to moderate their federalism, and that the centralists who ended up in opposition would begin just as promptly to question the overconcentration of power in the hands of the central authorities.

Politically both parties supported a liberal, constitutional, and representative form of state organization. At most, the Conservatives might define individual liberties in less absolute terms than the Liberals were wont to, and they might enlarge the relative weight of the executive branch vis-à-vis the other branches of government, although always surrounding it with explicit constitutional limitations. Yet in this, Colombian Conservatism was simply a moderate liberalism, and not even the constitution of 1886, which is still in effect, is an exception to this proposition. Drafted by the Conservative ideologue Miguel Antonio Caro in cooperation with Núñez, who just had cut his last ties with the mainstream of the Liberal party, the 1886 chapter was for some years denounced by Liberals in much the same terms as they had denounced the 1843 reform, albeit more vociferously. Yet it maintained all of the elements, including the separation of powers, that gave the appearance of popular sovereignty, and political liberty, however much it simultaneously strengthened the national executive and reinforced the social order through a close alliance (essentially tactical as far as Núñez was concerned) between church and state.

Some might object—and the Regeneration, as the increasingly Conservative-dominated post-1886 regime came to be known, would offer numerous examples—that the Conservatives, despite their profession of liberal principles, did behave differently from Liberals, violating constitutional norms more frequently than their adversaries precisely in their zeal to repress the latter. However, this would be a highly dubious proposition, since Colombia in the nineteenth century scarcely experienced "repression" worthy of the name, at least at the national level. The arbitrary acts committed by local bosses often escaped notice altogether outside their own districts; at least there was nothing comparable to the wave of lynchings of blacks in the southern United States in the latter nineteenth century and the first years of the twentieth. Even less did the few, thoroughly unimpressive, and eventually abortive Colombian dictatorships resemble the regimes of Juan Manuel de Rosas in Argentina or Gabriel García Moreno and Ignacio Veintimilla in Ecuador, to say nothing of the totalitarian dictatorships of the present century. In Colombia the most serious incidence of repression, in any case, was not that which was inflicted on political leaders but was the arbitrary mass exiling of Bogotá artisans after the defeat of Melo.

If one of the two parties was more guilty of violating constitutional guarantees, it was probably the Liberal party because of its minority status throughout the last century and really until the 1930s. Its status was a logical consequence of its quarrel with the church, since the clergy was in a better position to influence the political ideas and behavior of the masses than was any Liberal politician. As a result, although the Liberals introduced universal male suffrage first—and in the province of Vélez even briefly adopted universal woman suffrage for the first time in Latin America—they soon changed their minds on this issue. The elections carried out under universal suffrage under the constitutions of 1853 and 1858 produced more victories for the Conservatives than for the Liberals. Therefore, when the Liberals returned to power by armed force in 1861 they took several steps backward. Under the constitution of 1863 they left the right to vote to the discretion of the states. Some of the states reimposed legal restrictions on suffrage while others were content to practice massive fraud. The classic example is the presidential voting of 1875 as carried out in the state of Bolívar. The returns yielded a total of 44,112 for Bolívar's favorite son, Núñez, then running for the first time, as against just 7 votes for his principal rival, who, nevertheless, won the election in the nation as a whole.[15] The lifetime of the 1863 constitution, which was also a period of Liberal hegemony, was the golden age of electoral chicanery in Colombia. There was no lack of arbitrary electoral and other practices during the era of the Regeneration as well, when the Conservatives were mainly in control, but because of their majority status the Conservatives had less need to cheat in order to win. They did it rather to increase their majorities and to annoy the Liberals.

If in political matters there was little real difference between Liberals and Conservatives, in economic policy there was even less. There were disagreements, and important ones, in Colombia over economic matters, of which the most obvious was the conflict between tariff protectionism and so-called free trade. But the Liberals were not aligned on one side in these disagreements and the Conservatives on the other; rather, factions and subgroups of each party could be found on both sides in all of them. In broad-brush terms it can be said that the two parties accepted, without much serious questioning, the dominant economic ideology of the last century, that is, free enterprise and laissez-faire, which suited all sectors of the Colombian upper class quite well. Party leaders argued mainly about specific details but without opposing each other as two monolithic blocs. That dominant ideology was not always equally in keeping with the interests of the popular classes, and artisans waged a long battle against the policy of free trade—in the course of which they established transitory tactical alliances with factions of both parties but never achieved a really effective degree of tariff protection for their crafts.

If there were, then, no substantial differences on policy between the two parties, save in ecclesiastical matters, why were Colombian political contests so hard-fought, even violent? Up to a point, people no doubt believed that the differences between the parties were more clear-cut than they really were; and, as a motive for human action, belief is more important than reality. Neither can one exclude the thesis, so often stated, to the effect that political struggles in Colombia revolved around competition for control of bureaucratic positions, that is, for the meager booty contained in the public treasury or simply for the social status that official positions conferred. The amount of booty involved, at the local level particularly, was so slight that it is hard to see how anyone would risk his life fighting for it. But it is precisely in the small towns and villages that economic alternatives were most limited, and where control by one's own party of official decision making in such matters as the letting of contracts and adjudication of land titles might make the difference between poverty and modest comfort. Finally, there was the sheer cumulative effect of injuries given and received and of grudges passed down from father to son to grandson that inclined the rank and file of one party instinctively to expect the worst from the other and to rally to their own party's support in time of crisis.

The question of why the traditional parties showed much unusual staying power in the Colombian case remains. Most Latin American nations developed Liberal and Conservative parties (conceivably under different names but filling the same roles) at some point during the nineteenth century, but only in Colombia—and in Uruguay, whose Colorados and Blancos often are equated with Liberals and Conservatives, although there was even less doctrinal difference between them— have the original two parties continued to dominate the political scene to the present day. At least a partial explanation for Colombia undoubtedly can be found in the relative weakness of the military as an independent political force, so that consolidation of a two-party system was not disrupted by interludes of military dictatorship. As the frequency of civil warfare attests, military men played a role in Colombian politics, but they took part as much or more in their capacity as Liberals or Conservatives than they did as generals or colonels. To be sure, one may still ask whether the weakness of the military, which, as the century wore on, increasingly followed the leadership of civilian political figures rather than vice versa, was the cause of a strong party system or its effect. Obviously, we are dealing here with mutually reinforcing phenomena. But the ultimate causes of the military's subordinate political role cannot be explored within the scope of this essay.

It is hard to escape the conviction that another key factor—and one that contributed to Colombia's bipartisan system specifically—was the intensity of the religious question in nineteenth-century Colombian politics. This issue reflected the presence, on the one hand, of a strong institutional church and, on the other, of a sufficient number of liberal professional men imbued with modernizing and secularizing ideas who perceived the Church to be an obstacle to the changes they hoped to bring about. Wherever the Church was weak in Latin America, as it was in Venezuela, debate over ecclesiastical reform did not have quite the same polarizing effect as it had in Colombia, where the simple dichotomy of clerical versus anticlerical only could reinforce other tendencies making for a two-party system. The same dichotomy could probably be said to exist in Mexico. There, however, the development of a bipartisan system was cut short by the more active role of the military as well as by a backlash against the treason of the Mexican Conservatives, who never recovered from their fatal mistake of inviting Archduke Ferdinand Maximilian of Hapsburg to put on a Mexican imperial crown.

The Colombian party system, whatever the reasons for its longevity, constitutes the one obvious element of continuity between nineteenth-century political violence and the Violence of the twentieth century, at least in the latter's original bipartisan form (not in its leftist revolutionary offshoots). Once they were established, it was the parties that fought in both elections and civil wars and the parties that by their relative internal cohesion rendered the use of armed struggle so conspicuously ineffective. As already noted, however, the parties did not wage the Violence in exactly the same way as they had conducted the civil wars of the previous century. Not only were there intervals of relative peace of anywhere from a few months to a whole decade between the coups and revolutions of the nineteenth century, but also the close of the War of the Thousand Days ushered in nearly three decades of peace between the parties in the twentieth century, broken only by the scattered back-country shootings that seemed to accompany any national election campaign.

The outbreak of more intense, although regionally localized, partisan violence following the change of the parties in power (by election) in 1930 was soon quelled. Peace returned, except for the usual minor incidents around election time, until the beginning of the Violence in 1946. Certainly the prolonged hiatus in violence during the first part of the present century must be a warning against the tendency to equate one episode of violence with another just because they were waged under the same party banners as well as against the facile assumption that violence has always been a prominent feature of the Colombian political scene. Even so, one cannot escape the fact that the political system established after independence was prone to intermittent breakdowns in which presidents were seldom overthrown but people were killed and resources wasted. The ability of Colombians to avoid the bouts of military dictatorship so common in other parts of Spanish America and to maintain constitutional appearances, even at times in the very midst of civil armed conflict, is admirable. Yet their inability to absorb fully the lesson of the futility of violence in their own political context is distressing, and recent history suggests that too many still have not learned.

Notes

1. Malcolm Deas, "Algunos interrogantes sobre la relación guerras civiles y violencia," in *Pasado y presente de la violencia en Colombia*, comp. Gonzalo Sánchez and Ricardo Peñaranda (Bogotá, 1986), 41–46.

2. Gonzalo Sánchez, "La Violencia in Colombia: New Research, New Questions," *Hispanic American Historical Review* 65:4 (November 1985): 789 (emphasis in original).

3. Jesús María Henao and Gerardo Arrubla, *Historia de Colombia para la enseñanza secundaria*, 8th ed. (Bogotá, 1967), 815.

4. Charles Bergquist, *Coffee and Conflict in Colombia, 1886–1910*, 2d ed. (Durham, NC, 1986), 133.

5. Alvaro Tirado Mejía, *Aspectos sociales de las guerras civiles en Colombia* (Bogotá, 1976), 13–14, 61–64.

6. William Paul McGreevey, *An Economic History of Colombia, 1845–1930* (Cambridge, England, 1971), 88.

7. Ibid., 176.

8. Tirado Mejía, *Aspectos sociales*, 84, 88.

9. James Payne, *Patterns of Conflict in Colombia* (New Haven, CT, 1968), 143–52.

10. Helen Delpar, *Red against Blue: The Liberal Party in Colombian Politics, 1863–1899* (University, AL, 1981), 126–27. See also César Mendoza Ramos, "Los partidos políticos durante el siglo xix," *Huellas: Revista de la Universidad del Norte* 19 (April 1987): 23–32, for a discussion of the continuing disagreements among Colombian scholars concerning these questions.

11. The most influential statement of this thesis is in Indalecio Liévano Aguirre's *Bolívar* (Medellín, 1971), which has gone through multiple editions. It is presented even more starkly, however, in his *Razones socio-económicas de la conspiración de septiembre contra el Libertador* (Caracas, 1968).

12. The importance of the traditional location of power and prestige (or lack of same) is treated in Frank Safford, "Social Aspects of Politics in Nineteenth-Century Spanish America: New Granada, 1825–1850," *Journal of Social History* 5:3 (Spring 1972): 344–70, as part of a general review of alternative explanations for the origins of political alignments.

13. David Bushnell, "Voter Participation in the Colombian Election of 1856," *Hispanic American Historical Review* 51:2 (May 1971): 244–47.

14. David Sowell, "The Early Latin American Labor Movement: Artisans in Bogotá, Colombia, 1832–1919" (Ph.D. diss., University of Florida, 1986), 266–67, 271. Sowell recognizes that there is little firm evidence concerning the political sympathies of the artisans at the end of the nineteenth century and that the conclusion that a majority supported the nationalists must remain tentative.

15. David Bushnell, "Elecciones presidenciales, 1863–1883," *Universidad Nacional de Colombia Sede de Medellín: Revista de Extensión Cultural* 18 (December 1984): 48.

3

Agrarian Antecedents of the Violence*

Catherine LeGrand

In this chapter, Catherine LeGrand develops material that she first analyzed in her *Frontier Expansion and Peasant Protest in Colombia, 1850–1936* (Albuquerque, 1986) in order to chart the social implications of the privatization of public lands in Colombia during the fifty years after 1880. LeGrand argues that the privatization process, governed by liberal legislation passed in the 1870s and 1880s, resulted not in the creation of a large class of small farmers—the ostensible intent of the laws—but rather in the consolidation of large estates. Many of the farmers who colonized the land and expected to convert their parcels into freeholds were denied their rights and transformed into day laborers, tenants, and sharecroppers on the large estates that were created. Within this terrible historical irony LeGrand situates the agrarian protests of the 1920s and 1930s, which prefigure the struggle for land today.

Historians have long been aware of the general process described here. What is so distinctive and valuable about LeGrand's work is her effort to document this process systematically through time and space using the rich primary materials in the Public Land Archives of the Colombian government.

LeGrand teaches Latin American history at McGill University in Montreal, Canada. Among her recent publications is a critical review of the literature on land colonization in the contemporary period, "Colonization and Violence in Colombia: Perspectives and Debates," *Canadian Journal of Latin American and Caribbean Studies* (Summer 1990), which can be read in conjunction with Alfredo Molano's Chapter 9 in this volume.

Exporters of raw materials under Iberian rule, the nations of Latin America continued to perform a similar role in the world economy after

*This chapter originally was published in Gonzalo Sánchez and Ricardo Peñaranda, eds., *Pasado y presente de la Violencia en Colombia* (Bogotá, 1986). Reprinted by permission of the Centro de Estudios de la Realidad Colombiana.

independence. In the nineteenth century, however, a significant shift occurred in the kinds of materials exported. Whereas in colonial times the great wealth of Latin America lay in its mineral resources, particularly silver and gold, after 1850 agricultural production for foreign markets took on larger importance. The export of foodstuffs was not a new phenomenon, but in the nineteenth century the growth in consumer demand in the industrializing nations and the developing revolution in transport much enhanced the incentives for Latin Americans who would produce coffee, wheat, cattle, or bananas for overseas markets.

The growth of rural production for export after 1850 generated additional demands for labor. Indeed, one of the most pressing problems export entrepreneurs throughout Latin America had to confront was the problem of labor supply. Large landowners who aimed to profit from improved world market conditions by producing export crops had first to increase their labor force. In most countries the problem was resolved, and a thriving export agriculture developed. The question, in each specific case, is how and with what impact on peasant society?

One form of labor acquisition typical of Colombia in the late nineteenth and early twentieth centuries was the transformation of independent frontier squatters into tenant farmers and wage laborers. Agricultural entrepreneurs effected this transformation by asserting rights of private property over large areas of public lands occupied in part by peasant settlers; that is, they enclosed the peasants' fields. This form of labor acquisition gave rise to important resistance movements that provide insight into peasant motives and perceptions of the agrarian transformation process in which they were involved. Out of this labor acquisition and peasant resistance to it emerged one major thread of rural protest ideology that continues in the Colombian countryside to the present day.[1]

Since foreign immigration into Colombia was minimal, Colombian entrepreneurs had to rely on domestic resources to meet the ever-growing demands for labor generated by the agricultural export economy. The problem was that, whereas most of the rural population resided in the cold Andean highlands, the tropical products valued abroad could be grown only in the temperate midlands and hot lowlands. Such products included tobacco, quinine, indigo, and cotton, all of which enjoyed brief booms between 1850 and 1875, and coffee and bananas, which became the mainstays of the Colombian export economy thereafter. In the same period the introduction of new pasture grasses and breeds of cattle specifically adapted to lowland conditions encouraged the spread of cattle ranching throughout the Caribbean plains and interior river valleys. Although destined for the most part for internal consumption, some hides were exported and, after 1900, some live cattle as well. Most of the new cattle ranches, coffee estates, and banana plantations took form in sparsely populated wilderness areas that lay beyond the narrow reach of the Spanish colonial economy.[2]

This counterpoint of a dense highland population and a lowland export agriculture was not unique to Colombia. It also characterized the experience of other Latin American countries such as Guatemala and Peru. Studies of these countries indicate that coastal landowners successfully obtained estate workers from the highlands through a system of labor contracting.[3] In Colombia as well the highland population eventually would provide the major source of labor for export enterprise, but the passage from the highlands to the great estate was not so direct. Rather, in Colombia, an important intermediate step occurred: the formation through migration of a new smallholder peasant sector in the middle altitudes and lowlands.

To understand this process, it is essential to take account of the structure of landholding in regions of export growth. As late as 1850 there still existed immense areas of *terrenos baldíos* (public lands) in the middle altitudes and lowlands. The Colombian frontier was much more extensive than is often realized. Geographer Augustín Codazzi, studying Colombia in the nineteenth century, estimated that 75 percent of Colombian national territory was still public land in 1850. This figure included some twenty-four million hectares in the core areas of the country in the Andean region and along the Caribbean coast.[4] Not only in the Antioqueño area but also throughout the Andes and along the coast, vast properties formed in the colonial period lay interspersed with equally vast expanses of public lands of which no one claimed ownership.[5]

The first crops in Colombia were cultivated by large-scale entrepreneurs on private properties. But with the success of such crops, improvements in transportation, and development of local markets, a process of frontier expansion began, one of incorporation of public lands into the national economy. Peasants from the highlands led the way.

In the late nineteenth and early twentieth centuries, a constant stream of migrants wound their way out of the highlands of Antioquia, Boyacá, and Cauca into frontier zones in the middle and lower altitudes. These migrations reflected the stagnation and perhaps even contraction of the highland economy and the simultaneous appearance of new opportunities in the economically dynamic middle altitudes and valleys.[6] Some of these migrations received encouragement from merchants, road contractors, or large landowners who sought to develop new areas, while others were entirely spontaneous in nature. Migrants included rural artisans displaced by the influx of cheap European manufactures, smallholders impoverished by the overfragmentation of their properties, Indians dispossessed of their communal lands, and political refugees fleeing the civil wars. All were attracted to frontier regions by the promise of free land and by the hope of improving their economic situation through production for markets.[7]

The frontier settlers' concern with economic independence and advancement is revealed in their settlement patterns and productive activities. In choosing where to settle, for example, *colonos* (frontier peasants) manifested a decided preference for sites with market access. Most founded homesteads along rivers, roads, and railroads, while those who moved into isolated regions immediately pooled their labor to cut mule paths to the nearest town or waterway. Some frontier settlements also sent impassioned pleas to the government asking for penetration roads that would allow them to break into the market economy.[8]

Most families, working with family labor, cleared one to two hectares of land per year, finally achieving farms of ten to thirty hectares in size. Although limited to subsistence in the first few years, settlers tended to diversify production as soon as possible. In addition to the corn, beans, plaintains, and yucca that they consumed themselves or sold locally, Colombian frontiersmen also produced large quantities of sugarcane, rice, cotton, tobacco, cacao, wheat, and coffee for wider commercial markets.[9] Contemporary observers indicated that peasant cultivators of public lands produced a major portion of the food-stuffs grown in Colombia in the late nineteenth and early twentieth centuries.[10]

Many cultivators of public lands also showed a speculative bent. Often the first settlers to enter a region claimed large areas of unimproved land around their fields. They tried to keep other homesteaders out or else charged them for the right to settle there.[11] There was much buying and selling of *mejoras* (improvements) among *colonos*, and in many places they tried to use such negotiations to assert illegal claims to the land. Competition over land generated numerous controversies among settlers.[12] Despite these problems, most *colonos* sought to live in close proximity to other families. Wherever an expanse of public lands provided adequate marketing opportunities, the population grew rapidly and homesteaders grouped together to form nucleated villages known as *caseríos*. The first step in founding a *caserío* was to construct a chapel, a collective task. Then came the marketplace, the cemetery, and the jail. Later, perhaps, a school would be built and an office for the *inspector de policía* (justice of the peace). At the same time, shopkeepers and artisans appeared on the scene, eager to supply commodities the colonists could not themselves produce. Not infrequently, frontier *caseríos* included hundreds and even thousands of settlers, some living in town and others scattered throughout the countryside.[13] Thus, the growth economy in the middle altitudes and lowlands of Colombia stimulated the concurrent expansion of an independent, market-oriented peasantry in nearby frontier regions.

The availability of free land for settlement posed a major problem for the large estate owner who relied on hired labor. Clearly, where the lower classes had free access to land—that is, where they themselves controlled the means of production—they were less willing to accept work as tenant farmers or wage laborers. Throughout the late nineteenth and early twentieth centuries, landowners in the middle and lower altitudes complained constantly of labor scarcity.[14] Coffee growers in western Cundinamarca and Tolima tried to remedy the situation through *enganche*, a system of labor contracting, which brought peasants from the eastern highlands to work the coffee fields. Once they familiarized themselves with the region and accumulated some savings, however, even these workers tended to strike out on their own toward public lands nearby.[15]

The landlords' response to the labor problem was a logical one: they sought to tie labor to the estates by asserting control over the land, that is, by enclosing the peasants' fields. Few frontier settlers had property titles. Although by Colombian law frontier settlers after 1874 were entitled to free grants of the land they farmed, the surveying costs were prohibitive.[16] In contrast, for people of middle- and upper-class origin the titling of public lands was quite a simple matter.[17]

In the late nineteenth and early twentieth centuries, a massive privatization of public lands occurred. The Colombian government officially alienated 3.2 million hectares of public lands in this period, while an even greater quantity of land passed into private hands through illegal appropriations. Less than 10 percent of this territory went to the Antioqueño *poblaciones* (planned frontier settlements) of which so much has been written;[18] the rest was allotted in large tracts to merchants, politicians, and landowners who had the requisite political connections and who could pay the price.[19] Most of these individuals sought to form private properties in frontier regions in order to speculate on the land market or to produce export crops or livestock.

It is important to note, however, that the land that entrepreneurs chose to privatize was not public but was specifically land already occupied by peasant settlers. Furthermore, they sought to monopolize immense extensions of territory, much more than they possibly could put to use. The cumulative effect was to block the peasants from access to the most desirable land, thus encouraging them to sell their labor power.[20]

The means by which large proprietors dispossessed frontier settlers of their claims and transformed them into estate workers were as follows. First, well-to-do entrepreneurs sought to establish property rights to large tracts of public lands already occupied in part by peasant settlers. Some petitioned the government for grants, while others simply appropriated the territory. Various means were used to acquire public lands illicitly. Some individuals fenced off large extensions with barbed wire and sold the tracts; others staked imaginary mining claims in order to monopolize the surrounding land or inflated the boundaries marked in grant applications. Still others extended the borders of their rural estates to encompass adjacent public lands. Often these usurpations were confirmed in special court cases brought by landowners to "clarify" property limits. The subservience of local mayors, judges, and surveyors to the landlords' interests and the use of metes and bounds surveys considerably facilitated such usurpations. Ironically, although they were illegal, many appropriations received in time the sanction of the Colombian judicial system. Local judges customarily accepted wills, bills of sale, and court decisions as proof of property, so long as such documents showed possession for at least thirty years. Thus, much land that never officially left the public domain was incorporated into private properties through de facto claims and later sales or inheritances.[21]

Once they had established property rights, whether through legal or illegal channels, the land entrepreneurs turned to a second task, that of securing a labor force. Accompanied by the local mayor or a police picket, they informed the settlers who had opened the land that they had mistakenly occupied private property. The entrepreneurs then presented the peasants with two alternatives: They could vacate the property at once or sign tenancy contracts.[22] If the peasants agreed to become tenants, they abandoned their claims to the land and also relinquished control over their own labor. As rent for the continued use of their parcels, they were obliged to provide part-time workers for the alleged landowners. The precise terms of tenancy agreements varied from region to region, but all signified expropriation of the land and labor of independent peasant producers. If, on the other hand, the *colonos* decided to move on, they left behind the work of years. Some settlers probably were bought out, and these fortunate ones received some return for the work they had invested in the land.[23] Others, however, received no compensation. Many of those ejected remained in the area as day laborers or were hired as tenants on neighboring estates.[24] Others moved as settlers toward new frontiers where, with time, they often were displaced once again. Thus, with the growth of the Colombian export economy came a concentration of landholding that occurred through the cumulative dispossession of thousands of frontier squat-

ters. The formation of large properties and of a labor force to work
those properties proceeded concurrently.

The process of labor acquisition through territorial dispossession
gave rise to numerous social conflicts. It is important to describe these
conflicts and their evolution for they shed light on the emergence of one
major form of rural protest in Colombia. In the first part of the nineteenth century the tension between large land entrepreneurs, intent on
acquiring a dependent labor force, and colonists, concerned to maintain
their independence, rarely was expressed overtly. Generally, it seems,
the settlers accepted one or the other of the alternatives presented to
them without strong objection. After 1875, however, a significant
change occurred when *colonos* began to organize purposefully to defend
themselves against encroachment. In many parts of the country, small
groups of settlers, threatened by a single land entrepreneur, refused
either to sign tenancy agreements or to move off the land. Their
resistance precipitated open conflicts.

The decisive factor that persuaded the homesteaders to resist expropriation was the passage of national legislation supportive of settlers' rights. Before the 1870s the Colombian legal system made almost
no mention of independent *colonos* who did not form part of the
Antioqueño *poblaciones*. Then, in 1874 and 1882, congress passed two
important laws reforming public land policy, Law 61 of 1874 and Law
48 of 1882.[25] Intended to encourage the productive use of the public
domain, these laws advanced the principle that whoever cultivates
public land is its rightful owner. The new statutes not only permitted
peasants to form homesteads wherever they wished on the national
domain but also stipulated that the land they farmed was legally theirs
and should not be taken from them, even if they had not as yet obtained
written titles.

The land entrepreneurs paid this legislation no heed, but the law
profoundly influenced the settlers' perception of their own situation. It
gave them the sense that the national government was on their side, it
imbued their interests with legitimacy, and it provided a focal point
around which they began to organize in their own defense.[26] From 1874
on, settlers threatened with dispossession did their best to alert the
government to the violation of their legal rights. In the years from 1874
to 1930, settler groups sent hundreds of petitions to authorities in
Bogotá describing their problems with land grabbers and asking the
government to protect them.[27]

The drafting of such petitions required a concerted group effort.
Because most *colonos* were illiterate and ignorant of legal formalities,
they had to engage a country lawyer to write their appeals. A number of
families from the same area, all of whom were menaced by one land

claimant, generally pooled their resources to hire an attorney to argue their position collectively. More than four hundred such petitions, each signed by between five and one hundred *colono* families, are deposited in the Colombian Public Land Archives. In these pleas, the settlers expressed but one aim: to be left in peace to farm their land independently.

The legalistic orientation of *colono* protest made sense in Colombia. Given the existence of protective legislation, the settlers logically could suppose that the central government would support them, if only it were informed of their situation. Throughout Latin American history, Indians faced with threats to their communal lands have adopted similar protest strategies for similar reasons.[28]

Conflicts between settlers and land entrepreneurs, however, were not only played out on paper; they generally involved direct and sometimes violent confrontations as well. To assert *colono* status before the law, the peasants had to remain on the land without signing tenancy contracts. Faced with the settlers' refusal either to sign labor agreements or to vacate their parcels, the proprietors called on local mayors to evict them. Even if evicted, settlers often defied the authorities, returning doggedly to farm their fields once the officials had withdrawn. When this happened the landlords responded with more direct harassment. They threw pasture seed in the settlers' crops and turned cattle into their fields, pulled down bridges to cut market access, and jailed *colono* leaders on trumped-up charges. In some instances, landowners also formed vigilante bands to attack the most recalcitrant *colonos* in order to intimidate the others. Usually such tactics succeeded in forcing settlers to sign tenancy contracts or abandon the area. In some places, however, *colonos* refused for years to surrender their claims.[29]

Resistance tended to be most effective in regions where settlers were numerous and where they found middle-class allies willing to support them. Individuals who aided the settlers usually came from one of three groups. Some were *tinterillos de pueblo*, local lawyers, who hoped to profit by informing the peasants of their rights and writing their petitions for them. The dispute over the territory called Dinde in Cajibio and El Tambo (Cauca) shows that such hopes were not unreasonable. During the fifteen years of their struggle with the Vejarano family, the Indian *colonos* of Dinde, numbering 130 households in all, paid their lawyer more than 14,000 pesos in legal fees.[30]

Cultivators of public lands who possessed knowledge and resources superior to the average peasant sometimes also sided with the settlers. Usually these cultivators were local storekeepers, artisans, or administrators who had hired a few workers to plant crops or run livestock on public lands nearby. If outside entrepreneurs tried to appropriate their claims, these cultivators made common cause with peasants who similarly were threatened. One such individual was Tobias Enciso, a printer and former public market manager from Honda (Tolima). When Enciso's claim to public lands in the neighboring municipality of Victoria (Caldas) was challenged by the Isaacs Hermanos in 1917, he resisted in the name of the many small *colonos* living in the region. Enciso not only took his case and that of the settlers to court but also published a pamphlet presenting a vivid picture of the struggle from the *colonos'* point of view.[31]

Local authorities were the third group who occasionally provided settlers with aid, thus strengthening their resistance to land entrepreneurs. Local authorities favored the interests of wealthy and powerful entrepreneurs, but in some instances they supported the *colonos* instead. Generally speaking, the *personeros* (municipal advocates) and councilmen, who were most attuned to local affairs, tended to be more sympathetic toward the settlers, while the judges and mayors, through whom the crucial judicial and administrative decisions were made, backed the large land claimants.[32]

Whether lawyers, cultivators, or local officials, middle-class allies provided *colonos* with important leverage in their efforts to defend themselves against entrepreneurs. By informing the illiterate of their rights, drafting petitions on their behalf, and occasionally providing financial support, such individuals helped the settlers articulate their interests in opposition to the land entrepreneurs.

Confrontations between land entrepreneurs and peasant settlers during the period from 1875 to 1930 were widespread and numerous. More than 450 separate major confrontations (which I define as involving more than twenty-five settlers) took place in developing frontier regions during these years, some lasting for decades. Such disputes occurred most frequently in coffee areas in the middle altitudes of all three chains of the Andes, in cattle zones both in the interior and along the coast, and in the banana enclave created by the United Fruit Company near Santa Marta.[33]

During the period of growth, then, independent settlers actively resisted the appropriation of their land and labor by large landowners. Unfortunately, the archives do not permit a tracing of the resolution of every conflict. In some places, *colonos* may have been successful in their struggles for the land. Many smallholdings emerged, particularly in the coffee zones of the central branch of the Andes.[34] Elsewhere the ongoing expansion of large estates and the formation of a dependent labor force indicate that the entrepreneurs in many cases overcame the *colonos'* resistance.[35]

The landlords' apparent success, however, could not obliterate the settlers' memory of the experience through which they had passed. Dispossession, which touched so many peasant families, imbued them with a personal conviction of the illegitimacy of the properties on which they worked and an underlying resentment against the landlords. This rural consciousness lay inactive until structural changes in the 1920s provided the peasants with leverage to renew their struggles against the predominance of the great estates.

After 1920 the Colombian economy expanded at previously unheard-of rates, only to contract sharply with the onset of the Great Depression in 1929. Meanwhile, the national government extended its radius of influence, and new political parties that sought a popular base both in the cities and in the countryside developed. These changes occasioned a shift in the relative balance of power between landlords and peasants, permitting the peasants to reassert claims to that land of which they had been dispossessed.[36]

The precipitating factor was yet another reform in the legal system. Reflecting the state's tendency to take an interventionist role in the economy, the Colombian Supreme Court resolved for the first time to specify the legal criteria by which to distinguish private property from public land. When the Court ruled in 1926 that the only proof of property henceforth would be the original title by which the state had alienated the land from the public domain, the peasants listened.[37] Many knew that the large estates where they worked did not have such titles because they had been formed through the usurpation of public lands.

Thus, peasants in some places passed from the defensive to the offensive, and the squatter movements of the late 1920s and early 1930s began.[38] Tenant farmers in regions of recent frontier development suddenly argued that they were settlers, not tenants, and that the land was public not private property. They refused to pay their obligations any longer and continued to till their family plots embedded in the large estates. Meanwhile, groups of settlers, rural wage laborers, and construction workers laid off in the first years of the depression invaded outlying portions of the same properties. The newcomers also called themselves *colonos*. And, as *colonos* had always done, they built huts, cleared small fields, and petitioned the government to protect them against the attacks of the landlords who, they said, had robbed the nation of its patrimony.

In the wake of massive land invasions, many landlords in these regions retained effective control over only the relatively small areas that they had planted with export crops. Meanwhile, as dependent laborers who had been settlers declared themselves settlers once again, many large estates dissolved into their constituent parts. The tendency toward the concentration of rural property, so marked in the period of export growth, reversed itself in the early years of the depression. A popular agrarian reform was in the making.

The kinds of land occupations described here occurred in seven different areas of Colombia in the early 1930s. Organizationally unconnected, the various squatter movements were shaped by similar conditioning factors. Significantly, all emerged in regions of large estates with a recent history of land concentration and *colono*–land entrepreneur tensions. Moreover, the focal regions tended to be commercially important areas in which the impact of the Great Depression was felt with particular severity. The major regions included the coffee zones of Sumapaz, Quindío, Huila, and northern Valle, the Sinú cattle-ranching area, and the United Fruit Company banana zone.

The landlords, however, did not acquiesce in the loss of their properties, and a period of intense agrarian conflict ensued. In the course of the conflicts, peasants in frontier regions developed the protest strategies that they would use repeatedly in later years. During this period, non-Indian peasants first made use of the land invasion tactic, Colombian peasant leagues took form, and peasants in frontier areas began to identify with left-wing political parties. These parties included the Unión Nacional Izquierdista Revolucionaria (UNIR), founded by Jorge Eliécer Gaitán; the Partido Comunista de Colombia (PCC), which emerged out of the Partido Socialista Revolucionaria of the 1920s; and the Partido Agarista Nacional (PAN) of Sumapaz, led by dissident lawyer Erasmo Valencia.[39] The largest and most innovative of the settler organizations, however, was not a party but a "colony," the Colonia Agrícola de Sumapaz, which emerged in the mountains of Sumapaz to the southwest of Bogotá. The Colonia grouped together more than six thousand peasants who claimed the land of estates illegally consolidated in the 1830 to 1930 period and set up their own government, prefiguring the independent republic established in the same region during the Violence some twenty years later.[40]

Of particular importance during this period was the formulation of a rural protest ideology centering on the public land issue. As we have seen, tenant farmers and wage laborers, by claiming to be settlers of public lands, endeavored to reassert control over the land and labor of which they had been dispossessed. Those who participated in the hacienda invasions of the 1930s justified their actions with the argument that the land was truly public land. Against the written titles of the landlords, they advanced the idea that frontier land belongs first and foremost to those who work it.[41] From this time on the rural population was to appeal to this idea to justify the land invasions that have been a recurrent phenomenon in the Colombian countryside, particularly in periods of economic recession.

Thus, the *colono* movements of the 1930s constituted a distinct mode of agrarian protest adopted by diverse elements of the Colombian rural population. Tenants, rural day laborers, construction workers, plantation hands, all turned their sights toward the land because other economic options were few and because the government's agrarian policy made the reclamation of public lands a distinct possibility. In becoming settlers, these people sought economic independence, but they refused any longer to be relegated to distant frontiers. For them, as for the early frontier migrants, economic independence implied production for commercial markets and participation in the benefits of economic growth.

The tendency of the squatters' movements of the 1930s to spread and the growing intensity of the confrontations compelled the Colombian government to intervene in order to clarify the issue of property rights. The government's response was Law 200 of 1936, often called the first modern agrarian reform law in Colombian history. Ironically, in fact, the law appears to have given the landlords the upper hand. It reversed the Supreme Court decision of 1926, thereby sanctioning many landlords' property claims. At the same time, however, Law 200 strongly supported the concept of the social function of property; it stipulated that, if the great estates were not made productive within ten years, they should automatically revert to the public domain.[42]

Both landlords and peasants interpreted the new legislation as supportive of their own interests, and the conflicts continued under new guises. In the older frontier regions and in the new areas of frontier expansion, tensions between landlords and *colonos* have continued to be manifest in recent years. These tensions, however, have assumed new forms in response to changes in the larger socioeconomic and institutional environment. Recent research suggests that an awareness of the landlord-settler conflict is basic to understanding the Violence in certain of its regional manifestations, the land invasions of the 1960s and 1970s, and the success of guerrilla groups in building a support base in frontier regions today.[43]

Notes

1. The major source for this paper is the Colombian Public Land Archives, which contain all communications on public lands sent from the municipalities to the national government between 1830 and 1930. The archive consists of twenty-four volumes labeled *Bienes nacionales*, deposited in the Instituto Colombiano de la Reforma Agraria (INCORA), and seventy-eight volumes

designated *Ministerio de Industrias: Correspondencia de baldíos*, located in the Archivo Histórico Nacional in Bogotá.

2. Important works on Colombian economic growth in the late nineteenth and early twentieth centuries include Fernando Botero and Alvaro Guzmán Barney, "El enclave agrícola en la zona bananera de Santa Marta," *Cuadernos Colombianos* 4:11 (1977): 309–90; Roger Brew, *El desarrollo económico de Antioquia desde la independencia hasta 1920* (Bogotá, 1977); Orlando Fals Borda, *Capitalismo, hacienda y poblamiento en la Costa Atlántica* (Bogotá, 1976); William Paul McGreevey, *An Economic History of Colombia, 1845–1930* (Cambridge, Eng., 1971); José Antonio Ocampo, *Colombia y la economía mundial 1830–1910* (Bogotá, 1984); José Antonio Ocampo, ed., *Historia económica de Colombia* (Bogotá, 1987); Marco Palacios, *Coffee in Colombia, 1850–1970* (Cambridge, Eng., 1980); and James Parsons, *Antioqueño Colonization in Western Colombia* (Berkeley, 1949).

3. See, for example, David McCreery, "Debt Servitude in Rural Guatemala, 1876–1936," *Hispanic America Historical Review* 63:4 (November 1983): 735–59; Peter Klaren, "The Social and Economic Consequences of Modernization in the Peruvian Sugar Industry, 1870–1930," in Kenneth Duncan and Ian Rutledge, eds., *Land and Labour in Latin America* (Cambridge, England, 1977), 229–52; Peter Blanchard, "The Recruitment of Workers in the Peruvian Sierra at the Turn of the Century: The *Enganche* System," *Inter-American Economic Affairs* 336:3 (1979): 63–84; and Michael J. Gonzales, "Capitalist Agriculture and Labor Contracting in Northern Peru, 1880–1905," *Journal of Latin American Studies* 12 (November 1980): 291–315.

4. See Felipe Pérez, *Geografía física i política de los Estados Unidos de Colombia*, cited in Colombia, Ministerio de Hacienda, *Memoria al Congreso Nacional* (1873), 65; and "Informe del Sr. Visitador Fiscal de Ferrocarriles ... 8/12/1915," reprinted in Colombia, Ministerio de Industrias, *Memoria al Congreso Nacional* (1931), Vol. 5: 444–45.

5. Given the difficulty of determining municipal boundaries and possible errors in the data itself, it is difficult to map precisely the area still in the public domain at the beginning of the period of export growth.

6. The evolution of rural economy and society in the Andean highlands of Colombia in the nineteenth and early twentieth centuries is an important subject on which little research has been done. For some fragmentary information see McGreevey, *Economic History of Colombia*; Glenn Curry, "The Disappearance of the *Resguardos Indígenas* of Cundinamarca, Colombia, 1800–1863" (Ph.D. diss., Vanderbilt University, 1981); Orlando Fals Borda, *El hombre y la tierra en Boyacá* (Bogotá, 1972); David Church Johnson, "Social and Economic Change in Nineteenth-Century Santander, Colombia" (Ph.D. diss., University of California at Berkeley, 1975); and Fernando López G., *Evolución de la tenencia de la tierra en una zona minifundista*, Centro de Estudios Sobre el Desarrollo Económico (CEDE), Facultad de Economía, Universidad de Los Andes, Doc. No. 029 (Bogotá, 1975).

7. Much work has been done on these migrations for the Antioqueño colonization area of southern Antioquia, northern Tolima, Caldas, and northern Valle. See, for example, Brew, *Desarrollo económico de Antioquia*; Parsons,

Antioqueño Colonization; and Alvaro López Toro, *Migración y cambio social en Antioquia durante el siglo diez y nueve* (Bogotá, 1970). The Public Land Archives provide evidence that the colonization process was, in fact, much wider in geographical scope. Scattered information in regional studies supports this finding. See, for example, Jorge Villegas, "La colonización de vertiente del siglo XIX en Colombia," *Estudios rurales Latinoamericanos* 1:2 (1978): 101–47; Orlando Fals Borda, *Mompox y loba: Historia doble de La Costa*, vols. 1, 2 (Bogotá, 1979, 1981); and Carlos Enrique Pardo, "Cundinamarca: Hacienda cafetera y conflictos agrarios" (Tésis de Grado, Universidad de Los Andes, 1981).

8. See Archivo Histórico Nacional, *Ministerio de Industrias: Correspondencia de baldíos* (hereinafter cited as ANCB), volume 6, folio 99; v. 49, f. 202; v. 50, fs. 258, 424, 507; v. 54, fs. 203, 553–54; v. 58, f. 603; v. 71, f. 356; and v. 75, f. 371.

9. This information is drawn from a municipal survey of the extent and usage of the public domain conducted by the Colombian Ministry of Agriculture in 1916. The returns are to be found in ANCB, vols. 32, 39, 40, 43, 44, 46, 47, 48, and 67.

10. See Colombia, Archivo del Congreso Nacional (hereafter cited as AC), "Proyectos pendientes de 1859 (Cámara)," v. 3, f. 16; AC, "Leyes autógrafas de 1917," v. 6, f. 153; and ANCB, v. 43, f. 172. What is not yet clear is how much produce the *colonos* contributed to Colombian exports above and beyond their supply of domestic markets.

11. ANCB, v. 26, f. 384; v. 33, fs. 48, 246; v. 34, f. 366; v. 43, f. 273; v. 46, f. 166; v. 47, f. 302; v. 58, f. 364; v. 68, f. 36; v. 70, f. 75; v. 75, fs. 229, 295; and v. 76, f. 113; and Colombia, Ministerio de Agricultura, *Memoria al Congreso Nacional* (1922), 7.

12. See ANCB, v. 23, f. 24; v. 24, f. 359; v. 39, f. 232; v. 41, f. 191; v. 43, f. 254; and v. 44, f. 283. See also Colombia, Ministerio de Industrias, *Memoria al Congreso Nacional* (1934), 379–81.

13. For information on frontier *caseríos* and their formation, see Demetrio Daniel Henríquez, *Monografía completa de la zona bananera* (Santa Marta, 1939); Urbano Campo, *Urbanización y violencia en el Valle* (Bogotá, 1980), 17–55; Colombia, Departamento de Antioquia, *Informe del Secretario de Gobierno* (1930), 264; Colombia, Departamento de Tolima, *Informe del Secretario de Gobierno* (1933), 31; and ANCB, v. 13, f. 48; v. 20, f. 21; v. 22, f. 349; v. 24, f. 138; v. 43, f. 497; v. 64, f. 508; and v. 77, f. 385.

14. See *Boletín Industrial*, May 8, 1875; *El Agricultor* 2:5 (October 6, 1879): 77; ibid., 2:7 (December 8, 1879): 109; ibid., 4:6 (November 1882): 516; and ibid., 14:4 (May 1898): 213; and Fabio Zambrano et al., "Colombia: Desarrollo agrícola, 1900–1930" (Tésis de Grado, Universidad Jorge Tadeo Lozano, 1974), chap. 2.

15. No study yet exists of the Colombian *enganche* system. Scattered references indicate that owners of coffee estates in the eastern and central mountains sent labor contractors to the eastern highlands to hire seasonal workers for the biannual coffee harvests. Much of this work force seems to have been composed of women and children in the late nineteenth century.

See Palacios, *Coffee in Colombia*, 71, 89; and Malcolm Deas, "A Colombian Coffee Estate: Santa Barbara, Cundinamarca, 1870–1912," in Duncan and Rutledge, *Land and Labour*, 269–98. For information on women in Colombian agriculture, see Magdalena León de Leal and Carmen Diana Deere, eds., *Mujer y capitalismo agrario* (Bogotá, 1980); and Elssy Bonilla C. and Eduardo Velez B., *Mujer y trabajo en el sector rural colombiano* (Bogotá, 1987).

16. By Colombian law, every applicant for a land grant had to hire a surveyor to measure and map the territory. For a parcel less than fifty hectares in size, the surveyor's fee generally exceeded the value of the cultivated land. See ANCB, v. 4, f. 71; and v. 26, f. 713; and AC, "Leyes autógrafas de 1917," v. 6, fs. 148–49.

17. A compilation of the most important laws, legislative enactments, and resolutions concerning the titling of public lands from 1821 to 1931 was published in Colombia, Ministerio de Industrias, *Memoria al Congreso* (1931), vol. 3.

18. In the area of Antioqueño migrations in the central mountains, twenty-one *poblaciones* received corporate land grants from the Colombian government between 1830 and 1910. The people belonging to these settlements were among the few frontier settlers in Colombia to receive title to their holdings. Because many later became prosperous coffee producers, they have attracted a great deal of attention from historians. Indeed, the Antioqueño settlements gave birth to the myth of the "democratic frontier" that runs through much of the English-language literature on Colombia. See Parsons, *Antioqueño Colonization*, and Everett Hagen, "How Economic Growth Begins: A Theory of Social Change," *Journal of Social Issues* 19:1 (1963): 20–34. More recent studies of the Antioqueño area suggest that the formation of these settlements responded to the real estate development interests of Antioqueño merchants and landowners, who both stimulated the colonization movement and profited from it. Even within the Antioqueño area, many large estates took form through the dispossession of settlers, as described in this paper. The best of recent revisionist writings on the Antioqueño settlement movement include Brew, *Desarrollo económico de Antioquia*; Palacios, *Coffee in Colombia*, 161–97; Keith H. Christie, "Antioqueño Colonization in Western Colombia: A Reappraisal," *Hispanic American Historical Review* 58:2 (1978): 260–83; Joel Darío Sánchez Reyes, "Colonización quindiana: Proceso político-ideológico de la conformación del campesinado cafetero, 1840–1920" (M.A. thesis, Universidad de Los Andes, 1982); Carlos Ortiz, "Fundadores y negociantes en la colonización del Quindío," *Lecturas de Economía* [Universidad de Antioquia], 13 (1984): 105–39; Maria C. Errazuriz, *Cafeteros y cafetales del Líbano* (Bogotá, 1986), 31–44; and Keith H. Christie, *Oligarcas, campesinos y política en Colombia: Aspectos de la historia socio-política de la frontera antioqueña* (Bogotá, 1986).

19. This information is drawn from the list of all government land grants awarded to individuals, settlements, and companies for the years 1821–1931 found in Colombia, Ministerio de Industrias, *Memoria al Congreso* (1931), vol. 5: 249–410. More than 70 percent of the total land granted in this period went into properties greater than one thousand hectares in size.

20. For theoretical discussions of this point, see Evsey D. Domar, "The Causes of Slavery or Serfdom: A Hypothesis," *Journal of Economic History* 30:1–2 (1970): 18–32; Martin Katzman, "The Brazilian Frontier in Comparative Perspective," *Comparative Studies in Society and History* 17:3 (1975): 274–75; and Gervasio Castro de Rezende, "Plantation Systems, Land Tenure, and Labor Supply: An Historical Analysis of the Brazilian Case with a Contemporary Study of the Cacao Regions of Bahia, Brazil" (Ph.D. diss., University of Wisconsin, 1976). Several Colombian reports from the late nineteenth and early twentieth centuries allude to the labor motive for the creation of latifundia in frontier regions. A congressional committee, for example, reported in 1882 that "it is generally through the dispossession of the poor settlers that rich people acquire large landholdings. . . . Many . . . obtain immense extensions of territory which they hoard with the sole purpose of excluding settlers from those areas or else reducing them to serf-like conditions" (AC, "Leyes autógrafas de 1882 [Senado]," v. 2, fs. 250, 266). A letter from the Municipal Council of Espejuelo (Cauca) in 1907 was even more explicit: "In Cauca, the majority of the *hacendados* have taken over vast zones of public lands . . . which they neither work themselves nor allow others to work. By monopolizing the land, they aim only to undermine the position of the independent cultivators so as to form from their ranks groups of dependent laborers" (ANCB, v. 42, f. 177).

21. The various forms of usurpation and their geographical distribution and extent are described in Catherine LeGrand, *Frontier Expansion and Peasant Protest in Colombia, 1850–1936* (Albuquerque, 1986), 50–56. The Public Land Archives contain hundreds of examples of these usurpations. See, for instance, ANCB, v. 9, fs. 16–17; v. 12, f. 87; v. 13, fs. 48, 123; v. 14, f. 360; v. 25, f. 657; v. 26, f. 325; v. 33, f. 246; v. 72, f. 189; and v. 76, f. 113. The two court cases most frequently used by landlords to establish new property boundaries were *juicios de deslinde* (boundary actions) and *juicios de partición* (partition suits).

22. Scores of *colono* petitions collected in ANCB describe such meetings. For example, see ANCB, v. 11, f. 190; v. 14, f. 307; and v. 15, f. 246.

23. Malcolm Deas of Oxford University has suggested to me that for some settlers colonizing, improving, and then selling out became a way of life. There are hints that this was so in some papers from the Antioqueño colonization region (see INCORA, *Bienes nacionales*), but, unfortunately, the documentation is sparse.

24. Perhaps because historians of Colombia have yet to find the hacienda records that have proved so useful for the study of labor relations in Mexico and Peru, our knowledge of work roles and working conditions on Colombian estates remains rudimentary. Some forms of tenancy are described in Palacios, *Coffee in Colombia*, 55–120; Deas, "A Colombian Coffee Estate," 269–98; Mariano Arango, *Café e industria, 1850–1930* (Bogotá, 1977), 123–72; Absalón Machado, *El café: De la aparcería al capitalismo* (Bogotá, 1977); Luís Fernando Sierra, *El tobaco en la economía colombiana del siglo XIX* (Bogotá, 1961), 123–63; and Roger Soles, "Rural Land Invasions in Colombia: A Study

of the Macro- and Micro-Conditions and Forces Leading to Peasant Unrest" (Ph.D. diss., University of Wisconsin, 1972), 121–31. There were three major types of tenants in Colombia: 1) *arrendatarios* (also known as *agregados, terrazgueros,* or *concertados*), 2) *aparceros,* and 3) *colonos a partido. Arrendatarios* were service tenants who, as rent for a small plot of land on which to raise food crops, were expected to work or to provide labor in the landlords' fields. Such arrangements were common both in areas of traditional agriculture in the highlands and in some coffee regions, for example, western Cundinamarca and southern Tolima. In the coffee areas, *arrendatarios* often were paid for their labor, but at a salary considerably lower than that of day workers. Some of the more prosperous *arrendatarios* hired day laborers to perform their labor obligations, so as to devote themselves entirely to their own fields. In other coffee regions (for example, Santander, Antioquia, and Caldas), *arrendatarios* were few, and *aparcería,* or sharecropping, was the dominant form of tenancy. On the cattle ranches, yet a third form prevailed. Tenants known as *colonos a partido* were allowed to clear a parcel of land for their own use on the undeveloped outskirts of the property on the condition that they turn it over to the landlord planted in pasture grasses after two or three years. On ranches and to a lesser extent on coffee estates, *colonos a partido* were used to expand the productive area of the haciendas. Almost all large rural enterprises also employed some wage laborers for specific tasks; they were used on coffee estates at harvest time, on cattle ranches as cowboys, and on the United Fruit Company banana plantations, where some settlers of public lands also contracted for a wage, to work part-time in the banana groves. See Catherine LeGrand "Colombian Transformations: Peasants and Wage Laborers in the Santa Marta Banana Zone," *Journal of Peasant Studies* 11:4 (1984): 178–200.

25. The text of these laws is found in Colombia, Ministerio de Industrias, *Memoria al Congreso* (1931), vol. 3: 121–24, 149–51. In the early nineteenth century the Colombian government used the public domain primarily as a fiscal resource to support a bankrupt government. The Congress issued territorial certificates redeemable in public lands to finance the public debt and to pay military veterans and road and railroad contractors. Freely bought and sold on the open market, these certificates were relatively inexpensive for people of means, although clearly beyond the reach of the peasant population. During this period, the government also allotted a few grants to new settlements, mainly in the Antioqueño colonization area.

The reform of public land policy in the 1870s and 1880s responded to the Liberal concern to create a nation of small proprietors. It also reflected the desire of both Liberals and Conservatives to encourage the expansion of agriculture and stock raising through incorporation of the public domain into the national economy. From this time on, anyone who put public lands into production was allowed to petition for a free grant of that land and an additional area equal in size. Although the laws explicitly supported the rights of peasant settlers, most people who actually obtained land grants, "*a título de cultivador,*" were large farmers and ranchers.

26. This interpretation of settler ideology is drawn from a number of *colono* petitions in ANCB, which constantly refer to the laws of 1882 in their protests against land entrepreneurs.

27. See ANCB, vols. 1–78. These petitions date from 1874 through 1931. It is said that *colono* petitions from later years are deposited at INCORA in Bogotá.

28. See, for example, William B. Taylor, *Landlord and Peasant in Colonial Oaxaca* (Stanford, 1972); and Eric J. Hobsbawm, "Peasant Land Occupations," *Past and Present*, 62 (1974): 120–52.

29. For examples of confrontations between settlers and land entrepreneurs, see ANCB, v. 11, f. 190; v. 12, fs. 245, 286; v. 14, f. 307; v. 15, fs. 246, 342, 375, 378; v. 18, fs. 115, 468; v. 20, f. 130; v. 25, f. 31; v. 27, fs. 125, 132; v. 28, fs. 336, 340, 341; v. 29, f. 637; v. 35, f. 522; v. 36, f. 452; v. 43, f. 473; v. 45, fs. 626, 674; and v. 55, f. 477.

30. *Boletín de la Oficina General de Trabajo* 5:39–44 (January-June 1934): 152–54. For other examples of lawyers helping settlers, see ANCB, v. 10, f. 100; v. 14, fs. 342, 347; v. 28, f. 341; v. 34, f. 355; v. 50, f. 363; v. 62, f. 282; v. 63, fs. 4, 174; v. 64, f. 63; and v. 65, fs. 233, 471.

31. ANCB, v. 55, f. 477bis. For other cases, see ANCB, v. 10, f. 99; v. 43, f. 483; and v. 44, f. 435bis.

32. ANCB, v. 9, fs. 76, 86; v. 11, f. 111; v. 15, f. 267; v. 16, f. 69; v. 25, f. 41; v. 28, f. 122; v. 29, fs. 633, 774; v. 32, f. 451; v. 33, f. 503; v. 35, f. 591; v. 39, f. 199; v. 43, f. 283; v. 44, f. 390; v. 45, f. 629; v. 46, f. 235; v. 47, f. 132; and v. 57, f. 50.

33. The list was drawn up by the author from the *colono* petitions in ANCB, vols. 1–78. Because the petitions do not always state the number of peasant families involved in any given confrontation, it is difficult to be more specific concerning the magnitude of each conflict. Some, however, involved hundreds of settlers, and, in a few, more than one thousand peasant families took part. Major regions of ongoing disputes included Belalcázar (Caldas), San Antonio and Prado (Tolima), and Caparrapí and Pandi (Cundinamarca). I have in my possession detailed summaries of each confrontation that I would be willing to share with interested researchers.

34. See Parsons, *Antioqueño Colonization*; Palacios, *Coffee in Colombia*, 161–97; and Sánchez Reyes, "Colonización quindiana."

35. It is important to take into account the role the national government played in determining the outcome of the conflicts. In the 1870 to 1925 period the Colombian government seems to have had little direct power over what happened in the rural localities. Occasionally the government did reject applications for large land grants that took in settlers' fields. (See Colombia, Ministerio de Industrias, *Memoria al Congreso* [1931], vol. 3: 190; ANCB, v. 26, f. 680; and v. 46, f. 374.) But generally the settlers' petitions arrived too late or the directives of national authorities were undermined by local officials in collaboration with the landlords. (For examples of this, see ANCB, v. 25, fs. 709, 714; v. 36, f. 382; v. 44, f. 636; v. 45, f. 672; and v. 46, f. 419.) For a more detailed analysis of the government's ineffectiveness in protecting settlers' rights, see LeGrand, *Frontier Expansion*, 83–87.

36. The most informative works on the 1920s and 1930s in Colombia include J. Fred Rippy, *The Capitalists and Colombia* (New York, 1931); Miguel Urrutia, *The Development of the Colombian Labor Movement* (New Haven, CT, 1969); Hugo López C., "La inflación en Colombia en la década de los veintes," *Cuadernos Colombianos*, 5 (1975): 41–140; Jesús Antonio Bejarano, *El régimen agrario de la economía exportadora a la economía industrial* (Bogotá, 1979); and José Antonio Ocampo and Santiago Montenegro, *Crisis mundial, protección e industrialización* (Bogotá, 1984). The connection between these changes and the emergence of the agrarian movements of the 1930s is explored in LeGrand, *Frontier Expansion*, 91–108.

37. See "Sentencia de la sala de negocios generales de la Corte Suprema" (April 15, 1926), in Colombia, Corte Suprema, *Jurisprudencia*, vol. 3: 357. The shift in public land policy in the 1920s stemmed from the government's concern to increase the production of foodstuffs for domestic consumption in order to support industrialization. Recognizing that most foodstuffs for internal markets were supplied not by the large estates but by peasant producers, the government endeavored to facilitate colonization of the public domain by peasant settlers in order to expand food production. The uncertain status of landownership, however, frustrated the endeavor, leading the Supreme Court to define what was private property and what was public land in a way that would put the state and the colonization movement in a strong position. The government apparently had no idea of the magnitude of usurpations landowners had effected over the previous half-century.

38. Material on these squatter movements can be found in the *Informes* of the departmental governors and gubernatorial secretaries for the early 1930s; in the *Memorias* of the Ministry of Industries (1928–1936); in the *Boletín de la Oficina General de Trabajo* (1928–1936); and in the newspapers *Claridad, El Bolshevique*, and *Tierra*. See also Bejarano, *El régimen agrario*; Gloria Gaitán, *Colombia: La lucha por la tierra en la década del treinta* (Bogotá, 1976); Gonzalo Sánchez, *Las ligas campesinas en Colombia* (Bogotá, 1977); Victor Negrete B., *Orígen de las luchas agrarias en Córdoba* (Montería, 1981); and Colombia, *Informes que rindió a la honorable Cámara de Representantes la comisión designada para visitar la zona bananera del Magdalena* (Bogotá, 1936).

39. Although the leftist political parties were important in organizing peasants to resist the landlords, they did not create the conflicts; indeed, they began to organize the countryside only after the conflicts erupted. Both UNIR and the PCC formed peasant leagues, although UNIR was more successful in appealing to settlers while the PCC was more active in areas where tenants were involved in contract disputes and Indians sought return of their communal lands. On the activities of these parties in the early 1930s, see Sánchez, *Ligas campesinas*; Comité Central del Partido Communista de Colombia, *Treinta años de lucha del Partido Comunista de Colombia* (Bogotá, n.d.); Medófilo Medina, *Historia del Partido Communista de Colombia*, vol. 1 (Bogotá, 1980); Michael Jiménez, "The Limits of Export Capitalism: Economic Structure, Class, and Politics in a Colombian Coffee Municipality, 1900–1930" (Ph.D. diss., Harvard University, 1985), 440–513; and LeGrand, *Frontier Expansion*, 122–31.

40. Information on the Colonia Agrícola de Sumapaz can be found in Colombia, *Informe del Procurador General de la Nación* (1932), 39–43; Departamento de Cundinamarca, *Informe del Secretario de Gobierno* (1931), 31–34; Departamento de Tolima, *Informe del Secretario de Gobierno* (1932), 34–37; Academia Colombiana de Historia, Archivo del Presidente Enrique Olaya Herrera, box 2, folder 37, f. 82, and box 3, folder 21, "Informe del Jefe de la Sección de Justicia," 4–10; and *Claridad* (1932–1937), all issues.

41. See *Boletín de la Oficina General de Trabajo* 4: 33–35 (1933):1333; Departamento de Tolima, *Informe del Secretario de Gobierno* (1932), 31–34; Departamento de Cundinamarca, *Mensaje del Gobernador* (1933), 10; Ministerio de Industrias, *Memoria al Congreso* (1931), vol. 1:53; and Ministerio de Industrias, *Memoria al Congreso* (1934), 337.

42. For the text of Law 200 and its antecedents see AC, "Leyes autógrafas de 1936," v. 18, fs. 1–345. Marco A. Martínez, ed., *Régimen de tierras en Colombia (antecedentes de la Ley 200 de 1936 "Sobre régimen de tierras" y decretos reglamentarios)*, 2 vols. (Bogotá, 1939), is a useful compilation of all official documents relating to Law 200, including drafts of the bill, congressional debates, and committee reports. For interpretations of the law and its effects, see Darío Mesa, *El problema agrario en Colombia, 1920–1960* (Bogotá, 1972); Victor Moncayo C., "La ley y el problema agrario en Colombia," *Ideología y sociedad*, 14–15 (1975): 7–46; and Sánchez, *Ligas campesinas*, 125–29. To deal with the conflicts of the 1930s the Colombian government also initiated a "parcelization" program that provided for the purchase of underutilized estates and their subdivision, and it set up a system of land courts to handle disputes over rural property. The effects of these policies remain unstudied; indeed, Colombian agrarian history from 1936 to 1948 has yet to be seriously investigated. This period is of obvious importance for understanding the origins of the Violence and, more specifically, the connections between the agrarian conflicts of the 1930s and those of the 1940s and 1950s.

43. See Luís F. Bottia G. and Rudolfo Escobedo D., "La Violencia en el sur del departamento de Córdoba" (Tésis de Grado, Universidad de Los Andes, 1979); W. Ramírez Tobón, "La guerrilla rural en Colombia: Una vía hacía la colonización armada?," *Estudios Rurales Latinoamericanos* 4:2 (1981): 199–210; Mary Roldán, "The Political Dimensions of La Violencia in Antioquia," paper presented at the annual meeting of the American Historical Association, December 28, 1987, Washington, D.C.; Alfredo Molano, *Selva adentro: Una historia oral de la colonización del Guaviare* (Bogotá, 1987); Alfredo Molano, *Siguiendo el corte: Relatos de guerras y tierras* (Bogotá, 1989); and Catherine LeGrand, "Colonization and Violence in Colombia: Perspectives and Debates," *Canadian Journal of Latin American and Caribbean Studies* 14:28 (1989).

4

The Labor Movement (1930–1946) and the Origins of the Violence*

Charles Bergquist

In two books dealing with Colombia, Charles Bergquist has probed the connections between the coffee economy and political violence. In *Coffee and Conflict in Colombia, 1886–1910* (Durham, NC, 1978) he argued that the rise of the coffee economy was closely related to the origins and outcome of the most violent period proportionately in Colombian history, the War of the Thousand Days, 1899–1902. In *Labor in Latin America: Comparative Essays on Chile, Argentina, Venezuela, and Colombia* (Stanford, 1986), Bergquist developed the idea, outlined in this chapter, that coffee workers' struggles helped precipitate and explain the Violence of the midtwentieth century. This argument is novel in two important respects: first, because coffee workers usually are not considered part of the labor movement; and second, because blame for the Violence usually is placed at the doorstep of the elite. Bergquist does not blame coffee workers for the Violence. But he shows how, paradoxically, their democratic struggle for the land, accomplished within the context of the traditional party system, was the primary motor behind the complex series of events that culminated in the Violence of the post-1946 period.

Charles Bergquist teaches Latin American history and coordinates the Latin American Studies Program at the University of Washington.

The years that define the period under consideration, 1930 and 1946, are among the most decisive in the political history of Colombia. In 1930, a split in the Conservative party enabled the Liberal party to

*This chapter was originally published in Gonzalo Sánchez and Ricardo Peñaranda, eds., *Pasado y presente de la Violencia en Colombia* (Bogotá, 1986). Reprinted by permission of the Centro de Estudios de la Realidad Colombiana.

win the presidency, thus ending a half-century of Conservative political hegemony and ushering in a remarkable sixteen-year period of Liberal control and reform. In 1946 the tables were turned; the Liberal party divided its votes between two presidential candidates, and the Conservative party won control of the executive. These political events, it generally is accepted, helped to unleash the Violence, the longest and bloodiest civil commotion to affect a Latin American nation between the Mexican Revolution of 1910 and the current crisis in Central America.

For the Colombian labor movement these political events, and the period of Liberal political hegemony that they define, were no less decisive. During this period an insurgent, anticapitalist labor movement was deradicalized, its independent power destroyed, and its organizations successfully incorporated into the legal and political life of the nation.

What precisely is the connection between the events of 1930 and 1946 and the history of the Colombian labor movement? What is their relationship to the Violence, a phenomenon that, in contrast to the Mexican Revolution or the contemporary struggle in Central America, resists comprehension as a social and anti-imperialistic revolution? In other words, what does the history of the Colombian labor movement in the 1930s and 1940s have to do with the central questions of modern Colombian history?

Standard interpretations of this crucial period tend to ignore the importance of the labor movement to the outcome of national political developments. This is a curious state of affairs for two reasons. The first is that historical writing on this period, like that on the rest of twentieth-century Colombia, has been dominated by liberal and leftist scholarship. In terms of theory and political inclination, such scholarship could be expected to emphasize, more than would conservative interpretations, the interests and role of the working class. Second, most of these standard interpretations view the period in question as some kind of aborted social revolution. In this view, as the 1930s and 1940s progressed, the reformist Liberal leadership "betrayed the masses," frustrating their aspirations for a more just social and political order. Meanwhile, the Conservative political elite, in alliance with the Catholic Church, engendered the political reaction that eroded Liberal political hegemony and culminated in the establishment of the repressive Conservative regimes of the late 1940s and early 1950s. The result was the tragedy of the Violence, which pitted the Colombian people against themselves and left the bipartisan elite free to forge the nominally democratic dependent capitalist order that has existed, effectively unchallenged, to the present day.

Thus scholarship has focused primarily on elite political action as the key to understanding the period in question. It traces the initiatives and failings of reformist Liberal leaders, such as Alfonso López Pumarejo and Jorge Eliécer Gaitán, or the machinations of Conservative reactionaries, notably Laureano Gómez. Some social scientists writing in this tradition have broadened their study of elite political action by linking it to the dynamics of patronage and political exclusivism in Colombia's traditional bipartisan political system. But this work too neglects the struggle of Colombian workers when explaining the process that culminated in the Violence. Even students of the labor movement itself in general have failed to interpret national political events very differently. Although they are sympathetic to the workers, these writers tend to view the failure of the left and of popular forces as a problem of leadership—that is, of the alleged opportunism of the Communist party and of dissident Liberals such as Gaitán, or of clever manipulations by the Liberal or Conservative oligarchy in control of the traditional parties and the state.

This emphasis on the success of ruling-class conspiracies or on the failure of popular leadership significantly distorts the historical record. Focusing on the struggle of Colombian workers, I will argue, makes better sense of the dynamic of national political events that culminates in the Violence. To place the workers' struggle at the center of this historical analysis, however, it is necessary first to redefine Colombian labor history.

Conceptualizing Colombian Labor History

Traditionally, labor history in Colombia (and other peripheral capitalist societies) has been defined, following liberal and Marxist models constructed in core capitalist societies, as the history of urban workers, artisans and proletarians in manufacturing industry. Rural workers, "peasants"* and farmers in agricultural production, were separated from the labor movement, their struggles seen as involving a different problematic and obeying a different logic. The standard history of the labor movement begins in the nineteenth and early twentieth centuries

*A term derived from European experience and social theory. For reasons developed here, I do not find it useful in analyzing Colombian (or Latin American) rural workers, a class, which, unlike its European counterpart, emerged in response to the expansion of world capitalism. I have placed the word in quotation marks to distance myself from the bulk of the literature on the subject. The Spanish term *campesinos*, which means literally "people of the fields," usually is translated into English as "peasants."

with the study of the mutual aid societies and incipient unions and parties of urban artisans and manufacturing workers. It includes, as the twentieth century progresses, the history of transport (primarily railroad, river, and port) workers and those in the banana and oil enclaves, whose struggles reached explosive dimensions in the late 1920s. As Colombia's dependent capitalist society has matured in the half-century since 1930, standard labor history increasingly revolves around workers in the manufacturing and service sectors of the national economy.

Separated from this history of urban and industrial workers is the history of agrarian capitalism and "peasant" struggles. It traces the story of land and labor in rural areas from the colonial period on and, for this century, chronicles the rise of "peasant" leagues in the 1920s, analyzes the violent class struggle on the great coffee estates in the 1930s, speculates on the impact of the Violence on land tenure patterns in the 1940s and 1950s, and focuses on the process of rural proletarianization and on labor organization in the quarter century after 1960. Only for the recent period, when substantial proletarianization in the agricultural sector is achieved, are these previously separate histories of urban and rural workers allowed to overlap and be accorded simultaneous treatment.

The separate conceptualization and treatment of the history of urban and rural workers make good sense in terms of orthodox Marxist and liberal theory. In both cases such treatment derives from a well-developed theory of objective social processes (modernization for liberals, proletarianization for Marxists). Both theories try to explain modern history through categories of analysis (a modern sector or a proletariat) that predict changes in human consciousness and political action. Quite apart from their other problems, these theoretical models confront a serious obstacle in dealing with the reality of labor history in peripheral capitalist societies. Unlike in core capitalist countries, where the axis of economic growth and development has been located for two centuries in the industrial sector, in peripheral societies, at least until the midtwentieth century, economic activity mainly revolved around the export of primary mineral and agricultural products.

Should not, therefore, the history of workers in export production form the central theme in the history of labor in such societies? When one considers these workers' economic importance, such a focus clearly seems justified. Yet it has been ignored by historians and social scientists. In recent decades they have been quick to revise orthodox liberal and Marxist theories of economic development to take into account the special features of peripheral capitalism. Furthermore, they have adapted the categories of ruling-class description to accommodate the fact that in peripheral political development, power was wielded not by an industrial bourgeoisie but by those persons who controlled the means of export production and exchange. But, curiously, they have been remiss in modifying their categories of analysis for the working class. Why this has been true is itself worthy of investigation. Does it reflect the paternalistic and authoritarian elitism, however unconscious, of even the most "progressive" social science, including that conceived within the Marxist tradition?

Whatever the cause, the fact of the matter is that workers in export production and processing in peripheral capitalist societies, such as those of Latin America, refuse to conform to the conceptual categories of orthodox liberal and Marxist theory. How does one classify, for example, workers in the huge rural sugar export complexes at the core of the Cuban economy since the nineteenth century, or the miners of highland Peru who move in and out of subsistence agriculture? These workers are sometimes more rural than urban, sometimes more agricultural than industrial, sometimes free wage laborers, sometimes not. It was these workers in export production and processing, and those linked to them in the modern transportation network required by export production, who most fundamentally influenced the development of peripheral capitalist societies in the first half of the twentieth century. During this period they represented the most immediate obstacle to accumulation by the national and foreign ruling class. Strikes in the export sector most severely affected the economic and fiscal health of the nation. Export workers thus held the greatest objective and symbolic power to influence national labor and political developments. Their struggles tell the most about the fate and trajectory of the various Latin American labor movements. Their history most clearly reveals the mechanisms through which organized labor was effectively incorporated into the legal and institutional life of the various Latin American nation-states in the decades before midcentury.

In Colombia these workers were located in the coffee sector, the axis of the national economy during most of this century. Estimates of the numbers of full- and part-time coffee workers in the late 1920s range from five hundred thousand to almost one million, the latter number representing an astounding one eighth of the national population. Recent work by historians and social scientists has increased our understanding greatly of the varied and changing conditions under which coffee workers lived and labored. It also has improved our knowledge of the nature of their organized struggle, begun in the 1920s, for control of the land and the product of their labor. By and large, however, because of the conceptual impediments discussed earlier, the history of coffee workers has not been well integrated into the history of either the labor movement or the politics of the nation.

Emphasis on the struggle of coffee workers generates a different, more persuasive, and decidedly more democratic interpretation of the pivotal period of Colombian history defined by the Liberal Republic of 1930–1946. The elements of this new interpretation hinge on four sequential arguments advanced in the remainder of this essay. Each argument involves an appreciation of the meaning for national politics of class struggle within a changing world capitalist system. The first interprets the momentous transfer of power from the Conservative to the Liberal party in 1930. It places the events of 1930 in the context of the threat to ruling-class interests posed by the burgeoning anticapitalist labor movement of the 1920s, on the one hand, and by the advent of the worldwide crisis threatening the capitalist order at the end of that decade, on the other. The second deals with the Liberal Republic itself and argues that the increasingly victorious struggle of coffee workers for control of the land best explains the ebb and flow of social reform during this period. The third analyzes the crisis of liberalism and the transfer of power to the Conservative party in 1946. It focuses on the vulnerability of the Colombian labor movement to ruling-class initiatives during the resurgence and reorganization of world capitalism in the wake of the Second World War. The fourth reflects on the relationship of this whole social process to the phenomenon of the Violence.

The Advent of the Liberal Republic

Traditional interpretations of the victory of the Liberal party in 1930 tend to focus on either the vision of leaders such as López Pumarejo, or the ineptness of the Conservative leadership, confused by a Church hierarchy that signaled support of first one then another of the Conservative presidential candidates. Recent scholarship has broadened our understanding of these events by analyzing the declining fortunes of Conservative hegemony in terms of the government's failure to control through repression an insurgent anticapitalist labor movement and its inability by 1929 to ensure the flow of foreign investment into the economy. The massacre of perhaps one thousand workers and their families by government troops in the United Fruit Company banana enclave near Santa Marta, the infamous event that launched the political career of the dissident Liberal Gaitán, was the most blatant example of the first problem facing the Conservative regime.

The second problem was equally serious. For two decades after 1910 the growth and development of the Colombian economy, and the stability and legitimacy of the regime, had rested on the principles of classical liberal political economy. These principles were consolidated in law and policy by the bipartisan elite in the aftermath of the War of the Thousand Days. Under these policies, Colombia's development depended increasingly on the expansion of the coffee export sector and the large-scale infusion of foreign capital. A crisis for this system was triggered in 1927 by a U.S. government report critical of the credit worthiness of Colombia. The report led to virtual suspension of U.S. lending to Colombia in the following two years and contributed to the bipartisan decision to launch the candidacy of Enrique Olaya Herrera for the presidency in 1930. A Liberal then serving as Colombia's ambassador to the United States, Olaya Herrera was close to U.S. banking circles in New York. During his successful campaign he pledged himself to restore the flow of foreign investment needed to promote the continued growth of Colombia's coffee-based export economy.

Once in power, the government of Olaya Herrera set about dealing with the social and economic issues that had destroyed the legitimacy of the previous government. On the economic front it was initially unsuccessful. As the world depression deepened, the government proved powerless to restore the flow of foreign investment to the Colombian economy. As had other liberal regimes in Latin America during the world crisis, it was forced gradually to jettison the tenets of classical liberalism on which the export-oriented development of the nation had rested. The regime reluctantly abandoned the gold standard, defaulted on the foreign debt, and adopted exchange policies that favored the process of import-substituting industrialization.*

On the labor front, the policies of the new Liberal government, and those of its successors, met with greater favor. Through the labor law of 1931 the government promoted "responsible" labor organization, attempting to channel the labor movement into legal, moderate unions guided by the Liberal party. As a result, the number of legal unions mushroomed in the early 1930s, and eventually some of the more militant organizations, including the recently formed Communist party, chose to cooperate or ally themselves with the legal authorities and the Liberal party. They affiliated themselves with the Confederación de Trabajadores Colombianos (CTC), the first major Colombian labor federation.

*Widely used term to distinguish the kind of industrialization experienced by Latin America in the 1930s from the classical pattern witnessed in Western Europe during the nineteenth century. After 1930 the major Latin American countries increasingly began to produce the light and intermediate manufactures that they formerly imported. Compared to core industrial economies, however, they have been less successful in developing the autonomous capital goods (machine) sector of their economies.

Coffee Workers and the Logic of Liberal Reform

The policies and the intentions of the Liberal regimes, especially the first López Pumarejo government (1934–1938), traditionally have been viewed by leftist and liberal scholars as reformist and democratic. Some of these scholars have seen in López Pumarejo's "Revolution on the March" the hand of a "national bourgeoisie," a segment of the elite bent on increasing the scope and efficiency of capitalist agriculture and promoting, with the support of urban workers and manufacturers, the industrialization of the national economy.

Analysis of the major social reforms of this period—that is, the labor and agrarian reform laws of the early and mid-1930s—suggests a different interpretation for the motivations behind these policies. It also generates a different understanding of the reasons for the abandonment of these reforms by the leaders of the Liberal party during the government of Eduardo Santos (1938–1942), the second and ill-fated government of Alfonso López Pumarejo (1942–1945), and the short-lived transitional government of Alberto Lleras Camargo (1945–46), which paved the way for the Conservative restoration and reaction. These labor and agrarian reform initiatives generally are considered either as separate policies of democratic modernizers or as a function of the economic goals of a national bourgeoisie. Neither approach is very persuasive in explaining first their abandonment and then their reversal by the Liberal governments at the end of the period.

From the point of view of the Colombian working class, however, the nature and the unity of these labor and agrarian initiatives, codified in the constitutional reform of 1936, appear in a different light, and the rapidity with which they were abandoned and then reversed becomes more intelligible. Both sets of reforms were primarily a reaction to the perceived threat to the political and social hegemony of the ruling class posed by an insurgent labor movement. The concessions that the reforms to urban and rural workers involved were countenanced and tolerated by significant elements of the ruling class as long as the labor movement seemed a serious threat to their position. Once the independent power of the labor movement was broken and its organizations effectively channeled into cooperation with the state and alliance with the Liberal party, these reform policies were abandoned and then reversed.

The threat to the ruling class posed by the Colombian labor movement in the 1930s revolved around rural, not urban workers. With the coming of the depression, the strength and militance of urban and industrial workers, and of labor in the foreign-owned oil and banana enclaves, subsided rapidly. The downturn in demand for labor that accompanied the advent of the world crisis left militant worker organizations extremely weak and vulnerable. This was not the case, however, in the all-important coffee sector. There workers labored under conditions that ranged from wage labor, through various kinds of sharecropping arrangements, to petty commodity production by smallholders who rented or owned their land. During the boom in the coffee economy, which reached its apogee in the 1920s, most of these coffee workers, whatever the conditions of their labor, managed to improve their position vis-à-vis large landowners and capitalist producers. *Jornaleros* (day laborers) won higher wages, *arrendatarios* (leaseholders) managed to reduce their personal labor obligations to large landowners (or to hire others to fulfill them), and both joined *colonos* (homesteaders) and smallholders in increasing production of coffee and food for the market on land that they either owned, rented, or had gained access to. With the slump in coffee prices and the start of the depression, however, workers with access to land refused to yield to the large landowners who sought to salvage their declining profits by forcing workers to return to their former, more dependent position. In contrast to workers in the fully capitalist sectors of the economy, rural workers in hard times tended to strengthen their resolve and radicalize their demands.

The collective dimension of this struggle by coffee workers has received most of the attention of scholars. They have studied the formation of *ligas campesinas* ("peasant" leagues) in the late 1920s, especially in the departments of Cundinamarca and Tolima; the explosive struggles of *arrendatarios, jornaleros,* and *colonos* on the great coffee estates of southeastern Cundinamarca, which began in the late 1920s and gathered momentum in the early 1930s; and the political efforts, before 1935, of dissident Liberals led by Gaitán and his Unión Nacional Izquierdista Revolucionaria (UNIR) and of the Communist party to organize rural workers and mold them into a political force capable of challenging the electoral monopoly of the two traditional parties.

A less well-known, but highly significant, part of this collective struggle were the abortive national coffee strikes, organized by the Communist party in 1934 and 1935. Far more clearly than did their successors on the left, the organizers of these strikes recognized the centrality of the coffee labor force to the future of the Colombian labor movement. They sought to organize rural producers, female employees in coffee husking mills, and transport workers (muleteers, railmen, and stevedores) into a grand alliance at the very heart of the Colombian economy. Despite heroic struggle and significant but isolated successes, these strikes failed to paralyze the coffee sector and organize coffee workers into effective, enduring unions. This failure, and the unsuccessful efforts of UNIR and the Communist party to crack the electoral monopoly of the traditional parties, led the leaders of both parties to give up on the struggle to organize coffee workers. By 1936, Communists and dissident Liberals alike chose to pursue more modest reformist goals through alliance with the Liberal party.

The failure of these collective efforts was a result of many factors, the most important being the individual, and increasingly successful, struggle of tens of thousands of coffee workers for control of the land. This process is ignored or denied in leftist scholarship, and its exact timing and dynamics have yet to be thoroughly studied. Nevertheless, that this process was real is beyond doubt, and its general characteristics are clear. The process was well under way in the 1920s and seems to have gathered momentum in the 1930s and 1940s.

A comparison of the 1932, 1939, and 1955 coffee censuses reveals the direction and nature of this pivotal social process. Tables 1 through 3 provide information on the numbers and size of Colombian coffee farms over this whole period. Table 4 provides the only information on tenancy available in these coffee censuses.

Table 1 shows that by 1932 small farms with 5,000 or fewer trees already were producing almost half of Colombia's coffee. Somewhat larger small farms, those containing 5,001 to 20,000 trees, were producing an additional one fourth; large coffee farms the remaining one fourth. Table 2, with data from the partial coffee census of 1939, which was completed for only two coffee departments—Cundinamarca and Tolima—demonstrates the remarkable expansion of small coffee farms (those containing fewer than 20,000 trees) during the depression. It also reveals the virtual stagnation in the number of large coffee farms (those with more than 60,000 trees) in these departments during this same period. Table 3, based on information from the census of 1955, reveals that small coffee farms, those containing 2,500 to 25,000 trees, continued to be the most important unit of Colombian coffee production at midcentury. Unlike the earlier censuses, which were conducted by the National Federation of Coffee Growers, this census, undertaken by technical agencies of the United Nations, gives crucial information on tenancy. These data, summarized in Table 4, reveal that in the small farm category of 2,500 to 25,000 trees, more than three fourths of the farms were worked and administered by their owners. Estimates of the size necessary for a viable, family-owned and -operated coffee farm during this period range from 5,000 to 20,000 trees. This means that the bulk of the farm units in the one to ten hectare size, 77.9 percent of which were owned by their operators, were probably viable family farms. Table 3 shows that the number of such farms in 1955 was over 120,000.

It is risky to project this information on the importance of smallholders back onto the 1932 and 1939 censuses. It is quite likely that ownership was much less widespread in 1932 and that sharecropping, still important in 1955, was even more prevalent in the earlier period. But the 1955 census demonstrates what these earlier censuses had implied. It shows that land ownership was widespread in Colombian coffee production and that small family farms comprised the most numerous and important unit of Colombian coffee production. It seems likely that over the entire period, 1932 to 1955, property ownership in the coffee economy was widespread and that large and increasing numbers of viable family farms existed. At any rate, the historical trajectory of coffee production in Colombia during these years led to that result by 1955.

The secret to the growing preeminence of small family coffee farms during this period lay in the nature of the production process. It required neither large capital investment nor the application of sophisticated technology, but it did require heavy inputs of labor in all phases of coffee cultivation and processing. In their successful competition against large-scale coffee producers, small coffee farmers depended on rudimentary tools and machinery, on the ingenious use of natural resources and energy supplies, and on the full employment of the labor power of family members.

Landless and dependent coffee workers could acquire, augment, and sustain a freehold in different ways. They could colonize new land and win title to it through official procedures. They could organize to force large landowners to divide their estates and sell out. Or they could purchase land on the market. This last strategy was the most common. The politics of official distribution of public lands in the coffee zone, even in the Central Cordillera, favored large landowners, and over the years the struggle, which one observer appropriately called the battle of axes versus officially stamped legal paper, was usually won by the educated large landowners, merchants, and professionals. The parcelization of large coffee estates as a result of collective struggle by dependent coffee workers, already noted, affected several score coffee haciendas and a few thousand coffee workers and their families in important regions of Cundinamarca and Tolima. However, it cannot begin to account for the general fragmentation of landholding in all coffee zones revealed in the census data and the statistics on tenancy by the 1950s.

Successful pursuit of ownership of a smallhold involved families of coffee workers in a lifetime struggle in which ingenuity, hard work, and

Table 1. Coffee Properties Classified by Number of Trees in the Major Colombian Coffee-Producing Departments, 1932

Department	Number of Farms with the Following Numbers of Trees					Total No. of Properties
	Fewer Than 5,000 Trees	From 5,001 to 20,000	From 20,001 to 60,000	From 60,001 to 100,000	Over 100,000	
Antioquia	24,434	3,531	518	65	41	28,589
Caldas	36,475	3,411	260	23	5	40,174
Cauca	12,194	283	—	—	—	12,477
Cundinamarca	12,474	922	257	68	91	13,812
Norte de Santander	5,128	2,416	352	38	38	7,972
Santander	1,500	1,128	303	51	63	3,045
Tolima	9,610	2,670	369	62	60	12,771
Valle	18,477	1,514	71	3	4	20,069
Other departments	9,264	1,046	96	14	19	10,439
Totals	129,556	16,921	2,226	324	321	149,348
Percent of farms	86.75%	11.33%	1.49%	0.22%	0.21%	
Percent of trees	48.79%	24.67%	12.57%	5.51%	8.46%	

Source: Censo Cafetero, Boletín de Estadística 1:5 (February 1933): 122.

Table 2. Coffee Properties Classified by Number of Trees in Cundinamarca and Tolima, 1932 and 1939

	Number of Farms with the Following Numbers of Trees					Total No. of Properties
	Fewer Than 5,000 Trees	From 5,001 to 20,000	From 20,001 to 60,000	From 60,001 to 100,000	Over 100,000	
Cundinamarca						
1932	12,474	922	257	68	91	13,812
1939	25,826	3,874	406	76	88	30,270
Tolima						
1932	9,610	2,670	369	62	60	12,771
1939	22,555	5,021	511	68	62	28,217

Source: Table 1 and "Censo Cafetero en los departamentos de Cundinamarca y Tolima," Boletín de Estadística, no. 24 (April 1943): 62.

Table 3. Number and Production of Colombian Coffee Farms According to Size, 1955

Size of Farm	Number of Farms	Percent of All Farms	No. of Metric Tons Produced	Percent of All Production
Up to 1 hectare (fewer than 2,500 trees)	77,245	36.3%	19,129	5.3%
1.1 to 10 hectares (2,500 to 25,000 trees)	123,719	58.1	207,639	57.9
10.1 to 50 hectares (25,000 to 125,000 trees)	11,429	5.4	108,637	30.3
50.1 to 100 hectares (125,000 to 250,000 trees)	447	0.2	13,734	3.9
100.1 to 200 hectares (250,000 to 500,000 trees)	79	—	4,426	1.2
More than 200 hectares (more than 500,000 trees)	51	—	4,996	1.4
Totals	212,970	100.0%	358,561	100.0%

Source: Comisión Económica para América Latina y la Organización de las Naciones Unidas para la Agricultura y la Alimentación, *El café en América Latina: Problemas de la productividad y perspectivas. I. Colombia y El Salvador* (Mexico City, 1958), Table 18, p. 30.

Table 4. Percentage of Producing Colombian Coffee Farms According to Type of Administration and Size, 1955

	Up to 1 Hectare (Fewer Than 2,500 Trees)	1.1 to 10 Hectares (2,500 to 25,000 Trees)	10.1 to 50 Hectares (25,000 to 125,000 Trees)	More Than 50 Hectares (More Than 125,000 Trees)
Owner administrator	87.7%	77.9%	57.1%	14.3%
Administrator	2.0	4.6	17.2	71.4
Sharecropper	6.3	16.8	24.3	14.3
Administration by contract	3.9	0.7	1.4	—

Source: Same as Table 3: Table 23, p. 33. First column does not total 100% due to rounding.

a good measure of luck all played a role. The ingenuity included successful cultivation of a wide range of interpersonal relationships, from the choice of a spouse and godparents for children to the ability to gain sympathetic terms from relatives, friends, merchants, landowners, local political bosses, and government officials. Members of socially mobile families had to balance the expenses of material gifts and a certain liberality in the entertainment of strategic individuals with the desperate need to save in order to accumulate. This dilemma involved them in a complex and ever-changing social calculus that preoccupied coffee families, especially heads of households, throughout their lives. All family members had to cooperate and work hard to execute the multitude of agricultural, domestic construction, and artisanal tasks required for successful small farm operation. A healthy family, blessed with children, who happened to rent or agree to sharecrop land suitable for coffee production at a time when international coffee prices were low and then saw prices rise as the new coffee trees it planted came into full production, enjoyed optimal conditions for success in the struggle to accumulate capital and purchase land. Families that suffered the loss or partial incapacity of one or both parents, were barren of children, or invested in coffee production at an inopportune point in the unpredictable cycle of world coffee prices were almost certain to fail in the pursuit of a freehold. A family affiliated with one of the factions of the two major political parties in a locale where the other party or a rival faction was in the majority might be harassed by neighbors, merchants, and local officials in one historical era, only to see the tables turned as its own party or faction won control of national politics and local affairs.

In their struggle to survive and control enough land to ensure their independence, coffee families found themselves in constant and often violent competition with their neighbors, large landowners and small. Part of the reason lay in the structure of production in the coffee zone. Many small plots needed access to water, *trapiches* (sugarcane crushers), pasturage, woodlands, or marginal land for corn cultivation in the possession of others. Larger landowners depended on the labor of workers without a viable family freehold. Failure to meet an obligation or disagreement over the value of *mejoras* (improvements, especially plantings of new crops) made on rented or sharecropped land could lead to lasting grievances and protracted litigation between neighbors. Small coffee farmers, precisely because the margin between success and failure in their struggle was so narrow, were constantly denouncing their neighbors for alleged breaches of verbal and written contracts, or for damages allegedly incurred when pigs, mules, or cattle trespassed on their property and ate or damaged crops.

Coffee farmers were encouraged by their situation to use their wits to take advantage of their rivals at every conceivable opportunity. Some stole from rival farmers if they thought their action would go undetected. Most tried to cheat landowners of part of their portion in sharecropping agreements. Others sought to change boundaries of property that was typically unsurveyed and vaguely delimited in deeds by references to landmarks such as trees and stones and the course of creeks. In the constant struggle with his neighbors, the success of a small coffee farmer depended to a sizable degree on his manliness and tact. In areas far removed from effective control by civil and ecclesiastical authorities, those farmers capable of intimidating their fellows or of winning their respect, those able to bully their neighbors or impress them through equanimity and courage, had the best chance of surviving to old age, the best chance of acquiring, expanding, and maintaining a freehold.

Those coffee farmers who labored in production thus saw the central myths of capitalist and Christian ideology played out on an intimate scale. If they were successful, they attributed their good fortune to hard work, intelligence, frugality, and the moral virtues of their family and its members. If they failed, they blamed themselves or their rivals or attributed their misfortune to fate. As small property owners they identified with the capitalist, Christian values championed and disseminated by the Liberal and Conservative parties. Their loyalty to the two traditional parties, however, was not simply a consequence of the coincidence between ruling-class ideology and the vision of society fostered in their daily experience. The spoils distributed by local party bosses in exchange for rank-and-file loyalty and the competitive struggle between the parties for control over local affairs were features of Colombian politics, which individual smallholders enlisted in their efforts to create a social field of hierarchical interpersonal relationships favorable to their interests.

Through allegiance to one or the other of the major parties or its factions, coffee workers secured a host of strategically placed allies in their struggle to accumulate capital and control land. That such an affiliation also placed them in conflict with rivals and competitors of different political affiliation did not weaken their partisanship. In a local power structure completely at the mercy of partisan politics, one was potentially better (and no worse) off as a partisan of a possible victor in the political struggle than one was as a neutral, exposed without political allies in a Hobbesian world. The victory of one's party or party faction could mean anything from relief from military conscription for a teenage son to effective police protection from belligerent neighbors to a favorable resolution of legal disputes. For wealthier small farmers political victory could mean access to government jobs or an advanced education for their children, a favorable decision on the location of a rural road, or any of a hundred other political or legal favors.

The implications of the remarkable social process that left coffee smallholders partially victorious in their struggle for land were thus many and profound. The ability and willingness of smallholders to increase coffee production during the worldwide depression allowed them to expand at the expense of their inefficient large capitalist rivals in the coffee sector. It also helped to generate the foreign exchange and sustain the national market that were crucial to Colombia's recovery from the depression and the success of import-substitutive industrialization during the 1930s and early 1940s. Partly as a result of the smallholders' struggle, the industrial sector of the Colombian economy grew faster during this period than that of any other large Latin American nation. The social, political, and ideological results of this successful economic response to the world crisis of capitalism were no less important. For the first time in Colombian history, industrial workers became an important part of the labor force. Rural to urban migration freed migrants from the political control of local bosses from the two parties and helped make possible the rise of the populist urban politics of Gaitán in the 1940s. The success of petty commodity producers in the coffee sector and industrial capitalists in the manufacturing sector, coupled with the general growth and development of the Colombian economy, helped confirm in the minds of individuals in all classes the viability of an economic system based on the tenets of capitalism.

As we have seen, the successful struggle of coffee workers for control of land also served to reinforce the appeal and political monopoly of the two traditional parties. Coffee workers not only found some of their deepest aspirations and beliefs expressed in the dogma of the parties, but they also came to rely on and use effectively patron-client relationships embodied in the parties for protection and resources in their efforts to avoid proletarianization and secure a freehold. Consequently, the appeal of third parties, especially class-based ones, in the coffee zones that were at the core of rural society in Colombia was never great, and the monopoly of the traditional parties remained secure.

Moreover, the parties on the left, especially the Communist party, which valiantly tried to organize coffee producers and unite them with proletarianized urban and transport workers in the coffee export sector, never fully appreciated the democratic dimensions of the coffee workers' struggle. Even in Viotá, the southwestern Cundinamarcan coffee county (municipio) where the Communist party had its rare successes, the party began by trying to organize landless workers against their sometime employers, the *arrendatarios* and smallholders. Only after its efforts had failed, and after all these different kinds of coffee producers were unified through their mutual struggle against the large landowners, did the party acquiesce and support this alliance. But the party failed to elaborate on the democratic meaning of an alliance that included proletarians and small property owners, and it was either unable or unwilling to apply elsewhere the organizational formula that had proven successful in Viotá. The lessons and political potential of cooperative struggle for individual ownership of land largely were ignored. The relationship of worker control of the labor process to the issues of economic productivity and human alienation stayed unaddressed. Finally, the implications of the exploitation of labor by capital through control of the means of exchange, a relationship left untouched by worker ownership of the land, remained mostly unexamined.

The progressive, and in many ways democratic, victory of coffee workers in the core regions of the Colombian economy thus came to strengthen not the left but the traditional parties. The victory of rural coffee workers left the weak and peripheral unions in the less important sectors of the Colombian economy isolated and vulnerable. It also eliminated any social threat to Colombia's ruling class. Although the ruling class largely had lost control of coffee production, it still was unable to use its control of the state, ensured by the monopoly of the traditional parties, to exploit coffee producers through a progressively greater monopoly of coffee exchange and credit. This goal was accomplished primarily by expanding the power and activities of the National Federation of Coffee Growers in the decades following its creation in 1927.

The Crisis of Liberalism and the Beginning of Reaction

The Pyrrhic victory of coffee workers thus involved a paradoxical political and ideological process that both weakened their leftist allies and strengthened their class oppressors. The eclipse of a mobilized labor movement and the recovery of the national and world economies by the late 1930s allowed Colombia's bipartisan ruling class gradually to reverse the reformist social policies with which it first had responded to labor militancy and the world economic crisis. This dynamic was discernible in the steady movement to the right of the national government between 1938 and 1946, which led first to the halting of reform and then to the actual reversal of the land and labor laws that had been passed in the early and mid-1930s.

Thus, whereas the famous land reform law of 1936 (Law 200) passed at the zenith of López Pumarejo's reformist government sought to stem the tide of insurgent rural workers by legalizing the status quo in the countryside as well as by promising major redistribution of unused and poorly developed great estates within ten years, the land law (Law 100) passed in 1944 during López Pumarejo's second administration not only conveniently ignored the promised redistribution but also sought to strengthen the hand of large landowners in their dealings with their *arrendatarios* and tenants. The labor law (Law 6) passed the next year was not as openly reactionary. Its ambiguity undoubtedly reflected the growing numbers and importance of workers in manufacturing production, the strength of unions in the transport sector, and the political ties of many workers to the Liberal party. Moreover, war-induced prosperity created a high demand for labor, which probably also enhanced the bargaining position of these proletarianized workers. Parts of this 1945 labor law, such as its ban on the firing of union leaders, favored labor; other parts, particularly those that strengthened individual company unions at the expense of industrywide federations and expanded the definition of public-sector employees and banned them from striking, severely weakened labor.

During 1945 the government's ambivalent approach to organized labor turned openly repressive. By then the terms of the postwar international capitalist system, predicated on carefully controlled "apolitical" unionism and the renewed export of capital (much of it into manufacturing industry under the aegis of multinational corporations), had become clear. Following a pattern typical of capitalist societies in the postwar period, the Colombian government, in 1945, launched a major offensive against militant unions and the political left. After a bitter and protracted struggle, the Lleras Camargo government defeated the backbone of the Communist-led sector of the labor movement, the river transport workers' union (FEDENAL). Thereafter, confusion within the Communist party and the labor movement over the advisability of continuing their decade-old alliance with the Liberal party contributed to the dissident presidential candidacy of Gaitán, which split both the Liberal party and the labor movement in 1946. The result was the victory of the Conservative party, which in subsequent years used its control of the executive to limit further the autonomy of organized labor. With the support of the Catholic Church, the U.S.-government, and conservative U.S. unions, Conservative governments promoted the formally apolitical, economistic unionism typical of most of the new unions in Colombia's burgeoning manufacturing sector. These unions eventually joined the Unión de Trabajadores Colombianos (UTC), which became the largest labor federation in the nation.

The Labor Movement and the Violence

The postwar offensive against the left and the unions has led many scholars to view the Violence, which erupted full-blown following the assassination of Gaitán on April 9, 1948, as a premeditated process designed by the ruling class. According to this interpretation, the oligarchy sought to complement its urban labor policy by destroying the threat of independent class-based action on the part of Colombia's rural workers. By the late 1940s, however, such a threat no longer existed. It slowly had been eliminated in the 1930s and early 1940s by the victory of coffee workers in their struggle for land. Instead of a class struggle in the countryside, the competition for land in the coffee sector had degenerated into an increasingly desperate and violent effort by individuals to avoid proletarianization. Their struggle was sanctioned and its social content obscured by Colombia's traditional bipartisan politics.

It would appear that this struggle was made more serious by a series of economic factors that coalesced at the end of the world war. Coffee prices, held in check by wartime agreements with the United States, began a precipitous rise in the years following 1946. This price rise made large-scale coffee production profitable once more and stimulated a general inflationary process that squeezed small coffee farmers especially hard. Once largely self-sufficient, smallholders came to depend on the market for many of their needs in the decades after 1930. The growth of industry fostered by the world depression and by government policies that favored industry and urban consumers combined to hurt rural producers, especially smallholders unable to qualify for government credit. Their increasingly desperate efforts were pushed toward the complex phenomenon of the Violence by the political struggle for local control that was triggered by the transfer of national power in 1946.

The Violence, defined as the period of civil commotion that disrupted the nation between 1946 and 1966, was not a single, uniform social phenomenon. It was a multifaceted process whose social and political features as well as geographical focus changed as it evolved over two decades. The complexity of the Violence, however, should not obscure its essential unity. More than anything else, the Violence seems to have been the ultimate political expression of the ongoing struggle for land and social mobility in the coffee zones sketched in this essay. This was especially true during the earliest, most violent, and most "traditional" phase of the Violence, from 1946 to 1957.

Such, at least, is the most logical conclusion that can be drawn from Table 5, which reveals a close correlation (in 1955) between the intensity of coffee production by department and the intensity of the Violence (measured by a number of deaths per department attributed to it from 1946 to 1957). The three most important coffee departments in 1955, Antiguo Caldas, Antioquia, and Tolima, rank first, third, and second in number of deaths. To be sure, this is an argument based on correlation; testing of its causal links would require detailed analysis. Nevertheless, it is instructive to note that it was in these three departments, especially the first, Antiguo Caldas, that the small, viable family coffee farm enjoyed its greatest development.

Table 5. Deaths Attributed to the Violence in Colombia, 1946–1957, and Coffee Production, 1955, Ranked by Department

Deaths Attributed to the Violence		*Coffee Production*	
Department	*Deaths 1946–1957*	*Department*	*Tons*
Antiguo Caldas	44,255	Caldas	117,202
Tolima	30,912	Antioquia	59,600
Antioquia	26,115	Tolima	56,075
Santander (Norte)	20,885	Valle	50,042
Santander (Sur)	19,424	Cundinamarca	28,547
Valle	13,106	Huila	15,498
Meta	5,842	Santander (Norte)	10,484
Boyacá	5,359	Santander (Sur)	9,582
Huila	4,111	Cauca	9,464
Cundinamarca	4,037	All other	12,719
(Bogotá)	2,585		
Cauca	2,236		
All other departments and lesser administrative units	2,386		

Sources: Paul Oquist, *Violencia, conflicto y política en Colombia* (Bogotá, 1978), Table VI-2, p. 322; Comisíon Económica para América Latina y la Organización de las Naciones Unidas para la Agricultura y la Alimentación, *El café en América Latina: Problemas de la productividad y perspectivas. I. Colombia y El Salvador* (Mexico City, 1958), Table 2, p. 25.

Conclusion

The political events of 1930 and 1946, the years that mark momentous transfers of power between the two traditional parties and define the rise and fall of the Liberal Republic, were not the simple result of the actions of elite politicians. Neither can the progress of social reform and reaction during these years be attributed primarily to the visions of some leaders and the betrayals and conspiracies of others. The internal logic of the period, and its tragic outcome in the Violence, becomes truly comprehensible in terms of the democratic and largely victorious struggle of coffee workers for control of land. Therein lies the terrible historical irony of this pivotal period of national life.

The contemporary political implications of such an understanding of the period from 1930 to 1946, however, need not be pessimistic. Unlike traditional explanations, which work to empower not workers but their class oppressors, the interpretation advanced here shows how coffee workers influenced the history of labor and the nation profoundly in the 1930s and 1940s. They did so as they struggled for elemental human freedoms as yet imperfectly achieved in any contemporary society be it capitalist or so-called socialist. They sought the freedom to plan and execute productive labor and to enjoy the product of that labor. It is true that their efforts were channeled into the destructive nightmare of the Violence. But understanding how the democratic promise of their struggle was distorted, transformed, and subsequently ignored can be an important first step toward its realization in the future.

Part II

THE VIOLENCE

5

The Violence: An
Interpretative Synthesis

Gonzalo Sánchez

Gonzalo Sánchez was born and raised in El Líbano, Tolima, the Colombian *municipio* that suffered the Violence most intensely. He was seven years old in April 1952 when, as described in this chapter, the army's Colombia Battalion left an estimated fifteen hundred people dead in rural Las Rocas in El Líbano. The massacre occurred during the bloodiest week of the Violence, at the peak of the Conservative government's effort to crush the Liberal resistance.

A historian at the National University in Bogotá, Sánchez is recognized today as the leading student of the Violence. His work in social history includes *Los "Bolcheviques" de El Líbano* (Bogotá, 1976), a study of the revolutionary artisans of his hometown in the 1920s, and *Las ligas campesinas en Colombia* (Bogotá, 1977), an analysis of the mobilization of Colombian rural workers in the 1920s and 1930s. His work on the Violence includes *Los días de la revolución: Gaitanismo y 9 de abril en provincia* (Bogotá, 1983); a book coauthored with Donny Meertens, *Bandoleros, gamonales y campesinos* (Bogotá, 1984); and a book coedited with Ricardo Peñaranda, *Pasado y presente de la Violencia* (Bogotá, 1986). Sánchez also coordinated the work of the Commission for the Study of the Violence, whose findings were published in 1989. A selection from that work appears as Chapter 12.

The essay here is a major synthesis of the Violence. Building on his own work and on more than forty years of collective scholarship on the subject, Sánchez breaks new interpretive ground at every turn. He demonstrates the revolutionary social and political meanings of the movement led by Jorge Eliécer Gaitán. He reinterprets the dynamic and revolutionary potential of the *Bogotazo* of April 9, 1948, of its sequels in provincial cities, and of its projection into the countryside. He analyzes the parallel evolution of contending visions of Colombian society during the early 1950s: the repressive, reactionary projects of the Conservative government of Laureano Gómez versus the revolutionary social democratic platforms of factions of the Liberal resistance.

He offers a complex verdict on the military government of Gustavo Rojas Pinilla, showing how its pacification efforts ultimately aroused the class fears of the Liberal and Conservative political elite.

In his section on the National Front, which incorporates much new information from his current research, Sánchez addresses the two central issues of this volume. He surveys the complex struggle for land during the Violence and the insufficiencies of government efforts to address the agrarian question. He then outlines the transformation of the Liberal resistance into political banditry, which is suppressed by the bipartisan regime, and into revolutionary guerrilla movements, which have not been. The result is a new era of violence marked by a revolutionary struggle for land, the subject of Part III.

The Violence is a nodal point in the contemporary history of Colombia. Until recently, however, its position as an obligatory point of reference had paradoxical effects for the investigation of the phenomenon. Analysts of the history of the first decades of the century saw it as an indefinite horizon that enclosed both the processes they studied as well as their explanations. Those investigating the contemporary period were content simply to lay out some of its consequences. But the Violence itself, its complex trajectory, was left to some extent within parentheses. There was even an unspoken fear of entering its territory.

This situation has begun to change rapidly in recent years. The Violence has been demystified and now constitutes not only a privileged historical referent but also one of the poles of attraction for current social investigation in Colombia. Due to this collective research effort, it is possible to undertake a new interpretive synthesis of the phenomenon.

Gaitanismo and the Oligarchical Crisis

At the end of the Second World War, Colombia still had a basically oligarchical structure, questioned insistently by popular forces during the two preceding decades but not seriously threatened. The economic signals (coffee prices and the volume of imports, rates of industrialization and agricultural expansion) even permitted visions of a new era of prosperity. The elusive combination of economic development and political stability suddenly seemed within the grasp of the dominant classes. These classes enjoyed a peculiar hegemony. They themselves were united by social and cultural bonds. Their subaltern classes were sharply divided by partisan political differences.

A sanguine view of things, however, was confined to those in charge of the system. The majority of the nation was less optimistic and knew that it belonged in other statistical columns. Almost three fourths of the population was composed of peasants; more than half was illiterate; and 3 percent of the landowners monopolized half the land. Already workers and peasants had been hearing a language of intimidation. The workers had been put on notice by President Alberto Lleras Camargo during the strike of Magdalena River workers in 1945. Declaring the strike illegal, Lleras Camargo announced that the existence of one power in Bogotá and another on the river would not be tolerated. The second group, the peasants, had been put in dire straits by Law 100 of 1944. As frankly stated at the time in the *Revista Cafetera*, the organ of the powerful National Federation of Coffee Growers, the law established norms that "would adequately guarantee the rights of landowners, shielding them from the attempts of would-be squatters, so common before the passage of the law, to make themselves lords and masters of the parcels of land they cultivated."

This was obviously a potentially conflictive situation but not necessarily a revolutionary one. What made it truly explosive was the dynamic introduced into it by the movement led by Jorge Eliécer Gaitán, with its two clearly reformist themes of economic redistribution and political participation. These themes were backed by a social mobilization of such magnitude as to seem to transform their reformist content, leading the forces of the status quo to perceive a threat to the entire social edifice.

Gaitán arose in the 1940s as the inheritor of democratic tasks postponed or left inconclusive and frustrated. In just two years he gave the impression that he was turning Colombian politics on its head, uniting the people around him and the oligarchy against him. The Liberals, for example, seconded by the Communists, trumpeted the democratic cause of the Allies and portrayed Gaitán as the fascist threat on Colombian soil. The people were not fooled, however, and the tactic failed. The Liberals and Communists then tried another route, which, in the end, proved more effective. They penetrated the Gaitanista movement in an attempt either to neutralize it or to accentuate its internal tensions. At that price, Gaitán became the leader, the *Jefe Unico*, of the Liberal party in 1947. The Conservatives, for their part, moved in a different direction. With Laureano Gómez at the fore, they sought to turn Gaitanista discourse on the "moral restoration of the republic" to their own partisan purposes. The results of this tactic were notably ambiguous. It undoubtedly contributed to the rapid rise of Gaitán as well as to the Conservatives' principal goal, which was the defeat of the Liberals through internal division. It also gave Gaitán the opportunity to transmit his antioligarchical message to the Conservative masses, many of whom, out of conviction rather than as participants in a political ploy, began to feel strongly attracted to his ideas. The same process affected the police sent to monitor Gaitán's demonstrations and the Communists sent to sabotage them. As a result, the Conservatives were forced to adopt a different strategy. Alarmed by the imminence of Gaitán's triumph, which in fact was occurring already, they appealed to Colombians in the language of the Cold War. They described Gaitán as the cutting edge of communism, a representative of the dark forces that would destroy free enterprise and Western Christian values.

Whatever Gaitán's personal attitude regarding these maneuvers—and equivocation has been considered an essential element of his discourse and political practice—more important was the popular image of Gaitán that was being constructed, the collective representation of him, which might or might not have coincided with his own vision of himself. Everyone remembered his flaming oratory against the despotism of foreign capital, against the giveaway mentality of the oligarchy, in his speeches triggered by the massacre of Colombian workers in the banana zone in 1928. The peasants, especially those of Cundinamarca and Tolima, had had him by their side as a faithful interpreter of their aspirations in the struggle against landowner power during the agrarian mobilizations of the early 1930s. During that era, Gaitán's party, the Unión Nacional Izquierdista Revolucionaria (UNIR), had denounced the abuses committed by landowners (in Cundinamarca and Tolima, mostly Liberals) against squatters and tenants. In the 1940s migration, industrialization, and financial-mercantile operations had developed on a scale that made cities the decisive centers of power and capital, as well as of electoral results, and Gaitán was directing his appeal to the middle sectors—to shopkeepers, artisans, and industrial and service workers—to that whole stratum that the Bogotá aristocracy called "the lower depths of society." These middle sectors were to play an important role in the events of the *Bogotazo.*

By the mid-1940s, Gaitán had succeeded in creating a new historical force made up of the popular classes united across traditional party lines. His problem was how to maintain, and with what effects, his dual functions as radical reformist social leader and head of the traditional Liberal party. The evolution of and answer to this crucial question for Colombian politics came in the late 1940s.

It was in the urban conflicts, to which the oligarchy responded as a homogeneous bloc, that Gaitán's presence as a social leader seemed most noticeable. The workers' movement constituted the center of attention. The oligarchical offensive expressed itself, for the moment, in the systematic destruction of union organizations, in the reversal of workers' successes, and in the related promotion of new unions submissive to the bosses and to voices from the pulpits. Characteristically, Gaitán (who was a friend of the workers but not of the union apparatus, which he associated, not without reason, with the oligarchy) sought to shift the focus of worker activism to the street, that is, to a setting in which the workers' struggle could merge with that of the other popular classes. Against the model of negotiation between the unions and the state, the privileged formula of the Liberal Republic, Gaitán offered direct action: the march or demonstration whose setting was the public plaza. This was, first of all, a new strategy in which the demands of workers were transformed into a political struggle against the oligarchy. Second, it was a redefinition of traditional antagonisms. The idea of a bipartisan coalition against Gaitanismo, first suggested in early 1946 by former Liberal President Alfonso López Pumarejo and later realized under the government of Conservative President Mariano Ospina Pérez, was a response but also a spur to the formation of a popular bloc.

There was, however, a simultaneous process that was opposed to the one just outlined. This process served as a brake on the development of Gaitanismo as a united front made up of the oppressed, and cornered Gaitán in his role as Liberal chieftain. Gaitán's politics left exposed a rural flank, which progressively was exploited by the Conservative leader Gómez. Under Gómez's influence the dynamic of rural confrontation increasingly assumed a partisan character. Its starting point is clear. It began in the most notorious bastions of traditionalism, principally the departments of Boyacá and the two Santanders, where the memory of Liberal persecution against Conservative peasants during the government of Enrique Olaya Herrera (1930–1934) was still fresh. In that region debate over the presidential succession in 1946 had a particular angle, which was the organization of retaliation. And from that region would come one of the factors most directly associated with the generalization of the Violence, that is, the dismissal of the Liberal police and their replacement by peasants recruited from the Boyacá district of Chulavita.

These *chulavita* police were assigned to posts throughout the country, winning a reputation among Liberals as bloodthirsty criminals. In this context, it seemed as if the more traditional peasant communities were refusing to give way to the differentiated class conflicts of a society in the midst of capitalist modernization. It was the collision of conservative peasants with the social militants of the city. This overlapping of modes of conflict in the old and new society would constitute one of the dominant and characteristic features of the Violence. Indeed, in its very ambiguity "the Violence" as a term points out the complexity of the period being inaugurated.

The political significance of Gaitán and Gómez resides precisely in their having set themselves up as the spokesmen for the two historical tendencies just described. Gaitán attempted to impose the dynamic of social confrontation, and, although he knew that there were agrarian regions susceptible to that appeal, his locus of support was in the popular classes of the cities. Gómez, an aggressive, brilliant, and sectarian politician, encouraged rural partisan confrontation. He won over landlords threatened by peasant mobilizations; he offered guarantees to frightened capitalists, who saw in the language of Gaitán a disguised socialist program; and, above all, he inflamed passions in rural zones where a mentality of submission cultivated over centuries was combined with the social and political control of the Church. Gómez liked to portray himself as the interpreter of all of the most reactionary causes. Against the Spanish Republic he had taken the side of the Falangists, and against the Allied cause he had opted for the Axis. After 1946, against the supposedly conciliatory President Ospina Pérez, Gómez preferred the "blood and fire" line of José Antonio Montalvo, one of Ospina Pérez's most powerful ministers. Gómez put all of his political talent into maintaining the country's new social conflicts within the old vertical party divisions. Looking back, it must be said that he was very effective. Their two slogans, which dominated the era, precisely define these contrasting political figures: For Gaitán—"Against the Liberal Oligarchy and the Conservative Oligarchy, to battle!"; and for Gómez— "There are 1,800,000 false voter registration cards!," a declaration of the illegitimacy of the entire Liberal party.

Gaitán certainly had intended to escape this division of the social and the political. From his position in the Liberal party he systematically unfurled banners counterposing the oligarchy and the *pueblo* (people), the "nation of the politicians" and the "nation of the people." He invited political forces to regroup in a way that would transform the nature of the Liberal-Conservative confrontation. It is not entirely clear if he intended to achieve this goal by conversion of the Liberal party into a "party of the *pueblo*" (as implied in the Colón platform of 1947) or by maintaining the Gaitanista "movement," as happened in practice. In any case, Gaitán's preference for popular committees and distaste for an organizational scheme of directorates and cells revealed a predilection for "movement" over "party." This attitude had advantages, but also important limitations. It permitted broad diversification as the movement expanded and incorporated the masses into their own mobilization process; but it was an obstacle to ideological unity and disciplinary cohesion in moments of crisis. This attitude also magnified a role that Gaitán had reserved for himself and had carefully cultivated—

the role of sole interlocutor between the masses and the oligarchy, to be played in the setting of his choice, the public plaza.

The theatrical force of Gaitán's mediation was evident in its most spectacular episode, including the March of the Torches, which the Establishment associated with Mussolini's march on Rome. Most of all, it was manifest in the March of Silence (February 7, 1948), which left the *pueblo* with an immense though contained anger and left the oligarchy terrified and expecting the worst. The tragic vulnerability of this personalization of the movement became clear when Gaitán was assassinated on April 9, 1948. His assassination was not the start but was rather the culmination of the first wave of violence. Gaitán's *pueblo* had assumed the challenge and risen in revolt.

The 9th of April: The Two Faces of Colombia

During the opening days of April 1948, the oligarchical government was busy beautifying and embellishing Bogotá, since the coming 9th Pan-American Congress was to make the city something of a continental showcase. Diplomatic delegations from throughout South and Central America and the Caribbean were gathering to sign an anti-Communist declaration that U.S. Secretary of State George C. Marshall would be carrying with him. In anticipation of the meeting, Bogotá was cleansed of beggars, of shoeshiners, of street vendors, of *pueblo*. Gaitán had been excluded from the Colombian delegation to the conference. He belonged to and represented the Colombia that could not be shown off, the everyday Colombia, the one of misery. Gaitán's assassination on April 9 caused the hidden citizens of Bogotá and Colombia, the angry and frustrated *pueblo*, to erupt. Gaitán's assassin, an obscure fellow named Roa Sierra, was lynched on the spot, and his mutilated corpse was dragged—to cries of "to the [Presidential] Palace!"—along the same streets that two months earlier had witnessed the March of Silence. A multifaceted insurrection, perhaps the most complex of modern times, had begun. This rising of the multitude in legitimate self-defense had been predicted by Gaitán himself: "We are not cowards, we are the descendants of the brave men who annihilated tyranny on our soil."

When the political objective of seizing the Presidential Palace was frustrated by the intervention of a small but effective military detachment, the crowd grew angrier and its attention turned to destruction and looting. Two sorts of targets, and actions, came to the fore. The first face of the 9th of April was that of *social protest*, of an uprising against hunger, speculation, and the high cost of living. Its goal was the punishment of commerce, whose most notorious symbols were located downtown and whose representatives included a fair number of citizens with foreign names. Known generically in Colombia as *turcos*, these individuals were principally of Syrian, Lebanese, and Jewish descent.

Almost by instinct, the residents of Bogotá's poor outlying neighborhoods gathered downtown. The predominant form of their social protest was pillage, the objects of which were diverse. The crowd seized consumer goods, such as food, clothing, and household effects, as well as arms and metal tools that were useful not only in general but also for protecting one's loot. Liquor too was taken since drink supposedly can help one tolerate sadness, and that afternoon, on which the *pueblo*'s most important figure had died, was one of immense popular mourning. And since there was no tomorrow to consider, anything that could not be used immediately was better destroyed. The crowd's actions represented a mixture of anger, impotence, and rebellion.

The other face of the 9th of April was that of a *political uprising*. The palace held out due to the loyalty of the army and its reinforcement by troops and armed volunteers from Conservative Boyacá. But there were other places in the city that were associated with power, and they could be burned down, reduced to ashes. So during the afternoon and evening of that Friday in April, government buildings burned as did Church establishments and the offices of the newspaper *El Siglo*. (The house of *El Siglo*'s director, the politician Gómez, was set ablaze as well.) Every action seemed to stem from a single collective thought—that once the "Chief," the candidate for power, was no longer, power ceased to be a desirable objective and instead became a target of prepolitical hatred.

Nevertheless, there were those whose thoughts turned to the problem of power. The fact that the police had revolted nourished their visions. A revolutionary junta was created. It included two important figures of the intellectual left (Gerardo Molina, the rector of the National University, and the writer Jorge Zalamea) and a former minister, Adán Arriaga Andrade, among others. Also, National University students and radical Gaitanista professionals had had the audacity to seize the city's radio stations, and they not only transmitted to the whole country news of the assassination but they also gave out orders and instructions that played a crucial role in developments outside Bogotá. They broadcast calls for the formation of revolutionary juntas and for the gathering of arms, along with the insistent warning, "The slogan is Ordered Revolution! Organization!" They provided the provinces with the impulse and fervor for revolution. Often the broadcasts were unjustifiably triumphant and gave a distorted view of what was happening in Bogotá. "The *pueblo* rules for the first time in Colombia. . . . The Colombian Revolution is the greatest the world has known. . . . The true revolution in Latin America has begun!" were some of the proclamations.

They were seasoned with allusions to the French Revolution and to the independence struggle, which found powerful resonance in the provinces. The paradox was that the people in Bogotá, from where these voices originated, refused to listen to them, whereas the people in the provinces took them so seriously that it never occurred to them to march on the capital, which then had only a little over five hundred thousand inhabitants. Events thus unfolded on different levels—what happened in Bogotá and what happened in the provinces, based upon information (or, more accurately, disinformation) received on the radio. Except for officials in the palace who maintained telephone contact, inhabitants of the capital were unaware of what was occurring in the rest of the country.

During the two weeks following Gaitán's assassination, countless Colombian towns and rural districts lived under a formidable inversion of the institutional order. Police were "at the service of the Revolution" as they put it in the provinces; prisoners imprisoned or executed their guards; those individuals previously persecuted now exercised power in many localities; judges incited subversion; pulpits were silenced and priests either imprisoned, held incommunicado, or killed (principally in Tolima and Cundinamarca); peasants invaded haciendas, expropriated cattle, and gave orders to landowners (especially in the Sumapaz region and in southern Tolima); foreign companies, such as the oil refineries of Barrancabermeja, were seized by their workers; and so on. In these areas, protagonists rightly spoke of a new revolutionary order. In some cases they created an effective popular government backed by militias of the most diverse social composition, which suppressed anarchy and looting. It was as if the character of social and political development prior to April 9 had been dislocated, and it was no longer the city but the most remote provinces that displayed their full revolutionary potential. It seemed that a grand demolition of the oligarchical republic had begun.

Nevertheless, a stage of "dual power," such as was reached during the Paris Commune, was never manifest in Colombia at the national level. There was instead a constellation of alternative local power centers with no connections between them. And such local power could not last longer than a few days or weeks given the collapse of the insurrection in Bogotá. The capital's revolutionary junta was timid. Its members managed to pose the question of power, but they had neither the capacity nor the vocation for power. Like the masses in the street, they were content to await the results of the junta of notables led by the Liberal politician Carlos Lleras Restrepo. At great risk these notables had ventured to the palace not on the shoulders of the masses nor in their name but rather maintaining a careful distance from the *pueblo* in order to appear to the government as acceptable interlocutors.

The junta's class obligation and mission of the moment was to deactivate the rebellion, by negotiation insofar as that was possible; they sought to save the oligarchical republic at any price. When they left the palace after a memorable all-night session, the news transmitted on the radio stations (now controlled once more by the government) trumpeted the revival of the bipartisan National Union. The Liberal Darío Echandía (the representative of the oligarchy who was closest to Gaitán) was named the new interior minister. For his part, Lleras Restrepo, one of Gaitán's fiercest opponents, was to preside over his funeral on April 21, which the oligarchy would attend as well.

Bogotá had capitulated. Dispersal, popular resignation, members of the Gaitanista petty bourgeoisie alarmed by their own part in the events—truly, the *pueblo* had been disorganized. The provinces, it is true, tried to resist but in fragmentary form. Meanwhile, the oligarchical bloc recouped its unity with astonishing speed.

Could things have turned out differently? Probably. But for the 9th of April to have become a revolution (as Bolivian miners would demonstrate on the 9th of April exactly four years later) preparation and leadership were needed. Colombia's 9th of April was in its very essence a defensive and retaliatory popular reaction and not the result of any insurrectional political plan.

From Civil Resistance to Armed Resistance

Between the middle of 1948 and the end of 1949 the political discourse, alliances, and strategies of the oligarchical bloc had one common denominator: the ghost of April 9. Having crushed the rebellion was not enough. The possibility of its repetition had to be eliminated as well as the even more dangerous possibility that the workers' movement might become the articulator of social protest and political opposition. With the popular dispersal after April 9 these goals hardly seemed difficult, but the oligarchy had to take concrete steps to guarantee them. The firing of militant workers, the purging and imprisonment of union leaders, the attack on the strike as a legitimate instrument of protest, and the systematic destruction of a relatively united union movement were all parts of the government's new offensive. These measures complemented projects under way before April 9 and sought to establish the state as the right arm of the capitalist classes.

With an eye on the coming electoral fight, the Liberal party sometimes vacillated and sometimes was a silent accomplice, but generally the party cooperated with the repression. The repercussions from the employers' offensive were felt not only in the decline of labor militancy but also throughout the popular movement. In fact, from April 9 until the student agitation of 1954, there was no urban mobilization on a national scale. This was the principal legacy of President Ospina Pérez to his successor Gómez.

For Gómez, the reconstruction of order did not stop with the events of April 9, which had given him new reasons to extend the antipopular struggle into the countryside. He was obsessed with preventing what had occurred in Bogotá from happening in the rest of the country; that is, the siege of the center by the *chusma* (rabble). On the national level, his aim was to ensure that the provincial masses, who had shown such revolutionary vigor on April 9, would not threaten the *pax romana* imposed on the urban centers. Stimulated by Gómez's preaching, this task was carried out in the principal Conservative bastions of Boyacá and Nariño as well as in Antioquia. In Antioquia the clergy elaborated discourse that justified the murder of *nueveabrileños* (those involved in the uprisings following the assassination of Gaitán on April 9). It was from some of these zones that the Violence later advanced into Tolima, Valle del Cauca, and Viejo Caldas. In these regions peasants spoke not of "when the Violence started" but of "when it arrived," and this "arrival" usually is associated with the coming to town of a sinister force, the *chulavitas*.

In any event, Gómez now imposed the rhythm of politics. Full of resentment at the personal damage he had suffered on April 9, he voluntarily took the path of exile to Franco's Spain. One month prior to Gómez's return to Colombia in June 1949, the Liberal party officially left the cabinet of the National Union. That action greatly diminished the party's chances in the presidential succession, which would be decided by late 1949.

The Liberal withdrawal turned out to be a point of no return. During his exile Gómez had reached conclusions that rendered bipartisan cooperation impossible. According to Gómez, the social dynamic of the previous years was explained by the simple fact that there was an organic relationship between liberalism and communism. To describe this relationship he resorted to a mythological simile every bit as effective as his line about "1,800,000 false voter registrations." He formulated it in front of an enthusiastic crowd in the Plaza Berrio of Medellín:

> In Colombia one still speaks of the Liberal party to designate an amorphous, shapeless, and contradictory mass that can only be compared to or described as that imaginary creation of ancient times: the basilisk. The basilisk was a monster with the head of one animal, the face of another, the arms of yet another, and the feet of a deformed creature, and the whole was so

horrible and frightful that merely to look at it produced death. Our basilisk moves on feet of confusion and stupidity, on legs of brutality and violence that press into its immense oligarchical belly; with a chest of ire, masonic arms, and a tiny, diminutive, communist head.

In following the Liberal path, Colombia was, he said, on the brink of falling behind the Iron Curtain.

In practice, this analytical perception had various effects. It deepened the disorganization of the subaltern classes, and it drowned social confrontation in the blood of partisan confrontation. But it also disorganized the dominant classes, which lost their character as a political bloc. Indeed, an important Liberal fringe was thrown immediately into the opposition, or the "civil resistance" as it was known then.

Civil resistance had an essentially defensive character and fed the illusion that simple sabotage of the administration, where the Liberals were in the bureaucratic majority, would be sufficient to force the government to change its policies. Instead, the Liberal oligarchy, which after April 9 had shown itself to be useful and necessary to the government, found itself on the verge of political ostracism. An ever-increasing number of Liberals were being forced to renounce their political credo, the persecutions and assassinations at the hands of the *chulavitas* were unstoppable, and after the bloody October 1949 attack on the Casa Liberal in Cali words such as *massacre* and *genocide* were seen daily in newspaper headlines.

The Cali case involved refugees from rural areas for whom another term came into everyday use during the Violence, the term *exiles*. On October 9, 1949, the Liberal leader and president of the party's directorate in Boyacá, Gustavo Jiménez, was assassinated in Congress, and another leading Liberal was gravely injured. Following the ascending line of political terrorism, on November 26 the Liberal presidential candidate Darío Echandía was attacked in Bogotá, an attack in which his brother was killed. The Liberal leadership had no choice but to decree its electoral abstention, in a proclamation that evoked the prelude to past civil wars.

Just what a declaration of war might be was not really clear to Liberal leaders, who explored various possibilities starting with a military revolt that led only to the isolated insubordination of Captain Alfredo Silva in Villavicencio on November 15, 1949. The army as a whole remained loyal to the government just as it had on April 9. The Liberals then tried the path of the general strike, but that failed as well. They themselves had contributed to the liquidation of the workers' movement. All that remained was the response that the peasants had been preparing on their own, that is, armed resistance.

The armed occupation of Puerto López (Meta) on November 25, led by Eliseo Velázquez, and later that of San Vicente de Chucurí (Santander) by several hundred peasants under the command of Rafael Rangel, constituted the formal announcement that the struggle for democracy now rested on the shoulders of the peasant guerrillas. Rangel's action took place the same day as the presidential election, in which, thanks to the Liberal abstention, the sole candidate was Gómez. For the Liberal leadership this was an inevitable, although problematic, outcome. As part of the opposition they needed the guerrillas, but as members of the establishment they feared them.

The Visible and Invisible in the Violence

Laureano Gómez assumed the presidency in 1950 as the head of an extreme faction that had provoked the rupture of the oligarchical political pact created in the aftermath of April 9. With him had come an ultrareactionary solution to the central historical problem of the twentieth century—that is, the role of the masses in the game of alliances and political strategies. The chronology of this problem in Colombia may be sketched broadly in the following terms: subordination-integration under the Liberal Republic (1930–1945); repression-division after 1945 under the regimes of Lleras Camargo and Ospina Pérez; and beginning in 1950, repression all down the line. For Gómez there was no such a thing as the *pueblo*, or masses, only an *inepto vulgo*, a threatening mob.

This antipopular crusade rested on two factors that gave it ideological coherence in both its domestic and its international aspects. On the internal domestic side, the Catholic Church was central. After April 9 the Church breathed holy ire. In a country that called itself the most Catholic in the world, the Church's authority had been wounded, its properties ravaged, its personnel abused. It thus hardly needed formal arguments to become convinced of the truth of the basilisk theory. In consequence, although with some notable exceptions, the Church put all of its institutional weight on the side of governmental power. It simultaneously anathematized the opposition and offered the Kingdom of God to the government's terrorist bands. It not only legitimated the plans of the government, but it also helped to realize them, through, for instance, FANAL, the peasant affiliate of the conservative labor central and the only peasant organization in the country that managed to grow during the Violence. FANAL acted as an instrument of espionage in areas of rural unrest and as a cordon sanitaire in zones of convergence between the guerrillas and government forces. It has to be underlined that the *chulavitas* and the Church played complementary roles during the Violence.

On the international side, the principal support was the United States—its diplomacy, arms, and capital. This ideological context provided Gómez's government with, in effect, additional legitimation. These were the days of the Cold War and of McCarthyism, which were exacerbated by the Chinese revolution and the Korean War. It thus was easier than ever for Gómez to convince the United States that he, along with the Somozas, the Batistas, and the Trujillos of Central America and the Caribbean, was defending the strategic interests as well as values of Western democracy. Within the framework of this mutually reinforcing alliance, Gómez gave Colombia the dubious distinction of being the only Latin American country to send troops to Korea.

Significantly, the opposition characterized the regime as fascist or Falangist. The ideological influence of these corporativist and totalitarian models at last was made explicit in the constitutional reform project submitted by the government to a study commission. The proposal was torpedoed by the Liberal members of that body.

Under the Conservative regime, which, due to Gómez's illness, nominally was headed by Roberto Urdaneta Arbeláez after October 1951, the Violence reached new intensity, took on new forms, and affected new regions. Within its multidimensional character may be distinguished three general processes: terror, resistance, and the breakdown of social order.

Terror

The first and most visible process of the Violence, which left the greatest impact upon the collective memory, was a mixture of official terror, partisan sectarianism, and scorched-earth policy. This aspect of the Violence affected the lives, physical safety, psychology, and possessions of hundreds of thousands of Colombians. Its images are unerasable and in good measure have given the Violence its distinctive seal.

The extreme modality of this process was, of course, murder. Extreme not only for the number of victims but also because of the indescribable torture that surrounded these murders and marked for life the entire generation that witnessed them. Even children and unborn babies were punished for their parents' political choices. Those individuals spared execution were subjected to every depradation imaginable. New ones included the *boleteo*, or payment of security quotas. Old ones included the time-honored tactics of agrarian conflict—the destruction of plantings, the theft of animals, tools, and harvests, and the burning of houses and structures for sugarcane and coffee processing. Such tactics often led to the abandonment or forced sale of land.

Conflicts—between neighbors, between rural laborers and employers, between squatters and landlords, or between participants in simple barroom disputes—were resolved in bloodshed by those who, by virtue of their political affiliation, could count on the complicity of the authorities. In an incessant war of neighbor against neighbor, district against district, towns and hamlets established strict lines of political demarcation, the crossing of which could have fatal consequences. For Liberals, to wear a red tie or shirt or paint a door red was an invitation to death. For Conservatives, to possess an identity card indicating participation in the last, Conservative-only elections could result in the same fate. Atrocities involving mutilation, sexual violation, and the desecration of victims' corpses, in other words, the ritual of terror, were a pathological component that accompanied most intimidation.

Police and army detachments arrived like cyclones to terrorize defenseless towns. In November 1950 the huts of the Indians of the old reservations of Ortega and Natagaima in Tolima were burned and their inhabitants brutally expelled from the region. Yacopí, a town in northwestern Cundinamarca, suffered total obliteration in 1952. In early 1953, in Villarica, Tolima, one hundred forty peasants were lined up and shot. Some districts, such as San José de las Hermosas in southern Tolima, were even destroyed twice during the Violence. In a "pacification" operation (reminiscent of that undertaken by the Spanish general, Pablo Morillo, during Colombia's war for independence), the army's Colombia Battalion left an estimated fifteen hundred dead in the rural region of Las Rocas in El Líbano, Tolima. The events of Las Rocas occurred during the bloodiest period of the Violence, in April 1952. In a display of religious intolerance, whole communities of Protestants in central Tolima (in the towns of Ibagué, Rovira, and Armero) were decimated and their churches destroyed.

In lesser operations, which were more selective and continuous, victims were earmarked by one person and murdered by another. Murderers, called *pájaros* (birds), could often count on an extensive network of protectors, that is, on the complicity of the authorities and even on access to political figures who later, under the National Front, would occupy positions in Congress, the cabinet, or foreign embassies. El Condor in Valle del Cauca is the prototype and the best known of the *pájaros*, but there were many, many others, including those who swarmed over Viejo Caldas and Tolima. *Pájaros* were rewarded according to the importance of their victims, although the people who really got rich from their crimes were the *pájaros'* urban sponsors. Notaries and judges, sometimes out of well-founded fear but often because they were willing conspirators, facilitated the transactions in which the *pájaros* were hired and the subsequent impunity with which they operated. Victims often received printed cards announcing their deaths in advance. *Pájaros* discussed their plans in public places; the impunity with which they did so reduced chances of resistance and immobilized their victims. A café-bar in Armenia frequented by *pájaros* was known by popular wit as El Chamizo, a dead tree where vultures nest.

Daniel Pecaut has compared the *pájaros* to the *arditi*, the private groups that accompanied the rise of Italian fascism, and Eric Hobsbawm has seen in them a replica of the Sicilian Mafia. As a result of *pájaro* activities, the horrified residents along the banks of the Cauca River could count a daily flow of corpses carried along by the current. In towns in the western coffee zone a ghostly "red truck" roamed the streets in the early hours of the morning picking up the victims of the previous night. In this subculture of violence that was transforming social conduct, language, and values, and spawning leaders of the Liberal resistance with nicknames such as Desquite (Vengeance) and Sangrenegra (Blackblood), an entire generation was growing up whose attitudes toward their condition oscillated between fatalism, a thirst for vengeance, and repressed rebellion. This was the dimension of the Violence captured in the chronicles and novels of the era, including *Viento seco* by Daniel Caicedo, *Las balas de la ley* by Alfonso Hilarión, *Lo que el cielo no perdona* by Fidel Blandón Berrío, *Sin tierra para morir* by Eduardo Santa, and *Los días del terror* by Ramón Marique, to mention just a few of the more suggestive titles. It was also the dominant vision of the pioneering study by Germán Guzmán and his collaborators, *La Violencia en Colombia*.

Geographically, the terror extended throughout Colombia's interior, but it was especially prevalent in the smallholder regions of Boyacá and the Santanders and in the regions of Antioquian colonization of Valle del Cauca, Viejo Caldas, and Tolima, where that migratory process had resulted in a smallholder peasantry primarily dedicated to coffee production. More generally, it can be said that this kind of violence took hold in those zones where either government control, the structure of the economy, or topography prevented organized mass resistance to the policy of extermination.

This sort of political terrorism principally, although not exclusively, affected all social categories within the Liberal party but did so in an unequal manner. Landowners, businessmen, and the highest-ranking political chiefs could shield themselves from the Violence in the anonymity of the big cities or sometimes in foreign exile. This fact explains the great alarm caused by arson attacks in Bogotá on September 6, 1952, on the main Liberal newspapers, *El Tiempo* and *El Espectador*, and on the homes of Lleras Restrepo and López Pumarejo.

(Lleras Restrepo and López Pumarejo, however, unlike peasants in similar circumstances, later received indemnification under the regime of Gustavo Rojas Pinilla.) The message of such attacks was clear: high-level Liberals were also vulnerable. And in the prevailing atmosphere of retaliation, these attacks were an invitation to similar actions against Conservative leaders. In fact, Vicente Arbeláez, the son of the acting president came close to being killed in a guerrilla attack against an official convoy in Tolima. The anarchy threatened to reach into the capital of the republic.

Resistance

The second general process, and a major component of the Violence, was the guerrilla resistance. As already noted, this struggle became widespread when the oligarchical leadership of the Liberal party proved unable to stop the advance of the terrorist regime through simple civil resistance. The historic task of achieving democracy thus passed to the armed *pueblo*. In contrast to political terrorism, the real dimensions and achievements of the guerrilla struggle became publicly known only after the coup of Rojas in 1953.

Less visible, then, at the time, but no less important to understanding the Violence, was this eruption of the guerrilla enclaves. The guerrillas' actions gave the Violence the character of a war, making of it an organized and open confrontation between armed peasants and the government. This confrontation, however, was not like the civil wars of the last century. The great political chiefs and landowners did not participate directly as they had in earlier times. During the Violence they may have incited or influenced events, but they remained in the cities. Whereas it is true that the war was led in a large part by peasants tied to partisan loyalties, some of its leaders and rank and file were peasants who had fought independently for land in the 1930s. The war against the government was led by popular figures who had had revolutionary experience during the events of April 9 as mayors or as members of juntas or militias; by police who had deserted or been fired; by ordinary fighters who had gained respect and admiration during combat; and by migrants, muleteers, public works laborers, and, eventually, a few workers with urban labor experience. In sum, it was a conflict led by sectors representative of a Colombia that was very different from that represented by the leaders of the struggles of the nineteenth century. As a result, the war inevitably tended to become popular. This was, one might say, the "heroic" side of the Violence, in which it is often compared to the Mexican Revolution.

Large guerrilla centers acted as poles of attraction for refugees from either anarchy or official terror. Generally, these centers consolidated themselves in three types of areas.

1. Areas of recent colonization, such as Sumapaz and southern Tolima. As Darío Fajardo and Medófilo Medina have shown, the uncertainty of land titles in these areas was such that the "agrarian question" remained very much alive. These were also regions with considerable preexisting peasant politicization, through the Communist party, the Partido Socialista Revolucionario, and Gaitán's UNIR movement of the early 1930s.

2. Areas on the open frontier, where colonization was just getting under way (a process that was itself spurred by the Violence). These areas included the llanos, or eastern plains; the middle Magdalena River valley along the San Vicente de Chucurí-Barrancabermeja-La Dorada-Puerto Wilches circuit, and the Alto Sinú and Alto San Jorge river valleys on the border between Antioquia and Córdoba.

3. Less frequently, areas that already had a consolidated agrarian structure, such as southwestern Antioquia, but where other factors existed. These factors included a topography that lent itself to relative isolation from the centers of power, a certain level of Liberal political homogeneity, and support from or tolerance by Liberal landlords, at least in the initial stages of guerrilla formation.

In contrast to zones typical of either Antioquian colonization or highland smallholder agriculture, these were areas able to sustain economically large armed contingents during relatively long periods. This was possible because within the areas' productive structure an immediately available cattle supply coexisted with lands suitable for rapidly maturing subsistence crops. Between them, these zones may have sheltered some twenty thousand men in arms, half of them on the llanos alone.

These guerrilla fronts were associated with personages who came to symbolize their respective movements. The most important was undeniably Guadalupe Salcedo, who became a legend of the resistance on the llanos and, in the years that followed, became an icon of the armed resistance over the entire country. The next most important figure was probably Juan de la Cruz Varela, who gave to the resistance of his region, Sumapaz, its character as a peasants' war against the landlords' offensive that had begun in 1949. Only recently, the full stories regarding regional idols such as Juan de J. Franco Yepes (Capitán Franco) in southeast Antioquia and Julio Guerra in southern Córdoba have been rescued by historical investigation. About other figures, such as Rafael Rangel, in the Carare-Opón region of Santander, and Saul

Fajardo, in northeast Cundinamarca, we have only fragmentary information, although they live on in the collective memory of the peasantry.

Southern Tolima constitutes a special case in this regard given the complex evolution and fragmentation of its guerrilla movement. Perhaps the best-known figure in the region was Jesús María Oviedo ("General Mariachi"). But there were in reality as many generals as there were subregions and guerrilla commands: Leopoldo García ("General Peligro"), Hermógenes Vargas ("General Vencedor"), Aristóbulo Gómez ("General Santander"), Luis Efraín Valencia ("General Arboleda"), and Gerardo Loaiza ("General Loaiza"). Mere enumeration of these leaders illustrates the absence of a unified command and bosslike division of local influence.

Noteworthy figures in the guerrilla centers under Communist influence included the veteran peasant leader Isauro Yosa ("Major Lister") and the Indian guerrilla Jacobo Prías Alape ("Charro Negro"). But what was most significant about these centers in the long term was the evolution of peasants who migrated from other regions (Cauca, Huila, Quindío) and fought under the Liberal banner in bitter and sometimes bloody disputes with Communist peasants. By the 1960s these peasants had come to be counted among the founding members of the Communist guerrilla army Fuerzas Armadas Revolucionarias Colombianas (FARC). Such individuals include Major Ciro and Manuel Marulanda Vélez ("Tirofijo").

With the possible exception of southern Tolima, where periodic internal guerrilla rivalries left the resistance vulnerable to devastating incursions by the police, army, and paramilitary organizations, the guerrilla enclaves were effective centers of permanent refuge and often insurmountable barriers to the imposition of government authority. In these enclaves efforts were made to give the struggle a content, form, and perspective that differentiated it from the terrorism afflicting the vulnerable areas of the interior. Codes of revolutionary morality enforced respect toward women, children, and the elderly, and laws expressly prohibited the use of torture and scorched-earth policies against adversaries.

Codes also regulated the use of expropriations and the proceeds from them, subordinating individual appetites to the collective good of the resistance. In these areas, autonomous tribunals functioned and marriages were conducted before military chiefs. In some regions of greatest control, production and distribution priorities were set for the civilian population. This was the case on the llanos as well as in the Davis region of southern Tolima, once the Communists had managed to establish relatively stable and autonomous institutions there. Leaders in these areas also fought against sectarianism, albeit with mixed results; in Antioquia, Conservative peasants even sought the protection of Liberal guerrillas. The guerrillas also recognized the key role that women played in the resistance. "Women! Half the struggle!," recalled Eduardo Franco Isaza in his report on the guerrillas of the llanos. As the "eyes and ears of the guerrilla," women served as lookouts for the peasant fighters of southeastern Antioquia, groups carefully studied by Wilson Horacio Granados.

As seen from Bogotá, these unconnected forces seemed to constitute a purely defensive movement. Nevertheless, at the local and regional levels, given their popular roots and military audacity (they seized towns, destroyed "commissions" of *chulavitas*, and even shot down a pursuit plane in southern Tolima), they seemed quite capable of offensive projects. In these areas, one spoke of war and of revolution against the government; one did not passively await death but died in combat. Their offensive capability is illustrated in a legend recounted by Granados. According to the story, the Antioquian guerrilla leader Capitán Franco turned himself into a bull (the offensive symbol par excellence) and roamed the streets and countryside of Urrao, putting Conservatives, and especially the police, to flight. Residents of both government and guerrilla persuasion claimed to have seen him, and some even identified persons who had suffered his attacks.

Guerrilla movements took on a new dynamic by 1952. During the second half of that year, qualitative changes within the guerrilla groups were of profound concern to the national Liberal Directorate, the military, and even the governing Conservatives. The geographic center of these worries was the eastern llanos. On July 19 in Puerto López, Salcedo completely liquidated an army column of one hundred men. In August the principal guerrilla leaders presented the Liberal Directorate with a choice: either the directorate would lead the general revolt or the guerrillas would do so on their own. The Liberal oligarchy once again felt the fears that had assailed them on April 9, 1948. They responded through López Pumarejo: "If this is the last opportunity the Liberal leaders have to fulfill their historic destiny, as contemplated or interpreted by the chiefs of the armed revolt, then we are resolved to lose it! Moreover, if this means a definitive break with the *pueblo*, as the guerrillas would have it, so be it."

With a stroke of the pen the guerrillas had opened a new period in the revolution on the llanos. That same August 1952 saw the convening, in Viotá, Cundinamarca, of the so-called Boyacá Conference, attended by representatives of the country's most important guerrilla fronts (except those of southern Tolima). Although not fully successful, the conference transformed itself into the First National Conference of the Popular Movement of National Liberation; its work was to be directed by a national coordinating commission. On September 11 the First Law of the Llano was proclaimed, organizing the judicial system and distributing functions to civil and military chiefs, to *comisarios* (commissioners), and to agents of public order. It also defined offenses against the revolution, guaranteed individual rights, set limits and conditions on land use, promoted community labor, established dairies and agricultural colonies "belonging to the Revolution," and regulated cattle raising and the taxation of herds. The last act in this entire chain of events occurred at the very end of the year when, on December 31, a squadron of some two hundred peasants from northwestern Cundinamarca attacked the main Palanquero air force base near Bogotá and nearly seized it.

During the first months of 1953 the guerrillas' political and organizational concerns won priority over the strictly military aspects of their resistance. Preparations advanced for creation of a supreme national guerrilla command. Under the influence of the lawyer José Alvear Restrepo, the most notable ideologue of the resistance (and a figure unjustly forgotten today), the Law Organizing the Revolution on the Eastern Plains of Colombia—the Second Law of the Llano—was being written. It was sanctioned by a guerrilla assembly, the Revolutionary Assembly of Chiefs, on June 18, 1953, five days after the coup that deposed Gómez.

The 224 articles of the law were concerned basically with the organization of territory liberated as the war progressed. The law clearly envisioned the extension of the revolution to the entire country and the installation of a popular government. "The Revolution is a popular movement of liberation; it is the creation of all who participate in it." In general, the law embodied a much more radical program than that proposed by the Communists of southern Tolima. While the Communists certainly were raising the standard of agrarian reform under slogans such as "land for the tiller," they also were prisoners of an excessive localism, trapped in confrontations with the undisciplined and sectarian Liberal guerrillas of their zone. Their program thus was seen by many in the struggle as something of an artificial imposition. In contrast, the Second Law of the Llano was widely accepted as the natural result of the maturing of the struggle. The law of the llano was, in effect, the most complete democratic project proposed by the armed movement to counter the fascistic project of Gómez's Constituent Assembly. It thus deserves to be examined in some detail.

First, the law established a hierarchy of governing bodies: a congress, the "supreme authority of the Revolution," with representatives from both the army and the civilian population, would meet annually on May 1, Labor Day; a General Staff having five members, also including civilian representation, and charged with the political and administrative direction of the revolution's territory; a commander in chief (Salcedo), with supreme authority in military matters under the political direction of the General Staff; zone commanders; and *juntas de vereda* (district councils). In practice, the district councils would be the primary organs of government. Economically, they were to handle the organization and planning of production and the control of distribution and consumption. Politically, they were to call monthly open meetings (an example of direct democracy) for the discussion of community problems. They were also to serve as courts of first instance. The jurisdiction of the district councils was characterized in typical *llanero* fashion. A *vereda* (district) was defined as "the population group supplied with meat at a given slaughter site."

Second, the law established general guidelines for a war economy as concerned labor, property, production, and distribution. Production was described as "the principal obligation of the civilian population." Privately held small property was to be respected, but a socialist tendency was dominant. Within "liberated" territory natural resources and the means of production (land, water, and tools) belonged to the revolution and would be distributed among the members of the population according to work plans, the execution of which was the task of the district councils. "Once the maintenance of the Armed Forces is assured, goods will be distributed according to the needs of each person." These provisions were the revolutionary response to the periodic economic blockades of the region. They also served to bind the entire body of working people to the struggle.

Third, the law gave special attention to the relationship between the revolutionary armed forces and the noncombatant population. As was also true for district judges, the army was not considered to be an entity separate from the people. On the contrary, "The objective of the Revolutionary Armed Forces is the defense of the people and confrontation with the enemy in combat, until victory is obtained through the defeat of the tyranny and the implantation of a Popular Government in Colombia." The essentially democratic features of relations within the revolutionary army, which radically distinguished it from the regular army, included the obligation of the soldier to treat the civilian population and his fellow soldiers with respect. "In the Revolutionary Army all are comrades." This *compañerismo* was also extended to relations between superiors and inferiors. Inferiors had the right to criticize, discuss, and appeal the measures of their superiors, at least in theory. In addition, the decision of a citizen to join the revolutionary army was to be voluntary.

Fourth, since the educational role of politics in the armed struggle was recognized, the law made revolutionary instruction part of daily work: "At least one hour daily shall be devoted to revolutionary instruction for the troops, including notions of civic culture, national history, courtesy [*urbanidad*], hygiene, reading and writing, and especially, knowledge of the motives and objectives of the struggle, in accordance with a primer to be produced by the General Staff." This was basically a primary-school program with a revolutionary orientation. The General Staff also was charged with "compiling a history of the revolution, its military battles as well as its political, economic, and cultural development."

Fifth, one notes that in the context of the era and the circumstances a variety of the law's articles were quite novel. These included guidelines for dealing with civil marriage, divorce, and the legitimacy of children (all children were so considered); the equality of women and men; the protection of the indigenous population from the abuses of "civilized elements"; respect for the life, honor, and goods of Conservatives in occupied territory; and the prohibition of scorched-earth policies.

Finally, among the leaders of the *llanero* revolutionary army was a clear understanding that consolidation of revolutionary tendencies on the llanos also depended on their development in the rest of the country. Thus the movement was organized for projection and not just for defense. This goal is expressly manifest in one of the functions assigned to the General Staff: "To direct the relations of the llano with the other guerrillas and revolutionary groups, in Colombia as well as other countries, and to seek union and cooperation with them in all ways possible."

The guerrilla chiefs who participated in the June 1953 assembly concerned themselves with themes and issues that were entirely new to the course of the Violence. The possibility of elevating their activities to the category of a national revolution had been forcefully raised, its military dimensions, under the direction of Salcedo, fully contemplated.

It is worth noting that both this revolutionary democratic program and the corporativist policy of Gómez matured simultaneously over the first half of 1953. Before either could be approved, the government fell. The two projects represented a new polarization whose implications, had the coup not occurred, could have been extraordinary.

The Breakdown of Social Order

The third process, derived from both terror and resistance, was that of the social effects of the Violence. Although apparent to contemporaries in its most dramatic expressions, many of the deeper structural dimensions of this process still remain hidden. In a sense, the social aspects of the Violence constitute the period's most ignored aspect, one that is visible only at a distance, over the long term, by a new generation. As will be discussed, it is an aspect revealed panoramically only when the ending of the Violence is known. Here it is sufficient to catalog the outstanding social manifestations of the era.

The Violence, wherever it extended, deeply affected the structure of rural property holding. As a precaution or because of extortion, thousands of harassed peasants either abandoned their parcels or were forced to sell them at prices far inferior to their value. They then joined the migratory flow to distant colonization zones, or the army of the unemployed, or the petty merchants and slum dwellers of the cities. Some displaced peasants eventually joined the ranks of the guerrillas. The lands they abandoned had varied destinies. Sometimes they passed to a landholder in the area, sometimes to peasants of the opposing side, and very frequently to a new group of merchants, people affiliated with both parties, known as *aprovechadores* (those who take advantage), which came into existence as a commercial and landholding class through the turbulent dealings of the Violence. Modest shopkeepers and muleteers became rich overnight through the sale of stolen coffee and cattle or of abandoned peasant properties. Many large landholders in guerrilla zones and areas of generalized anarchy, were subject to similar temptations, but they had, as did the wealthier peasants with some liquidity, a wider range of options. They could sell off their investments or restructure them. Above all, they could take refuge in a large city where they could wait for the situation to improve.

Apart from some notable cases of continuity, such as the uninterrupted expropriation of the indigenous communities in the triangle formed by southern Tolima, northern Huila, and Tierradentro in Cauca, or the advance of capitalist agriculture in the sugar zone of the Cauca Valley and the flatlands of Tolima (Armero, Espinal, and Guamo), the process of social breakdown underwent continuous pendular movement. Where on one day only Conservative peasants might establish themselves safely, on the next day only Liberals could do so. In zones of recent agrarian agitation, such as the Sumapaz region of Tolima and Cundinamarca, if the initiative had belonged to the landowners at the close of the 1940s, in the 1950s the peasants mounted an effective counterattack. In these zones the peasant movement had armed itself rather than disappearing, as commonly is thought.

Over the course of any single year, there were also certain economic rhythms to the Violence. In the coffee departments, murders, robberies, and assaults intensified during the harvest period. In contrast, on the llanos, the period of greatest activity in the cattle trade, the year's end, was accompanied by a truce, achieved through the active intervention of the landowners with the army as well as with the guerrillas.

In all zones affected by the Violence, cheap land and high rural salaries, results of the general insecurity, combined to discourage landowners and would-be investors of a capitalist bent. The exodus of the landowners to the cities had some disturbing effects on the old hacienda structure. De facto occupants of land in areas of guerrilla presence could remain, uncertain as to how long, under the watchful but impotent eyes of local landowners. The crisis in the countryside also brought with it an internal reorganization of the haciendas. It forced revitalization of sharecropping and labor rent on coffee plantations where such tenancy forms had begun to disappear following the land law of 1936. This revitalization occurred with important modifications, however. The sharecroppers, renters, and similar tenants "charged" for the risks to which they were subjected daily by failing to provide full accountings to their absentee landlords and by exercising increased control over the processes of coffee production and commercialization. That is to say, they took on functions that went well beyond what the landowners either would have ceded voluntarily or would have tolerated were they not absentee. Sharecroppers and administrators even entered into agreements with guerrillas in many zones. These conditions represented an unraveling not only of landowner authority but also of deeply rooted aspects of hacienda operation.

Although in certain localities in certain periods it was impossible to harvest the coffee, the conflicts did not produce abrupt changes in the national volume of marketable coffee; what came into play was simply a substitution for the regular mechanisms of commercialization. This may explain in part the euphoria of the National Federation of Coffee Growers, even during the most critical movements of the Violence. But it should be made clear that this euphoria did not reflect the real situation of the proprietors. In other words, the harvest might have been lost to the direct producers but not necessarily to the commercial circuit.

The economic impact of the Violence on cattle ranching was much more obvious for three reasons: first, because of the scale and

frequency of cattle thefts, which affected both small and large proprietors; second, because as already noted, the destruction of cattle constituted a principal form of punishment of political adversaries; and
third, because cattle, unlike coffee, was a basic element in sustaining
large guerrilla groups. Expropriation of cattle in order to feed the
combatant population (in southern Tolima, southeastern Antioquia, and
the eastern plains especially) and forced taxation meant that the guerrillas
were in fact a very costly burden to the ranchers.

As a corollary, new poles of attraction for agricultural investment
were created, most notably on the Atlantic Coast, where the Violence
was minimal or nonexistent. New centers of accumulation also sprang
up. At their head was a new breed of merchant-landowner, who commonly held strings of rural properties concentrated in a form that the
anthropologist Jaime Arocha calls "dispersed latifundio." There was
also a reordering of urban productive space with the dismantling of
light industry in many intermediate towns and the rise of new sites of
industrial concentration in larger ones. Finally, there emerged new
kinds of migration and colonization, which, linked to the demolishing
impact suffered not only by peasants but also by owners of properties in
those sectors of the dominant classes in clear decline (that is, large
landowners and ranchers), suggests an acephalous, subterranean social
commotion that threatened to upset the foundations of the traditional
order, though nobody knew exactly how.

Seeing in this perspective the simultaneous evolution of the three
general processes already analyzed—terror and anarchy, novel aspects
of resistance, and gradual social dislocation—makes more understandable how an emergency exit to the crisis was sought. An atypical coup
d'etat, which would delegate the political task of pacification to the
military, seemed to open a hopeful vista for Colombians. On June 13,
1953, the commander of the armed forces, General Gustavo Rojas
Pinilla, assumed power, to the delight of nearly everyone, especially of
the Liberals who saluted him as a second Liberator.

Rojas, the Amnesty, and the Problems of Peace

When Rojas assumed power in mid-1953 he found a country devastated
by terror in some areas and in a state of generalized insurgency in
others. The nation seemed on the verge of an irreversible social and
political crisis. In enunciating the goal of his government, "Peace,
Justice, and Liberty," he thus was responding to a national desire. (It

was indeed unusual that in Colombia a de facto president from the military was received with the widest and strongest support to greet any ruler in the history of the republic.) The Liberal leader Echandía spoke of a "coup of opinion," and the dimensions of the change were measured in the verse of the national anthem that begins, "The horrible night has ended." The essential tasks of the new government were three: to end the terror and anarchy, demobilize the guerrillas, and reconstruct the areas affected by the Violence.

The Pacification

The first task of the Rojas regime, to end the terror and anarchy, seemed fulfilled by the very impact of the political shift that had just occurred. Gómez, who had made terror a government policy, had taken the path of exile once again, leaving his political allies leaderless, incoherent, and on the defensive. In contrast to the language of war, talk of reconciliation flooded the country, spearheaded by the president and systematically reaffirmed by the political and economic elites, the Church, and the press. The rebels in arms, who before had been treated as criminals and bandits, were now recognized as a rebel force and belligerents with whom negotiation was conceivable. In place of appeals to the partisan heroes of the respective parties the common inheritance of Simón Bolívar and the Christian tradition was stressed. The sectarian symbols of blue and red were replaced by the national flag. "Fatherland before the parties" was the slogan of the new era that was promised. This emphasis upon the national, it must be noted, would be made explicit in all of Rojas's efforts to forge organizations to compete with the two traditional parties. It would materialize in the effort to form a new labor central and would reappear in the Alianza Nacional Popular (ANAPO), the political party formed after the fall of Rojas from power.

For the moment, the positive effect of these recent events and new attitudes and values was undeniable. During his first year of government, Rojas created the impression that a new collective psychology had been generated, one that was open to a reorientation of Colombian political culture. Thousands of uprooted peasants undertook the journey back to their former homes. An atmosphere of tranquility, all the more apparent when compared to the chaos that had reigned in the immediate past, began to be felt throughout the country. To some extent, this calm was more apparent than real since continuing disorders were no longer reported. It seemed an easy triumph. The many-sided evolution of the Violence had made peace a necessity for peons and landowners alike, for insurgents as well as for those who wielded power.

The Amnesty

Parallel to his ideological campaign and using all of the political capital that it had produced for him, Rojas began his second task, to disarm and demobilize the guerrillas. He did so with an audacious initiative, the effects of which were quite complex: he offered a general and unconditional amnesty. To give credibility to the offer, during his first week in power Rojas ordered both the suspension of hostilities and the massive distribution of fliers, to be dropped by planes and helicopters on the principal guerrilla fronts, with messages of peace and promises of specific guarantees for those who laid down their arms.

Although officials had set their sights particularly on the eastern llanos, the government operations assumed the character of a general peace offensive. A circular was sent on June 15, 1953, by the army commander, General Alfredo Duarte Blum, to all military posts, instructing local officials on the procedures to be followed. The fact of partial or total fulfillment of the peace objectives in any region was to be used to pressure the guerrillas of the llanos, who were the most numerous, the most feared, and the most important rebels in the national context.

It must be recalled that when the first fliers fell on the plains, the guerrillas had just completed the Revolutionary Assembly of Chiefs. After approving the Second Law of the Llano on June 18, they had dispersed to their respective commands and territories with the aim of informing their followers about the content and implications of the latest stage in the guerrilla struggle. When the guerrillas learned of the overthrow of Gómez and were convinced that the helicopters indeed were delivering gestures of friendship instead of bombs and bullets, they reacted with surprise and incredulity. Still, in order to respond to the show of government goodwill and to gain time to permit internal consultations with their national command in Bogotá and to evaluate the general situation in the country, they ordered a suspension of guerrilla hostilities beginning June 22.

The military precision of the government's negotiations, undertaken simultaneously throughout the country, gave the impression of a pincers operation directed at the plains and showed its first fruits after only one month. The chain of guerrilla resistance broke, naturally at its "weakest link." With the support and intervention of local political bosses, landowners, and merchants, the government obtained the first unconditional surrenders in central Tolima. In order to heighten their exemplary character these ceremonies were given the widest publicity imaginable. The government also extracted from the Liberal guerrillas in the south and north of Tolima a promise to surrender in August, a promise announced with great public fanfare even though it was fulfilled only in October. Similarly, but with less public attention because the guerrillas involved were not as well known, combatants led by Rafael Rangel in the Territorio Vázques of northwestern Cundinamarca were also turning themselves in. In Antioquia the best-known guerrilla leader, Captain Franco Yepes, had announced on July 24 not the surrender but the dissolution of his forces. He was captured a month later by troops who had gone back on their word and imprisoned in La Ladera, in Medellín, until the end of the Rojas regime.

It was within this context that the government's military chiefs on the plains advanced in their separate negotiations with second-rank guerrilla leaders. These leaders' communications with the overall commanders, Salcedo and Franco Isaza, were almost completely severed, as is made clear in the records of contacts made prior to the surrender and collected by Germán Guzmán and his coauthors. After the guerrillas presented a twenty-four-point petition, for which they demanded presidential approval as a condition for finalizing negotiations, the military corralled the principal guerrilla leaders, including Salcedo, in the village of Monterrey. They in fact were held as hostages until the guerrilla fighters under their command completed their surrender.

What permitted a successful outcome from the government's point of view was the personal prestige of the president, which was greater every day. Rojas's intervention in the process was decisive. He continued to be the supreme arbiter. The problems, treason, and extortion that had appeared on the path were attributed to the bad faith of the local or regional implementers of his policies. Moreover, it was not procedures but results that counted, thanks in part to the selective coverage of the press controlled by the two parties. By the end of October, these results were convincing. In the country as a whole, 3,500 men had turned in their arms according to official reports. On the plains alone, 1,489 combatants had done so. And, although the general tendency was to surrender only shotguns and inoperable arms, the *llaneros* made their gesture more definitive by turning in around five hundred rifles as well.

In making its economic plans, the government felt obliged to treat the llanos with particular consideration. As a result, as late as January 1955—a critical year for Rojas—the president was triumphantly received in Yopal and Tame, two bastions of the now-demobilized guerrilla forces. On that occasion, in Tame, he even shook Salcedo's hand. There, at least, the peasants seemed willing to admit that the government indeed had kept its word.

Nevertheless, the peace process remained suspended in two vital regions, much preoccupying the government: the Communist-influenced regions of southern Tolima and Sumapaz. The Communists had reacted cautiously to the prospects created by a regime that was, after all, military. After bitter internal debates, they opted for a simple demobilization, without surrendering their weapons. But their isolation made the "self-defense" tactic that they had practiced no longer viable. Under siege by the army and by Liberal former guerrillas instigated by landowners, the Communists undertook a silent and systematic migration to the mountains of Sumapaz in the eastern chain, which were closer to Viotá, their center of logistical support in the Tequendama region. Others moved toward Riochiquito, Cauca, on the edge of the central range. Those who took the Sumapaz route were welcomed by that veteran agrarian leader of Gaitanista tendencies, Varela, who had been led by the Violence to make common cause with his old rivals, the Communists. With an astuteness derived from many years of struggle, Varela had made a politically calculated gesture of surrender in October 1953. To neutralize the military pressure he surrendered, according to newspaper accounts, 1,200 men; however, to prevent imminent landowner reaction, he held onto their arms. Under these conditions there began what later would be called a "truce" in the region.

The most politically articulate guerrilla fronts formulated, over the course of their various responses to the amnesty, an essentially democratic program, which can be seen as either a derivation or a continuation of the programs that they had developed in the years of armed resistance. This program included demands for basic guarantees, such as the right to life and physical integrity; the disarming of the counterguerrillas; the recognition that they were guerrillas, not bandits; freedom for political prisoners; the lifting of the state of siege and the holding of free elections; and freedom of written and verbal expression. In the economic field, guerrilla demands expressed the pressing necessities of their regions, including government credits for the reconstruction and productive use of lands belonging to peasant communities; indemnification for regions devastated by the direct actions of government forces; return of the "exiles" to their places of origin and aid for the repatriation of those forced to flee to Panama or Venezuela; restitution of properties to their former owners; and, eventually, distribution of land to peasants based on the principle of "land to the tiller." In sum, the guerrillas had formulated, in 1953, the basic tasks of the democratic forces as well as the central points of the agrarian problematic for the next ten years of the Violence, first during the Rojas years and later under the National Front.

The Economic Reconstruction

The reconstruction of the rural economy surely would have been a huge task for any government. Approximate statistics were gathered only in 1957, and they reveal a dramatic picture. In Tolima, for example, from 1949 to 1957, 361,800 persons had emigrated, either temporarily or permanently; 34,300 homes had been burned; and more than 40,000 rural properties belonging to over 32,000 proprietors had been abandoned, either temporarily or definitively. This last figure amounted to 42 percent of the rural properties and proprietors of Tolima. The figures—although not the proportions—were even greater in the more populous Valle del Cauca, thanks, as later would become known, to the continuous actions of the *pájaros*. And, beyond these obvious effects were others not immediately visible, such as those resulting from irregular mechanisms of land, cattle, and crop commercialization, which were manifest in prices that were sometimes tantamount to confiscation.

To respond to the challenge of these figures, Rojas initially had in his favor a buoyant coffee economy. Unprecedented coffee prices (U.S. $0.81 per pound in 1954) brought in large additional resources to the state. Rojas imposed new taxes on bond and stock dividends. He began to talk of agrarian reform to alleviate the anguish of the peasants. However, the coffee bonanza would disintegrate by the following year. Meanwhile, the industrialists, bankers, and insurance executives had become the disguised enemies of the government. Many protested the redistributive impact of lifting import restrictions; for them it meant a drain of foreign exchange, although the middle and lower classes considered it a relief for their daily budgets. Finally, the promises of agrarian reform were subsumed in a project of capitalist development, which, with its typical landowner perspective, combined the notions of productivity and colonization.

It is true that some projects of national interest did receive a boost under the Rojas regime. These included the reordering of petroleum production through the creation of the state oil company ECOPETROL and the strengthening of the state steelworks at Paz del Río. For the purposes of this exposition, it is convenient to note that most new financial resources were invested in two well-defined sectors. First, they went toward certain types of agricultural investment, such as the purchase of machinery and fertilizers, and into the setting up of irrigation zones, whose immediate beneficiaries were the great sugar barons of the Cauca Valley and the emergent rice and cotton entrepreneurs of the plains of Tolima. Second, they went toward financing infrastructure projects, such as construction of hydroelectric plants, the Atlantic Railway, the Eldorado International Airport in Bogotá, and the national television center—works that, on the whole, fed the pace of capitalist reproduction in both urban and rural Colombia. The regime's plans clearly sought not to aid those who had been ruined by the Violence but rather to reward and stimulate those who, either directly or indirectly, had come out on top in the process.

In regard to colonization—which may be considered the second focus of the government's agrarian policy—the centers of greatest disturbance, which were the coffee zones, were avoided instead of emphasized. "Directed colonization" was presented as the panacea for the tensions in the country's interior, on the pretext that the key problem was not the distribution of land but rather was excessive demographic pressure. This policy was not surprising. The National Agriculture Council, which was put in charge of designing these plans, was made up mainly of groups representing the interests of the largest landowners, of the federations of coffee and rice growers, and of ranchers. The Immigration and Colonization Institute, under whose auspices were founded towns such as Cimitarra, Santander, turned out to be essentially inoperative due to administrative chaos, a shortage of funds, and lack of coordination between government agencies. Its functions were reassigned to the Agrarian Bank in 1956.

It appeared as though the government were waiting for the Violence in the most conflictive zones to generate its own solutions. And, in part, one might say that the Violence did, in its own way. In effect, the "spontaneous colonizations" by refugees of the Violence played an important role in the post-1948 population growth of some zones of the middle Magdalena River valley and the Catatumbo, growth that accelerated after 1955 with the arrival of migrants from the Valle del Cauca, Tolima, and Viejo Caldas. These three departments, in descending order, were the only ones to experience a decline in population between 1951 and 1964. But such spontaneous colonizations had a tragic aspect. The colonizers tended to settle in various regions according to their political affiliations and in doing so set deadly boundaries to their settlements. They thus succeeded in transferring to these new regions the same conflicts that they just had fled.

There was, however, a new state agency that was devoted to economic and social reconstruction. It was poorly funded but surrounded by a publicity campaign comparable only to the campaign that accompanied the amnesty process. This agency was the Office of Rehabilitation and Relief, founded in 1954 under the National Social Assistance Service. It created a controversial celebrity in the person of its director, the president's daughter María Eugenia Rojas. The creation of this office by the military regime did imply a certain recognition that merely disarming the peasants was insufficient to resolve the calamitous consequences of the Violence. Nevertheless, the agency's accomplishments hardly justified the exaggerated optimism with which it was viewed by contemporary observers (such as the U.S. historian, Vernon Lee Fluharty). The reconstruction of the devastated town of Yacopí, Cundinamarca, which had been chosen as the showcase for a wider plan, only generated frustration in other regions that had had a similar fate under Gómez, especially in Tolima. For instance, the displaced inhabitants of Santiago Pérez (or Ataco), in southern Tolima, a prosperous Liberal coffee district in 1949 that was totally destroyed and later "conservatized" in the fifties, were, in late 1958, still demanding indemnification from the state for reconstruction.

The way in which credits were issued revealed a notably paternalistic streak in the rehabilitation program. By giving miniscule grants, designed to resolve the specific situations of those individuals who had gained recognition as *damnificados* (victims), the government sought to throw a veil over the true social dimensions of the problem. The 26,000 requests that displaced proprietors had filed by January 1955 may have covered the agency's desks in Bogotá, but they did not find a solution.

All this notwithstanding, the regime's programs, especially those involving credits, made manifest yet again the privileged place accorded the eastern plains in the government's plans. Of the total 20,700 loans made by January 1955, nearly half (9,000) flowed to the dominions of the guerrilla forces once led by Salcedo. It was in other conflictive regions, however, where these efforts were to receive their real trial by fire—that is, in zones of traditional agrarian conflict and great political heterogeneity, such as Sumapaz and southern Tolima. In Chaparral in southern Tolima, for example, peasants encountered a series of problems. First, the loans offered them for the recuperation of parcels of land were limited to 1,000 pesos, or about U.S. $300, each. Second, since this was a region still undergoing colonization, many of its peasants lacked property titles, creating an impossible obstacle to receiving state assistance. Third, the sectarian criteria by which petitions were often either accepted or ignored led to complaints—sometimes justified and sometimes not—that those who were benefiting were not the victims but rather had been the beneficiaries of the Violence.

Starting in 1956, demands were made for a moratorium on or a pardon of interest and other payments owed to official entities, such as the Agrarian Bank, in certain zones affected by the Violence. These demands were advanced under the banner of the rehabilitation plan but not by the government agency responsible for the plan. Rather, they were made by landowners from towns in southeastern Tolima, such as Purificación and Dolores. These requests were soon followed by others, such as one asking that urban and rural property taxes be reduced. For these reasons, getting recognized as a "zone affected by the Violence" came to be a very important component in the struggle to obtain an advantage in the division of the tax burden and in the haggling over local and departmental budgets. Success for individual or collective petitions frequently depended, just as it did in the case of the *damnificados*, on political and social influence, that is, on having powerful "godfathers." In any case, the demands of those affected were increasingly beyond what the government was either able or willing to offer.

Quite apart from the effectiveness of the official measures taken in response to these demands, there was something that secretly worried leaders of the traditional political parties. They were increasingly concerned that Rojas, who had arms but no autonomous political force, was trying to build a political base through the rehabilitation funds. Since many chunks of the budget for public works and services were being channeled either through the Ministry of War or under the label of "rehabilitation," it was becoming the norm at each inauguration of new highway, school, or clinic to see a military chief preaching the virtues of the *pueblo*-armed forces alliance." In a country where the spoils system was deeply rooted and helped to ensure the monopoly of the two traditional parties, this development clearly threatened the elite.

One Step Forward, Many Steps Backward

Many factors militated against the sought-after national pacification. Some were the fault of the government or of its agents, but other problems were due to the parties' strategies of destabilization. The first signs of what could be considered a shift in the official attitude toward the regime's critics and opponents came in mid-1954, that is, after the first full year of the Rojas administration.

On June 8 and 9, 1954, during the first urban antigovernment protests in several years, thirteen university demonstrators were shot by the army in events that culminated in the appointment of a colonel as rector of the National University. From that moment the government became defensive before public opinion and sought to neutralize its fiercest adversaries from within the traditional parties, the deposed followers of former Conservative President Gómez. As part of his newly conciliatory attitude toward the previous regime, Rojas signed a decree on June 13 extending amnesty to those persons imprisoned for "exaggerated support or adhesion to the [Gómez] government." In other words, while the politically persecuted were released through the front door of the jails, their killers were being released through the back door.

Whereas the government had displayed the photograph of Rojas with Salcedo as a symbol of what had been achieved on the llanos, the more critical Liberals were circulating a different picture in Tolima, Valle del Cauca, and Caldas; a photograph of the president with the infamous Leon María Lozano, "El Condor," and his political protectors. The picture showed graphically just how the regime was moving backward. El Condor and his cohorts, upon regaining their freedom, returned to their exploits in towns such as Tuluá and Cartago in Valle del Cauca and extended their activities to Génova, Calarcá, and Armenia in Quindío and to several areas of central and southern Tolima. In that latter department, agents of the secret police, especially those of the Colombian Intelligence Service, used the newly released killers to assassinate individuals who had been amnestied, demobilized guerrillas who had not turned in their arms, and defenseless peasants. The killings were so open that even the army expressed its unease.

What happened next is by now well known. Those guerrillas who had not laid down their arms were further convinced of the need to hold onto them, and those who had surrendered their weapons regretted doing so. Many Colombians began to view the amnesty as a ploy of the government. The partisan violence soon regained its dynamic of past years. Former guerrillas, such as Teófilo Rojas ("Chispas"), found it easy to recruit new fighters and to convince old comrades that peace was an illusion and that they had to rearm. In Quindío the coffee growers and Liberal political bosses felt so persecuted by the Conservative bands of *pájaros* that they decided to make contact with the Liberal guerrillas of southern Tolima. They sent emissaries to Chispas to convince him to set up a "self-defense zone" in the region with their economic support and political protection. Since the offer gave Chispas an opportunity to attack his rivals in the north, he responded by alternating his activities between Tolima and Quindío, the two slopes of the central Andean range.

The government's measures to placate the Laureanistas helped neither the amnesty nor the peace processes. Moreover, the traditional parties, which had remained in a sort of recess during Rojas's first year in power, now emerged as a factor. The parties began to use the daily acts of violence as instruments of political mobilization. While on the one hand they condemned the resurgence of the Violence, on the other hand they stimulated it and declared Rojas solely responsible for it. The newspapers of both parties echoed this two-sided tactic. In fact, the parties' newspapers became the privileged terrain of the opposition and a pole of organization and unification for the dominant classes against the "dictator," as they now began to call him.

Rojas responded erratically to these provocations, sometimes, at mass rallies, denouncing them as an oligarchical plot and, on other occasions, alleging a Communist conspiracy. His censorship and closing of newspapers was but a symptom of his weakness and only served to strengthen his adversaries. They flouted the government's measures simply by changing the titles of the newspapers affected. Meanwhile, from exile and through his Bogotá newspaper, *El Siglo*, Gómez loudly demanded a "freedom of the press" that never had existed under his government. In the context of the government's daily decay and with the support of the press and even of the Liberal politicians, Gómez now could present himself as the new standard-bearer of democracy.

A final and unequal battle thus was unleashed on the political scene. While Rojas zigzagged, trying to build an independent power base, the political establishment, with more than a century of experience, moved with particular skill and security—this was their turf. When, in late 1954, the government was rumored to be considering a "National Action Movement," former president López Pumarejo managed to abort the initiative merely by suggesting a bipartisan coalition. As a result, when Rojas did launch his "third force" on June 13, 1956, the bipartisan Civic Front already had been in operation for months under the leadership of Lleras Camargo. Rojas was trying to work from below in a long-term project, while the Civic Front was working from above for immediate agreements. One month after the formal announcement of the Third Force, Lleras Camargo and Gómez signed the Pact of Benidorm in Spain. An exultant Gómez reaped the fruits of the advancing crisis on the economic as well as the political front, saying that the country had not understood his government and had gotten what it deserved.

When Rojas announced in early 1957 his intention to stay in power for another four years, the economic interest groups and the Church already had prepared the general strike that would force his resignation on May 10. The victors were greeted with support similar to that enjoyed by Rojas four years earlier. The new panorama was quite clear—politics would continue to be under the control of the parties while a military junta of five members, led by General Gabriel París, would administer the economy.

Lleras Camargo had been the architect of the Civic Front, but the big winner was Gómez. Already, in debates over the economic crisis, which had deepened after 1955, the "pragmatic competence" of the preceding regime in economic affairs commonly was conceded. Now came the moment of formal recognition: the military junta gave the finance portfolio to Antonio Alvarez Restrepo, an old minister of Gómez. After his return to the country, Gómez ran in the congressional elections of March 1958 and won a seat in the Senate, and that body elected him as its president. It was in that capacity that he placed the presidential sash on Lleras Camargo in August. Gómez was the symbol of the new legitimacy. In this context the subsequent trial of Rojas before the Senate can be seen as, among other things, the political reaffirmation of Gómez. To put it in the lexicon of the era, Gómez was the real *rehabilitado* of the Violence.

History's Judgment on Rojas

The picture presented to this point would seem to suggest an ambiguous verdict on Rojas's government. After an initial phase of wide popular expectation, there came a period of growing frustration. It had fulfilled its role as a transitional government, as an arbiter, and its efforts to stay in power by dislocating the political spectrum only served to spur the reunification of traditional bipartisan dominance, which rapidly reappropriated all democratic space.

In examining the relative weight of the pros and cons, the best-known chronicles of the period have left divided opinions. The most enthusiastic apologists, such as Fluharty, see only the regime's beginnings and its transformative potential. The harshest critics, above all those seduced by the National Front, such as John Martz, wish to see only the regime's final months and to uncover at every step the expected figure of the stereotypical Latin American dictator. Perhaps what the complex trajectory just described really shows is the impossibility of finding such comfortable and schematic solutions to judging the period.

It should also be noted that *rojismo* did not end on May 10, 1957. The ANAPO party of the 1960s was formed using much of the political discourse of Rojas's initial period in power. It even can be added that, over the long term, Rojas made an undeniable contribution to the political thawing of Colombia. ANAPO created, for the first time, the possibility for movement by sectors of the Conservative party toward the left. In the 1978 elections several leftist coalitions contained old ANAPO figures on their lists. Jaime Piedrahita Cardona, one of ANAPO's founders, was the presidential candidate of the Popular Unity Front, and one of his regional chiefs, Julio César Pernía, was the presidential candidate of the National Opposition Union. The histories of the "Socialist ANAPO" and of the guerrilla group M-19, as seen in the personal trajectory of Carlos Toledo Plata, serve to illustrate yet another path taken by the militants of *rojismo*.

A decisive component of any effort to evaluate the Rojas regime is the landowner-military offensive against Sumapaz. It was this action more than any other that made the Rojas era one not of transition or truce but rather a further chapter in the Violence. As was pointed out earlier, Sumapaz was left after late 1953 in a sort of limbo, but it was closely watched by the military. The basic problem was one of land. It was expressed in the conflicting answers to one basic question: what did peace mean?

For peasants, peace meant, above all, that they would be recognized as the legitimate occupants of the land for which they had fought for decades, and which they had won with their blood albeit aided by the landowner exodus of the 1940s and 1950s. For those landowners, acceptance of the new status quo in the region amounted to legalizing an unacceptable result of the Violence. For them, the Violence in Sumapaz had led to an agrarian revolution pure and simple. The arrival of the Communists of southern Tolima, who were very active in mass organization through "democratic fronts," exasperated the landowners still further since they believed that the situation was becoming irreversible. For landowners, peace only had one acceptable outcome: their guaranteed return to their properties and eviction of the peasants. It thus transpired in the latter half of 1954 that, in what might be characterized as the counterattack of the latifundia against the peasant economy and organization, the government, acting as the armed agent of the landowners, began to prepare a military assault on the region.

Counting on the more or less consolidated results of the disarmament in other regions, government officials thought that Sumapaz's capacity for resistance would be minimal and that a rapid and total victory over poorly armed peasants thus could be assured. The first major military provocation came in November 1954 when approximately one hundred peasants, who were awaiting safe-conduct passes in the plaza of Puerto Nuevo, were executed. That same month, in response to constant aggression, the army undertook a sweep in which they captured the Communist agrarian leader Isauro Yosa, one of many rebels in southern Tolima who had abandoned the guerrilla ranks after the initial truce. On May 4, 1955, Sumapaz was declared a Military Operations Zone, and from that date "pacification" once more came to be a synonym for devastation, machine-gunning, and bombardment. At least six battalions, around one third of the army's total force, were involved, supported by a torture center known during the era as the concentration camp of Cunday.

The first results showed that the government, the military, and the landowners had underestimated the peasants' capacity for resistance. An operation expected to take days or weeks became a long war lasting two years. During this war, many peasants, including women and children, were killed, but thousands managed to escape encirclement. Some took refuge with Varela in the Alto Sumapaz; others fled toward Marquetalia, in extreme southern Tolima. Old guerrilla zones felt threatened and began to mobilize in a general revolt against the military regime. When Guadalupe Salcedo was murdered in June 1957 in Bogotá, he was exploring the possibilities of coordinating guerrilla solidarity with Sumapaz.

The military invasion succeeded in geographically displacing a problem too large to permit so close to the capital, but it did so at an incalculable political cost. It eroded the prestige that Rojas had won at the moment of coming to power through his treatment of the crucial issues of war and peace. The historical verdict of the peasants on his government had also changed. The judgment that German Guzmán reported from a peasant woman who had been a guerrilla in Sumapaz may serve as a closing note for this section on the Violence. The woman was asked, "And what do you think of Rojas?" She responded, "He did some good things, but also some really bad things. Don't you see that he pacified the eastern plains but tried to get rid of Tolima?"

The National Front: Colombia at the Crossroads

With the installation of the National Front in 1958, one cycle of Colombian political history came to an end, and the strategies of domination were redefined. In addition there occurred a multiplication of the forces questioning what was becoming known as "the system." The Liberal and Conservative oligarchies, whom the government of Rojas had done the great service of uniting, achieved a long-term pact whose central feature was the peaceful sharing of power as enshrined in a constitutional amendment approved by a plebiscite. Power sharing was to be brought about through a combination of alternating the presidency every four years and the mandatory equal distribution of public posts (including all legislative offices) between the two parties. Political forces outside the bipartisan process were formally excluded.

This political pact simultaneously covered two fronts. First, it cleared the path for interoligarchical relations that had been blocked, with tremendous destabilizing effects, since the 1940s. Second, it was a preemptive response to a new factor that had evolved from the course of the Violence itself. The Violence was an ambiguous process resembling both a nineteenth-century-style civil war and an embryonic peasant revolution, and, as the former problem was resolved, the second took the fore. In theory a negotiated way out of the Violence, the National Front, in practice, actually inaugurated a new phase of it.

A Fragile Legitimacy

The first real test of the new political project's legitimacy was the theatrical trial of Rojas before the Senate. The plan was to unload all responsibility for the Violence on the shoulders of the dictatorship, thus exonerating the creators of the National Front. But the trial had unexpected complications, and the accusers were forced to call a precipitous halt to the proceedings. The sentence, which stripped Rojas of his political rights, also gave him a new role to play in the coming years. He became a living symbol of those Colombians left out of a pact whose oligarchical nature would become more obvious every day.

The contrast between the growing popular disillusionment with the National Front and the growing popularity of Rojas would become clear in electoral returns throughout the 1960s. In the congressional elections of 1960, not only did abstentions reach 50 percent, but also the candidates of Rojas's old collaborators in the Conservative party, the followers of Ospina Pérez, greatly outpolled the Laureanistas. This result was not yet an open rejection of traditional party politics, but it was a clear indication of who was acceptable and who was not. In 1962 the partisans of Rojas entered the electoral arena with ANAPO, the independent movement that they had founded two years earlier. It had a modest initial result, 104,829 votes, but the party's subsequent growth was stunning. It created real problems for the National Front, which felt its legitimacy threatened. ANAPO tripled its support by 1964, drawing 309,678 votes. It received 523,000 votes in the congressional elections of 1966, and in the presidential election of that year, fielding a Liberal of Gaitanista tendencies, José Jaramillo Giraldo, the party received 742,133 votes. ANAPO reached its zenith on April 19, 1970—a date intimately linked to the founding and name of M-19—in the presidential election that nearly consigned the National Front to oblivion. The electoral count gave an early lead to Rojas over his National Front opponent Misael Pastrana Borrero. However, after a televised speech by the interior minister, which was interpreted as a public announcement of fraud, the count gave a narrow victory to the official candidate.

Over the course of the decade of the 1960s ANAPO became a magnet for popular discontent, above all in the larger urban centers. It really never produced any specific program for the rural zones devastated by the Violence. When ANAPO did consider the agrarian question it did so from a landowners' perspective. In short, it might be said that ANAPO's political discourse remained only on the "frontier" of the Violence; the party never confronted the heart of the issues raised by that phenomenon.

Itinerary of the Agrarian Question

In rural areas peace continued to be, on the whole, only a distant promise. The true dimensions of the conflict, especially its social nature, were beginning to be recognized, but this did not guarantee that effective measures would be taken to deal with them. For instance, the direct link between the Violence and the agrarian problem, which had been raised by the guerrillas in 1953, was "discovered" only after 1957 by official agencies, politicians, and military commanders.

A military man, Colonel Alfonso Guzmán Acevedo, was among the first to bring the problem to national attention. As civil and military chief of eastern Tolima, he had confronted the issue during the punitive operations against the peasants of Sumapaz. In early 1957, acting as governor of Tolima, he presented to the national government a proposed decree in which he indicated the mechanisms that he felt were required to compensate those persons who, since November 9, 1949, "had, without order of a competent authority, been stripped of the lands they had been occupying and developing peacefully." In the same vein, a report on the socioeconomic effects of the Violence between 1949 and 1957 made by the head of Tolima's Agriculture Department, Hugo Pascualy, concluded that "peace cannot be a reality, without first establishing an equilibrium of property." Politicians who had visited the Casa Verde district of Ataco, in extreme southern Tolima, observed that it had been occupied massively by members of the opposing political party who had come from the neighboring municipality of San Antonio. Their diagnosis was also unequivocal, "The problem of Casa Verde is essentially one of land."

If, however, these diagnoses indeed suggest gradual public acceptance of a new understanding of the Violence, there was still important resistance in the realm of political policy. The predominant responses were still those left over from the Rojas regime. They included the promotion of new colonization schemes under the sponsorship of the Agrarian Bank (in the Ariary region of Meta, for example) and the expansion of the activities and coverage of the rehabilitation plans. The office in charge of these plans was elevated to Special Rehabilitation Commission status and attached to the president's office; its budget was raised from 27 million pesos in 1958 to over 100 million in 1959, with more money to be devoted to recuperation of affected properties than had been in the previous year. The government's basic outlook, however, had not changed substantially. It continued to work from the assumption that the current occupants of rural properties were the legitimate owners and that the state's role, therefore, should be only that of giving the landowners credits, technical assistance, and so on to help them rehabilitate their properties. The urgent and difficult problem of land theft was left outside the agency's legal scope. Moreover, the issuance of credits was conditioned on the possibility of the state's exercising control over the beneficiaries. This aspect is clearly shown by the unusual restrictions introduced in a circular dated July 23, 1958, which barred loans for "those areas where the authorities do not control the situation, and where there remain serious abnormalities preventing the return of the inhabitants."

It was in order to restore the confidence in the state of just these peasant inhabitants, as well as to decentralize the functions of the Special Rehabilitation Commission, that the so-called *equipos polivalentes* (multifaceted teams) were set up. They were advertised as "a new stage of rehabilitation." Each team was composed of a doctor, a nurse, a home economist, an engineer, and an agricultural expert. The teams were supported by an equally diverse infrastructure, including social welfare centers, schools, sewing centers, playgrounds, branches of the Agrarian Bank, churches, first aid stations, demonstration farms, and even bulldozers and heavy trucks to open up regional penetration roads. Fourteen such teams were located in towns of the five departments still under a state of siege: Riosucio and Génova in Viejo Caldas; Páez in Cauca; Colombia, Baraya, and Aipe in Huila; Rioblanco, Chaparral, Dolores, Ataco, and Líbano in Tolima; and Caicedonia, Ulloa, and Ceilán in Valle del Cauca.

The goal of the teams was to integrate these regions into the political, economic, and social life of the nation by simultaneously addressing several different aspects of community development, such as education and health (through school and hospital construction). In particularly fast-growing urban centers, such as Cali, the teams also undertook housing construction. Their favorite activity, however, was road building, which best met two of the government's goals, stimulating economic development and providing employment for former fighters. Road building also reaffirmed the state's presence in zones where it had been diminished under the impact of the Violence. It was to some extent a way of linking former guerrillas to programs that sought to eradicate the material conditions that had caused them to become guerrillas. The director of the Special Rehabilitation Commission, José Gómez Pinzón, summarized road building's functions in the following manner:

> There were many regions where owing to the long years of violence the money system had completely disappeared and trade between regions was carried out by a primitive barter system. So what we did was to flood these vast areas with cash, and since the only way to do that was by creating sources of employment, so that the population could get money and reinvest it in their region, we initiated a vast program of public works. We began to build paths and penetration roads with the aim of connecting these regions to centers of consumption, permitting access to the authorities, and getting the money flooded in.

The multifaceted teams linked to the rehabilitation effort were only the beginning of more elaborate efforts at social control, such as *acción comunal* (community action). The teams also had direct connections to plans for the militarization of the rural zones through "civil-military action." These plans were laid out by General Alberto Ruíz Novoa at the Conference of American Armed Forces held in the Panama Canal Zone in 1963.

Perhaps the most novel initiative of the Special Rehabilitation Commission under the National Front was the creation of *bolsas de propiedad raíz*, real estate exchanges, where rural property could be registered for sale or trade in order to facilitate the relocation of proprietors to areas that better suited their political affiliations. In mid-1959 a list of eighty-seven properties in Tolima was published, most of them in the southern part of the department (in Chaparral, Rioblanco, San Antonio, Valle de San Juan). The desperate situation of many proprietors was reflected in cases such as that of a farm called La Dalia in the district of Ambeima in Chaparral. Although thirty hectares in size the property was offered for only 800 pesos. It finally sold for a sum sufficient only for the transportation expenses of the owner and his family.

Finally, it should be noted that, despite enormous pressure and resistance from politicians and the military bordering on sabotage, several former guerrilla chieftains did benefit briefly from rehabilitation loans. Examples include Teófilo Rojas ("Chispas"), Leopaldo García ("General Peligro"), and Roberto González ("Pedro Brincos").

One thing about these rehabilitation efforts remains clear. The legal issue of property, as affected by land theft and other de facto situations, and the issue of agrarian structure still had not been addressed. These issues did not fit into what might be called (with perhaps some exaggeration) the philosophy of rehabilitation. Only with the creation of the Tribunals of Equity and Conciliation, which began to operate in 1960, were the first, albeit limited, steps taken to deal with these issues.

The tribunals, with seats in the five departments defined by decree as violent (Caldas, Cauca, Huila, Tolima, and Valle del Cauca), were given the mission of resolving these de facto land and property situations. They also were to address the question of economic injury caused by any transaction that took place under coercion and were to sort out rival claims engendered by the opportunistic atmosphere of the Violence in a given zone. They aimed at resolving a critical problem, but the solution they offered was a false one.

Lasting just one year, the tribunals managed to demonstrate only their impotence in solving problems of such magnitude. Their operational limitations were overwhelming, and it will suffice to point out but a few. For example, if the property in question were already in the hands of a third party when the tribunal began to function, then the claim would be paralyzed. This was an enormous flaw since among the tactics used by land usurpers was the employment of *comisionistas* (intermediaries) in the deal, or the swapping of parcels with others in similar situations. A second cause of inefficiency derived from the nature of the tribunals—they were "conciliation" bodies and thus lacked coercive power to impose resolutions. If the two sides did not display a "spirit of conciliation," then the tribunal had no alternative but to file away the claim for good. And even if the tribunal were to issue an opinion, to accept that there had been an economic injury in the original transaction and embargo the property in question, a new series of obstacles presented itself. The eyewitness inspection required for appraisal of the property necessitated the presence of judges and appraisers in regions where nobody could guarantee their safety. The appraisal itself would occasion endless arguments over the multiple factors entering into the calculation. In appraising coffee properties, for example, one had to consider annual variations in coffee prices, whether production had declined before or after the initial sale, or whether the de facto proprietor had introduced improvements that had to be compensated. In short, the process was governed by principles foreign to the reality being addressed.

The tribunals were not operating in areas only of past violence, as their regulations and their very conception seem to imply, but were in areas of immediate violence, areas in which merely by filing a claim before the tribunal one put one's life at risk. Besides—because this was what was really at issue—how could it be expected that social groups that had made their fortunes from the Violence would voluntarily present themselves before the tribunals in order to renounce their gains? Evidently the problem was not seen in these terms but rather as a question of certain individuals having become impoverished and others having gotten rich.

It was only around 1960–61 that various pressures made it no longer possible to ignore the social dimension of the Violence. Peasant land invasions had resumed in many regions. Representatives of opposition groups, especially those tied to the peasants of Sumapaz and southern Tolima (whose spokesman was Juan de la Cruz Varela), had been elected to Congress on agrarian reform platforms. Even the official sectors that were led by the future president, Lleras Restrepo, had reached the conclusion (by a different path) that if the migratory avalanche to the cities that the Violence had produced were not halted, the urban situation could explode and endanger the conditions needed for capitalism in Colombia.

All of the implications of the long agrarian reform debate set off by these first alarm bells need not be discussed here. What is important to note is that the real beneficiaries of the reform were the large landowners of Sumapaz and southern Tolima, who had been trapped in a conflict they realized they could not win. The agency formed to carry out the limited agrarian reform, the Colombian Institute of Agrarian Reform (INCORA), began its operations in just these regions and bought the landowners' problems from them. In contrast to the defiant landowners that INCORA encountered in other regions, such as the Cauca Valley and the Atlantic Coast, the absentee landowners of Sumapaz actually called in INCORA. Many of them not only hastened to offer for sale unproductive latifundia, abandoned over the previous decade, but they also managed to strike attractive deals by overvaluing lands that nobody else would have bought. The National Front provided the landowners with the solution that military invasion could not. The peasants of other regions drew the appropriate conclusions. A few years later—during the crisis spawned by ANAPO's electoral success— these peasants undertook the popular path to agrarian reform under the direction of the National Peasant Association (ANUC). They reminded the nation that the National Front had left unresolved one of the fundamental components of the Violence, the agrarian problem.

The National Front and Political Banditry

Other dimensions of the Violence under the National Front were of a predominantly political nature. These factors had deep roots, and they resurfaced with the reactivation of electoral competition under the National Front's conception of legitimacy. This conception was defined by the bipartisan accords and by the limited amnesty decree. For the

movements toward centralization and state revitalization that gained
expression through the National Front, peace and collective renunciation
of a bloody past were seen as necessities. Only thus could the oligarchy
restore its political hegemony. However, at the levels of local and
regional power, it was almost impossible to erase the past. The Violence
was still part of daily events and formed the substance of rural and
small-town political discourse.

To a large extent, the politics of the 1960s were waged in terms of
struggles and pacts between different levels of power. And it was in the
interstices of these struggles that the characteristic expression of the
Violence during this era, *bandolerismo* (political banditry), lived and
died. This phenomenon is detailed in Gonzalo Sánchez and Donny
Meertens, *Bandoleros, gamonales y campesinos*, and only a few aspects of the evolution of *bandolerismo* need be presented here.

Bandolerismo was, above all, a phenomenon of Liberal peasants
who had suffered from official terror or participated in the resistance
during the 1940s and 1950s. (There were a few notable exceptions,
such as the Conservative Efraín González, who operated first in Quindío
and later in Santander and Boyacá.) Some peasants sought revenge;
others found it incomprehensible that the National Front would invite
them to forget, to capitulate, without first eradicating the causes of their
rebellion. Their greatest presence was in the coffee belt of the central
range (northern Tolima, northern Valle del Cauca, and Viejo Caldas),
where political motivations were joined to the economic stimuli of the
Violence.

The evolution of these bandit groups was marked by several stages.
In an initial phase, the bandits could count on a wide political space. On
one side, space was provided them by the local bosses (whether or not
the bosses supported the National Front). A web of alliances and
rivalries resulted, born of mutual need. On the other side, space was
provided by dissident factions of the traditional parties, such as the
Liberal Revolutionary Movement (MRL). These factions had sprung
up under the simultaneous and ambiguous banners of sectarianism and
popular nonconformity, processes fostered by the politics of the National Front. The *bandoleros* thus were one dimension of local political
power. They were an armed force whose function was to protect a
social fringe group comprising peasants and landowners of a given
party, which was threatened by political adversaries.

In this early stage the bandits received, in return for the armed
protection that they provided, the voluntary economic support of even
the large landowners. As already noted, Chispas was called in by the
Liberal coffee hacendados of Quindío to counteract the activities of the
Conservative band of Efraín González. For his part, González was

funded by the coffee wealth of his Conservative supporters in the town of Pijao.

In urban centers, bandit groups could count on the professional services of doctors and lawyers, the sympathy of storekeepers who kept "deliveries" coming, and the collaboration of tailors in the manufacture of uniforms. They had, then, a considerable network of loyalties. Although the terror the bandits inflicted on their adversaries (who were defined in partisan political terms rather than in terms of social class) was frequently barbarous, the protected community did not deny them their status as guerrillas but rather idealized them and made them figures of legend.

The second phase in their evolution witnessed the expansion of these armed bands and was marked by the economic and political implications of that process. The maintenance of permanent bands, in which a few members were engaged even partially in productive activities, began to modify the initial picture of allegiances and hostilities. *Bandolero* leaders gradually were becoming involved in the internal organization of the coffee properties. They named employees and administrators, contracted for workers, and distributed harvests. They also raised the protection quotas that the owners had to pay. As owners resisted these changes, they were increasingly drawn to a policy of state repression. Expansion of the *bandoleros* led to the breakdown of their alliance with the landowners, with far-reaching implications. It threatened to lead to the breakdown of rural hierarchies. "Desquite" in northern Tolima, "Chispas" in Quindío, and their fellows in other regions developed closer ties with estate personnel and administrators. These employees became, in effect, the economic arm of the armed groups, which increasingly ignored the authority of the proprietors. The bandit groups never really questioned the structure of rural property. They did not have to as long as they could control production. Moreover, it was in the bandits' interest to protect production. This fact helps explain why in Quindío, despite the endemic violence and the absence of the proprietors, the amount of coffee produced for market actually rose during this period.

The increasing hostility of the proprietors was interpreted by the *bandoleros* as a desertion from the cause and cost the landowners dearly. The *bandoleros* resorted to tactics that gave the Violence a visibly economic character. Their two principal instruments were *boleteo* (extortion) and kidnapping. *Boleteo* was indeed common in the 1950s, but it was used then only against political adversaries. Now it had acquired a class content, and it was employed indiscriminately against proprietors of either party. Kidnapping, however, was a relatively new tactic. The departments most affected were Tolima, Valle del Cauca, and Huila, in descending order. The critical year was 1963, not only because of the total number of cases that year—around thirty, according to official reports—but also because the total amount paid as ransom, estimated at around 7 million pesos, was so high.

In political relations, the growth and multiplication of the *bandoleros* generated trends similar to the economic and social problems faced by proprietors. From simple instruments of electoral control, the *bandolero* leaders came to be at the center of political realignment in the rural zones. They now were in competition rather than in alliance with the bosses—challenging their power in some zones, trying to take their place in others. One obvious example of this process is "Desquite," who proclaimed himself Civil and Military Chief of Northern Tolima. Clearly, his declaration cannot be taken at face value, but it does reveal an explicit will to gain autonomy from his earlier political protectors by reducing their room to maneuver. Now even local bosses discovered the advantages of political centralization and joined in the National Front's pacification plans. Along with the proprietors, they decisively took the side of the army. Even the MRL turned its back on the bandits and collaborated closely with the military. When the MRL died, so too did the Liberals' guerrilla past.

A third stage in the bandit groups' evolution now began. The *bandoleros* had had their links to the landowners and bosses broken and their last ties to the traditional parties, especially the Liberal party, cut. In addition, they were standing alone against an army trained and equipped with U.S. aid and given almost unlimited powers to combat them. They might have appeared, therefore, to be on the verge of an irreversible process of radicalization. However, this was not entirely the case. Certainly, there were individual examples of *bandoleros* joining new opposition or revolutionary movements, such as Efraín González, who joined ANAPO, or "Pedro Brincos," who became allied with the Worker-Student-Peasant Movement (MOEC), which was devoted to the violent seizure of power. But for the majority of *bandoleros* there was no further political development. They were left bewildered by political transformations that seemed to take place in spite of them. Amid the confusion, they contributed to their own destruction by turning their weapons on the peasants who were their surest supporters. They interpreted as a deliberate withdrawal of peasant support what was in reality the neutralization and blockading of their communications and bases of support by the army.

In their diversity the *bandoleros* had taken the multiple paths possible in the Violence: anarchy and terror, as in the case of "Sangrenegra"; the eruption of peasant power, as in the case of the mythical "Capitán Venganza" in Risaralda; and the encounter of the old struggles with the new revolutionary war, as in the exceptional but illustrative case of "Pedro Brincos." They represented a past that had not yet gone, and a future that had not yet arrived.

Thousands of peasants were killed in the war of *bandolerismo*. At last the National Front could proclaim *its* peace. With the liquidation of the "bandits," a whole era of national history had played itself out, the era of party warfare. However, the announced peace was but a partial one. Even before the old war was over, a new and entirely different war had begun. Many of the combatants of the Violence had shifted ranks, transformed by their struggle as well as by the revolutionary winds that invaded Latin America in the era of the Cuban Revolution. There was a multiplication of fronts and of nomenclature; new social groups were drawn in, especially the urban middle class (students, professionals, white-collar workers). In all of them could be detected, in some form, the sectarianism of the past wars. They bore the traumatic inheritance of the Violence but were now inscribed in another history, in a history still not concluded today.

In sum, one can say of the three basic components of the Violence analyzed in this synthesis that the first, anarcho-sectarianism, was partially suppressed; the second, the resistance, was transformed; and the third, the social impact, was left unresolved.

Bibliography

Alape, Arturo. *El Bogotazo: Memorias del olvido.* Bogotá, 1983.

Arocha, Jaime. *La Violencia en el Quindío.* Bogotá, 1979.

Braun, Herbert. *The Assassination of Gaitán: Public Life and Urban Violence in Colombia.* Madison, 1985.

Fajardo, Darío. *Violencia y desarrollo.* Bogotá, 1979.

Fluharty, Vernon Lee. *Dance of the Millions: Military Rule and Social Revolution in Colombia, (1930–1956).* Pittsburgh, 1957.

Franco Isaza, Eduardo. *La guerrilla de los llanos.* Bogotá, 1959.

Gilhodés, Pierre. "Agrarian Struggles in Colombia." In *Agrarian Problems and Peasant Movements in Latin America*, ed. R. Stavenhagen. New York, 1970.

Granados, Wilson Horacio. "La Violencia en Urrao, Antioquia, 1948–1953." Monografía de Grado, Universidad de Antioquia, Departamento de Sociología, Medellín, 1982.

Guzmán Campos, Germán, Orlando Fals Borda, and Eduardo Umaña Luna. *La Violencia en Colombia.* 2 vols. Bogotá, 1962 and 1964.

Henderson, James D. *When Colombia Bled: A History of the Violence in Tolima.* University, AL, 1985.

Hobsbawm, Eric J. "The Anatomy of Violence." *New Society* 28 (1963): 16–18.

Martz, John D. *Colombia: A Contemporary Political Survey.* Chapel Hill, 1962.

Molano, Alfredo. *Amnistía y violencia.* Bogotá, 1978.

————. *Los años del tropel.* Bogotá, 1985.

Oquist, Paul. *Violence, Conflict, and Politics in Colombia.* New York, 1980.

Palacios, Marco. *El populismo en Colombia.* Bogotá, 1971.

Pecaut, Daniel. *L'Ordre et al Violence: Evolution socio-politique de la Colombie (1930–1953).* Paris, 1986.

Ramsey, Russell. *Civil-Military Relations in Colombia, 1946–1965.* N.p.; 1978.

Ortiz Sarmiento, Carlos Miguel. *Estado y subversión en Colombia: La Violencia en el Quindío años 50.* Bogotá, 1985.

Sánchez, Gonzalo. *Los días de la revolución: Gaitanismo y 9 de abril en provincia.* Bogotá, 1983.

————. "Raíces históricas de la Amnistía o las etapas de la Guerra en Colombia." In *Ensayos de historia social y política del siglo XX*, ed. Gonzalo Sánchez. Bogotá, 1985.

————, and Donny Meertens. *Bandoleros, gamonales y campesinos: El caso de la Violencia en Colombia.* Bogotá, 1983.

————, and Ricardo Peñaranda, eds. *Pasado y presente de la Violencia en Colombia.* Bogotá, 1986.

Urán, Carlos. *Rojas o la manipulación del poder.* Bogotá, 1983.

6

The "Business of the Violence": The Quindío in the 1950s and 1960s*

Carlos Miguel Ortiz Sarmiento

This essay focuses on the coffee business and on land transactions during the Violence in the Quindío, a region where smallholders predominate in the heart of the coffee zone of the central chain of the Colombian Andes. Carlos Miguel Ortiz Sarmiento advances a revisionist argument based on the importance of what he calls "intermediaries" in the production and commercialization of coffee. One intermediary is the independent estate manager, who procured labor for large coffee farms. Labor arrangements on such estates may have included day labor at a set wage or piecework as well as a variety of sharecropping systems and tenancy contracts. Under sharecropping and tenancy workers gained access to land that they could cultivate in exchange for their agreeing to labor for the landowner several days each month. These labor arrangements had the effect of shielding the landowner from his workers, of muddling the distinction between capital and labor in coffee production. The other intermediary is the small-town coffee merchant, frequently the operator of a small general store. These merchants mediated between often very poor coffee smallholders and the great domestic and foreign coffee exporters. They thus acted, in Ortiz's words, "like a curtain of smoke that blurred the alchemy of accumulation."

Class-based politics were thus unlikely to appear in the Quindío. What was likely to appear in the region, given the context of Colombia's partisan political system, is what the author calls the "business of the Violence." He argues that after 1950, as partisan violence spread in the region, the intermediaries took advantage of the terror, even promoted it, in order to

*This chapter originally was published in Gonzalo Sánchez and Ricardo Peñaranda, eds., *Pasado y presente de la Violencia en Colombia* (Bogotá, 1986). Reprinted by permission of the Centro de Estudios de la Realidad Colombiana.

accumulate land and capital at the expense of both the smallholders and the large landowners. The upward mobility of such intermediaries—in the context of an overall distribution of land that seems to have changed little—is the primary finding of Ortiz's research. He thus challenges much leftist scholarship that sees in the Violence some kind of conspiracy by the landholding elite or by a nascent bourgeoisie in the manufacturing industry to dispossess smallholders of their land and create a labor reserve army for agriculture and industry.

Although the author's interpretation is based on his research in the Quindío (research, it is important to note, that is sensitive, therefore his need to maintain the anonymity of his subjects and to leave his documentation unspecific), it is not unlikely that the process he analyzes also operated in other regions of the coffee zone where smallholdings were numerous. His emphasis on the conservative, individualistic ideological and political dimensions of the struggle for land thus complements and extends the argument advanced in Chapter 4 on the connections between smallholder production and the origins of the Violence. Together these two chapters help to answer the question, posed throughout this volume, of why the ongoing appeal of the two traditional parties to the majority of Colombians, as well as helping to answer its corollary, of why third, class-based parties of the left had only limited success.

Carlos Ortiz, a sociologist, is the author of *Estado y subversión en Colombia: La Violencia en el Quindío años 50* (Bogotá, 1985). He is currently a member of the Department of History at the National University in Bogotá.

The regional history that had unfolded since the colonial era laid the foundation for the specific connections that arose between the Violence and economic activity in the Quindío.[1] In other regions of Colombia historical antecedents made it feasible for more or less class-based confrontations to be expressed through the Violence under party slogans: the eviction of squatters or tenants by large landowners, the recovery of land by tenant farmers expelled in the 1920s, or the recuperation of indigenous homelands, for example.

One must remember that in the Quindío, by contrast, society had not tended to structure itself in a predominantly class-based fashion, except in certain limited and well-defined zones and time periods. Several factors contributed to this outcome: the proliferation of medium and small landholdings in coffee cultivation; the large percentage of regional coffee production accounted for by such units; the fact that large-scale capital accumulation occurred primarily in the commercialization of coffee, rather than in its production; and that, simultaneously, trade offered numerous "opportunities" for the lower classes through enterprises like muleteering.

Two features above all account for the lack of class-based politics in the Quindío coffee zone. First, there is the importance of the intermediary, who in commerce was the small general store owner, and in production was the *agregado*, or farm foreman, whose duties included the hiring and firing of farm labor, and who usually received a portion of the harvest. The second factor is the social mobility generated by the colonization and expansion of the agricultural frontier. This process was still going on in the first half of this century, with coffee estates being established and public lands being adjudicated to private owners, especially on the high mountain slopes. The mediation of the store-keeper put a rural world of traditional smallholder coffee production in touch with the world market, ruled by the laws of capital, but at the same time it interposed itself between the poor cultivators and the great exporter like a curtain of smoke that blurred the alchemy of accumulation. The agricultural foreman, in turn, who was both an autonomous purchaser of the auxiliary labor force and a direct boss, cushioned the contact between day laborers and landowners, making confrontation between them nearly impossible.

In this type of society, where people were grouped in factions through the parties and the local political bosses, the new circum-stances created an outlet for peoples' needs, frustrations, and hopes through the use or support of armed partisan attacks. On the other hand, these new organizational forms, once created, made their imprint on certain already existing patterns of economic behavior but without modifying them substantially. This was true of the forced sale of land, the enrichment of storekeepers through the purchase of cheap coffee, the already mentioned social mobility, and the intangible and disinter-ested nature of the economically powerful sectors, who were able to maintain their position, generally unaffected by the violence around them.

Various types of businesses tried their luck successively in the Quindío; their emergence and degree of success depended largely on what stage the partisan conflict was passing through. In a first stage, before the gangs were consolidated and firmly rooted in the population, the business of buying stolen coffee or coffee collected on the numer-ous abandoned estates and parcels began to be profitable; likewise, the job of independent foreman on the properties of fugitive landlords became more profitable.

The most notable fact of these early years was, then, the promotion of buyers/storekeepers and of independent foremen. Since at first those expelled from the land were Liberals, it is obvious that the beneficiaries would be Conservatives, and the most rewarding zones would be the *municipios* made Conservative by force.

During this first stage the coffee-buying small general store, which, along with muleteering, had been so important as an avenue of upward mobility for poor migrants during the 1920s and 1930s, continued to be profitable; it would reach its last peak before being replaced by more centralized forms of commercialization following the Violence. And, although the circumstances were new, the secret of wealth was the same as always: to buy coffee at lower-than-average prices, taking advantage of the fact that it was incompletely dried, that credit had been extended in advance of purchases, or—as in the present case—that the coffee in question had been stolen.

A second stage began with the consolidation of the gangs from both sides and the consequent partisan homogenization of the rural neighborhoods. Those owners who had temporarily abandoned their lands were increasingly led to sell them at whatever price they could get, thus opening up another path to economic advancement that was already well known in the Quindío from earlier times: "deals," or bargains gotten from sellers in distress. Pressure on sellers was often increased by means of a kind of extortion known as the *boleteo*, or by insinuating to the gangs that they target certain victims who owned desirable properties. Such opportunities were open to Conservatives as well as Liberals, since the processes of homogenization operated on both sides, depending on the neighborhood. On the large farms and estates, the homogenization of the rural neighborhoods opened up new opportunities for foremen who were connected with the gangs (or who at least belonged to the same party the gangs represented). They either did not turn over or began to falsify their employers' accounts.

In rural commerce, the stealing of livestock was widespread, becoming the most distinctive activity of the Liberal gangs and their henchmen, just as stealing coffee had especially characterized the Conservatives. The reason is that the zones occupied by the Liberal guerrillas often were located either at the edge of the coffee-growing district or in the area devoted exclusively to livestock.[2] On the other hand, the Liberal gangs from the coffee-growing districts of the La Vieja River valley were also, like the Conservatives, first and foremost dealers in plundered coffee.[3]

Finally, as control of the rural neighborhoods was divided among gangs of either Liberal or Conservative persuasion, seizures by Conservative authorities and their private enforcers or thugs in the urban centers favored another kind of business operation there. This was the transfer of stores or of coffee-buying establishments to Conservatives, either through outright sale or through means of an administrator who would later accede to ownership. In some cases, Conservatives went as far as the physical elimination of a Liberal competitor to assure their little local monopoly on meat, phonograph records, movies, or whatever.[4] In those settlements where, in spite of sectarian Conservative government control, a process of "reliberalization" took place with the aid of Liberal urban thugs and the two forces became equally fearsome, two commercial streets for the opposing parties appeared in the center of town. There were stores for Conservatives and stores for Liberals and to cross the threshold of the wrong one meant risking one's life.

The order in which these themes will be presented is not strictly chronological. I prefer to study each of the major sets of economic activities in relation to the Violence so as to be able to retain, within each set, certain milestones in its evolution. Thus, everything relating to commerce, both rural and urban, will be dealt with first, followed by topics concerning the labor force and the appropriation of the products of labor—that is, the relations between owners, foremen, and workers. Finally, the question of changes in the ownership of land, whose effects are a little more comprehensible than the other phenomena and, further-more, have a bearing on the present state of affairs in the principal coffee-growing department in the country, will be analyzed.

Business and the Violence

The Coffee Business

The first conclusion to be drawn from an examination of coffee statistics during the Violence is that from 1950 to 1964 the national export volumes basically remained constant, with ups and downs but without any perceptible overall tendency toward a decrease (see Table 1). The years of the Liberal diaspora in the country—1951, 1952, and 1953—show increases in the number of sacks of coffee exported. The year 1954, which, at least during its first half, saw less armed partisan activity, shows the beginning of a decline in exports. After some oscillations, exports recovered their previous level in 1958. Another notable decline occurred in 1965, when the official task of exterminating the gangs was completed. Subsequent years did not see increased exports, as might have been expected by anyone believing that the gangs had been an obstacle to the coffee trade.

Although I did not have direct access to the statistics from the export houses of the towns of Armenia and Sevilla (the two regional centers of the Quindío),[5] I did obtain figures for the two coffee brands marketed as "Armenia" and "Sevilla" (see Table 2). Exports of Arme-nia coffee show a more positive picture than the nation as a whole during these fourteen years. The percent annual growth figures in 1951, 1952 and 1953 were higher than those for the country as a whole, and except for a decline in 1954, in the other years the quantities exported

Table 1. Colombian Coffee Exports, 1950 to 1965 (in 60-Kilogram Sacks)

1950	*1951*	*1952*	*1953*
4,472,357	4,793,983	5,032,058	6,632,336
1954	*1955*	*1956*	*1957*
5,733,320	5,866,891	5,069,777	4,823,733
1958	*1959*	*1960*	*1961*
5,440,625	6,418,379	5,937,741	5,650,972
1962	*1963*	*1964*	*1965*
6,561,432	6,133,673	6,412,257	5,651,544

Source: Federación Nacional de Cafeteros, *Boletín de Estadística* 34 (July 1956): Table 13, p. 21; 40 (July 1966): 40.

Table 2. Exports of Armenia Coffee, 1950 to 1965 (in 60-Kilogram Sacks), and Annual Percentage Change, Armenia versus All Coffee Exports

Year	Exports, Armenia Coffee	Annual Percentage Change, Armenia Coffee	Annual Percentage Change, All Coffee Exports
1950	975,453	—	—
1951	1,129,008	+15.7	+ 7.2
1952	1,236,687	+ 9.5	+ 5.0
1953	1,687,410	+36.4	+31.8
1954	1,633,386	- 3.2	+13.6
1955	1,679,037	+ 2.8	+ 2.3
1956	1,683,218	+ 0.2	-13.6
1957	1,719,335	+ 2.1	- 4.8
1958	1,875,902	+ 9.1	+12.8
1959	2,487,032	+32.6	+17.9
1960	2,404,148	- 3.3	- 7.4
1961	2,513,490	+ 4.5	- 4.8
1962	3,068,808	+22.1	+16.1
1963	3,152,667	+ 2.7	- 6.5
1964	3,243,225	+ 2.9	+ 4.5
1965	2,841,645	-12.4	-11.9

Source: Same as Table 1.

show a more definite upward trend than the national totals. By 1958, the fourth year of the activity of the bandit Chispas in the mountains, the number of sacks exported was already double that of 1950, and by 1962 the figure had tripled. After 1965, on the other hand, just as the Violence came to an end, the volume of trade began to decrease.

It is worth noting, furthermore, that during the time span under consideration, Armenia coffee, along with Manizales, figures at the top of the national list (in volume of exports), never leaving first place after 1953 (see Table 3). Medellín coffee, which encompasses the total production of the major coffee-producing department of Antioquia, only occupies third place. The same pattern, however, does not occur with Sevilla coffee. Having performed very well until 1954 (during the years of the violent Conservative takeover of the two main *municipios* that supply this coffee), it suffered a progressive and uninterrupted decline. In 1964 it exported only one twentieth of the amount it exported in 1954. In the intervening years the Conservative persecution had been answered by a Liberal counterattack of equal, or greater, intensity of violence.[6]

Table 3. Exports of Manizales, Medellín, and Sevilla Coffee, 1950 to 1965 (in 60-Kilogram Sacks)

Year	Manizales Coffee	Medellín Coffee	Sevilla Coffee
1950	1,144,236	876,069	295,993
1951	1,135,878	963,608	329,171
1952	1,248,808	1,164,843	309,487
1953	1,386,178	1,391,149	380,824
1954	1,308,523	1,142,962	354,978
1955	1,363,691	1,385,512	294,192
1956	1,115,367	1,224,874	236,472
1957	1,227,225	1,011,573	174,118
1958	1,214,971	1,183,337	158,107
1959	1,474,564	1,168,573	108,492
1960	1,142,797	1,285,774	82,207
1961	950,056	1,164,674	56,133
1962	1,055,507	1,545,975	44,042
1963	729,923	1,494,701	52,429
1964	910,581	1,686,422	18,958
1965	439,921	1,683,724	—

Source: Same as Tables 1 and 2.

How did it happen that coffee everywhere continued to reach the exporters during the years in which Liberal owners were abandoning their estates? And how did it happen that, in the area covered by Armenia, growth soared until 1964, in a parallel line with the expulsions and forced sales by Liberals and Conservatives and in the absence of nearly all the wealthy estate owners? These facts can be explained largely by the chain of intermediaries that had always characterized the circulation of coffee between the direct producer and the exporters.[7]

In point of fact, the exporters, whether they were natives of the Quindío, other Colombians, or foreigners, neither profited nor lost from the Violence, nor were they interested in knowing the moral circumstances surrounding the origin of the coffee beans they bought. For the exporters, as for the banks, it had been true always that the product of the social labor they appropriated depended very little on local vicissitudes. Even in this convulsed period, they did not need to become involved in regional political squabbles. They seemed to float safely above the storm, but nevertheless they walked off with a large portion, if not the largest portion, of the capital produced in the region.

Rural Storekeepers Enriched by the Violence

At the other end of the chain, very close to the direct producer, one finds undoubtedly the most decisive link, the storekeeper/coffee buyer of the rural neighborhood. His new role of facilitating the "laundering" of stolen coffee was simply an aspect of his essential function, which was to bring together the two different worlds of rural production and world commerce. In his hands the loot from rural neighborhoods could be converted into an exportable commodity. He charged a high price for his alchemy: my interviews confirm that generally the stolen coffee was bought for less than half the regular price. Since the gang members, or the merely casual looters (the most numerous group), had not had to work the long hours or meet the same demands as a regular worker under normal conditions, and since in addition they considered it a favor to be able to "legalize" their operation and buy other merchandise, they never argued about the price.

It should come as no surprise, then, as many court records reveal, that the storekeepers encouraged the gangs' activities and sometimes provided them with arms. Even in cases in which they did not influence the persecution of any specific proprietor, they nevertheless had an interest in the maintenance of the system as a whole. Another person interviewed, who had been an independent muleteer during this period, unexpectedly summed up the traffic in one intensely violent rural neighborhood. "Several other muleteers and I could not even handle the job of bringing all the coffee the storekeeper [who was his friend] brought every day to the village." This testimony implies that a great number of coffee estates had been abandoned in that region.

The coffee brought to the stores had been collected in various ways. Sometimes it was the quota demanded by the gangs from the person immediately in charge of the estates (small owners or foremen). In some parts of the *municipios* of Caicedonia and Génova, for example, there were even fixed locations where a sack of coffee for the gangs had to be left periodically. Sometimes it was sacks of dry coffee from the storeroom, at other times undried coffee piled up in the processing area that was taken by force. In the mountains, gangs of men with sacks carried out repeated nocturnal raids. The better organized groups used mules or, in the vicinity of Armenia, Montenegro, and Quimbaya, ghostly camouflaged jeeps. Sometimes the coffee for sale had been picked directly from the tree. This was especially the case on lands abandoned in urgent circumstances. Gleaners, frequently the neighbors themselves, would enter the coffee fields at night. A common practice during the first years in zones where the Liberals were being perse- cuted, in later years it was still going on in other neighborhoods where it was especially the Conservatives who had to pay the piper. One of the beneficiaries told me that the Liberal gangs would pass the word: go pick the coffee on such and such an abandoned estate. Of every ten twenty-five-pound sacks, three or four would go to the gang. The remaining six or seven belonged to the pickers. Both groups would sell it at half price to the storekeeper.

One thing is absolutely clear according to the most diverse interviewees. The coffee was never lost; it all reached the market. At least in the first years of the trouble coffee was abundant because the fields yielded their crops without needing any maintenance. This factor is peculiar to coffee, and would not have been possible in wheat or sugarcane growing areas. As time passed, those coffee plantings that remained abandoned wasted away. They became overgrown with weeds, and the coffee trees became diseased or died. But in general the fields did not remain abandoned this long, provided that they were not in certain zones of the *municipios* of the south (Sevilla, Caicedonia, and Génova).[8] Some estates reverted to their owners when they returned under the gangs' protection, while others acquired new masters (new owners or stewards).

The rural store was not the only place to convert stolen goods into merchandise, but it was the easiest. Urban buyers also received stolen coffee, also at low prices. However, in dealing with these buyers, the seller had to hurdle certain official controls, such as the obligation to keep a written record that was subject to eventual inspection by the

National Office of the Treasury. This meant that the buyers were more careful in order to avoid being fined, for in principle the names and quantities recorded in this record book had to match the declarations of the sellers. The roadblocks located along the roads in urban centers as well as the safe-conduct "passes" required for coffee sellers were additional annoyances for anyone carrying contraband to town. However, records and roadblocks could be overcome. Doing so depended on a good match between party affinity and bribes offered, a combination that was not regularly accessible to Liberals nor within reach of all Conservatives.

It is obvious that the stability of the storekeeper who collected the fruits of the plundering depended on the same system of kickbacks. Some storekeepers had begun as estate stewards who had the stolen coffee registered in the name of their employer when they sold it to the village purchaser. Those among them who had done well (the interviewees were unanimous on this point) had excellent relations with the local bosses and Conservative politicians in the *municipio*, as well as contacts with political leaders in the departmental capitals. This is why the majority of storekeepers who became rich were Conservatives. Nevertheless, the storekeepers themselves were usually not part of the political scene (I found isolated cases of new storekeepers who became politicians in mountain *municipios*). Of course, they did stand out in the rural neighborhoods as "good citizens" before their fellow partisans, and in the eyes of the opposition some more than others gained a reputation for being sectarian. On the whole they had migrated to the coffee zone in the decades before the Violence and became property owners only after it began.

The Urban Buyers

The urban buyers who came from the lower social strata and became wealthy during the period were also Conservatives. The reason is, a fortiori, the same one that applies to the rural storekeepers. In the five *municipios* in which the Violence hit hard, all of the coffee-buying establishments ended up in Conservative hands. (Today the picture has changed somewhat, although Conservative predominance is still appreciable.) It is surprising that even in the *municipio* that suffered violent "reliberalization," coffee purchasing remained in the hands of Conservatives. This situation held even though Liberals returned to take control of their farms and installed managers from their own party and even though other kinds of stores were divided up violently between the two sides. One explanation is that, in addition to the backing of the official authorities and the dose of bipartisanship that these businessmen could count on, the buyers found ways to transcend their initial sectarianism. Some took advantage of societies of brothers in which at least one passed for a Liberal. Others counted on marriage alliances with prestigious Liberal families or on friendships with Liberal leaders, even persecuted ones. After 1957 the general affection on the part of all of the coffee buyers for the conciliating spirit of the National Front helped them maintain their position.

Among the Conservatives who took over the urban coffee trade in the *municipios* studied, the means of access were diverse. Some were already established buyers, while others were simple wage earners who initially assumed the administration of the business affairs of their absentee Liberal bosses. Some did not have direct links with the gangs or with thugs, while others were known to have financed bullying and taken care of the subsistence and safe-conduct of certain thugs. Whatever their route to success, all today enjoy not only land and wealth but also recognition of their social standing.

The Business of Selling

The story of the proprietors of the three or four large businesses in each small town is similar to that of the coffee buyers, although the Conservative concentration in this sector is less marked. It is important to emphasize that when it comes to businessmen, Liberal or Conservative, the Violence did them no harm. On the contrary, the interviewees all agreed that during that period business was good in their *municipios*. They dealt in groceries, clothes and housewares, medicines, radios and records, pawned used goods, and, not least, liquor and amusements. In the liquor business departmental governments handled production while merchants handled distribution. A businessman from one of the *municipios* most heavily disturbed by the Violence told me: "All that money [referring to proceeds from extortion and the stealing of coffee and livestock] stayed and was spent in the *municipio*; today, on the other hand, it is very difficult for that amount of money to circulate in the area, because the landowners don't live here, but in Armenia, Pereira, Bogotá, Cali, Medellín." He was right. During the Violence the rich owners did not live in such *municipios*, but their share of the farm earnings was reduced, if not liquidated, through the mechanisms of the Violence. A much larger portion, therefore, remained at the disposal of those who lived in the *municipio* and who, furthermore, were inclined to "blow their money," to put it bluntly, rather than to save it. This was true of gang members, robbers, laborers, and a good proportion of the estate managers themselves. The gang members preferred to pay for their purchases less out of discipline or tactics than for the pleasure that they got from being "big spenders."

Thus the Violence brought economic benefits of the kind attributed to "democratic" systems and at higher levels than in normal periods. It worked to sustain the market (and commercial profits) through maintenance of or growth in the buying power of the majority of people.[9] Only the market for exclusive articles for the upper echelons suffered a decline, which was logically due to the exodus of well-to-do families or the occupation of their property by families of more modest tastes. In Sevilla, for example, the automobile dealers and some of the appliance stores closed, which produced the sensation of recession. By way of compensation, these sectors of the market were absorbed by the larger urban centers of the coffee zone, the cities of Cali, Armenia, and Pereira, which profited from the shift.

To the positive picture that the Violence offered to businessmen in general—whether they themselves were peaceful or violent—one must add other circumstances related strictly to party politics, which could raise profits even more. Whether some people intentionally provoked the execution or expulsion of others, or whether they simply took advantage of opportunities created by the violence of the partisan struggle, the fact is that the expulsion of some long-established wealthy businessmen opened the way for others to rise from the lower classes. In one of the *municipios* studied, newly emerging Conservatives little by little appropriated the wholesale business. Meanwhile, some of the former owners took refuge in neighboring towns, and others invested in land and moved to the country, into neighborhoods well protected by the Liberal gangs. As one can see, the migratory movements occasioned by the Violence and the transfers of capital that accompanied them spread out in all directions. Some of those who had known only rural business sold part of their rural property in order to try their luck in the cities. Since, as we have seen, business was not going badly, the move for them was the occasion for a new era of prosperity.

Among the Conservatives who did well in the anonymous *municipio* whose story is reported here, there was an exemplary case of social mobility. It concerns a migrant who arrived in town in poverty at the end of the thirties. He began as a shopkeeper, setting up a modest grain store in the village marketplace. In the fifties he began to deal, small scale, in the buying of coffee, and when the Liberal owners of the main retail store in town had to flee, he took over the management of the business for them. There are rumors that he did not keep accounts in the stipulated manner. I can offer no opinion on these remarks, but the custom was common during that period. After a while, he became the owner of the business, and later he invested in land. Although the store is now gone, he is known today as a rich local landowner.

Most of the Conservative or Liberal businessmen who advanced in this way in the shadow of sectarian party politics were not directly involved in politics. Only in the mountain *municipios* does one encounter cases of emerging businessmen who were also local political strongmen. Usually, one can see the signs of bipartisanship that I have pointed out in the buyers. Even in a *municipio* indisputably controlled by Liberal guerrillas, I discovered a prosperous Conservative businessman who was able to accommodate himself to the situation and is still patronized by his old clientele from both parties. He benefited from the existence of Liberal brothers in the family, and it was not unusual for him to do business with the gangs of the opposing party.

The Violence and the Social Division of Labor in the Countryside

As previously mentioned, during the Violence the proportion of wealth accruing to large proprietors in the agricultural sector was reduced by a degree never experienced either before or after the period. Here a few observations are necessary on the way in which different sectors of rural workers—distinct from the armed groups—participated in the new distribution of wealth.

The Independent Foremen or Estate Managers

As in the case of the commercialization of coffee, so also with that of its production: the central figure, the estate foreman, is a mediating agent. This person, who traditionally functioned as an "insulating link" and a catalyst between other workers and the rentiers or landlords, now saw the frontiers of his own domain expand. This second "boss" (as his workers called him), in exchange for being dependent on the gangs and paying tribute to them, was freed from the control of his own boss. His natural role as an intermediary meant that the benefits of the Violence touched him in two areas. He could make good use of the pressures or simply of the atmosphere of insecurity in dealing with his employer, and he could take advantage of the same factors with regard to his employees, the laborers. The first case is illustrated abundantly in stories of foremen who not only did not render accounts to but also extorted money from the owners they worked for, made up tales of being held up on the road to cover up their swindles, or spread false rumors so as to blackmail their bosses.

The nature of the foreman's role vis-à-vis the workers and the owner during these years was undoubtedly particularly advantageous to the foreman. In fact, due to the circumstances of the Violence, it had become common to entrust the entire estate to a single foreman, thus diminishing not only the labor unrest caused by the labor legislation of 1936 but also the risks of partisan banditry. This single foreman was called the "straw boss" on coffee-growing farms and the "contractor" on cattle ranches.

The Violence was a most profitable period for foremen and, furthermore, strengthened their function. Paradoxically, the institution was at the same time in decline since, in the view of the owners, foremen encouraged the Violence and under its influence became much more problematic and uncontrollable. They were kept on only because under the circumstances the proprietors could not see any other means of holding onto their properties. After the Violence, statistics show that foremen rapidly were replaced by salaried managers on the large farms and estates. They only survived in substantial proportions on small- and medium-size properties belonging to urban owners, since, as one of the interviewees said, "The foreman is the method when you don't have any capital."

Where the relations among owner, foreman, and gangs were most convergent, that is, where all belonged to the same political party, it appears that the institution of the foreman lasted for a longer period after the Violence.[10] Even in such cases, however, the profitability of the new type of manager soon wiped out the vestiges of the independent foreman. In one of the rural neighborhoods controlled by "Chispas," a wealthy Liberal rancher still had independent foremen in 1977; nevertheless, he decided to replace them with salaried managers "because," he said, "then the political problem no longer exists."

The foremen also had the option of taking advantage of the Violence when it came to their workers, just as the small and medium owners who worked on and managed their own farms did. I learned of several extreme cases where pickers were murdered by foremen or owners, sometimes using a highly trusted fellow worker to do the deed, in order to appropriate the wages that the pickers had accumulated over two weeks or a month. Pickers' wages were paid according to the piecework system, that is, by the "can" of coffee beans picked, and, according to estate records, they usually were paid once or twice a month. One of the people interviewed participated directly, a few years ago, in the exhumation of the bodies of missing persons on a farm where years before there had been cases of "disappeared" workers. The owner of the middle-size farm, who is no longer the proprietor of this "cemetery," is today an affluent planter and continues to live in the same *municipio* (it is said that he got rich primarily from selling stolen livestock). In other locations, people talk (one cannot say on what basis) of two foremen who did the same thing.

Other kinds of behaviors reveal the tension between foremen and workers and provide material for acts of revenge either during the Violence or later. Only a few years ago, in one of the *municipios* where I was conducting interviews, an owner from a certain large city was killed while making an inspection of his property. Three different versions of the motivation behind the crime were advanced. The version having nothing to do with the Violence attributed the crime to the revenge of a worker who recently had felt himself unjustly treated by the way in which the owner had settled his accounts. The second version dealt with family revenge by the relatives of people forced off the land by thugs that the deceased had employed in previous years. The third version, finally, also invoked latent revenge but involving labor practices. Twenty-five years earlier, the deceased had worked as a foreman for various large estates (at the same time he was a small owner); he had a reputation for excessive despotism with the workers, and since that time his grave had been dug.

It should be said that the extreme methods resorted to by the foremen, including murder, also could be applied against them under certain circumstances. I have in mind the type of tenant farmer/foreman with whom the owner had contracted to plant seedlings in the areas most recently opened to coffee cultivation. There were cases of homicides performed in order to avoid paying debts pending for the expansion.

Pressure by the foreman on the owner, on the other hand, could lead the latter to sell his title, although this was not the trend among large landholdings, as we shall see in the next section. In fact, examples are rare of foremen who became legal proprietors of estates where, because of the Violence, they had freely enjoyed the profits of production. I learned of only one estate in this category in the mountain region. It is still in litigation today, and the occupant claims, against the heirs of his former employer, the rights of "effective occupation" recognized by the law.

The foremen who are today millionaire planters do not seem to have become rich exclusively through their earlier occupation. They are, on the contrary, the few who instead of "blowing their money" (an expression used by the interviewees) invested it in a variety of business ventures. That is, they joined the world of trade as buyers/storekeepers, butchers (some of whom trafficked in stolen livestock), moneylenders, or buyers of, initially, small farms at low prices.[11] The average acquisition was only one or two medium-size farms or one or two houses in town, property that many of them still have. As to the question of their social background, they were migrants into the coffee zone during the 1930s and 1940s.

The Workers

Day laborers and migrant pickers, the principal source of recruits for the gangs, were without doubt the most frequent victims of the Violence. They were vulnerable not only because their tendency to disappear into the woods made the army suspicious of them at all times, but also because they and the foremen were the cannon fodder in the intimidation of owners. In fact, the first step in threatening a farmer or a planter consisted of "killing" one or several of his laborers; immediately, the ominous *boleta* (extortion note) was delivered. If the owner did not give in, the gangs tried to kill the foreman and his family and sometimes set fire to the estate house. Finally, they set their sights on the person of the owner himself who, being absent from the land and having protection, was the hardest target to hit.[12] Nevertheless, the very atmosphere of extreme insecurity that worried rural wage earners had a positive overall effect on the price of the daily wage or of the "can" of coffee picked. All of the owners and stewards interviewed recall that the cost of labor was high, at least higher than it is now.[13]

Whereas the itinerant condition of the pickers and the nature of labor relations in coffee production contributed to the nonexistence or weakness of union organizations, it did operate in favor of the law of supply and demand. The scarcity (real or apparent) of pickers at harvesttime due to unsafe conditions was heightened by the more attractive and (one hardly need mention) safer opportunities for employment offered by the gangs or the crews of thugs. On the other hand, the demand for help remained high if one takes into account the volume of coffee exported during these years (not all of which, of course, was harvested by paid laborers). The official figures for "agricultural day-labor" for 1949 to 1953 confirm this, at least insofar as the global data of the department of Caldas apply to the twelve *municipios* of the Quindío of Caldas that are the focus of this study.[14] In fact, according to these statistics, from 1950 on, Caldas occupied first place in the average price of labor, a position it regularly had enjoyed for many years (although it dropped comparatively in 1948 and 1949). Another violent department, Tolima, also found itself near the top of the list, having been in earlier years a zone of rather low wages. The departments along the Atlantic Coast, however, which were in a good position in this regard until 1946–47, fell progressively behind after 1950 in rural wage levels; as we know, this area was not affected by the Violence after 1948 and is not coffee country. Finally, the department of Nariño, which was not hit by the Violence of the 1950s, remained in last place in the country in agricultural wage levels for the whole period in question.

It remains to be seen whether the Violence determined the prolongation in the Quindío of economic conditions favorable to the continuation of the migratory cycle when circumstances in the 1940s signaled a change of direction. The slowdown that rural wages had begun to show in the mid-1940s went hand in hand with a reduction in opportunities for migrants to accumulate capital or acquire property. Might the Violence have opened, in fact, an aperture in this impasse?

The Violence, however, also could be used as an extreme recourse by owners to contain the pressures that laborers were able to exert through union organizations in the last years when and in the few places where such expressions occurred. At least that is the impression one gets from scrutiny of a court proceeding relating to the murder of four workers from one estate. It was the year 1963. Labor unions were being created on certain estates where modern methods of operation based on salaried labor created more favorable conditions for unionization. On the estate where the massacre took place, a second union, independent of the owners' control, was being formed. On the neighboring estates the owners, skilled politicians in every sense of the word, had managed to win over the union leaders. They offered union officials modest opportunities in the political world, products of the leverage that they had as members of congress. It was rumored that they also offered them sums of money.[15] On the estate in question, however, the situation seemed less manageable, perhaps partly because of the influence of political groups (among them the Communist party) outside the party machine of the local bosses. One fine day a Liberal gang made a raid. Three of the murdered laborers were Conservatives, which supports the partisan version. But the fourth, a Liberal, was none other than the principal organizer of the disobedient union, which, at the time, was drawing up a list of demands. After my colleagues and I had studied the various declarations made in the proceedings, listened to several witnesses who had testified in court, and discussing this material, the unanimous conclusion was that it was very likely that the administrator of the estate, a member of the owner's family, had been involved in the affair.[16]

The Violence and Land Transactions

The exchange of rural property during the Violence actually continued in the direction that had given its particular stamp to the pattern of land tenure in the Quindío. Three trends, already established in the region, synthesize this history of transactions under the new circumstances of the Violence: first, investment in land by people who had become wealthy through trade (from the business of the Violence, in this case); second, the purchase of land at below-average prices from distressed sellers; and third, the dispossession of smallholders and their possible transition to another social group. (This smallholder exodus did not substantially modify the pattern of land distribution due to the permanent replacement of these smallholders by others or by workers who previously had no property.) This changing of the guard now carried a political stamp—Liberals for Conservatives and vice versa. It was obviously more accelerated than in other times of rapid change, such as those caused by inflation or by falling coffee prices. And, furthermore, it affected people all at once; it was not a gradual process.

Forced Sales at Low Prices

In the face of the pressure mechanisms described for the abandonment of land, the response was not usually immediate sale nor was it the same response for different sized properties. The land registry reveals the following statistics for two *municipios*, Salento and Circasia. The frequency of transactions fell substantially from 1949 to 1953, accentuating a decline already apparent since 1945. From March 1953 until the end of the year transfers increased in both *municipios* (this coincided with the period of preparation for and transition to the military government of Gustavo Rojas Pinilla, with which a return to normalcy was expected). From 1954 to 1960 (the last year that my study covered) there was practically no exchange of large properties. Instead, during this period, the frequency of transactions involving small parcels was rather high, especially between 1954 and 1957. Prices (at least those registered, which were not necessarily the actual prices) were ostensibly low, considering the value of acreage in the neighborhood both before and after the period.[17]

Given the magnitude of the task, research in the land registry books was limited to these two *municipios*. Circumstances, in fact, differed in the heart of the same region. Some municipalities experienced official attacks either to a lesser degree than others or to such a high degree as to change their political alignment. In some municipalities the gangs were formed early on, in others later. In the *municipios* of Salento and Circasia, for example, it seems that because of their more benign social and partisan features there were many fewer forced sales.[18] This sample using two *municipios*, however, pointed to aspects of the problem that were clarified through interviews in the rest of the *municipios*. The focus was on the steps that led to the sales and the differences in ability to resist selling.

Among the several ways in which proprietors reacted to threats was a more or less generalized trend. There existed from the start a tendency to resist, to refuse to sell, which was as effective as the sellers' capacity to hold out. The unwillingness to sell, of course, can be explained in part because the drop in prices due to the unsafe conditions made selling unattractive. Therefore, the owner's first step was usually to abandon the property and take refuge in the small "urban" nucleus where friends and relatives lived, usually in the town where the family in question shopped and sold its coffee. This move was intended to be only temporary. But since the situation usually prolonged itself, poor refugees tried to find other ways to earn a living, yet always hoping to return someday to their property. Some worked as laborers in less hostile areas while others found themselves temporarily in the ranks of the underemployed (frequently after moving to a medium-size city). They made their decisions in the midst of uncertainty and fear. During this period of resistance, the coffee buyers, and moneylenders in general, played a very important role. Some peasants, because of the lack of security, deposited their savings with them, and they in turn loaned money to refugees and wrote mortgages.[19]

When at last the situation became economically unfeasible, the refugee would sell his land. Or he could decide to sell it when he found another parcel of land, also at a low price, in a zone taken over by his own party. Those individuals who showed greater resistance to selling were evidently the large landowners, and thus transactions for their properties were delayed except when, as with the smaller landowners, they found good buys for land in zones covered by gangs of their own party affinity. The ability of large landowners to resist selling was based not so much on the size of their holdings as on the availability of additional capital, which was common among agricultural proprietors of the Quindío. When they themselves had little capital, it was often supplied by banking contacts.

Those persons least able to resist selling were the widows of large landowners. They were the easiest prey for the real estate agents; they sold without delay. The women of the Quindío typically were excluded from productive activity other than domestic duties. The murder of her husband would take a woman unawares and leave her totally unable to manage the responsibilities of earning a living for the family. After a few days in the nearest hamlet, the widow would move with her children to a place, frequently a medium-size city, where she could hope to receive help, either because she had family there or because she could appeal to friends or business associates of her husband.

The Question of Terrateniente Violence

Nothing could be less applicable to the Quindío than that old legend according to which the Violence was a plan conceived by the *terratenientes*, the large landowners. First of all, it must be noted that, as the term classically has been understood, there were no *terratenientes* in the Quindío. But let us assume that the word simply designates an owner of a large coffee and/or livestock estate or of scattered farms that added up to an extensive holding. It is already known that most of these properties were in the mountains, where Liberals predominated. Although it is true that when and where the guerrillas took hold some of them acquired new and attractive acreage (a fact verified in the registry books), it is hardly credible that the supposed *terrateniente* plan to create an era of prosperity would have posited a first, painful stage during which they themselves became the victims of official and paraofficial attacks. Furthermore, both before and after the gangs, the profits yielded by the properties were for a long time at the mercy of the new networks of control in the rural neighborhoods.

As for the Conservative large estate owners, most of whom were in the west-central area of La Hoya, the registry books reveal certain names linked to the purchase of small- or medium-size properties.[20] Nevertheless, the interviews do not show a link to the Violence either through these few names or through the names of the most important Conservative landowning families of the period. They did not, then, make direct use of the gangs for the purpose of real estate transactions, unless it was done with extreme prudence or the adjudications were registered under fictitious names. The satisfactory rate of accumulation these landowners had achieved leads one to think that although many of them had become rich by taking advantage of special occasions to buy land and by exploiting homesteaders and tenants long before, they now had no need of resorting to these same strategies, especially if they involved irregular practices.

The legend attributing the Violence to a plan by the *terratenientes* arose from a misunderstanding. This misunderstanding was based, on the one hand, on the fact that the Liberal gangs had installed themselves in the rural neighborhoods due to the diligence of and financing by the great Liberal landowners of the mountain region. What people forget is that this was not the beginning of what is known as the Violence and that initially the function of the armed men was to protect property (a rather conservative function). The fact that the landowners, as did the rest of the populace, heeded the gangs seems normal under the circumstances. (When the state proved capable of handling the situation, the landowners deserted the gangs; many of them meanwhile had collaborated with the guerrillas and the army at one and the same time.) The fact that in soliciting the presence of the guerrillas the landowners spoke for all their copartisans in the area also seems normal. They were best able to finance the operation as well as the most suitable persons to organize it, some because they were in fact local bosses and others because they had good contacts with Liberal leaders. The second cause of the misunderstanding may have been the confusion between the nature of a big landowner and that of a businessman, distinct roles that at times might be played by the same person. The profits of rural business (from coffee, livestock, and land) certainly were linked closely to the Violence, although it is hard to prove that the businessmen who benefited from it were those who engineered it. The third source of the fallacy rests on the fact that those who became rich or richer under the aegis of the Violence invested in land, following the venerable custom of the Quindío. Today, therefore, they are large landowners, but many of them were not so before.[21]

The legend assigned a complementary responsible role to industrialists, as if they and the landlords had acted together in a magnificent synchronization of will of a kind difficult to find outside of imaginary schemes. The volume of poor peasants dislodged by the landlords, it was said, was just what the "industrial bourgeoisie" needed in order to secure an optimal cost of labor. But in the Quindío manufacturing had not created any such imaginary demand for a labor force. Manufacturing was stagnant for reasons other than the lack or shortage of a labor force. The increase in migration to urban centers in the region, particularly Armenia, had not waited for the Violence to manifest itself. It began years earlier and coincided for different reasons with the period of industrial stagnation. The urbanization of Armenia, as of the country in general, was not accompanied by industrialization, which meant that the peasants who migrated were not destined for industry or to become prisoners of this "bourgeoisie." When migration was accelerated even more by the Violence, manufacturing industry in Armenia showed no sign of improvement.

Quite another matter is the question of whether other urban activities might have been encouraged and stimulated by the low cost of unskilled labor, whose availability increased because of the migration to Armenia of peasants and people from neighboring towns. One such activity was construction.[22] The favorable cost of construction labor, which in its two lowest categories of workers was even lower than the official minimum subsistence wage, was accompanied by the other variable essential to the expansion of this industry, a growing demand for buildings of every kind. While commercial buildings were erected in the central zone of Armenia, farther out different types of neighborhoods grew up. Sometimes these neighborhoods were composed of shacks built by the migrants themselves along the railroad tracks, sometimes they were of modest houses, as in the southern end of town, and sometimes they were made up of homes for relatively rich refugee peasants, such as the ones that swelled the neighborhood of Granada. Once his farmland was lost, the first bit of security that the migrant sought was to buy a house that was within his reach so that he could at least put a roof over his family's head.

It is possible that much capital originating in the countryside was invested during this period in construction, just as capital had been diverted to urban commerce. In addition, construction became another means of making money for young, recently graduated architects, with no capital at all, who began prosperous careers as builders.

In one city a well-known founding family reverted in 1953 to an enterprise common at the beginning of the century, the subdivision of its land abutting the city so as to resell it (revalued at higher prices) as small building lots. The donation of a lot for a school in 1952 preceded this activity. The total acreage of the family's land was not diminished by these resales; in fact, the reverse was true because at the same time they annexed several abutting estates inside the city limits. One of these properties was originally public land whose title they acquired in 1960, seven years after they gained control of it.

Who Bought the "Lands of the Violence"?

A good businessman is one who knows when to buy and when to sell, taking advantage of propitious circumstances—and the Violence was one of those times. In the part of the *municipio* of Quimbaya convulsed by the Violence, coffee land planted in high-yielding coffee, whose value remained constant between 1950 and 1964, is now worth more than one hundred times what it was then.[23] Whether they admit it or not, virtually all merchants had something to do with land purchases during the Violence. Due to the time of resistance that intervened between the threat by the gangs or the thugs and the moment of sale, it was extremely difficult to prove whether a person obtained land by killing or threatening its owner. Between the buyer and the persecuted owner a series of intermediaries interposed themselves. "Agents," people who worked full time putting buyers and sellers in contact with each other for the purpose of making vehicle or real estate transactions, were one kind of intermediary. Interested parties also made use of friends or associates of the person in need; the fact that they might have used the gangs against the owner previously did not stand in the way of this contact.[24]

Nevertheless, the link between the gangs and purchases at reduced prices and, in general terms, the support of the gangs by the agents, was not always established by the interviewees, despite the signs that they trusted the interviewer and identified with the objectives of his research. In addition to the mediation of time and the interposed agents, other factors inhibit people today from making such connections. Thus, when a person in an influential position continues to maintain the political contacts that were connected with his bossism (part of which involves doing favors for family and community), he enjoys an immunity that does not fall equally upon those who concern themselves exclusively with their private business affairs, much less on those who abandoned the region after becoming rich. Forgiveness is greater when it comes to Liberal leaders, since all their transactions are covered under their initial condition as the persecuted and as patrons of local defense. It is also obvious that those persons most vulnerable to accusations are those who were transformed rapidly from dispossessed to millionaire landlords rather than those individuals with old money who benefited, in the course of events, by becoming richer.

Propertyless Conservatives who supported the first gangs and bought land from Liberals through what was called the "politics of shakedown" were more likely to have the finger pointed at them if they also left the *municipios* where they had lived. (Yet some had emigrated with the appearance of the first Liberal "guerrillas.") These Conservatives, however, were not the only individuals who participated in the politics of land shakedowns, although they are the most easily identified. Frequently, public opinion has blamed them additionally for the wealth acquired by others, in accordance with the common moral tendency to personify evil in an absolute manner.

Even after paying special attention to oral testimony and to the contradictions between such testimony and the deeds in the land registry books, the analysis I have presented is weakened to some extent by the limitations mentioned.[25] Nevertheless, certain additional conclusions emerge. First, the most numerous transactions of large farms and estates took place in zones of more recent coffee culture development to which migrants were attracted in the immediately preceding decades. One example is the mountain zone southwest of Calarcá, which includes several *municipios*. Another example is the border between Filandia and Quimbaya, a zone where small- and medium-size properties alternated—and still do—with large ones and where the richest men of that time had made their fortunes in the 1920s and 1930s. By way of contrast, in the realm of the great estates of the *municipios* of La Tebaida and Montenegro, dominion of the most famous potentates of the whole region, the few registered operations took place, as they had before, within families or within the same circle of friends and business associates. Second, in the zones where a lot of large properties changed hands, the Liberal families who at the moment of the persecution were the largest owners in their *municipios* continued in that position once the Violence was over.[26] One thus can formulate the trend in the following terms: People from the lower strata of former migrants joined the class of large landowners, but the recomposition did not bring about the ruin of those who previously belonged to that class.

Thus, in one of the *municipios* that underwent violent "Conservativization," the majority of large landowners continue to be Liberal, descendants of those persecuted during the Violence. (The Conservative large landowners in this *municipio* usually date from the Violence.) However, the majority of the population of this *municipio* is Conservative, and the largest number of parcels and medium-size farms is in the hands of Conservatives (they had belonged to Liberals before the Violence). Only two large landowners are mentioned who were impoverished by the Violence. One now works as an itinerant butter merchant in Armenia, and the other is a vendor of fried foods in a neighboring town in Tolima.

There is no doubt that the small farms were not the most desirable real estate to the buyers. Since they had the resources, they tended to look for cheap offerings of a certain size. Often the harassed peasant, unable to find a buyer from his own social class, considered it a favor if a rich merchant from town, or the buyer of his crops, consented to buy his land so that he could remain solvent. This situation tended to be taken advantage of by individuals who specialized in the accumulation of many small pieces of property either by conventional purchase or at low prices caused by mortgage foreclosures.

In general, those persons most likely to amass significant amounts of acreage by buying at low prices were those who combined the following characteristics: they had available, that is, liquid, capital; they managed their capital personally; and they kept in contact with potential sellers. This is a different problem from the argument about whether they intentionally used gangs or not to further their dealings. I have already mentioned the social groups who eminently combined the three traits listed—that is, lenders and urban and rural merchants, each in a different sphere.

While individually the people easiest to contact by those owners anxious to sell were their neighbors, friends, and relatives,[27] there was another especially important group because its members were known by everyone and people trusted them because of their services. I refer to the politicians and the professionals, already quite visible with respect to the mobility that the epoch lent them in party organizations and within state institutions. Whether they were politicians or nonpolitical professionals, the regular duties of their jobs put them in an advantageous position as "emergency" buyers. In one of the Conservative rural neighborhoods most afflicted by the gangs, a doctor collected several good farms during these years. The known supporters of the armed bands were, on the other hand, medium-size owners. When this professional, who came from another region, settled in the major town of the *municipio*, he had no resources except his university degree. Later, while the Violence was still going on, he moved to another city, returning to the rural neighborhood only for annual visits. Other doctors and several dentists are included on the lists I compiled.

Public Lands

The zones most recently opened to coffee farming that saw intense movement of property also had undeeded land when the Violence began.[28] Several of the large estates that Liberals were constrained to abandon in the 1950s and were later sold to Conservatives were classified as "improved public lands" that had no titles. The "good" contacts of the buyers, in circumstances in which partisanship had invaded government offices, made the negotiations easier. Large estates bought cheaply received adjudication of the title by the Ministry of Agriculture one or two years later. The ministers' resolutions, whose texts appear in the land registry books, recognized the rights of a new owner by virtue of his having lived on and improved the land for fifteen years, some say, or twenty, in other cases, thus satisfying the stipulation in the law. In fact, these were years in which the retreating Liberal seller actually had been improving the land, but, due to political favoritism, these years were credited to his Conservative successor.

Most of the adjudications of large parcels granted by the agriculture ministry in one of the *municipios* studied benefited two Conservatives (both formerly day laborers) and took place in 1953 and 1954. One received the title to six large parcels and the other to five. The Liberals, however, were not excluded from the feast; the manipulation of the law (and possibly also the use of leverage) reveals the same features here as elsewhere. The Liberal who registered the largest number of important land purchases from 1953 to 1957, according to the documents studied in two *municipios*, was one of those who had had to sell his estates in the Conservative zone. He acquired two large public tracts in 1953–54 and two more in 1957. Three of the four were located in areas with Liberal gangs.

A final example of the fate of public lands during the Violence is Romerales, a rural neighborhood located on the highest mesas of the

mountain range. This neighborhood was inhabited during the Violence
by tenant farmers who for twenty or thirty years had lived on pasture
and potato cultivation on their public land claims. Most of the allot-
ments averaged around forty hectares and in the absence of titles, sales
or successions of land were certified with simple receipts stamped by a
court. There had been months of a harvest so abundant that its like,
some said, had never been seen before, when the hurricane of the
Violence scattered the two thousand tenant farmers. One day the police
of the neighboring town committed an outrageous massacre, leaving a
total, it is said, of forty-two dead. During the years in which, as a
consequence of fear, the land remained uninhabited, a rich Conservative from Medellín took possession of thousands of hectares in this
region, claiming that they were part of an inheritance that his wife had
received. Neither he nor she, however, had ever been heard of in the
area before. The case was decided, after interminable proceedings, in
favor of the tenant farmers as a result of the intervention of a high-
ranking army officer and of legislators from Tolima who were national
Liberal figures. They brought letters on the matter at the request of the
only large landowners in the area, a Liberal family with good contacts
in both parties. The family also obtained the installation of an army post
in order to guarantee safety from the region's various armed bands (the
family had lost three children and their mother in the massacre). In the
process, the family had communicated with Conservative friends who
had connections with the Sixth Tolima Brigade and had ceded to them,
in exchange for their help, the forested zone of their estate.

Conclusion

Such are the sui generis paths followed by the Violence in the
redistribution of the social division of labor and in the restructuring of
property-owning social groups through persons emerging from the
lower classes. If the Violence had not occurred, the opportunities for
upward mobility that were known in the Quindío from earlier times
might have been extinguished sooner.

Since the Violence, the Quindío has not been the promised land for
the waves of poor migrants that it once was. Now those persons who go
there are just passing through as seasonal coffee harvesters. Of course,
the purchase of land "bargains" from people in dire circumstances
continues, but the deals are not as profitable as they once were. And
certain groups, especially agricultural laborers, are excluded more now
from buying land than before. As for the businessmen and professionals who became wealthy and became rural landowners, in this regard
the Violence perpetuated a trend that had been manifest since colonial

times. The absenteeism of large landowners, however, is a phenomenon more specific to the circumstances of the Violence and has proven
to be irreversible. The apogee of the storekeepers and foremen was akin
to the lucidity of a dying man.

This period of history gave rise to most of the individuals who at
the present time are the leaders of business and of the private and public
entities of the newly created department of Quindío. This is not to say
that their careers always are linked directly to the Violence but rather
that they proceeded from various situations related to it: for example,
the young Liberals who began their careers in the government of Rojas,
the merchants who profited from movements in local markets, or those
persons who benefited in the construction business because of the
demand for housing. As for property and capital, the families who were
well off before the Violence in general conserved their positions, with
some exceptions. But now they share their businesses, their clubs, and
their prestige with many nouveaux riches who sprang up during the
Violence.

Notes

1. The material in this essay is extracted from Carlos Miguel Ortiz
Sarmiento, *Estado y subversión en Colombia: La Violencia en el Quindío
años 50* (Bogotá, 1985).

2. For a discussion of the nature of these Liberal guerrillas, in contrast to
those of the eastern plains and elsewhere, see my unpublished paper, presented
at the Fourth National Colombian History Congress, Tunja, December 1983.

3. It should be understood that the focus here is on predominant features
since the armed groups from one party or the other took part in both forms of
pillage and in many other kinds of businesses. Among the activities not
discussed here for lack of data is commerce in contraband weapons. According
to oral sources, this business was lucrative and widespread and involved
gangs, politicians, and personnel from official ranks.

4. These three examples are cases that I was able to document in specific
municipios.

5. Figures for bags of coffee exported, published in the *Boletín* of the
Federation of Coffee Growers, only distinguish between the different regional
centers up to 1944.

6. It also is possible that transportation variables, rather than those of
production and collection, account for the enormous decline in the percentages.
For example, it might have been that many rural communities or general store
owners, formerly clients of Sevilla, now preferred, for reasons including lack
of safety and party politics, to bring their coffee to Armenia. If this was the
case then the interpretation of the percentages cited for Armenia would have
to be adjusted downward.

7. The other part of the explanation concerns the independent foreman, a subject that will be addressed. Some people took on both jobs at the same time, with obvious benefits. Estate managers whose employers had been chased away invested the "extras" that came with their jobs in the purchase of stolen coffee. These were the managers who succeeded.

8. The zones that remained abandoned in the *municipios* referred to are primarily devoted to livestock rather than coffee.

9. In asserting this I am provisionally ignoring national factors that had a negative influence on buying power, that is, factors that attenuated these favorable local conditions.

10. This is neither the only factor nor the most decisive one in the persistence of the independent foreman in the Quindío; it is merely the factor that has the most bearing here.

The sketch that I have drawn suggests factors that acted in the contrary direction. Determinants of more or less importance according to the zone might include the choice of whether or not to introduce cultivation of high-yield strains of coffee and the increase of investment in technology, such as chemical fertilizers, that this choice necessitates; the modes of communication and the cost of shipping; and the state of rural unionization in the sector.

11. This list itemizes only the precise cases uncovered in the research. These people then lived in three different *municipios*.

12. The method that developed in the 1960s, kidnapping, evolved when the planters did not have the scapegoats interposed; this accounts for their increased collaboration with the army during that period.

13. According to figures from the Bank of the Republic, in the first half of 1960, for example, the daily wage on the coffee farms in the Quindío fluctuated from 10 to 14 pesos during the harvest, plus food, and from 6.20 to 9 pesos in the off season. Meanwhile, a journeyman in construction drew between 6.50 and 10 pesos, and in the same industry, an unskilled worker earned a daily wage of only 5.50 to 7.50 pesos. Workers in the coffee-machine industry in Armenia received daily pay of 8.50 pesos, those in the chemical and soap industries from 6.50 to 12 pesos, and workers in public works, 7 pesos.

14. I could not find figures differentiated by *municipio* for the period before 1953, only global figures for Caldas. The trend observed until that year in Caldas can be verified for the whole Quindío region according to figures supplied by the Bank of the Republic (see note 13). I have analyzed these statistics over twenty-four six-month periods from 1954 to 1965. The comparison with the rhythms of some urban wages in Armenia during the same period helps to portray the level sustained by agricultural day labor.

15. One of the union leaders who confirmed this was a beneficiary. Until recently, he held local political office, and he still has not retired from politics.

16. The court called the administrator to testify in the final stage of the proceedings. He was ordered detained for several days, but he was set free due to the services of a competent lawyer. All those who testified at the hearing, except the two trustworthy laborers involved (whose stories contradicted each other), agreed on these points: the administrator drove past the site in his car at the time of the attack; the chief of the gang ordered his people not to bother the

administrator or disarm him; the administrator continued on, having seen the victims tied up before they were killed; the administrator did not tell the military police, who were stationed approximately three minutes away by car; when a few moments later some workers came to tell the administrator what had happened, he ordered them back to work as usual; someone offered to go immediately to the authorities, and the administrator refused the offer; finally, the administrator himself ordered that the police not be notified. (The judicial proceeding is not cited so as not to cast any blame of an individual nature. It is up to the judicial system, according to its own criteria, to decide who is at fault when it comes to individual responsibility; this study is concerned only with the analysis of the social determinants of events.)

17. This calculation is for the moment imprecise and only can be approximate; thus, I have not provided the figures.

18. This does not mean to say that they did not exist. In Circasia there was at least one case of a person who consolidated quite a few small parcels, allegedly through blackmail.

19. The guerrilla bands also held money; often their depositors were the butchers who bought stolen livestock from them.

20. Curiously, in a partnership established in 1953 for this purpose, one of the two partners was the same landowner who in the first decade of the century had made his fortune by, among other things, purchasing parcels abutting the land of needy peasants or tenant farmers; in the 1920s he confronted the tenant farmers from his own estate and took advantage of the conflicts between the tenant farmers and owners on the neighboring estate. I was able to establish the movements of this businessman, who was always surrounded by notoriety, not only through oral reports and written articles but also by studying the registry books back to the beginning of the century.

21. Here I have outlined certain factual conditions that encouraged the theory to spread through the region, as it did in other parts of the country. But one cannot ignore the influence of the prevailing intellectual climate over the way things were explained. Countering the interpretations of Conservatives and Liberals on the Violence—interpretations that, by the way, are not difficult to refute—the third explanatory direction taken was nourished by a positivism that was very characteristic of the period among those who used Marxist terminology. It consisted, roughly speaking, in gathering global statistics from official sources (for example, data on the distribution of land parcels by size, on migration, or on the distribution of occupations) and "applying" to them the formulas from Karl Marx's *Das Kapital* or the European classics in general, without elaborating specifically on the mechanisms of the relation involved. In the case of the Violence the analysis seemed similar to the peasant expulsion provoked by the "enclosures" in England and also to the notion of the "industrial reserve army" formulated by Marx apropos of English industrialization in the nineteenth century. "The Violence in Colombia," thus, could not have any other answers than those possible under a single question, which was considered the "a priori" of the necessary "theoretical frame": how did the Violence accomplish its (only) goal of adapting the structure of land in the direction of

"capitalism," or, ultimately, how did the great landlords use the Violence in order to sabotage the logic of capitalist evolution?

22. Street vending by large numbers of underemployed was also a channel for bringing products from several industries located outside the Quindío into the market of the expanding city.

23. Meanwhile, day wages, which from 1962 to 1965 varied from 12 to 21 pesos in that *municipio* (during harvesttime), had risen only to 120 pesos.

24. Complications introduced by intermediaries were one of the main obstacles to the work of the Court of Conciliation and Equity in the Quindío. The court was formed to indemnify those directly dispossessed by the Violence. None of the courts created for this purpose in the country in 1960 fulfilled their purpose, and they all disappeared before the year was up.

25. Data from the registry office present their own difficulties. These problems include not only those of scattered farms belonging to a single owner and of fictitious names, but also those created by the high level of inaccuracy of the statistics for property size. In more than half of the cases the sizes are not noted; in other cases, the sizes have to be reconstructed by laboriously tracing distant transactions; and in any case, the reconstructed sizes usually do not correspond to the (much larger) sizes verified through fieldwork.

I was concerned only with the class of proprietors who owned more than 80 hectares in coffee before 1946 and more than 60 after 1965 and those owners whose livestock acreage totaled more than 500 hectares in both periods. Given the spurious character of the figures already noted, in order to establish (approximately) the measurements with which to identify the classes just mentioned, I had to combine the questionable figures from the tax and registry offices (using them only as guides and proportional measures) with figures from oral and newspaper sources.

26. Many Liberal families, at the limits of resistance, were obliged to sell one or several parcels, but sooner or later they bought in guerrilla-influenced zones. Their alienation from their home neighborhoods, caused by the insecurity of the moment, later became permanent. Today, these families live in the cities (Bogotá, Manizales, Pereira, or Armenia), and very few are seen in the country.

27. Stories such as follows are not rare in the field: "I had to sell my little farm and it was bought by a next-door neighbor, because I begged her to since no one was buying because they were afraid; she, who had a big farm, finally agreed." Another time a respondent told me: "I had to sell my farm to a Conservative who was a close friend. I gave it to him for 7,000 pesos, although I had practically sold it before the threats for 36,000."

28. In the 1960s titles were still being adjudicated in several *municipios* of the Quindío. And in the 1970s, for example, almost one hundred small parcels were deeded in the rural district of the Congal in the *municipio* of Filandia.

7

Violence and Economic Development: 1945–1950 and 1985–1988

Medófilo Medina

Medófilo Medina currently directs the graduate program in history at the National University in Bogotá. A student of the social and political history of modern Colombia, he has focused on popular protest and the evolution of the Colombian Communist party. He is the author of *Historia del Partido Comunista de Colombia* (Bogotá, 1979; 2d ed., 1980) and *La protesta urbana en Colombia durante el siglo XX* (Bogotá, 1984). Among his recent publications is an essay on one of the themes central to analysis of Colombia's violent politics: the failure of third parties to challenge effectively the political monopoly of the two traditional parties. That essay, "Los terceros partidos en Colombia," appears as Chapter 11 in Volume 2 of a major survey of modern Colombian history directed by Alvaro Tirado Mejía, the *Nueva historia de Colombia*, 7 vols. (Bogotá, 1989). For readers of Spanish this multivolume work is an excellent point of reference for all aspects of twentieth-century Colombian history.

In his comparative study here, Medina focuses on the curious symbiosis between economic development and violence in Colombia during two periods in national life. The violence has intensified greatly since this article was written in 1988, but Medina's analysis remains valid today. Medina moves far beyond the simple notion that drug dollars stimulate the Colombian economy. He explores the debilitating effects of drug-related violence on organized labor, and he suggests that there are subtle links between the cultural values promoted by the drug trade, conservative ideology, and neoliberal economic policy.

The Violence that descended on Colombia in the middle of the present century occurred at a time when the country was entering a phase of accelerated economic growth (1945–1953). October 1949 was precisely the least likely time for a Colombian to utter optimistic comments about the condition of the country. In fact, a series of terrorist-style collective killings had taken place as a prelude to the presidential election to be held the next month. Imperturbably, however, the president of the Asociación Nacional de Industriales (ANDI) commented on the state of the economy: "In recent weeks I have repeatedly stated my opinion on the matter, which is very optimistic and is based on concrete facts, such as the price of coffee, the very considerable increases in agricultural and industrial production, the level of international payments, and the equilibrium in the balance of payments."[1] Perhaps more forthright than his predecessor, a later ANDI president, Fabio Echeverry Correa, stated mysteriously at the beginning of 1987 that "the economy is fine, but the country's not well." By then the violence had taken on all the trappings of a dirty war.

The coincidence of violence and the expansion of the economy during two different periods suggest a relationship between the two phenomena that is not simply fortuitous. Of course, there is no reason to assume, at least at the national level, the existence of "intentional strategies" in this association between economic boom and high levels of political violence. It is a matter of more complex causal factors, which, more often than not, are more powerful than the social agents that they call forth into action.

Economy and Violence, 1945–1950

In the mid-1940s, after a period of recession, economic indicators began to shoot upward. Between 1945 and 1949 the gross national product, the national per capita product, and gross national income grew at annual rates of 5.9, 3.6, and 7.5 percent, respectively.[2] Between 1945 and 1953 industry grew at a record annual rate of 9.2 percent. Agriculture saw a 77 percent increase in the volume of production for 1948, and 113 percent for 1949.[3] Meanwhile, the Colombian economy was undergoing two processes: on the one hand, a trend toward monopoly, and on the other hand, the reactivation and diversification of foreign investment, particularly by North American capitalists.[4] These processes are the backdrop for the central pair of variables analyzed here, economic growth and the Violence.

At the same time that the indicators just cited reflected the healthy state of the economy, the Violence was advancing inexorably. By 1947 most of the country's departments were experiencing violent episodes. In the cities, workers' demonstrations were being repressed. The Gaitanista enclaves were also claiming victims. By the end of 1949 massacres had taken place in Belalcázar in the Cauca; El Playón in

Santander; Betania, Ceilán, and San Rafael in Valle del Cauca; and Arauca, in Caldas. In Cali, army troops set fire to the Liberal party headquarters and killed several people. The chronological distribution of deaths of violence during the second half of the 1940s is as follows: 13,968 in 1947, 43,557 in 1948, 18,519 in 1949, and 50,253 in 1950.[5] In all there were 126,297 victims of the Violence during this period.

At the beginning of the 1940s a consensus among the economic and political elites began to crystallize concerning the need to dismantle the "ideology of state regulation" in favor of the explicit adoption of orthodox liberal principles for economic and social programs. The political crisis that beset the regime between 1943 and 1945, and that served as the introduction to the Violence, was conditioned by these efforts to adapt the statist, social welfare, and prolabor policies inherited from the 1930s to the postwar liberal order. Daniel Pecaut has skillfully documented and conceptualized the implications and patterns of this change of direction.[6]

The withdrawal of state intervention in favor of a liberal economic model coincided with a change in the level of political participation by social movements. In 1936 there had been a kind of historical compromise among a constellation of bourgeois elites and a combination of forces representing the popular and middle sectors of society. This compromise created some room—limited, of course—for the labor movement. It allowed the establishment of paternalistic channels of political communication between the government and organized labor.

The initiative for these changes was taken by economic associations, first of all, by the large coffee growers, through the Federación Nacional de Cafeteros, and second, by the industrialists and merchants. The industrialists formalized their national organization, ANDI, in 1944, and the merchants established theirs, the Federación Nacional de Comerciantes (FENALCO), in 1945. In contrast to earlier years, government cabinets after 1943 reserved no seats for bold thirty-year-old kids, nor did they include outstanding journalists or professionals unless they had major connections with powerful economic interests. The ministers in the second government of Alfonso López Pumarejo (1942–1945) and in that of Mariano Ospina Pérez (1946–1949) were either prominent financiers, solid entrepreneurs, or lawyers for foreign oil companies.

The resignation of President López Pumarejo on July 19, 1945, and congress's choice of Alberto Lleras Camargo to succeed him cemented the change of direction of the state and of its policies. A few months later the new president had the opportunity to demonstrate the direction that the changes would take with respect to social movements. At the beginning of December 1945 the port and river transport workers on the Magdalena River who were organized under the Magdalena River Transport Workers Union (FEDENAL), an affiliate of the Confederación de Trabajadores Colombianos (CTC), went on strike. Their movement was declared illegal by the minister of labor. On the second day of the strike, President Lleras Camargo announced that it was necessary to eliminate a supposed "national belief" in the existence of two governments, one in Bogotá and one on the Magdalena River. The president supported management's intransigent position and authorized military repression against the strikers. Spokesmen for the owners' associations, as well as the leaders of Colombia's two traditional parties, applauded the president's actions.

The Magdalena River conflict offered the government an exceptional opportunity to show unequivocally to workers and to the public at large what the official line would be in the future with regard to union organization and the handling of industrial conflict. At the time that it was repressed FEDENAL was the most important organization in the CTC, then the only national labor federation. The workers affiliated with FEDENAL had achieved more gains than those in any other union in Colombia. Moreover, since members of the Communist party played an important leadership role in FEDENAL, the government's repression notably affected the influence of the party in union organization. At the same time, the repression dealt a severe blow to the CTC, which saw its most important affiliate crushed. In every aspect of this matter, the regime's treatment of the strike by the Magdalena River workers had an unmistakable demonstration effect.

Prior to this incident, a general strike called by the CTC in solidarity with a strike at the Monserrate textile mill in Bogotá was declared illegal. The textile strike lasted two months and was settled with no gains for the workers. As would be the FEDENAL strike, this was a sign of things to come.

The government's antiunion offensive developed in several directions between 1945 and 1950. Among them were: 1) the outlawing of strikes; 2) the bloody military repression of workers' demonstrations, principally in Bogotá and Cali; 3) government authorization of worker firings, which were particularly numerous in 1947; 4) an offensive against the CTC in the courts as a result of which the federation's legal standing was suspended; 5) encouragement of division within the CTC, which temporarily split in two at its Eighth Congress, held in Medellín in August 1946; and 6) the encouragement of pluralism in union organization, expressed through protection for the founding of a new national labor federation. This newly created organization was the Unión de Trabajadores Colombianos (UTC), which was formed under the auspices of the Catholic Church on June 16, 1946. It was recognized as legal in 1949 after President Ospina Pérez's government, in Decree 2785, repealed measures that had prohibited plural union organization.[7]

The policy implemented through these concrete steps developed alongside an ideological campaign that denounced the union movement and denigrated it as an independent factor in the political system. The voice of the Catholic hierarchy was not silent in this outcry. Among the prelates heard from were Archbishop García Benítez of Medellín and Bishop Miguel Angel Builes of Santa Rosa de Osos, who prohibited workers from joining FEDETA, a CTC affiliate in Antioquia, under pain of excommunication.

The union sectors assembled under the CTC resisted the antiworker offensive. This resistance was expressed between 1945 and 1950 in the following ways:

1. Growth in the strike movement: the number of strikes per year between 1945 and 1948 did not drop below twenty, a relatively high average for the strike movement in the 1930s and 1940s.

2. Repeated calls for national strikes by the CTC and for regional strikes by its affiliated federations. Some of these strikes took place.

3. Radicalization of other labor sectors, such as the oil workers, who stood firm for the nationalization of the oil industry.

The disintegration of the ideology of state regulation and the process of adopting a liberal scheme with a consequent reduction in the role of the unions also met with resistance from workers. At the time, as will be discussed, some of this resistance found political expression through the Gaitanista movement. The regressive shift by the elites thus was accompanied by a simultaneous popular radicalization. But the trajectories of popular, union, and political resistance advanced according to different, and frequently conflicting, logics.

When one examines the course of politics in Colombia after 1945, what is obvious is the advance of the antipopular offensive and the debilitation of the union movement, which would become displaced definitively as a political factor. With this defeat an entity capable of channeling social conflict was eliminated. The union movement disappeared as a symbolic point of reference for many urban sectors, which then found themselves at the mercy of sectarian bipartisan political confrontation.

The process of political radicalization through Gaitanismo was abruptly interrupted with the assassination of Jorge Eliécer Gaitán on April 9, 1948. Now the violence, which had been increasingly steadily since 1945, could not be contained. Although after 1948 this violence would be mainly a rural phenomenon, its gestation had been urban and its first stages had been both urban and rural.

After 1948 the association between violence and economic expansion appeared in a new guise. Whereas between 1946 and 1949 the government's antiunion offensive had helped assure high profits, after the 1948 assassination of Gaitán, threats and exile promoted different forms of capital accumulation. For the coffee-growing areas, Jaime Arocha and, especially, Carlos Miguel Ortiz Sarmiento have documented convincingly the way in which a reshuffling of land ownership took place.[8] Professionals, merchants from the county seats, storekeepers, and estate foremen were able to dominate coffee commerce and become strong links in the "business of the Violence."

The noncoffee rural economy also was affected. For example, in the northern part of the Valle del Cauca, in the mountainous region of the department, coercion meant replacement of small farmers by small- and medium-sized cattlemen who could supply milk to an affiliate of a transnational dairy company. In time, laborers left the mountains for the flatlands of the department to work in the sugar mills.[9] Even in the llanos, fortunes were being amassed in livestock as a result of the Violence, and it is clear that in the post-1953 phase some people, who had played important roles in the military confrontation between the state and the Liberal guerrillas, remained in the region at the service of the cattlemen, who used them to rid their property of tenant farmers.[10]

In regions that had been the scenes of agrarian struggles in the 1930s, the large landowners, in more than a few cases, saw the Violence as an opportunity to dispute the property rights of former tenant farmers who had managed to become smallholders. This was true in the southern and eastern parts of Tolima and in the Sumapaz region in Cundinamarca.[11] The manifestations were different in each region, but the logic was the same—the Violence was a factor in capitalist accumulation.

Economy and Violence, 1985–1988

How does the relationship between the economy and violence manifest itself in the present? The first half of the 1980s was characterized by a worldwide economic recession. Colombia was no exception, although its statistics were less drastic than those for other countries. By the middle of 1986, however, the economy began to show positive indications, and these signs developed into a true recovery in 1986 and 1987. In these years the growth of the GNP was about 5.1 percent. Manufacturing grew at a rate close to 7 percent. Automobile sales increased notably as did the sales of other durable consumer goods.

Activity in the private building sector increased, and the agricultural sector showed a satisfactory performance starting in 1986, with a growth rate of 4.1 percent in 1987.

Since the middle of 1985 there has been a constant flow of capital to industry. Between the beginning of 1986 and the first months of 1987, authorized imports of capital goods grew by 25 percent. In practically all branches of manufacturing there were miracles. Businesses that had been on the brink of ruin or already had begun bankruptcy proceedings not only overcame their critical situations but also were able to show profits in the next quarter. Among the most important examples were the steel mill at Paz del Río, the large textile firms of Fabricato and Coltejer, the national airline Avianca, and the sugar manufacturer Ingenio de Río Paila. The case of IBM is especially interesting. While its parent company was having one of its worst periods ever, the Colombian affiliate's profits climbed to 3,510 million pesos.[12]

As had occurred in the 1940s, so also in the second half of the 1980s good economic conditions coincided with a recrudescence of violence. Taken together the growth of paramilitary gangs, the proliferation of *sicarios*, the systematic elimination of leaders of the leftist political party Unión Patriótica (UP), the emulation of Peru's Sendero Luminoso by certain guerrilla organizations, the assassination of state officials by drug traffickers, and the increase in clashes between the guerrillas and the armed forces form a patchwork quilt of violence. Might there be, then, a relationship in the present between economic expansion and violence? For the midcentury period, research has shown that there were internal links between one phenomenon and the other. For the present period, one can only hazard hypotheses.

High rates of capital accumulation awaken extraordinary expectations of profit making. This tendency, which is natural in business, in Colombia becomes a powerful reason for violence because the rules upon which labor-management relations rest are in a permanent state of legal challenge. Aspects of the country's labor law are subject to constant revision. It is as though no firm ground were under this body of law and almost everything were open to dispute. Likewise, no real guarantees exist for the implementation either of the labor laws or of agreements reached in collective bargaining. When one compares the motives behind workers' strikes, it is clear that, in the eighties, the extraordinary increase in strikes was triggered not by new demands but in opposition to the violation of either labor laws or points gained in mediation. Between 1981 and 1984 such opposition was behind 31 percent of the strikes in manufacturing, 70 percent in services (excluding teaching), and 80 percent in transportation. For these same categories, in the period 1971 to 1980, strikes for the same reason were almost half these rates.

These figures are taken from a study by Rocío Londoño Botero, who concludes her analysis by noting that "the reports on inspection visits by the Labor Ministry between 1982 and 1985, covering 12,452 companies, show that only 8.4 percent of these companies were in strict compliance with the law, and that 91.6 percent violated, on average, 3.85 percent separate rules.[13] In addition, the legitimacy of the unions was always in doubt. Union coverage tended to become smaller. The creation of new unions confronted severe regulation, and, at the same time, large sectors of the labor force were excluded from union organization. Of 915,307 employees working in government jobs, only 17 percent had the right to participate in collective bargaining. The prohibition of strikes covered an even larger number of workers because those working in nongovernment jobs that were considered to be "public services" were excluded from this right.

A study of the extent of the violence that has surrounded union activity in several areas during recent years casts some light on the dynamic between economy and violent conflict. One example is the important case in the banana zone of Urabá in Antioquia. In recent years, Colombia has become the third largest producer of bananas in the world, and profits for the fruit companies are simply fabulous. Although banana production in Urabá began in 1952, it was not until April 1987 that a labor agreement was signed by the Ministry of Labor, the business association of the growers, and spokesmen for the Sintagro and Sintrabanano unions, which represented 32,200 workers.[14] These unions were affiliated with the workers' federation created in the mid-1980s, the Central Unitaria de Trabajadores (CUT). During the negotiation of this agreement, 17 workers were assassinated.

The agreement reached between the owners and the workers in Urabá has turned out to be very fragile. Deterioration of the political situation in the region has continued, and the violence has not subsided. The murder of workers has not stopped either; to date, the most sinister of these episodes took place on March 4, 1987, when a paramilitary group forced 26 banana workers, all union members, from their houses and shot them. Since 1988 scores of union members have been killed in Urabá by rightist paramilitary groups that the left has denounced as instruments of the growers. Government militarization of the zone and efforts to impose a special system of identity cards for workers have met with strong union resistance and endemic strike activity.

The opinions that different national sectors hold about Urabá are telling. Businessmen tend to identify the violence with union actions, and they call for national support for an economic sector that looks so promising. The armed forces claim not to see anything behind the union movement other than subversive guerrilla pressure. The Bogotá daily, *La República*, mouthpiece for the mainstream of the Conservative party, summed up the situation this way: "It is pernicious for each one of the 267 farms in Urabá to have a union. Sintagro threatens the country's economy by promoting strikes. It is necessary to change the policy on the labor front and prevent the nation's banana companies, which are hemmed in by Communist unionism, from having to abandon cultivation."[15] Bishop Héctor Rueda told the press on June 30, 1987, that the banana strikes had a subversive bias.

The intolerance demonstrated in some branches of the economy toward union organization and the inclusion of large doses of cruelty in worker-owner relations in some regions have their corollaries on the national level. In 1986, following agreements among various union groups of differing ideological and political orientations, the CUT was created. During the brief time that it has been in existence, the CUT has been subject to harsh persecution. Between November 1986 and January 1988, seventy members of the organization were murdered. This appalling figure is surpassed only by the number of victims from the UP, which has counted hundreds of its members killed since January 1988.

In analyzing both the economy and the violence of the eighties, it is necessary to incorporate the influence of the drug trade. A network of communicating arteries exists between what is called, euphemistically, "hot money" and the formal economy. It is difficult to measure how much the drug traffic and other illegal economic activities, such as contraband and commerce in emeralds, count for in the economy as a whole. The time is past when drug lords could name a company openly after themselves, as for example, Carlos Lehder did with his automobile dealership.

Nevertheless, the flow of money continues and increases, and there is indirect evidence of money laundering as well. For example, the amnesty provided for in President Virgilio Barco's tax reform program brought more than 190,000 new taxpayers to the tax rolls, taxpayers who declared a total of more than 755,000 million pesos (8,757 were corporate entities, which accounted for 153,000 million pesos, and 182,955 were private persons, who accounted for 602,179 million pesos).[16] Also needing to be studied are the moneys that have entered the economy through the so-called sinister window of the Bank of the Republic. In a country that has had a low rate of domestic savings, it is not realistic to think that the formal sectors of the economy could generate the kind of cash flow revealed in these figures; so much cash could be supplied only through the activities of drug dealers.

In his statements to the press in October 1987, Comptroller Rodolfo González García linked Colombia's economic revival to the influence of hot money, especially to that invested in housing and commerce. The economic upswing that began in mid-1985 hardly can be interpreted exclusively on the basis of favorable trends in the coffee sector, which unquestionably has seen some very good times during the last few years. It is also difficult to attribute the upswing to the fluctuation of long-term debt in the public sector, at least as recorded for 1987.[17] In short, the economic renewal cannot be explained solely by the impact of the coffee sector and the outcome of external indebtedness.

The communications media, particularly the press and political spokesmen, have encouraged a dual morality. They harshly condemn the drug traffic in public discourse but close their eyes to its active penetration in the illegal economy. The magazine *Semana* was close to the truth when it called the drug mafia "a small but supremely powerful group." "There are no social or economic sectors which the drug traffic has not managed to infiltrate," the weekly stated. "Diplomatic relations, exports, aviation, sports, the armed forces, banks, parliament, political campaigns, private enterprise, construction, the Church, the courts, and even the guerrilla movement have been victims of the tentacles of the traffic in drugs."[18]

From the perspective of the present analysis, the most important issue is how, when money is moved from one sector of the economy to another, some social values are enhanced and others negated. The pursuit of wealth at any price, the audacity of the methods employed, the use of terror as a means to dissuade or eliminate rivals—in one way or another these conditions all influence economic relations, especially worker-owner disagreements. Yet rarely taken into account in these relationships are the dimensions of the violence that emanates from an illegal and clandestine economy, such as the existence of personal armies, the training of *sicarios*, and corruption in the government's armed forces.

Also understandable is the ideological evolution of drug dealers toward anticommunism and extreme nationalism. This trend may have been retarded in the past by the dealers' coexistence with guerrillas of leftist orientation in regions of recent colonization where drug plants were being cultivated. (See the essay by Alfredo Molano, Chapter 9 of this volume.) The importance of drug trafficking in the present stage of Colombian economic development has caused violent methods—methods that historically accompanied the primary stages of capital accumulation—to reappear in contemporary economic activity.

In assessing the association between violence and economic growth in recent years, the significance of the shift in economic policy should not be underestimated. Following a period of protection and of overseeing certain elements of the public welfare, government changed its policy, in the mid-1970s, to give it a neoliberal focus. This focus involved, for instance, the elimination of subsidies for products and services that had helped hold down the cost of living, the dismantling of the agency supervising price control, the elimination of so-called political prices, and the raising of the sales tax. In this change of focus, too, the present period is analogous to the 1940s when official policy resulted in the dismantling of the ideology of state regulation.

Notes

1. *El Tiempo*, October 21, 1949.
2. Miguel Urrutia Montoya, *Cincuenta años de desarrollo económico colombiano* (Bogotá, 1979), 16.
3. Absalón Machado, ed., *Problemas agrarios colombianos* (Bogotá, 1986).
4. For an analysis of these processes see, among others, Rafael Baquero, *La economía nacional y la política de guerra en Colombia* (Bogotá, 1972), and Konrad Matter, *Inversiones extranjeras en la economía colombiana* (Medellín, 1977).
5. Paul Oquist, *Violencia, conflicto y política en Colombia* (Bogotá, 1978), 17.
6. Daniel Pecaut, *Orden y violencia, 1930–1954*, 2 vols. (Bogotá, 1987).
7. The postwar offensive against Colombian labor was part of a general world pattern.
8. Jaime Arocha, *La Violencia en el Quindío* (Bogotá, 1979). For Ortiz Sarmiento, see Chapter 6 of this volume.
9. For the socioeconomic content of the Violence in the northern part of Valle, see Urbano Campo, *Urbanización y violencia en el Valle* (Bogotá, 1980).
10. These impressions were formed on the basis of personal interviews conducted by the author in 1981 with former participants in the Violence in Los Llanos.
11. Medófilo Medina, "La resistencia campesina en el sur del Tolima," in *Pasado y presente de la Violencia en Colombia*, eds. Gonzalo Sánchez and Ricardo Peñaranda (Bogotá, 1986), 233–65.
12. This brief summary is based on data from Moshe Syrkin, "Crecimiento económico y cambio estructural en Colombia," *Coyuntura Económica* 17:4 (December 1987); and "Las cien empresas mas grandes de Colombia," *Semana*, May 26, 1987.
13. Rocío Londoño Botero, "Los sindicatos y la política laboral en Colombia" (paper, Departamento de Sociología, Universidad Nacional, Bogotá, 1988), 50.
14. A methodical description of the conflicts in the banana zone can be found in Julián Delgadillo, "La Violencia en Urabá" (Paper presented at the VI Congreso de Historia de Colombia, Ibagué, November 1987).

15. *La República*, July 8, 1987.
16. *El Tiempo*, November 15, 1987.
17. *Coyuntura Económica* 17:4 (December 1987): 6.
18. *Semana*, December 30, 1986, January 12, 1987.

Part III

THE CONTEMPORARY CRISIS

8

Revolutionary Guerrilla Groups in Colombia*

Eduardo Pizarro

In this path-breaking essay Eduardo Pizarro provides a short yet comprehensive analysis of the origins, nature, and trajectory of the various guerrilla groups operating in Colombia. Published in Spanish in 1986, it has proved to be remarkably accurate in distinguishing the various styles of the guerrilla groups and in predicting the groups' behavior during the government's long efforts— begun in earnest during the presidency of Belisario Betancur (1982–1986) and continued through the presidency of Virgilio Barco (1986–1990)—to achieve peace through negotiation with the guerrillas.

More detailed treatment of these issues and coverage of the peace effort since 1986 is available in Pizarro's recently published book, *Historia de la guerrilla en Colombia* (Bogotá, 1990). The peace effort reached an important milestone in 1989–90 with the negotiated settlement that ended the armed insurgency of the M-19. The group's former commander, Carlos Pizarro, subsequently ran for the presidency in 1990. Pizarro was murdered by a paid assassin as he flew from Bogotá to a campaign appearance in Barranquilla. He was replaced by Antonio Navarro Wolf, who won a surprising share of the vote.

Eduardo Pizarro is a sociologist at the Institute of Political Studies and International Relations at the National University in Bogotá.

Since 1986 the Colombian guerrilla movement has been developing around two central axes. One is the political program of the leftist coalition party Unión Patriótica, under the leadership of the guerrilla organization Fuerzas Armadas Revolucionarias Colombianas (FARC), and the other is the military-style Coordinadora Guerrillera

*This chapter was originally published in Gonzalo Sánchez and Ricardo Peñaranda, eds., *Pasado y presente de la Violencia en Colombia* (Bogotá, 1986). Reprinted by permission of the Centro de Estudios de la Realidad Colombiana.

Nacional, headed by the M-19 guerrilla group. This growing unification of insurrectionary armed groups coincides with two converging processes now taking place in Colombia. The first process is related to the increasingly active political role of the guerrilla groups. In recent years, guerrilla groups have entered into real dialogue with the government and have become a source of proposals for national policymaking (such as their calls for democratic reforms, for the naming of a "peace cabinet," and for a national dialogue on reform and reconciliation). The second process is the growth of a surprising number of social movements—civic, regional, neighborhood, and cultural—that have raised citizen participation levels. The participation of citizens in these new movements has occurred in a context of continuing apathy and indifference toward traditional institutional structures of social and political participation, as revealed, for example, in the high rates of electoral abstention.

Regis Debray, analyzing Ernesto "Che" Guevara's failure in Bolivia, asserts that "if the guerrilla vanguard, the 'little motor,' can be called the external cause, and the Bolivian mass movement, the 'big motor,' can be called the internal cause, there should be no objection to the notion that the external cause appeared on the national scene without any immediate or obvious relation to the internal cause, which was in its vicinity but not in its orbit, or, more directly, was moving parallel to its course but was not directly pushing it along."[1] The guerrilla movement in Bolivia was suffocated by its own isolation since it never achieved any real link with the popular movement of the country.

The course along which popular struggles and the guerrilla movement have unfolded in Colombia parallels the Bolivian case, except for rare regional exceptions. This condition accounts for the relative ineffectiveness in Colombia of guerrilla military action for more than two decades. However, the two processes cited earlier—political activism on a national scale and the emergence of social movements—have begun to produce a qualitative and quantitative change in the insurgent movement, whose consequences are still difficult to measure.

One fact is undeniable: the armed movement has passed from being a bit player in national life to becoming a central actor on the political scene. In the future, the country will find it necessary to take the armed movement into account given the insurgents' role in the plan for national reconciliation initiated by the government of Belisario Betancur.

The object of this essay is not a historical one. It is at once more modest and more ambitious. It aims, above all, to delineate the actual profile of each of the armed groups (its social composition, its political strategy, the structure of its activities, and its ideology) in order to understand its stance vis-à-vis the process of national reconciliation and to try to elucidate what each group's political strategy might be in the future.

The Emergence of the Guerrilla Movement

External Factors

Internal as well as international factors contributed to the birth of the armed revolutionary movement in Colombia. Under the impact of the Cuban Revolution and the theses of Guevara and Debray, the revolutionary struggle for the control of political power based on the *foco*, or "insurrectionary armed enclave," affected many Latin American countries in the 1960s.[2] The spokesmen for this new structure of political action came from the radicalized urban sectors: in Peru, Héctor Bejar of the Ejército de Liberación Nacional (ELN) and Luis de la Puente of the Movimiento de Izquierda Revolucionaria (MIR) in 1963; in Guatemala, Luis Turcios, Antonio Yon Sosa, Turcios Lima, and Luis Trejo of the Fuerzas Armadas Rebeldes (FAR) during 1962; in Argentina, Jorge Ricardo Masseti, leader of the Ejército Guerrillero del Pueblo (EGP) in 1964; in Nicaragua, Carlos Fonseca Amador, Silvio Mayorga, Noel Guerrero, and Tomás Borge founded, in July 1961, the Frente Sandinista de Liberación Nacional, which initiated military operations a year later; in Brazil, various political-military organizations were formed throughout the sixties, such as the Vanguardia Popular Revolucionaria (VPR), the Comando de Liberación Nacional (COLINA), and, above all, Carlos Marighella's Acción de Liberación Nacional; in Bolivia, under the inspiration of Che himself, the Ejército de Liberación Nacional (ELN) was born in 1966; and in Uruguay, following the principle of the urban insurrectionary enclave, the Tupamaros arose under the leadership of Raúl Sendic.

In Colombia, the debut of the first political-military organizations similarly would arise from the enclave conception. The Movimiento Obrero Estudiantil Campesino (Worker Student Peasant Movement, MOEC); the Fuerzas Armadas de Liberación (Armed Forces of Liberation, FAL); the Ejército de Liberación Nacional (Army for National Liberation, ELN); and even the Partido Comunista Marxista-Leninista (Marxist-Leninist-Communist party, PCML), a Maoist-leaning group, sought the consolidation of armed enclaves in different parts of the country after 1962.[3]

The principles that inspired the *foco* concept had been synthesized by Che in his "General Principles of Guerrilla Warfare," in which he pointed out:

We consider that the Cuban revolution made three fundamental
contributions to the mechanics of revolutionary movements in America:
1) popular forces can win a war against an army; 2) it is not always
necessary to wait until all the conditions of revolution exist; the
insurrectionary enclave can create them; 3) in underdeveloped America
the field of armed struggle must be fundamentally the countryside. Of
these three contributions, the first two pit themselves against the quietist
attitude of revolutionaries or pseudorevolutionaries who hide, and hide
their inactivity, behind the pretext that nothing can be done against a
professional army. They also contradict those others who want to wait
until all the objective and subjective necessary conditions automatically
appear, without doing anything to accelerate the process.[4]

Colombia was witnessing the revival of the popular struggle after the
military interregnum of Gustavo Rojas Pinilla. Che's call for armed
struggle, with its celebration of voluntarism, would make a profound
and lasting impact. In light of this situation, the last sentence in Che's
text was not taken into consideration: "Where a government has risen
to power by some means of popular consent, whether fraudulent or not,
and maintains at least the appearance of constitutional legality, guerrilla
uprising is impossible because all the possibilities of the civic struggle
have not been exhausted."[5]

A second decisive international factor was the Chinese-Soviet rupture during the first years of the 1960s and the subsequent division of
the pro-Soviet Communist parties into two wings. In Colombia, the
mechanical attempt to reproduce the experience of the Chinese revolution instigated by the PCML followed the installation of what would be
called the "Ejército Popular de Liberación" (Popular Army of Liberation, EPL) in northwest Antioquia.[6]

Internal Factors

While external factors served as a spark to kindle the enthusiasm of
certain sectors for the initiatives of *foco*-style guerrilla activity, there is
no doubt that only the presence of a complex array of factors on the
internal front made it possible for the guerrilla groups to come into
existence and, above all, to consolidate themselves. In the absence of
these internal factors, the Colombian guerrillas very probably would
have met the same fate as their fellow insurrectionaries elsewhere in
South America.

One significant internal factor was the approval by the Colombian
Communist party of the resolutions of the 20th Congress of the Soviet
Communist party concerning the possibility of a peaceful road to
revolution. Such a stance was totally contrary to the tremendous spirit

of expectation that had been produced by the Cuban Revolution among radical urban groups at the beginning of the Frente Nacional. It was also an ironic position for the Communists to take since the government had declared the party illegal in 1956 and, in 1958, had launched a military offensive against the Communist stronghold of Villarrica.[7] The radical urban groups denounced the Communist party as a lame organization and advanced new political options that would end the Communist monopoly of the revolutionary opposition in the country.

In 1958 the Communist party's reaction to the birth of the Frente Nacional was recorded in *Tribuna*, the organ of the party's 8th Congress:

> under these new conditions, when our party has declared at various meetings that it is decidedly in favor of the peaceful, constitutional, and legal route of development in the social and political struggle, it would be contradictory to maintain in the platform that we propose to overthrow the government by means of a revolutionary uprising by the Colombian people. On this matter our platform must bring together the lessons given us by our people, learned at the cost of great sacrifice, and apply, to our concrete situation, the thesis of the Twentieth Congress of the Communist Party of the Soviet Union. This means that we must consider the advantage of inserting into the Party platform, in place of the call to overthrow the government, *a call for peaceful revolutionary struggle through the progressive democratization of the country, the strengthening and unity of the workers' movement and the worker-peasant alliance, and the development of the democratic Frente Nacional.*[8]

Other groups, influenced by radical urban politics, emerged to oppose the Communist party's position. On the one hand, there appeared an insurrectionary left, which insisted that an imminent revolutionary situation existed, and which sharply criticized reformism and pacifism and favored armed struggle and electoral abstention. These groups included the militarist sector of the MOEC, the ELN, and the PCML. On the other hand, groups such as the Frente Unido de Acción Revolucionario (United Front for Revolutionary Action, FUAR) and the future Movimiento Obrero Independiente Revolucionario (Revolutionary Independent Labor Movement, MOIR), although they shared this radical perspective, nevertheless denied the immediate viability of armed action. Instead, they placed their main emphasis on the organization of urban movements.

The early 1960s, then, witness the breakup of the Communist monopoly on revolutionary rhetoric and action and mark the emergence of a broad range of radical political efforts that constitute the basis of the present-day guerrilla movements in the country. It must not be forgotten that during this stage there was an unusual awakening, following the long, dormant period of the Violence and the military dictatorships, of the popular forces, especially of labor and the student movement. There were strikes, demonstrations, and confrontations whose central actors came from the ranks of white-collar workers (bank clerks, teachers, and other public employees) and students. These social groups proved receptive to the radical discourse going on around them.

In another development, the Frente Nacional installed a "limited democracy" in Colombia, one founded on an exclusive bipartisan monopoly, a stable government, the autonomy of the military branch in the management of internal public order, and the extreme centralization of state decisions in the executive branch, to the detriment of the congress. The absence of real democratic space for political forces other than those sanctioned by the narrow channels of the bipartisan system blocked the aspirations of the popular sectors and had as an immediate consequence the deinstitutionalization of social and union-based political struggles. These struggles overflowed the legal boundaries and resulted in "civic strikes," illegal strikes, armed movements, and so on. These new forms of mobilization and struggle came to have at least as much importance as the forms of political participation provided for in the law.[9]

What facilitated the rapid development of the first insurrectionary guerrilla groups in Colombia was the persistence of forms of the earlier political violence,[10] especially the "political banditry," which survived until at least 1965. In fact, the first attempts to form guerrilla enclaves were based on the desire to "integrate urban revolutionary feeling with rural violence, with the goal of undertaking guerrilla actions."[11] The students and professionals involved with these emerging political organizations wanted to attract former Liberal guerrilla leaders and active bandit groups to the political platform that they were formulating. This was the case, for example, with the attempt by a founder of the MOEC, Antonio Larrota, to recruit the guerrilla chieftain Adán de Jesús Aguirre ("El Aguila"), whose group in the department of Cauca was rapidly disintegrating. Later, a medical doctor, Tulio Bayer, tried to recruit Rosendo Colmenares in the northeastern territory of Vichada. And the nascent EPL wooed Julio Guerra in the northeast part of the department of Antioquia. In fact, during the early days of the ELN, Eriberto Espitia assumed the duties of leadership; he was a former comrade of "Chispas," a one-time Liberal guerrilla fighter who had become, in effect, a political bandit. The former Liberal leader of the guerrillas of the llano, Eduardo Franco Isaza, was active in the MOEC. And Roberto González Prieto ("Pedro Brincos") maintained relations with both the MOEC and the FUAR, headed by Gloria Gaitán and Luis Emiro Valencia, respectively.[12] (Ricardo Otero, a university professor of the same generation as Larrota, died fighting at González Prieto's side.)

The role of a person or a group born in the previous stage of the Violence was not, however, the Violence's only influence on the first attempts to form guerrilla enclaves. Even the location of the areas chosen to initiate guerrilla activities was determined by this tradition. For example, the selection of the so-called zone X of the nascent PCML was influenced by the fact that, in the past, a Liberal guerrilla chieftain named Rafael Rangel had been active there, and the people were familiar with the presence of armed groups.[13] Personages, regions, and traditions involved in past violence all contributed, then, to the formation of the first armed nuclei in the country. In terms of their objectives, a great chasm existed between the old guerrillas and the new, but the continuity between one stage and the next of the Violence rested on more bridges than normally is recognized.

There is no doubt that in the nuclei of survivors of the old Liberal guerrilla groups there was enormous frustration. They joined the Movimiento Revolucionario Liberal (Revolutionary Liberal Movement, MRL) in massive numbers and, in many cases, allied themselves with new revolutionary guerrilla groups. The map of the old violence and the map of the new had no substantial differences; both coincide with the map of the MRL and the Communist enclaves, forming the map of the resistance and of national rebellion.

The surprisingly close relationship between the Violence and the birth of the contemporary guerrilla movement is equally evident in the biographies of a large number of the leaders and rank-and-file militants in the various guerrilla movements. Alvaro Fayad (former commander of the M-19) was an eyewitness to the assassination of his own father by thugs in the service of the Conservative party.[14] Fabio Vásquez Castaño lost family members in the region where he was born, the Quindío.[15] Dr. Bayer always was influenced heavily by his experiences in the department of Antioquia during the period of the Violence.[16] Iván Marino Ospina had contact from his youth with political bandit leaders.[17] The great majority of the present leaders of the FARC participated in the guerrilla gangs of the fifties, including Jacobo Arenas, who had participated in spite of his urban origins.[18]

As Hernando Gómez Buendía astutely asserts, in Colombia one cannot speak of the "guerrilla movement" in the abstract, but rather one must speak of "guerrilla movements" in the plural given the extreme heterogeneity and dispersion of the armed insurrectionary groups.[19] The social composition of these groups, their ideologies, strategies, and military tactics, and the very conflicts that served to spark their emergence all differ greatly. It is this fact that best explains why, despite two decades of attempts at unification, dispersion still continues to be the groups' dominant feature. The formation in 1986 of the Coordinadora Guerrillera Nacional, which united six guerrilla organizations, led to a few joint military actions, but that organization is still far from the formation of a joint General Staff, a stage long since achieved in Guatemala and El Salvador.*

MOEC

The awakening of the non-Communist guerrilla movement begins with the MOEC, which appeared in 1959 and held its first congress in Cali in July 1960. Its principal promoters were a group of radical students that included Eduardo Aristizábal, Max Santos, Robinson Jiménez, and Larrota. For Juan Tairona, one of its leaders, it "initiated a new stage in the Colombian revolution, a stage which is characterized by the repudiation of the old reformist, pacifist, and electoral political line, and by the shift to an organized offensive by the masses."[20]

From the beginning, however, the MOEC contained two internal factions, one impatient to form guerrilla enclaves, and the other more oriented toward the task of urban political organization, especially among workers. The radical sector's attempts to launch the first enclave-style experiments in the country ended in disaster. Larrota traveled to Cuba in the middle of 1959, and on his return in 1961, he repaired to the mountains in the department of Cauca, where he tried to win over to his cause the leader of the political bandits in the area, "El Aguila," who ended up liquidating him. In Santa Rita, on the banks of the Infrida River (in the territory of Vichada), Colmenares, one of the few guerrillas of the llano who refused to surrender arms in 1953, launched a new enclave plan. He was urged on by Dr. Bayer, the physician from the city of Manizales, and by a brother of Antonio Larrota, Ramón. After several military operations in the area, internal conflicts and the military attacks by the Colombia and Vargas battalions under the command of then Lieutenant Colonel Alvaro Valencia Tovar shattered the experiment.[21]

The extreme heterogeneity of the Vichada group is a mirror of the ambiguity of these initial projects. The "Estado Mayor" was composed of the previously mentioned former Liberal guerrilla chieftain Colmenares, an army sergeant major who had fought in Korea named Flavio Barney (who ended by entering into secret negotiations with one

*The negotiations that led to the peace pact between the government and the M-19 in 1989 sharply divided the Coordinadora and deprived it of one of its strongest elements.

of his old commanders in Korea, Valencia Tovar, and betraying his companions in the venture), a former Communist who had been expelled from the party, Leonidas Castañeda, a rancher and militant of the MRL, Alfredo Marín Ospina, plus Dr. Bayer of the MOEC.

At the end of 1964 the MOEC split. One fragment was the sector that later would constitute the nucleus of the Maoist group MOIR, which would serve as a base for other failed guerrilla experiments. Another fragment was the FAL. There was a third sector that would disappear eventually, to be absorbed by other organizations. The FAL would give rise to several additional attempts to create armed enclaves, with more or less obscure ideologies, such as was the case with the Ejército Revolucionario de Colombia (Revolutionary Colombian Army, ERC). This group was formed in October 1961 by González Prieto in the town of Turbo, in the northern part of Antioquia. The group was annihilated later by the Fourth Brigade of Medellín.

ELN

The story of the ELN begins with the arrival of a group of Colombian scholarship students in Cuba at the height of the missile crisis of 1962. Part of this group asked for and obtained military training and began a series of discussions on the need to "form a group in order to go back to Colombia to develop the theory of Che Guevara, the theory of the guerrilla enclave or *foco*."[22] On November 11, 1962, stimulated by Fabio Vásquez Castaño, a militant in the Youth of the Revolutionary Liberal Movement (Juventud del Movimiento Revolucionario Liberal, or JMRL) and the only member of the group who had gone to Cuba to undertake future military action, the Brigada pro Liberación Nacional José Antonio Galán was created in Havana. The group was initially under the direction of Víctor Medina Morón (former regional secretary of the Communist party from Santander), Fabio Vásquez of the JMRL, and Eriberto Espitia, a former comrade of "Chispas."

Later, in Colombia, on July 4, 1964, on a ranch belonging to a Captain Parmenio, the ELN officially was born. The original team of sixteen men departed from the ranch.[23] On January 7, 1965, the ELN opened fire on the town of Simocota, Santander, and distributed the "Manifesto of Simacota" to attract national public attention. Simultaneously, the ELN began talks with the radical priest, Father Camilo Torres, and his Frente Unido.

The initial cadres of the ELN came primarily from the university sector and included Ricardo Lara Parada, Jaime Arenas, Medina Morón, and Juan de Dios Aguilera. Because of their initial implantation in a zone where the Violence had been very intense and the contemporary social conflict was great, involving as it did the struggles of militant petroleum workers and peasant land colonizers, the guerrillas made rapid strides at first.

Yet after decades of military action the ELN still has not been able to get past the simple survival phase. Its second stage, as planned from the beginning, was to have been one of relative equilibrium with the military, making it possible for the guerrillas to defend the areas in which they operate. This stage has not been reached.*

The central error of the first guerrilla organizations to emerge in Colombia, as illustrated by the fates of the MOEC, the FAL, and the ELN, was that the guerrillas thought an imminent prerevolutionary situation existed, that the possibility of national development was blocked totally, and that a political crisis was gestating. As one jailed militant of the ELN put it, "Wasn't this a sign that, from the very beginning, the ELN wanted to accommodate national reality to a conception of struggle, and not the reverse?"[24]

A number of causal factors explain the long stagnation of the ELN and the failure of the MOEC. Among the factors are these two groups' mechanical belief in the peasantry as the vanguard element (a position that ignored the rapid urbanization that was taking place in the country); extreme militarism, as reflected in the early incorporation and sacrifice of Father Torres as well as in the attempt to make his Frente Unido—the germ of a broad popular movement—into a simple appendage to their own military projects; emphasis on the military initiative in the absence of a political party and a mass front; consideration of the agricultural zones as simply settings for armed actions and not as regions where the concomitant building of peasant support and sustaining organizations was required; and guerrilla actions carried out with total autonomy from the level of organization and political consciousness of the masses that they were supposed to affect.

PCML

The birth of the PCML and, later, of its armed branch, the EPL, was determined not only by the general factors outlined for all the pioneer guerrilla organizations (radicalization of urban sectors, the Cuban

*In recent years the ELN has focused its activities almost exclusively on efforts to disrupt and destroy the oil industry (which it believes must be nationalized), attacking with great success the pipelines of the north. Effective economic sabotage (a strategy denounced even by other revolutionary groups) has not increased its political support, however, and may even have distanced it further from the general public it hopes to win over to a revolutionary position.

Revolution, exclusion from participation in the Frente Nacional) but also by a special factor, the Chinese-Soviet rupture. The party grew out of the concerns of a group of leaders, including Pedro León Arboleda, Pedro Vásquez Rendón, Libardo Mora Toro, and Francisco Garnica, of the youth wing of the Communist party (Juventud Comunista, JUCO). This group formed the Comité de Integración de los Movimientos Revolucionarios Colombianos (Committee for the Integration of the Revolutionary Movements of Colombia, CIMREC), and in May 1965, they held the new party's constitutional congress. A few months later, in December 1965, operating under the conception that there was an "incipient insurrectional situation" in the country, the 2d Plenary Session of the Central Committee convened. At this meeting the military line was elaborated and the leadership was ordered transferred to the countryside and there also was harsh criticism of the guerrilla enclave experiments that initially inspired the armed groups, including the PCML itself. CIMREC also adopted the Chinese thesis of "prolonged popular war" as a basis for their action on this level.

In fact, the first armed experiments of this organization were inspired by the *foco* theory, which led to such dismal failures as the defection of Uriel Barrera, the commander in zone X; the liquidation in its embryonic stage of the group led by Jesús María Alzate in the north of the department of Valle; and the capture and assassination under torture by the army of Garnica, of Carlos Alberto Morales, and of Ricardo Torres. On December 17, 1967, the first PCML guerrilla unit, or *foco*, was formed in the northeast of the department of Antioquia under the leadership of Vásquez Rendón and Francisco Caraballo. This was the "Francisco Garnica" front, the first embryonic entity of the EPL. The EPL, together with the so-called Patriotic Juntas (at the regional and local levels), sought the establishment of "liberated zones" in Colombia. From its beginning this experiment had the support of Julio Guerra, a former militant Liberal guerrilla leader from the MRL who made a decisive contribution to the implantation of the PCML in this area.

In subsequent years the PCML and the EPL were often on the verge of total extinction. This situation was due in part to the scope of the military offensives launched against them in the 1960s and in part to the deep schisms that affected them internally, resulting in separate groups such as the Marxist-Leninist League, the Marxist-Leninist Tendency, and the urban group, Pedro León Arboleda (PLA).

Reconstruction of the PCML began with its 11th Congress, held in April 1980, in which the group broke with Maoism and its sequels. "Then we adopted the strategy and objective of building bases of support, surrounding the cities from the country, and recognizing the role of the working class and sectors like the intellectuals. We thus abandoned the idea of prolonged popular war, which is the Maoist theory, and we stopped overestimating the peasantry."[25] The PCML's overcoming of extreme sectarianism, its reevaluation of the political process as a basis for rejuvenating the armed groups, and its infiltration into union and urban popular media all explain the fact that, contrary to expectations, the PCML was one of the groups to sign the ill-fated truce agreements with the Betancur government in 1984.

FARC

While the formation of present-day Communist guerrilla groups has its immediate origin in the military aggression against the self-defended peasant regions in 1964, the groups' roots lie much deeper in time.

> At the beginning of the thirties, the agricultural workers who put into effect the Communist slogan of "the revolutionary taking of the land" by occupying the large estates and establishing agricultural settlements on public lands in several departments, employed self-defense to protect their conquests. . . . Self-defense organizations, such as the "Guardia Roja," the "Correo Rojo," the Peasant Leagues, and the Litigation Commissions effectively combined three fronts of struggle: defense against aggression, using arms if necessary; solidarity; and the search for "legal" solutions.[26]

From its beginning the Communist party was an important presence in certain rural areas, especially the Sumapaz and Viotá regions in the southwest of the department of Cundinamarca and the southern part of the department of Tolima. Beginning in the fifties, armed nuclei aligned with the party appeared in some of these areas. As early as October 22, 1949, the Central Committee of the party issued a clandestine appeal that circulated all over the country proposing "to the proletariat and the people the necessity of defending themselves, answering the violence of the fascist bandits with the organized violence of the masses." Later, the 13th Plenary Session of the party presented Communists with the concrete task of "organizing self-defense in every region threatened by reactionary attacks." In 1949 "resistance committees" composed of both Liberals and Communists were formed in opposition to the Conservative dictatorship. Later, the first Communist-oriented guerrilla units were mobilized, but they ceased to function during the process of pacification undertaken by General Rojas in 1953.

In 1955, however, government violence began again. This time it was directed against the Communist-influenced regions where the guerrilla movement had been weakened. This was the war of Villarrica, where once more the military was mobilized. "History confirms the fact that out of self-defense the guerrilla movement arose, a transformation wrought in the face of circumstances. [Self-defense] is the guerrilla's waiting room, the immense 'forest' where a guerrilla movement can disappear when national political conditions were adverse to its continued existence as such."[27]

This new stage culminated with the amnesty of President Alberto Lleras Camargo and the beginning of the Frente Nacional. Then came a renewed attack against the zones in which the old guerrillas had gone into hiding. These regions were called "independent republics" by then Conservative Congressman Alvaro Gómez Hurtado; the name helped to justify the military's iniquitous action.

> *It is not an exaggeration to conclude that in Colombia, from a strictly military point of view, the enemy was invented in the name of a continental response....* The inspiration for this ideological-military offensive at the beginning of the sixties came from outside the country. A weak president was pressured to appoint a new kind of officer as head of the military, someone who was sympathetic to ideas being advanced by the Alliance for Progress.[28]

The result was truly a Pyrrhic military victory with tremendous implications. The use of thousands of soldiers to dislodge a few hundred peasant families resulted in a situation, twenty years later, in which the Communist-inspired guerrilla groups of the FARC had a network of twenty-seven armed fronts.

Initially, nuclei of militants from the zones afflicted by the military offensives, including Marquetalia, Riochiquito, and areas in the east and south of Tolima, held a meeting on July 20, 1964. Calling themselves the Southern Bloc, they issued the guerrillas' agrarian program, and, two years later, at the 2d National Conference of Guerrilla Groups, the FARC came into being.

The FARC did not arise—as had been the case with the first guerrilla experiments reviewed here—from a strictly voluntarist decision or as a mechanical effort to transplant the Cuban Revolution. On the contrary, as had happened in 1949 and 1955, the FARC emerged as a people's response to official violence and militarist aggression. This extensive political experience is central to understanding the maturity demonstrated by the leadership of the FARC in their response to the change in the political situation produced under the administration of President Belisario Betancur.

The 10th through the 13th congresses of the Communist party, however, viewed the FARC as a "simple strategic reserve" useful in case a military dictatorship ascended to power. Since there was not any imminent plan to seize the government, the FARC developed during these years in response to local situations in which rural workers and smallholders united to defend their interests in the face of violence on the part of large landowners or the military. (Both kinds of violence were superimposed in areas of land colonization.)[29] The guerrilla movement thus was constituted in the form of a regional structure of social warfare, of individual and collective survival, which explains why it has been so deeply rooted in the areas where it operates. In such areas, guerrilla groups, the Communist party, and agrarian organizations mutually reinforce each other, generating a regional power to be reckoned with. In this way, the countryside ceases to be a simple theater for fighting and becomes instead a setting for the building of real local power.

When the truce with the guerrilla movement was signed in 1984, rebel organizations unquestionably obtained the status of recognized belligerents. With this political development, the FARC rose above its condition of peasant guerrilla movement and established itself, through the legal party Unión Patriótica, as one of the two axes around which the destiny of the Colombian guerrilla movement revolves at the present time.

M-19

The M-19 was to revolutionize the Colombian guerrilla movement as it sought to make the armed movement into a genuine interlocutor of the government and a generator of proposals for national policy making. It arose as a product of the merging of a sector that had been expelled from the Communist party and the FARC (Jaime Bateman, Alvaro Fayad, Iván Marino Ospina, and Carlos Pizarro) and a sector that came out of the socialist wing of ANAPO (Carlos Toledo Plata, Andrés Almarales, and Israel Santamaría).

At first, those members who came from the FARC had the idea of forming urban guerrilla enclaves under the name Movimiento de Liberación Nacional (MLN), as the Uruguayan Tupamaros had done. But the popular tide that was sweeping the country at the time, under ANAPO's dynamic force, "produced, among the leaders of the MLN, a more realistic course that led to the choice of a name based on a national event (the allegedly stolen presidential election of April 19, 1970, when ANAPO's candidate barely was defeated by the candidate of the Frente Nacional)."[30]

The M-19 was born in 1972 at a meeting held in Bogotá attended by twenty-two people. The group's first act was to steal the sword of the Liberator, Simón Bolívar. This event underlines the profound split between the M-19 and the rest of the country's guerrilla organizations: if, through ANAPO, they wanted to put the guerrilla movement into the nation, through the recovery of Bolívar's tradition they wanted to put the nation into the guerrilla movement.

The new guerrilla organization started from the premise that national symbols were a national heritage and not a simple set of bourgeois values; therefore, the guerrilla movement had to rescue the nation's roots and its historical traditions. Between the stealing of Bolívar's sword and the formation in 1986 of the Batallón América,[31] there is an undeniable connecting thread: the conception of the present struggle as a continuation of the crusade for freedom, as the "second independence." The M-19's good judgment in exploiting the symbolism of national roots is one of the factors that made it possible for the guerrilla groups to assume a role as protagonists in state affairs during the government of Betancur. One is no longer dealing here with forces manipulated from the outside but with national organizations identified with the historical heritage. As with the resurrection of Martí by the Cuban Movimiento 26 de Julio, of Sandino by the Nicaraguan FSLN, or of the Salvadoran Farabundo Martí, the resurrection of Bolívar by the M-19 symbolizes the "Latinamericanization" of popular struggles on the continent, the demarcation of their boundaries from those of the international sphere.

Something that has become evident, however, only with the passing of the years is the enormous disparity between the M-19's capacity to rejuvenate—which stimulated the subversion of subversion—and its weakness in the area of forming an organizational machine and a coherent political platform. The M-19's attempt to make itself into a decisive factor in the internal power structure of ANAPO failed. In fact, the socialist ANAPO group, which published the newspaper *Mayorías* and which had managed to elevate one of its leaders, Israel Santamaría, to third in the national hierarchy after General Rojas and his daughter, María Eugenia, ultimately was expelled from that party. "Our error when we came to ANAPO was that instead of merging with this group and piercing its soul with the M-19's banner, we began a fight to strip it of its own ideology and impose leftist ideology on it."[32] The socialists were expelled without having been able to consolidate themselves internally. As a result, the rank and file of the party either remained within the traditional organization or entered a phase of political apathy.

A later attempt to join FIRMES, a reformist Liberal group, in order to convert it into a channel for political expression, likewise ended in a disastrous failure. The roots of these setbacks are found in a permanent feature of the M-19's political strategy, the group's tendency to substitute audacious political-military feats for the patient work of building a political movement. These feats included stealing Bolívar's sword, assassinating José Raquel Mercado (the controversial leader of the CTC labor federation), stealing weapons from the army's north Bogotá arsenal, unleashing guerrillas in Nariño and Chocó, seizing the embassy of the Dominican Republic, and, in 1985, taking the Palace of Justice. By behaving in this manner, the M-19's importance as a protagonist on the national level was characterized more by its "lucky hits" than by its shaping of a political-military movement with grassroots support and a solid organization. A sui generis movement,[33] in spite of its ups and downs, the M-19 produced a revolution in the heart of the guerrilla movement after the taking of the Dominican embassy. Through that action it succeeded in moving from the guerrilla as protagonist fighting against the military forces to guerrilla as political protagonist fighting the state. The guerrilla movement switched its main target—now it uses military means to make the government negotiate on matters of national policy, that is, to pay attention to proposals put forth by the opposition.

This new modality took the form of armed opposition under the administration of President Julio Cesar Turbay Ayala since it was the only kind of behavior possible within the policy implemented under the repressive security statute. And, in spite of the provisional formation of some committees to promote dialogue with the guerrillas, the armed opposition continued under Betancur. In fact, at times of crucial political decisions, the leadership of the M-19 always favored the continuation of the military route and systematically rejected the option to become an important force in the democratic process. Its idea always has been to establish a military force as a negotiating factor with the state, at first by consolidating a southern front in Caquetá and, later, a western front in Valle, a policy orchestrated with the encouragement of the Coordinadora Guerrillera Nacional.*

---

*Since these words were written, the chain of events unleashed by the M-19's takeover of the Palace of Justice in Bogotá in 1985 has had unexpected, even paradoxical, consequences for the M-19, the guerrilla groups in general, and the peace process itself. This bloody event resulted in the deaths of scores of government officials, including the majority of the Supreme Court justices, and the massacre by the Colombian army of the M-19 cadres who had taken them hostage. On the one hand, this outcome seems to have discredited in the eyes of public opinion all of the parties involved—the M-19, the government of Betancur, and the military. As a result, the promising peace initiatives of the Betancur regime, which had advanced to a cease-fire and a dialogue with

The Process of National Reconciliation and the Guerrilla Movement

During the administration of President Alfonso López Michelsen (1974–1978), the government tried, for the first time, to open negotiations with the armed groups in search of a solution to the political violence. This effort was frustrated by various factors, among them the systematic blocking by the military of any kind of dialogue with the ELN, which was considered to be on the brink of total annihilation.[34] The civilian-military crisis of 1975, in which General Valencia Tovar, then commander of the army, was relieved of his command, was a consequence of this fact. After this dialogue failed due to the inflexibility of the military establishment, the country would have to wait until 1982 to begin this process in earnest.

During the government of President Turbay Ayala (1978–1982), guerrilla actions, especially those instigated by the M-19, reached new, unexpected levels compared to the previous decade. It was during this period, for example, that the M-19 stole hundreds of weapons from the army's arsenal in northern Bogotá and engineered the taking of the Dominican embassy. The government sought to resolve the situation through an authoritarian response. It put into effect a draconian security statute and gave virtually total autonomy to the military forces in the management of internal public order, a policy that led to widespread torture, arbitrary arrest, and political assassinations. By the time Turbay Ayala's term was over, he had managed only to aggravate internal conditions, and the country found itself on the edge of a generalized confrontation.

This scenario was the background to President Betancur's (1982–1986) reformist platform, which sought to defuse the time bomb that was ticking in the country. To accomplish this, the government tried to implement—as was strictly necessary—a policy of democratic reform and a peace pact with the guerrillas.[35]

the major guerrilla groups, including the M-19 and the FARC, were derailed. On the other hand, these same events eventually led a weakened M-19 into negotiations with the regime of Virgilio Barco (1986–1990), a process that resulted, to the surprise of many, in a negotiated peace between the M-19 and the government. The pact that they signed called for national dialogue and reform (long-standing goals of the M-19), amnesty, and an end to the M-19's insurgency against the state. These developments, consummated in 1989, left only the Marxist guerrilla groups (most importantly, the FARC and the ELN) still in arms against the government.

Betancur's idea was to be developed in five steps. At the beginning of his term, the president convoked a multiparty political summit (September 8, 1982) to discuss political reform. Subsequently, a peace commission was formed (September 19, 1982), an amnesty law was passed (November 19, 1982), a truce agreement with the main guerrilla movements was signed (March and August, 1984), and, finally, during 1984 and 1985, a series of legislative proposals was presented to the Congress of the Republic, oriented toward cementing the democratic advances.

In response to this government project, two different strategies were developed gradually by the guerrilla organizations, the FARC's "democratization of war" and the M-19's "guerrillization of democracy."[36] These two sequences of action can be compared (using Vladimir Zabala's scheme) as follows:

FARC-EP

1. Growth in the countryside.
2. Movement from the agrarian to the urban through political action.
3. Appeal to social sectors excluded from access to land, credit, and commerce.

Goals

1. Control of territory as key to control of population.
2. Political route, including participation in electoral politics.
3. Involve the people in politics in order to move on later to other forms of struggle.
4. Use of the principle: "War is the continuation of politics using other means."

M-19

1. Growth in the cities.
2. Movement from the urban to the rural through military action.
3. Appeal to marginalized social sectors in the city, especially professionals and the underemployed.

Goals

1. Impact population regardless of territorial control.

2. Use politics to mobilize population to military action regardless of position on electoral politics.
3. Involve the guerrilla in the nation in order later to involve the nation with the guerrilla.
4. Use of the principle: "Politics is the continuation of war using other means."

In spite of their differences, in both cases we find a qualitative and quantitative leap beyond earlier positions. Two factors converge to explain this phenomenon. On the one hand, there is the overt activity in the political arena by the guerrilla groups, who passed from the limitations of "armed propaganda" to the status of a pole generating political proposals for the whole society. On the other hand, during the last decade, social movements of all sorts have been multiplying at a geometric rate, and they are now at the stage of national organization. Examples are the Coordinadora Nacional de Movimientos Cívicos, Organización Nacional Indígena de Colombia, the national meetings of the Movimientos Políticos Regionales, and the Coordinadora Nacional de Acción Comunal.

Let us take a brief look at these two factors.

The assumption of a major political role by the armed movement began on a national scale after the seizure of the Dominican embassy with the M-19's proposal for a "truce for peace" and with the opening of a great national dialogue. Bateman's attempt to hold a political summit in Panama was aimed in the same direction. However, as already pointed out, the authoritarianism in this period only allowed this nascent national political presence to be expressed in the form of an "armed opposition." The opening created by Betancur established new possibilities for guerrilla expression. Guerrilla demands—amnesty for political prisoners, national dialogue, democratic reform, truce, and pacification—became the axes around which national debate revolved during subsequent years.

These developments constitute a genuine rupture with the past. In the first stage of the guerrilla movement, the insurgent forces above all stressed the ideological and military aspects of their activities and had a disdainful attitude toward political activity. Among others, the Frente Unido, Golconda (a radical Catholic movement), and ANAPO were sought out by the guerrillas to orchestrate military enterprises, but these entities were not considered important or decisive in themselves. The fate of FIRMES, which the M-19 tried to convert into a vehicle for its own maneuvers, is the best example of this tendency.

As for the second factor, there is no doubt that the systematic blocking of citizen participation that was due to the narrowness of proper political channels in a "limited democracy" had led, first, to a growing skepticism with respect to the ruling institutions and, above all, to the emergence of noninstitutional forms of participation, often in open defiance of the legal system (civil strikes, for example). This dynamic of the deinstitutionalization of social and political struggle was of such magnitude that, in the midst of the negotiations for peace, three new organizations were born: the Quintín Lame, Patria Libre, and the Ejército Revolucionario de los Trabajadores (ERT); all three were members of the Coordinadora Guerrillera Nacional.

After the crisis of the national peasant organization in 1978, the indigenous movement was the only rural organized force that existed on both the regional level and the national level. Although the Quintín Lame was hardly an armed branch of these legal organizations, it was a factor in the general context of the growing viability and deepening of the indigenous struggle.[37] Likewise, in the case of Patria Libre and the ERT, one cannot ignore the emergence of popular urban fronts, which, like "A Luchar" (To Fight), the "Movimiento Pan y Libertad" (Movement for Bread and Liberty), and others, were an expression of the efforts to centralize nationally the scattered social movements. These factors explain the dynamism of the two poles of the guerrilla movement today.

The creation of the Batallón América and the formation of the Coordinadora Guerrillera Nacional followed the M-19's successful actions in the urban area of Cali. These actions had the broadest impact in the whole agitated history of guerrilla fighting in the country and gave the M-19 the initiative on the military front at the regional level. The M-19 had been the first guerrilla force to move beyond guerrilla warfare in its classic version (founded on mobility and surprise) to achieve a second phase, which enabled it, as a result of the concentration of men and firepower, to sustain, in a prolonged fashion, the structure of a war of positions held, a war of territorial control. Still, the M-19's salient failing has been its manifest inability—or simply its disdaining—to generate a complementary political platform that would allow it to act effectively on the political stage. It relies on the militarization of the fight for democracy, military action with little mediation. Only as an afterthought has it formed ad hoc, feeble, and short-lived political committees.

As for the FARC, its rate of growth truly has been unexpected. After the armed colonization of zones such as Marquetalia, Riochiquito, Guayabero, and El Pato it shed its local character and became a phenomenon that embraced extensive regions. Today, the FARC, through the Unión Patriótica, is the fundamental force in a territory that extends from Arauca to Caquetá, with zones of influence in other regions in the center of the country as well, primarily in the departments of Antioquia, Santander, and Tolima. In this process the FARC has begun to overtake the Communist party and has been emerging slowly as a political movement, heterogeneous in its composition and heterodox in its postulates. The impact this process will have in future years on the languid and sectarian Communist party undoubtedly will be enormous.

The development of the Unión Patriótica can be explained above all by the fact that in the Communist party-FARC dynamic, the latter took the historical initiative, shattering the immobility, the stereotyped language, and the destructive sectarianism that long had characterized the Communist organization.

Conclusion

In recent years there certainly has been a qualitative and quantitative advance in the armed movement. Its roots go back to the Liberal administrations of Lopéz Michelsen and Turbay Ayala, which deepened social inequalities (using neoliberal development models) and brutally suppressed popular protest, thereby generating an unanticipated legitimation of the armed movement. This growing legitimation is expressed in the increased appeal of the tactic of "armed colonization" utilized by the FARC,[38] and in the formation of the Coordinadora Guerrillera Nacional, with its visible and invisible, explicit and implicit, ties to the popular movement.

However, this relative strengthening of the guerrilla movement does not mean in the least that it has historical viability. On the one hand, the guerrilla advance has been accompanied by an unexpected development of paramilitary groups all over the country, which threaten to plunge the country into the horrors of a generalized "dirty war."* Here is a partial list: Muerte a Secuestradores (Death to Kidnappers), El Escuadrón de la Muerte (The Death Squad), El Grupo (The Group), Muerte a Abigeos (Death to Rustlers), Castigo a Firmantes e Intermediarios Estafadores (Punishment to Swindling Intermediaries),

*Here, Pizarro touches on a theme that has grown dramatically in importance in recent years and which reinforces his conclusions. By the late 1980s several of the guerrilla groups, including the FARC, had become involved deeply in the cocaine trade while the paramilitary right, at times indistinguishable from the drug mafia, had stepped up its war on the legal left (particularly on leaders of the Unión Patriótica and the labor unions) and on the state itself. These issues are discussed more fully in Chapter 13.

El Embrión (The Embryo), Alfa 83, Pro Limpieza del Valle del Magdalena (Pro Cleanup of the Magdalena Valley), Los Tiznados (The Soot Faced), Movimiento Anticomunista Colombiano (Colombian Anticommunist Movement), Los Grillos (The Crickets), El Escuadrón Machete (The Machete Squadron), Falange, Muerte a Invasores, Colaboradores y Patrocinadores (Death to Land Invaders, Their Collaborators and Supporters), and Los Comandos Verdes (The Green Rangers).

The excessive and demoralizing prolongation of guerrilla warfare, on the other hand—far beyond anything expected by its initiators—has led to the spread of reprehensible activities of common criminality such as kidnapping and extortion. These crimes have weakened the ethical bases of guerrilla action and affected its social legitimacy. What is the difference between the common criminals eliminated by the FARC in order to win popular support and those assassinated by the group Terminator, which is financed by large local landowners? Finally, as leftist leaders themselves have recognized, the guerrilla movement does not have the capacity to liquidate the army, nor does the army have the capability of destroying the guerrillas. Twenty years of political violence have demonstrated this fact and have created a climate of fratricidal confrontation that shows no hope of resolution.

If civil war should occur, though, have the guerrilla chiefs even thought of the national cost of a generalized confrontation and of the unheard of costs that the eventual national reconstruction would entail? A civil war in Colombia would be a new Armero,* from the Guajira to the Amazon. Now more than ever the process begun by the Betancur administration to implement a policy of democratic reform accompanied by sustained negotiations with the insurgent movement seems irreversibly to be the country's only alternative.

Democratic reform is a policy that must be carried out without the ambiguity manifested by the Betancur government. Betancur's government took advantage of the truce with the FARC to try selectively to wipe out the rest of the armed movement. Even less needed is the disgraceful project implemented under Turbay Ayala's government, which brought the country to the brink of the abyss. The process of pacification is not dependent solely on the goodwill of the guerrilla chiefs. It is a national responsibility in which the armed forces, the labor unions, the traditional parties, and especially the right have to accept that any negotiation process implies mutual concessions.

*City in the department of Tolima totally destroyed by a volcanic eruption in 1986.

Notes

1. Regis Debray, *La guérilla du Che* (Paris, 1974), 170.

2. The second wave would take as its model the triumph of the Sandinista revolution, which was founded not on a presumed guerrilla base but on an extensive front of popular masses. "Nicaragua revived the enthusiasm of the vanguards for armed struggle," Jaime Bateman would affirm in one of his last interviews (Ramón Jimeno, *Oiga hermano* [Bogotá, 1984], 16).

3. Initially, the Marxist-Leninist Communist party, which was formed on July 17, 1965, as an organization separate from the Colombian Communist party, promoted three guerrilla zones—"X," "H," and "FLOR"—within the framework of the guerrilla enclave tradition. See Fabiola Calvo, *EPL: Diez hombres, un ejército, una historia* (Bogotá, 1985).

4. Ernesto Guevara, "La guerra de guerrillas," in *Obras, 1957–1967*, 2 vols. (Havana, 1977), 1:31.

5. Ibid., 32.

6. Due to the failure of the first guerrilla enclave experiments, the PCML adopted as its own the Maoist theory of "prolonged popular war," which in turn would be questioned in 1980 at the organization's 11th Congress.

7. The Communist party was declared illegal by the National Constitutional Assembly, which had been convened under the government of Rojas Pinilla, in Legislative Act No. 6 of 1954 (which was made into law in Decree No. 0434 of 1956).

8. (Emphasis in original.) This is the general tone that characterizes all of the declarations of the period either by the Communist party or by the guerrillas whom they influenced. See Gilberto Vieira, "Informe al VIII Congreso del Partido Comunista," in *Documentos Políticos*, 13 (Bogotá, 1959), 36: "The possibility of a peaceful transition from capitalism to socialism is based on the new world balance of power and the changes that the existence of the socialist camp, headed by the Soviet Union, is producing all over the world." Equally revealing is the document signed by Manuel Marulanda and Ciro Castaño (Communist guerrilla chieftains) in support of the pacification campaign of President Alberto Lleras Camargo in 1958, transcribed by Gonzalo Sánchez in *Ensayos de historia social y política del siglo XX* (Bogotá, 1985), 272.

9. "A considerable proportion of the 'members' do not accept the ruling political system, questioning, in this way, the legitimacy of the government, and routing their mobilization through instruments that are marginal, informal, and legally barred from political action. The result is a growing polarization between informality and formality in political matters and the chronic deinstitutionalization of the political struggle." Thus the accurate verdict of Gabriel Silva in his article, "Desarrollo económico, paz y reforma política: Un conflicto latente," in the March 1986 publication *Documentos* issued by the Medellín newspaper *El Mundo*.

10. In his chronology of the stages of political violence that the country passed through during its Republican phase, Gonzalo Sánchez states that "the third stage is the one that began to gestate during the course of the Violence

itself, but particularly in the 60s: this is the stage we are still living in today."
It is a stage born in "the very guts of the Violence." Sánchez, *Ensayos*, 218, 274.

11. Russell Ramsey, *Guerrilleros y soldados* (Bogotá, 1981), 297.

12. See Gonzalo Sánchez and Donny Meertens, *Bandoleros, gamonales y campesinos: El caso de la Violencia en Colombia* (Bogotá, 1983), 135.

13. Calvo, *EPL*, 31.

14. Patrica Lara, *Siembra vientos y recogerás tempestades* (Bogotá, 1982), 55.

15. Cristina de la Torre, "Nacimiento del ELN: Revelaciones de Ricardo Lara Parada," *Trópicos* 3 (1980): 23.

16. Ramsey, *Guerrilleros y soldados*, 297.

17. Lara, *Siembra vientos*, 66.

18. Jacobo Arenas, *Cese el fuego: Una historia política de las FARC* (Bogotá: 1985), 81.

19. Hernando Gómez Buendía, "Procesos de reconciliación nacional en América Latina, Colombia: Un punto de vista liberal," mimeograph (Bogotá, 1985).

20. Proletarización, *¿De dónde venimos, hacia dónde vamos, hacia dónde debemos ir?* (Medellín, 1975), 86.

21. Tulio Bayer, "El levantamiento del Vichada," *Trópicos* 2 (1979).

22. De la Torre, "Nacimiento del ELN," 22.

23. *Insurrección* 33 (1970).

24. Mauricio Trujillo, "Un guerrillero escribe desde la cárcel," *Trópicos* 9 (1981): 19.

25. Calvo, *EPL*, 121 ff.

26. José Modesto Campos, "Las formas superiores de lucha en Colombia: Experiencia creadora de las masas," *Estudios Marxistas* 10 (1975): 3.

27. Ibid., 6.

28. Pierre Gilhodés, "El ejército colombiano analiza la Violencia," a report presented at the 1st International Symposium on the Violence in Colombia (Bogotá, 1984), 305.

29. W. Ramírez Tobón, "La guerrilla rural en Colombia: ¿Una vía hacia la colonización armada?" *Estudios Rurales Latinamericanos* 4:2 (1981).

30. Vladimir Zabala, "La toma del Palacio de Justicia," mimeograph (San Cristóbal, 1986), 5.

31. The America Battalion is made up of two national organizations, the M-19 and the Quintín Lame; members of the Túpac Amaru group (Peru) and Alfaro Vive Carajo (Ecuador) attend as honorary members.

32. Olga Behar, *Las guerras de la paz* (Bogotá, 1985), 85.

33. Malcolm Deas, "El rompecabezas de la paz," *El Tiempo, Lecturas Dominicales*, April 19, 1986.

34. Arturo Alape, *La Paz, la violencia: Testigos de excepción* (Bogotá, 1985), p. 367.

35. Ricardo Santamaría and Gabriel Silva, *Proceso político en Colombia* (Bogotá, 1984), 69.

36. Zabala, "La toma del Palacio de Justicia," 21.

37. Ibid., 32.

38. A recent work, which could not be taken into consideration in this essay, questions the general use of the concept "armed colonization" to explain, in every case, the implantation of the FARC. See Jaime Jaramillo, Leonidas Mora, and Fernando Cubides, *Colonización, coca y guerrilla* (Bogotá, 1986), 72.

9

Violence and Land Colonization

Alfredo Molano

There are many different stories of land colonization and its relationship to violence in Colombia. Best known (and the subject of a classic work in English, James Parsons's *Antioqueño Colonization in Western Colombia* [Berkeley, 1949]) is the story of the nineteenth-century movement of settlers south from Antioquia in the central range into the vast region that would become the heart of the country's coffee economy in the twentieth century. This area, composed of the modern departments of Caldas, Risaralda, and Quindío, and parts of southern Antioquia, northern Tolima, and northern Valle del Cauca, became the core of the smallholder coffee regime, with all of its ideological and political implications for the Violence (see Chapter 4).

There is also the story of the alienation of public lands during the late nineteenth and early twentieth centuries told in this volume by Catherine LeGrand (Chapter 3). It concentrates on areas generally outside the smallholder coffee zones, where colonization led, violently, to the consolidation of large estates and engendered movements of agrarian protest in the 1920s and 1930s. And there is the story of the struggle for land during the Violence, a story begun in the essays by Gonzalo Sánchez (Chapter 5), Carlos Miguel Ortiz Sarmiento (Chapter 6), and Medófilo Medina (Chapter 7).

This chapter, by Alfredo Molano, picks up the story of agrarian struggle during the Violence and follows its implications for colonization and violence up to the present day. Molano begins with an account of the offensive undertaken by the government of Gustavo Rojas Pinilla against isolated areas in southeastern Cundinamarca and eastern Tolima where rural workers had taken possession of large estates and, under radical Liberal and Communist leaders, were seeking to maintain their gains by force of arms. (These are the regions referred to by Molano as the Independent Republics.) Eventually, forced out by the army's offensive, these groups marched southeast, over the eastern chain of the Andes, and into the virgin forests of the piedmont of the national territories of Meta and Caquetá, where they colonized the land as subsistence farmers.

Molano takes great pains in describing the process through which these settlers eventually entered into economic crisis in the 1960s and 1970s. Faced with the loss of their land to big ranchers and to large-scale commercial farmers, the settlers proved receptive to revolutionary guerrilla groups, especially to the FARC, who protected them and often provided the basic services and justice that the Colombian government had proven unable or unwilling to extend them. The final chapter in this saga of colonization and violence begins around 1980, when drug dealers enter these areas. Molano describes the complex, violent relationships that have resulted from the contention between smallholders (who often grow coca) and their guerrilla protectors (who exact tribute from the drug trade and now participate directly in it), the drug processors and traffickers and the right-wing paramilitary organizations that they finance to protect their interests, and, finally, the Colombian army and government officials sent to defeat the guerrillas and destroy the drug trade.

Alfredo Molano is a sociologist. His widely read books, *Los años del tropel: Relatos de la Violencia* (Bogotá, 1985), *Selva adentro: Una historia oral de la colonización del Guaviare* (Bogotá, 1987), and *Siguiendo el corte: Relatos de guerras y de tierras* (Bogotá, 1989), are based on oral sources.

Land colonization has been a permanent feature in the history of Colombia. The search for new land and its improvement and integration into economic production has never ceased from the moment the conquest was abandoned as a military enterprise. And violence has characterized and still characterizes Colombia's civil and political life. Naturally, the relation between the two phenomena cannot be reduced to a simple correlation. On the contrary, it is a correlation marked by phases or modalities of intertwined relations.

General Considerations

The modern phase of land colonization began in the 1930s and 1940s, when latifundios, traditional large landed estates, slowly began to be converted into commercial agricultural enterprises, still conserving, however, their most characteristic feature: the control over vast expanses of land, which assured easy dealings with labor. Clear testimony to this expansion is the agrarian struggle of the so-called Liberal Republic. By the 1950s, colonization was linked to other factors: the crisis of the peasant economy, demographic growth, political violence, industrialization, and the most dramatic consequence of all these phenomena, urban unemployment.

Political violence is not merely an expression of economic factors, that is, it is not a demonstration of the so-called disintegration of the peasant economy. Violence in Colombia is the result of multiple factors, one of which is the constriction of the political system and its inability to welcome and integrate the new social interest groups unleashed by economic change. The power monopoly of the Liberal and Conservative parties and the alignment of the people under these two banners—which have an aura almost of religious trappings—prevented the great economic and social changes unleashed by development from finding suitable avenues of political action. The parties wanted to govern the new reality under the same power system as before. This impossible match emerged as a contradiction, which was expressed as political violence. But at the same time, it prevented violence from assuming a social and progressive cast, up to a point. In the long run this pattern was counterproductive for the system itself since in Colombia all movements for social progress have had to pursue a path of political opposition and to use violence as their method.

In the 1960s and 1970s land colonization accelerated. On the one hand, the peasant economy—composed basically of tiny plots and situated primarily in the mountainous areas—found itself in a profound state of crisis. On the other hand, demographic growth reached its climax, and the violence began to shed its partisan colors as it sought social expression and overflowed the narrow political channels in which it hitherto had been confined. Thousands of peasants were driven from their land by economic and political circumstances; many others reached adulthood and found themselves landless. Simultaneously, the market for urban and rural employment became saturated. The agrarian reform begun in the 1960s was a failure even in its efforts at internal colonization, and the new peasant contingents had to move to vacant public lands in the piedmont of the eastern plains, the middle Magdalena River valley, Perijá, the Sierra Nevada de Santa Marta, and Urabá.

The land colonization of the 1950s and 1960s must be distinguished from that of the 1970s and 1980s. The main driving force of the first wave was traditional partisan political conflict since usually political motivations concealed the stealing and concentration of land parcels and the expulsion of peasants. This is what happened in the department of Valle del Cauca, in some coffee regions, and in quite a few regions of the Atlantic Coast. Many peasants from these areas joined guerrilla groups loyal to one party or the other and, for reasons of physical and social survival, settled in inhospitable places reputed to be public land. This is how the colonization of the middle Magdalena River valley and the lower Cauca River valley began as well as the colonization of a large part of the piedmont of the eastern plains, from Támara and Pajarito to Granada and Fuente de Oro.

Origins of Armed Colonization

The regions of Sumapaz and Tequendama in the eastern part of the department of Tolima and the southwestern part of the department of Cundinamarca were exceptions to the trend just described. In these regions large coffee estates prevailed, and the struggle for land, whose antecedents went back to the 1930s, had achieved solid forms of organization that little by little became separate from traditional party conflict and emerged as movements with clear social missions. Persecuted by the army and the large landowners, the agrarian leagues of the 1930s gradually became an armed movement that combined the agrarian reform experiments of the radical Liberal Juan de la Cruz Varela and the organizational and military experience of the Communist party. Veterans of the struggle for land in the coffee zone of southwestern Cundinamarca, these different versions of the same experience took place in the eastern part of the department of Tolima, a region colonized by peasants who came from the Tequendama and the Sumapaz areas and also by some peasants from among those driven out of the *municipios* of Chaparral, El Líbano, and Rovira, in central and northern Tolima (to mention only three localities for which there is data).

Military fortification began in these regions before 1953, and political organization solidified between 1953 and 1955, the year in which Gustavo Rojas Pinilla unleashed an unprecedented military offensive in the government's fight against the guerrillas. That offensive, called the war of Villarrica, gave rise to two processes—the regrouping of the guerrilla movement and peasant marches—which, with the passage of time, have become vital factors in explaining the current situation of violence that is overrunning the country.

In the regrouping of armed men in the southern part of Tolima the names Charro Negro, Tirofijo, Ciro Castaño, and Isauro Yosa have become famous. Here the armed self-defense movements were founded that organized themselves into the so-called Independent Republics of Marquetalia—El Pato, Riochiquito, and Guayabero—and that later evolved into the Fuerzas Armadas Revolucionarias Colombianas (FARC). The activities of these groups not only were military in nature but also were economic, and thus the groups colonized vast regions. Their accomplishment has been called armed colonization. The main threat to these movements arose from harassment by the army and from the interests of the large landowners, who wanted to occupy these lands themselves. In any case, at root there was a desire on the part of the armed colonists for the land and for autonomous forms of production and defense. They had come to realize that unless they were armed the land and the work they had put into improving the land would tend to fall into the hands of the large landowners.

These colonists did not believe in the state because of their personal experience with social and economic partisanship and their discovery of the double value system upheld by the ruling classes. They were a people, furthermore, who had lost or been obliged to relinquish the principal underpinning of their values and their traditions, that is, their ownership of land. From then on, therefore, and perhaps even until the present day, the colonist is a man who is ready to bear arms and who believes in them only; he does not know any other means of political action. His enemies also resort to weapons to settle every conflict that threatens their interests or aspirations. The colonists believe this, and they are not mistaken. The almost calculated failure of the agrarian reform of the 1960s, the bipartisan blockade, and the gradual abandonment of the regions of colonization by the state, all demonstrate its truth. All of the Independent Republics of the 1960s were inspired by the experiences of guerrillas who had to work the land for their livelihoods and had to organize in order to govern and defend themselves. Their goal was not to overthrow the system but to defend their economic independence and embryonic form of political organization. With the founding of the FARC this revolutionary character, which in its time was not understood, has evolved greatly.

As noted earlier, the Villarrica war gave rise to guerrilla regrouping, in the south of the department of Tolima and the north of the department of Cauca, as well as to two impressive peasant marches. The difference between the two phenomena is that the guerrilla reorganization began as a response to a short-term military offensive, whereas the peasant marches were a way to defend the civilian population against a sustained army attack. The famous marching columns, organized by the Villarrica movement, were two large displacements of hundreds of families, who were defended by mobile guerrillas basically seeking to survive the war. Both the column of El Duda and that of the Alto Guayabero headed for the forests of the piedmont of the eastern plains.

Once in possession of this territory, these groups retained their defensive armed character, which implied a form of organization that ignored the state and upheld their right to govern themselves independent of the traditional parties and of the always weak institutions of the state. In economic terms, the peasants' activity consisted of colonizing and improving the land to satisfy their own domestic needs, for the most part quite basic, resorting on principle and by tradition to collective forms of labor.

This colonization coincided with the rehabilitation programs that were begun by the first government of the Frente Nacional but were soon left to their own fate. Its epicenter was the settlement of the fertile lands of the Ariari River basin. This zone saw the convergence of various colonization forces, not only those oriented toward Communist agrarian reform, which have just been described, but also those formed of groups of dispersed Liberals after their defeat in the war of the eastern plains, and by Liberal groups in the departments of Tolima and Valle, who had been defeated by government troops between 1955 and the early 1960s. Government programs were limited to deeding public lands and offering superficial technical and financial aid, which was soon exhausted by the demands of colonization. Even so, this assistance was enough to create a difference, at least at first, between the evolution of the groups that went to the south of the department of Tolima and to the north of the Cauca and those who settled in the Ariari.

During the period called the Violence, from 1946 to 1966, an intense process of colonization was taking place in which political and economic factors converged and led to an enormous expansion of the agricultural frontier. In some zones, as, for example, in the middle Magdalena Valley (parts of the departments of Santander and Santander del Norte) and in the northern reaches of the Cauca River, the Violence tended to recede. The armed groups were controlled, exterminated, or dismantled, and these regions gave in to a more or less peaceful colonizing impulse. In the piedmont, fundamentally in Meta and Caquetá, peasant colonization developed without any consequent solution to the Violence. In this way, the marching columns became axes of colonization, and, although they modified some or many of their main characteristics, they did not abandon either their weapons or the forms of organization that sustained them.

The Evolution of the FARC

Another process involved the organization of the FARC, armed nuclei that progressively consolidated themselves and became more powerful as the colonization regions entered a state of crisis. This process was typical of the piedmont of the eastern plains (Meta and Caquetá) and of the Magdalena and the lower Cauca River valleys. (The Sierra Nevada of Santa Marta and the Perijá represent zones that for the moment—and for many years—followed a separate evolution.)

The evolution of the nuclei of the FARC has been described in a variety of studies. Here it is important to highlight the long military siege that they had to confront, both when they constituted the Independent Republics and later, after the republics had failed or were suspended and the FARC nuclei were scattered into dispersed military fronts. In order to advance in this direction they revived old relations with the organizations of the piedmont or tried to reactivate the dispersed Liberal guerrilla organizations of the lower Cauca and middle Magdalena valleys. In economic terms, these nuclei were foci of colonization, and in that sense the colonies around them were no different from any other form of colonization. These colonists also burned, planted, and harvested under very basic and precarious conditions. Theirs was a subsistence economy based on the power of family labor and that of neighbors, using simple tools and very primitive technology. Naturally, there was no capital formation process either as a base aimed at or as a result of production. Nevertheless, as time passed, depending on the quality of the soil, communications networks, and commercial centers, the colonists were able to amass very small amounts of capital. This accumulation could be detected in the scope of improvements to the land or in the acquisition of cattle.

The difference between colonization in this region and the process in other zones of the country was based on two features: first, the greater extent of collective organization of labor, and second, the existence of a social organization that provided the social services that the state should have offered. This system also supported armed organizations, which, in turn, presided over the whole set of social relations thus established. There are, of course, other important elements, particularly the political plan pursued by the leaders. The organization of these nuclei was not simply a form of armed defense of the colonists' achievements or a manner of coping with political persecution by the traditional parties and the army. It was also an instrument of action with a view toward the transformation of political power. Here, and only here, can the role of the Communist party in the process be located.

The Crisis of Colonization

The elements discussed in the preceding section evolved historically; they were not a project that originated from a deliberate, conscious plan. On the contrary, they arose and developed slowly and circumstantially. Many features were abandoned along the way, others were modified, and still others were changed from top to bottom. In my view, the most lasting feature, after undergoing some changes, has been the political program. Through it the whole phenomenon can be seen as an astute process of improvement and articulation of organization toward a political end. That story is yet to be written. Nevertheless, some general outlines of its evolution already can be discerned. There were two essential factors that determined the changes in organization. One was pressure from the large landowners and the role that they played in the development of commercial agriculture, and the other was the role of the state and the political parties.

With regard to the first factor, one must emphasize the fragility of the peasant colonist economy, especially during the first phase. In general, the colonist, through his own labor and using primitive tools and technology, produced a marketable surplus that usually was placed in the hands of commercial middlemen. The family's labor basically produced only enough for subsistence; the surplus was determined by the natural fertility of the soil and, therefore, as the soil inevitably became exhausted, the surplus declined as well. The colonist confronted this dilemma by working more land, but extension of his productive unit was limited by the availability of family labor. He improved his initial acreage either by using the small profits that the merchant had not managed to snatch away or by extraordinary additional hard labor.

There is a critical moment in the colonizing process that occurs when the land that the colonist has put into cultivation begins to return decreasing yields, and he is unable to arrest this tendency by cultivating new fields since he has neither enough hands within the family nor enough money to hire outside labor. He then has three choices: to sell his land and start the colonization process again but further inland, that is, to start again where the virgin soil is a match for his limited techniques; to sell and go to work for wages; or to find a way to obtain financial aid from the state or from a private investor in order to overcome the crisis and become an agricultural entrepreneur.

Overall, this type of crisis affected not only the individual colonist but also the entire settlement. This was the moment when the land buyer appeared, often a merchant or a cattleman. But whoever this person was made no difference. The colonist ended by selling, and since he was not the only one to sell, the buyer ended by purchasing his farm and that of his neighbors. Through such concentration of parcels large cattle ranches were formed. The capital that financed their purchase nearly always had been generated in the commercial sphere, that is, through the economic transformation of the colonists' surplus.

It must be pointed out that the colonist, in this early stage, cultivated only a few crops, such as dry-farmed rice, corn, bananas, and yucca. On a sporadic basis some of these crops, especially rice, found a market and generated earnings for the colonist. Corn, bananas, and yucca basically fed the family, the pigs, and household fowl. Pigs and fowl in large measure constituted the liquid surplus that accumulated. This is so because the agricultural products, the corn and the bananas, had to compete in markets that tended to be saturated not only with the products of the central peasant economy but also with those of the commercial agricultural enterprises that produced them at lower cost. Thus the peasant economy as a whole, but particularly the colonization economy, was hurt by competition from the commercial farm economy. It was the equivalent of closing off or blockading the typical products of colonization. In these ways, the colonist found himself hemmed in little by little by circumstances that limited him and led him into crisis: the decline of the natural fertility of the soil, an inability to accumulate a surplus in a reproductive way, and competition from commercial agriculture.

The role of roads, transporters, and merchants, in fact, the very development of the local population and commercial economy, mitigated against the peasant economy and precipitated the crisis. Whether a colonist could or could not pass this crossroads and begin his journey toward commercial farming depended on his ability to obtain capital from a source external to his own productive unit. I do not deny the possibility that under very favorable conditions and without an external source of capital he might be able to overcome the crisis. However, the great majority of colonists gave into pressure from large landowners and sold their farms.

The other side of the picture was its business aspect. First of all, the colonist generally was shy. Unfamiliar with urban centers, he was awkward and ill at ease in such environments. Second, roads were scarce and in terrible condition. The transporter, who was generally also the merchant or his associate, bought the colonists' produce at lower than market prices given the high cost of transport. Wearing any of his hats, the merchant, a kind of economic strongman who might also play a political role, was not only the buyer of the colonist's produce but also the seller of most of the merchandise that the latter needed. Between these two operations, the merchant functioned as a lender as well.

Pressure from large landowners was real and permanent. In the economic sphere it was exerted through the complex relations between the colonist and the merchant and tended to eat up the former's surplus. Also, the merchant's extension of credit at excessively high interest rates tended to absorb part of what the colonist needed to satisfy his basic subsistence. Although it is true that the colonist was able to cushion this pressure through the domestic economy properly speaking, it is no less true that the hand of the merchant reached even there. In addition, the merchant functioned as a creditor and a real estate buyer. His strategy was clear and his objective deliberate—to acquire the colonist's land. Since working the land increased its value, transforming it into an object to be bought and sold, his final goal in his multiple transactions with the colonist was to obtain this "merchandise" and bring it to market. Whether the merchant kept it and made it into his own place or whether he sold it matters little here. The fact is that, in the short run or the long, he became the owner of the parcel that the colonist had created.

If there had been only colonists in the zone, in equally bankrupt circumstances, there would have been no demand for the land, and it would have had no value. For the concentration of land to happen, there had to be other methods of production that could overcome the conditions that they faced. A necessary condition for concentration, then, was the existence of cattlemen and farmers with the capital to rescue the productive unit from the bankrupt condition in which the colonist was working. Only through this capital, which was in the hands of the merchant, the cattleman, and the commercial farmer, could the productive unit be saved. Sometimes, however, the state managed to delay the colonist's defeat and help him with a loan (which had to be subsidized) because otherwise the crisis would worsen and accelerate.

The cattleman who established himself in a colonization zone was without exception a man who possessed a capital base that he reproduced and accumulated in the cattle business. To do this, he needed land in quantities that would permit him to reduce substantially his investment in labor, land improvement, and infrastructure. This logic led him to search for new land. Generally, in the colonization zones there tended to be a clearly visible frontier between colonists and large landowning cattlemen. The large landowner pressed for the sale of parcels using all of the legal and illegal methods within his reach and drawing help from merchants, lawyers, the police, and the army. Lawsuits over boundaries, possession of parcels, and water use were typical conflicts used by cattlemen to uproot the colonists. Government authorities heard complaints at the request of the cattlemen and almost invariably (there were exceptions) decided in the cattlemen's favor. It must be remembered that the land in these zones did not fall under the criterion of ownership but only under that of possession. There were no customary norms regulating water or servitude, and the cattlemen, in general, were people who had social, economic, and political influence over local authorities. Thus the colonists found themselves unprotected and at the mercy of the cattlemen's strategy. The merchants did the rest.

Some students of the subject have pointed out the close relations that existed between the cattlemen and the army. Many cattlemen were retired from the military and belonged to what might be called the local elite. Quite a few of the ranchers had important business relations with each other. Most of them considered the colonist to be more a convenient laborer than a citizen with rights. In the face of this power structure, the colonist found himself backed against the wall and ended up by giving in and selling his land. The colonists suffered not only economic pressure from merchants but also noneconomic pressures either from the community of large landowners or from the violence that accompanied dispossession and its side effects. Those colonists who managed to survive the Violence and tried to continue on in the colonization zones had to cope with the hostility of government armed forces acting in the service of large landowning interests. To the colonist the army's violence was the same as any other and had the same consequences: to take away from them their land or, better said, the value of their labor accumulated in the form of improvement to the land.

Guerrillas and Colonization

This is the situation that the guerrillas found in all the zones of colonization in which they were active and became a peripheral local power. In the so-called Independent Republics of the 1960s, the colonists were on the brink of ruin because of poor market conditions and the absence of government aid. They did not lose their land, however, because the guerrillas helped them, and to an extent, this help prevented large landowners from acquiring and concentrating the land into large tracts. Insofar as the guerrillas were able to create defenses for the colonists they tended to control the roles of the merchant and the intermediaries and to provide for or attend to the population's most basic needs, such as education, health, and justice. Economically, the guerrillas' power was based on contributions or taxes from the colonists, paid either in cash or commodities or with labor. The colonists' obligations usually were fulfilled through collective work, either on "organization farms" or on the private property of others.

The purpose of organizing the colonists into juntas presided over by an armed corps was to prevent large landowners from taking over the colonists' land and—to the extent that the organization was strong enough economically—to eliminate or delay the other factors that threatened colonists. Behind the pretense of the independence of these republics, what really existed were first, the right to independent action, to self-defense through internal laws independent of the laws of the free market and the ambitions of the large landowners, and second, access to basic services not offered by the government, such as health care, education, credit, roads, and price controls. The difference in the trajectories followed by the groups in the mountain zones of Marquetalia,

Riochiquito, and El Pato and those of the piedmont, such as Medellín del Ariari, was precisely that in the latter region the state assisted colonization through the assignment of land titles, extension of credit, and provision of roads and some services. Here the guerrillas practically disappeared; they reappeared only when the disintegration of the peasant colonization was in an advanced stage, and the government had abandoned the communities to their own resources.

In the zones where the FARC had no influence in the 1960s, the process of dismantling peasant colonization and transferring land to large landowning interests proceeded without interference. In these regions, the guerrilla organizations of the 1950s were dispersed or eliminated. Rafael Rangel's guerrillas in the middle Magdalena and Julio Guerra's in the lower Cauca were either dead or under control, and land concentration advanced without difficulty. Large estates were formed from Puerto Boyacá to Şan Pablo and from Puerto Valdivia to Montelíbano on the Sinú River. This was the state of affairs in these regions when the student groups of the middle sixties proposed the development of proselytizing armed actions, the Ejército de Liberación Nacional (ELN) in the middle Magdalena and the Ejército Popular de Liberación (EPL) in the northern Cauca Valley and in the upper Sinú Valley in the region of San Jorge.

The speed and violence of the process of dismantling the peasant colonization economy depended on the fertility of the land and the amount of resistance exerted by the colonists against the pressures of the large landowners. In short, where the land was fertile, and the dismantling slower, pressure from the landowners was the strongest. Also, the better organized the colonists were, the more violent the methods of the landowners. This appears to have been the case in Caquetá and El Pato, for example, places with good land and a high degree of peasant organization. In the middle Magdalena, although there was good land, violence did not appear until peasant organizations had developed. In other places, like the Sierra Nevada de Santa Marta, where in general the soil is poor and peasant organization nonexistent, violence was delayed.

The pressures on colonists organized into Independent Republics were not limited to those exerted by the large landowners. There were also a military siege and the army's offensive strategy. The republics were considered to be bastions of the banditry of the Violence—which in fact was not untrue—or of Communist organizations, which was not untrue either, at least in the minds of some of their leaders. In defining these republics as gangs of Communist bandits, the government had an excuse to launch military attacks against them, condemn them politically, and blockade them economically. Thus to the pressures exerted by the landowners was added pressure from the army, and the colonists' attempts at political autonomy and economic self-determination were blocked by the government. The only outcome possible was war. One by one the republics fell to the army, and once they were under government control the land became concentrated in the hands of the large landowners. A close look shows, however, that this result was ephemeral both in military and economic terms.

After Marquetalia, the FARC nuclei relocated to other regions where economic and social conditions were similar and where an organizational basis for struggle already existed. The FARC learned their lesson well and modified their strategy. They gave up their attempts at autonomy and strengthened the military aspects of their organization. Above all, they decentralized the fronts, scattering them across the country, but maintained a single command. These changes accentuated the political component of the program and allowed the ideological orientation of the Communist party to be emphasized. The peasants came to understand that without a political program of national scope their struggle was doomed to failure.

A process of uninterrupted growth then ensued. The scattered nuclei, located in new zones where the same laws of colonization were in effect, became military fronts. The social and economic organization of these regions developed somewhat independent of the military organization, which was always organized and efficient. Gradually, fronts appeared in the middle Magdalena, the lower Cauca, and the upper Sinú, where conditions were ripe. In the northwest part of Antioquia, the high zones of the middle Magdalena, Caldas, Cundinamarca, and Antioquia, actions took place in zones still linked militarily to organizations like those of El Pato, Guayabero, Caguán, Ariari. These zones included regions of Tolima, Cauca, and Huila that had been taken by the army in showy but short-lived operations. From 1966 to 1976 this process continued without interruption. The government had new and more complicated conflicts to cope with, including economic and social deterioration on the national level and the political weakening of the traditional parties, which obliged the state to turn its attention to matters other than colonization. The agrarian reform stimulated peasant mobility. Strikes and student revolts brought the struggle to the urban context, and the Alianza Nacional Popular (ANAPO) seriously threatened the monopoly of the traditional parties. Meanwhile, ELN and EPL guerrillas occupied the army's attention. The FARC, in turn, sometimes silently, sometimes openly, advanced into regions where the presence of the state was imperceptible and colonization was proceeding actively.

Colonization and Coca: The Cases of Guaviare and Guayabero

Leaving aside the evolution of the situation in other sections of the country, let us now focus our attention on the special case of the piedmont of the eastern plains, particularly the regions of Guaviare and Guayabero in the national territories of Meta and Caquetá. Here the links forged since the 1950s between land colonization and guerrillas took special and particularly violent form in the 1970s and 1980s under the influence of the cocaine trade.

These regions were colonized by peasants who fled from the Violence between 1950 and the late 1960s. Most of these colonists had lost their land and belongings and escaped with only their lives. A few, very few, had been organized by the marching columns after the war of Villarrica. The column of El Duda spread out and, loosely organized, settled in the piedmont of the eastern plains between La Uribe and Medellín del Ariari as well as in the middle courses of the Ariari, Guape, and Güejar rivers. Dumar Aljure, the local strongman in this region, and, later, the government set limits on expansion during the years 1960 to 1970. The other column originally headed toward the Alto Guayabero and then spread out toward El Pato and Caguán and eventually, toward the Caquetá River.

The columns split up because of their need to survive, but they did not abandon totally either their weapons or their forms of organization, both of which had proven useful in confrontations with the army. On the contrary, they used these means to confront yet another enemy, different but no less powerful—the forest. These colonization nuclei, disunited and without links to a central organization, armed themselves with axe and rifle. Their activities in taming the land were basically economic, almost indistinguishable from the work of the hundreds of peasants who arrived individually to settle and colonize these empty lands. At first, state institutions, the agricultural reform agency (INCORA), and the Agrarian Bank stimulated the settlement with programs such as the one in La Mona in Caquetá and in El Canaguaro in Meta. These institutions created opportunities by extending credit and offering services.

In a context of understandable economic difficulties, colonization of the south of the Meta and the Caquetá progressed between 1960 and 1970. Soon the first symptoms of decline began to appear, however, and lands reclaimed from the forest were transferred—legally and illegally, violently and peacefully—to large landowners, primarily cattlemen. But since most of this land was (and remains) very fertile, the cattle ranch was followed by the commercial farm with its rice, sorghum, combines and tractors, and, above all, its hired labor.

Three zones of colonization can be distinguished according to three different systems of labor: peasant colonization, cattle-raising colonization, and commercial agriculture colonization. The first system is based on the unity of land and labor. The second develops out of the crisis of the first and is sustained by monopoly of the land and large capital investment. The third represents an intensification of these conditions, above all, in the area of wage labor. In this way, the repression of the colonist was determined by cattle interests and intensified by the ambitions and role of commercial farmers.

Government services, which might have stemmed the disintegration process through subsidized credit, commercialization, land titles, and roads, became weaker and weaker. Instead of helping the colonists' efforts, the government stimulated the large landowners' voraciousness by selectively extending credit and building infrastructure and following policies in accordance with the landowners' interests. If the state had concerned itself with subsidizing the upward step from colonist to entrepreneur, lowering the cost of money, and prohibiting the concentration of land, while, at the same time, improving services, controlling prices, and building roads, the fate of colonization might have been altered. But the state did not concern itself in these areas and perhaps it could not since the colonists played no direct role in national politics, and their political representatives were persons whose interests were different and even antagonistic to the rulers' own. Thus the process of dismantling, which began in the middle of the 1970s, was stimulated by the government and the army. The role of the military and former military men in this process, in these regions, was definitive in creating explosive conditions, which soon led to violence.

Nevertheless, as the dismantling developed, and cattlemen and commercial farmers accumulated the land that had been opened and tamed by the colonists, the nuclei of self-defense were reactivated. For the moment the Independent Republics were silenced but not beaten, and the new structure of the FARC was imposed as an organizational system among the colonists and the peasants under its influence.

The activities of the armed self-defense nuclei became more assertive. Rather than relying exclusively on its original adherents, the movement broadened and strengthened its radius of action. A colonist faced a difficult choice: join the army of the unemployed, either in the city or the country, or try again—perhaps for the third time—to settle new land. Armed resistance, in contrast, offered a different prospect in the few zones where the guerrillas were strong, zones where the crisis of peasant colonization and the concentration of land were either not occurring or at least tapering off. For this reason, the nuclei of self-defense soon became guerrilla fronts. Furthermore, the conditions brought on by the dismantling of the colonization economy later allowed other organizations, such as the M-19 in Caquetá and the EPL in Meta, to establish themselves and win several victories.

The government responded to the growth of the insurrectionary fronts with military repression. In the context of the economic crisis affecting peasant colonization, government repression became a stimulus to armed reaction. Villages were taken regularly, ambushes were an everyday occurrence, and, little by little, the fronts consolidated their positions.

In spite of military activity, or, perhaps, precisely because of it, the nuclei of armed peasants, in becoming fronts, did not neglect economic, social, and political organization in the zones where they had influence. The new organizational structure of the FARC did well, in part, because the government did not provide the services that the FARC extended to the people, services that were supplemented, sometimes generously, by the fronts. Another reason was that the mere activity of the fronts prevented large landowners from advancing onto the lands of the colonists. Even though the colonists alone were unable to make the leap into the business economy, the relative weakness of the large landowners prevented the dismantling from becoming complete. Moreover, there were zones where, through cooperatives, credit, and other resources, including some provided by the state, these communities prospered astonishingly. Finally, as a result of the legalization of the Communist party these communities achieved representation on the national political scene.

The social and economic organization of the colonists through legal or extralegal entities enabled the creation of labor collectives and were a means of politicization. These entities recognized the authority of the political organizations that backed them. The communities influenced and defended by the guerrillas tended toward autonomous forms of political and economic organization, but this tendency did not prevent them from participating in traditional political contests as well. In any case, this situation enabled them to have political independence and forms of accumulation that would have been otherwise impossible.

At the end of the 1970s, in the midst of sustained growth of the FARC and EPL fronts and the appearance of new guerrilla forces like the M-19, the heyday of coca began. On the guerrilla fronts there was active discussion of this issue. To tolerate coca cultivation involved obvious dangers but to oppose it meant opposing a higher standard of living for the colonists. Even more serious was the fact that the peasant saw from the beginning that the cultivation of coca could become the vehicle for the accumulation of capital that he so ardently desired as a way to escape from a subsistence living. Yet this prospect was precisely what the armed groups feared since it would have a negative effect on politicization and organization.

The pragmatism of the M-19, to all appearances, broke the impasse. In those days this group was involved in changing its urban focus for the rural struggle, and it accepted the opportunity presented it first by the drug traffic and later by mass production of coca leaf. This set of events opened the way for the FARC also to admit the possibility of becoming involved with the coca business in their zones of influence. Furthermore, drug traffickers were cultivating coca successfully, although the alkaloid content of the Colombian leaf was lower and of poorer quality than that of the Peruvian or Bolivian leaf. Given the poverty of the colonist, the breadth of the market, the crisis of values among the people, and above all the traffickers' capacity to organize and mock the law, dealers deduced that Colombia was an optimal country for them to operate in and that imported pulp, brought in by Colombians from the south, could be replaced by Colombian pulp.

It is possible that the agreements between cocaine dealers and guerrillas were not explicit and in fact might have been negotiated organization by organization. The arrangements and agreements must have been local and must have been based on already existing situations since coca cultivation spread with amazing speed in zones of colonization, especially in the piedmont of the eastern plains, where a kind of infrastructure already existed to handle the importation of pulp from Peru, Ecuador, and Bolivia.

What, then, did coca mean—and what does it mean now—to the colonizing peasant, the guerrillas, and the Establishment? For the colonist, it represented simply the possibility of his getting the additional economic benefit that his farm was not providing and without which he faced ruin. Coca meant that he would have the opportunity to make the transition to cattle raising and, perhaps, to commercial farming and that he would probably not have to lose the years of accumulated labor represented by his improved land. In sum, coca prevented the dismantling of the economy of colonization.

However, the coca boom did not have implications solely for the economics of colonization. Word of the boom spread rapidly, and soon the army of urban unemployed and underemployed saw the prospect of getting rich on the horizon. The same idea occurred to the commercial farmer, the cattleman, the merchant, the prostitute, the judge, and the policeman, and one and all got in line to dip their cups into the torrent. The population of some towns multiplied by as much as ten, and villages sprang up overnight. The impact of colonization on the forests in these years is still to be studied. Clearly, after 1978 colonization advanced more rapidly than it had in the preceding twenty-five or thirty years.

This nervous, risky world of money, which lacked scruples, literally invaded the forest, breaking every norm and custom. The drug bosses and their henchmen did as they pleased. The authorities either did not exist, or they too observed the law of the survival of the fittest. Violence—bribery, murder, and robbery—took hold in these previously quiet lands. The guerrillas' lack of preparedness for this anarchy permitted the drug lords to consolidate their power. But little by little the guerrillas reacted, first by tolerating and then by participating in the boom. This course of action led to the definition of clear rules governing relations between the insurrectionary armed groups and the armed drug traffickers' groups. The existence of a common enemy, the Colombian state, facilitated accord between these groups. The guerrillas were supported by the colonists and by those people who saw the possibility of getting rich quick because anarchy was a serious threat to their own interests. Therefore, sympathy for the guerrillas increased and overflowed the confines of their traditional sectors of support. Agreement between the guerrillas and drug lords was not easy. It was the result of violent strife whose heavy toll of resentment persists today.

At least until the end of the 1980s, the guerrillas progressively managed to impose their law in the coca-producing territories. With blood and with fire, resorting to intimidation or argument, they established clear rules: the ousting of thieves, *sicarios* (hired assassins), spies, and informers; the prohibition of the use of the cracklike substance *bazuco* as a means of payment or an article of consumption; fixed wages for coca harvesters; the proscription of processing secrets; and the requirement that other crops be cultivated in addition to coca. These conditions were in addition to those that the guerrillas normally maintained in their areas of influence, that is, their provision of basic services, their monopoly on force, and their dispensing of justice. In these ways, the guerrillas created optimal conditions for the production of coca. In return, the guerrillas extended the system of tribute that already existed—a contribution left up to the judgment of the contributor—to cover the whole population that profited from the boom, whether directly or indirectly. Producers paid 10 percent, and merchants 8 percent. Extortion, kidnapping, rustling, and bribery disappeared in the zones where the guerrillas became powerful.

Coca and the Guerrillas

The cultivation and processing of the coca leaf from the outset created enormous difficulties for the guerrillas even though it placed huge sums of money in their hands. From a logistical point of view, it is clear that the tribute they imposed on the population as a tacit reimbursement for maintaining a social order favorable to the new production allowed the guerrillas to profit indirectly from the economic benefits of the boom. This type of profit, of course, was not confined to the guerrillas. The boom led to the accelerated and indirect enrichment of organized business, of the so-called informal sector, of the transportation industry, both on the rivers and overland, and of local banks, landlords, and developers. The institutional sector had not remained apart and indifferent either. Value-added taxes had risen along with increased buying power. The participation of government employees in the cocaine business, from the army and the national police to rank-and-file officials, was widespread. They also profited through their receptiveness to generous bribes. Every government employee who had direct or indirect connections to the production or transport of coca was a possible tool, a potential pipeline to the flood of riches.

The guerrillas did nothing exceptional, then, when they charged or received "protection money," and this tribute was not perceived as an abuse by many people. Adherents and supporters of the movement paid it without complaint as a legitimate and voluntary contribution. For those persons who were either politically indifferent or hostile, however, the tribute was a compulsory tax, which, like any tax, was resented. A person's response depended, therefore, on his degree of political sympathy with the guerrillas. However, when the price of coca fell, sympathies cooled because payments to the guerrillas became more of a burden. In any case, the merchants and the coca-growing colonist knew that if it were not the guerrillas demanding payment it would be the army or the police exacting tribute in exchange for insuring their safety and freedom.

The army and the police now had a new reason, in addition to their ideological and constitutional ones, for wanting to control strategic points or production zones. In places where the guerrillas had been displaced by the army, the latter extracted its own kind of tribute. There is no question that behind their fulfillment of the army's constitutional obligation to control every corner of the national territory lay the hidden desire by soldiers and officers alike to use official force for their own benefit. The guerrillas aspired to control the movement of persons and merchandise because this made it easier for them to collect tribute without competition from the army. In fact, the colonists and peasant settlers viewed the government's armed forces with hostility not only because all their lives they had been victims of army assaults but also because they saw the army as more arbitrary than the guerrillas.

Bribery was not regulated by any set of laws but tribute paid to the guerrillas was. Bribes went directly into the soldiers' pockets, but money paid to the guerrillas had a specific political destination. The two groups behaved very differently. Whereas the soldier saw the colonist as a bandit and a political enemy, the guerrilla saw him as a real or potential partisan, whose poverty was the ideal cause behind the guerrilla's struggle. These differences are behind the fact that the guerrilla's tribute and the soldier's "bite," or bribe, did not weigh equally on the colonist's scale.

In any case, tribute collected on coca indisputably enabled the guerrillas to strengthen themselves militarily and socially. On the military side, the guerrillas invested a good part of the money collected in the modernization of weapons, in troop salaries, and in raising the operatives' standard of living. Socially, guerrilla authority had consolidated and broadened itself without interruption. The economic circumstances of the colonist, national social conflicts, and the weakness of the state as a promoter of development and as protector of the lives, honor, and belongings of its citizens all determined and guaranteed the role of the guerrillas in the colonization zones. The fact that the guerrillas were economically and militarily strong contributed to their position as the local power. They extended services in the areas of credit, education, health, justice, registry, public works, and ecological and cultural programs. Consequently, the insurrectionaries not only were the recognized local government but also were a civilizing agent in an environment that otherwise would have been, as one local priest put it, a "veritable vortex."

Coca and the situation that emerged because of it also brought to the nation serious problems with subversion. The migration to every region of the country of hundreds of settlers who came from the most heterogeneous social conditions and had the most dissimilar and contradictory interests, has been and remains a real and an imminent threat to order in the colonization zones. These groups, besides being a threat to the government, are also a challenge to the guerrillas.

In spite of this motley crowd, the guerrillas have broadened their geographical and social coverage. No doubt their dispensing of rapid justice, guided by clear and simple rules, partly explains the guerrillas' success. A great deal might be said on this subject. Although it is a justice ruled by a simple peasant code, a conservative one even, it is enormously flexible due to its common law components. Although guerrilla justice has a partisan bias, adjusted to political ideals, it is recognized and considered legitimate by a large part of the population. For example, rich merchants from Guaviare, after exhausting official means of justice, have resorted to settling their differences by appealing to guerrilla intervention. The law of the hills, as it is popularly known, enjoys legitimacy and support. Of course, the guerrillas' capacity both to dispense justice and to impose a system of tribute is based on the existence of the armed movement.

The guerrillas also have had to confront the consequences of the enrichment of one sector of colonists. Coca, as we have seen, offered farmers an opportunity to accumulate capital and to make the transition into the business economy, that is, into a system based on the reproduction of capital. Many colonists increased their scale of production considerably and themselves became employers of hired labor, thus raising their volume of accumulation. Although the guerrillas' political program is flexible enough to include this stratum of colonists, it is no secret that these colonists have become more and more disturbed by the course of events in these zones. Many colonists have chosen to plant ordinary crops, and these farmers definitely exert considerable pressure as they seek the tranquility of sustained economic growth. How much influence they actually have on the ideology of the armed movement remains to be analyzed. The recent reform that permits the popular election of mayors provides this sector with an occasion to express their support for pacifist, electoral trends. In addition, popular election of mayors permits the colonizers' aspirations for political self-determination to be realized in part.

Finally, confrontations with drug mafias and paramilitary groups have serious implications for the guerrillas. As has been noted, for a fairly long period there was a tacit agreement between the guerrillas and the drug dealers, which later was formalized. Given the growth of the guerrillas' military might, the drug bosses were obliged to accept their conditions. These conditions were threefold: first, a monopoly on arms by the insurrectionaries; second, the payment of taxes, just the same as any small cultivator; and third, the prohibition of payment in *bazuco* to coca pickers. This agreement led to full acceptance of the guerrillas' local authority. For the drug bosses, the transaction was convenient considering the extent of the territory dominated by the guerrillas.

As might be expected, this marriage of convenience between the guerrillas and drug lords did not last. Pressure from the army and the police, who had successes in several operations against drug trafficking, abuses committed by both parties, and the fall of international drug prices all opened breaches in the agreements until a break occurred. The army and the police were concerned with the outcome because the guerrilla-drug mafia alliance not only was a threat to the state, but it also prevented soldiers and officers from profiting individually from the drug trade.

After the alliance was broken, the mafia chose to organize its own forces to fight the guerrillas and those groups that they considered their civilian and political extensions, such as the political party Unión Patriótica, the labor unions, and the Juntas de Acción Comunal (government-sponsored community action committees). The persecution of the representatives of these organizations has intensified and can only be explained by the authorities' toleration of these activities, if not their actual participation in them. The wave of assassinations has had serious political implications for the armed movement's electoral hopes since it neutralizes the activity of popular leaders, intimidates the voters, impedes alliances, and threatens to lead to a breakdown of the current truce with the government.

What is the relation, then, between the armed guerrilla groups and the drug traffickers, the army, and the police? What is the relation between the police and paramilitary groups? What is the role of the traditional political parties? What is the function of the landowning sectors, greedy for lands reclaimed from the forest? For the moment, there is a well-founded fear that the *chulavita* experience of the Violence (named after the town from which the armed thugs sent by the Conservative government into areas of Liberal resistance hailed) might be repeated. The organization of armed civilian bands by local authorities or by soldiers acting individually could unleash a full-blown regime of private justice. Until now, there have been restraints on these processes partly because no one can guarantee a limit on or can control the activities of these groups and partly because the guerrillas are obliged to defend themselves. Today, there is discontent among the guerrillas over the disadvantageous situation that they have been put in by the truce on this point. Who knows what will happen if the assassinations continue?

10

Guerrillas and Violence

Daniel Pecaut

Daniel Pecaut, of the School for Advanced Study in the Social Sciences in Paris, is the leading French social scientist specializing in Colombia. He has published three books on Colombian politics: *Política y sindicalismo en Colombia* (Bogotá, 1973), *Orden y violencia: Colombia 1930–1954* (Bogotá, 1987), and *Crónica de dos décadas de política colombiana, 1968–1988* (Bogotá, 1988).

The analysis Pecaut presents in this chapter is actually much broader than its title suggests. Pecaut first frames what seems to be a paradox. He describes how during the last thirty years Colombia, unlike some major South American countries, such as Brazil, Chile, and Argentina, has avoided authoritarian military regimes and has maintained a functioning limited democracy. Yet during the same period Colombia has witnessed the rise and consolidation of powerful guerrilla movements, which have become central actors in the politics of the nation. Exploration of this apparent paradox allows Pecaut to review the whole period since the Violence. He concentrates his analysis on the implications of the political solution, the National Front, adopted by the Liberal and Conservative elites to bring the Violence to an end. He agues that since 1958 Colombia's limited democracy and the guerrilla movement are but two sides of the same coin. Both express—and perpetuate—a new violence born of the disjunction between socioeconomic modernization and channels for political representation.

Other students of Colombian politics, notably the U.S. political scientist Jonathan Hartlyn in his *Politics of Coalition Rule in Colombia* (Cambridge, Eng., 1988), have developed a more sanguine view of Colombia's political system. They emphasize in particular its ability to articulate the interests of a wide array of economic groups and to promote the vigorous, sustained economic growth that also distinguishes the history of Colombia from that of most Latin American countries over the last quarter century.

At the heart of this debate is the issue of the ability of popular sectors—rural workers and smallholders, organized labor, the urban poor and marginalized—to express their interests through the political system. All

analysts agree on the central features of contemporary Colombian politics that
bear on this issue: the continuing loyalty of the great majority of Colombian
voters to the traditional parties, and the inability of parties of the left to attract
the electorate to their programs of radical social reform.

The question thus becomes: who or what is responsible for this state of
affairs? Pecaut finds his answer in the legacy and contemporary expressions
of the violence itself, and he places particular responsibility on the National
Front. His prognosis for the future is not optimistic about the ability of
Colombians to break out of the vicious circle defined by limited democracy
and violence. This same question is discussed from another angle by Luís
Alberto Restrepo in Chapter 13.

For more than thirty years now Colombia has preserved a limited
democratic regime. It also chronically has been affected by social and
political violence and, more recently, by the rise of powerful guerrilla
organizations. What are the connections between limited democracy
and violence? Do contemporary guerrilla actions express, to some
extent, the crisis of the democratic system, or do they simply continue
traditional violence? These are the questions raised in this study.

Colombia is one of the rare South American countries that has
continuously maintained a civil democratic regime throughout this
century. The only military interlude, from 1953 to 1958 (with the Rojas
Pinilla government until 1957 and then the one-year military junta),
only slightly contradicts this general rule. It was the civilian elite that
brought General Gustavo Rojas Pinilla to power, ensured the essentials
of government administration, and ended this brief digression. It was
the elite that set in place in 1958 a coalition regime between the
Conservative and Liberal parties, which had monopolized the electorate since the nineteenth century. Designed to last sixteen years, this
National Front system, based on strict division of governmental functions
and public offices, is still in effect today with only minor changes.[1] Of
course, this civil democracy quite often has resorted to exceptional
measures, beginning with an almost permanent state of siege,[2] and has
raised many obstacles to the development of opposition parties.[3] Since
1975 it also has given the military an increasingly wider margin of
action. Nevertheless, Colombia has escaped the introduction of the
authoritarian military regimes that have appeared almost everywhere
else in Latin America as the means of coping with popular movements
aroused during populist periods.

Colombia is also the only South American country where for forty
years guerrilla warfare has formed the permanent background of social
and political life. The phenomenon, known quite accurately as the
Violence, raged from 1947 to 1956, leaving a death toll of two hundred
thousand. From this period sprang armed peasant movements—self-

defense groups at first, then guerrilla forces. In the mid-1960s various guerrilla organizations appeared, beginning with the Armed Revolutionary Forces of Colombia (FARC), which was linked to the Communist party and encompassed the peasant movements in numerous regions marked by the Violence; then the National Liberation Army (ELN), inspired by Cuba and the *foquista* (guerrilla enclave) model; and finally the Popular Liberation Army (EPL), driven by Maoist ideology. Despite the number of areas affected, these rural guerrilla forces did not have serious political repercussions, and around 1973–74 they seemed to be merely marking time.[4] After 1978, however, the guerrilla movement took on new importance. To the groups just listed were added M-19, a perpetrator of far-reaching actions and large-scale military operations,[5] and soon a multitude of other organizations of varying strengths, from the Quintín Lame group, with its links to indigenous peoples in Cauca, to terrorist-oriented groups such as the Autodefensa Obrera (Workers' Self-Defense).

Henceforth armed actions affected the cities and took on an offensive character in rural areas. For the first time, several of these organizations openly avowed a revolutionary plan to take power. Both in the cities and in the countryside a diffuse social violence spread, as evidenced by the growing number of bloody confrontations, explosions of local unrest,[6] and kidnappings and killings. As early as 1980 the rise of guerrilla forces was becoming a major political problem: their strength was estimated at ten to fifteen thousand. The army was present throughout a large part of the national territory, and the excesses of repression caused anxiety in certain elements of public opinion. Many of the leaders of the two traditional parties recognized the necessity of a "political solution." In 1982 the newly elected Conservative president, Belisario Betancur, took the initiative to restore peace. An unconditional amnesty at the end of 1982 freed hundreds of imprisoned guerrillas, but the fighting did not end. In fact, at times it reached an unprecedented intensity.

It was not until mid-1984, after long negotiations, that Betancur's policy seemed to bear fruit with the signing of cease-fire agreements with the FARC and then with M-19 and the EPL.[7] But these were precarious agreements. While Colombia was in difficult economic straits, the president tried to devise and negotiate political and social reforms with the signatory organizations. Most of the sociopolitical elite, skeptical of the entire peace process, proved reticent to consider these measures. Within the army itself there was much resistance to a cease-fire without disarmament of the guerrilla forces, and paramilitary groups became active. Many sectors watched fearfully as M-19 and the FARC tried, often successfully, to gain a foothold in working-class districts in the big cities, under cover of the cease-fire. At the same time, the guerrillas were reinforcing their military potential considerably, acquiring ever more sophisticated weaponry.

By mid-1985 the results of the political overture seemed limited: the ELN had not agreed to negotiate, and M-19 resumed large-scale hostilities. In and around the town of Cali, in the department of Valle del Cauca, M-19 claimed to renounce guerrilla tactics for direct military confrontation.[8] In Bogotá in October 1985, M-19 took over the Palace of Justice in an effort to indict President Betancur by holding the Supreme Court magistrates hostage; the action ended in a bloodbath. Other organizations also renewed the fighting.

There was one positive result. The FARC, numerically the strongest organization and commanding the greatest number of fronts, declared that it would respect the truce and began an electoral strategy. On the ticket of a new party, the Patriotic Union, and assisted by the Communist party, it presented candidates in the parliamentary elections of March 1985, as well as a candidate in the presidential election on May 1985 who won nearly 4 percent of the vote. Given the instability of the situation, however, it would have been premature for the FARC to exclude a return to military action. Some of its most important leaders indicated that this was merely a provisional tactic to extend their organization's political audience.[9]

Should we consider as pure coincidence this dual continuity—civil democracy, on the one hand, and social violence and guerrilla warfare, on the other? The hypothesis of this study is that it is not merely coincidental. Violence is the flipside of Colombian democracy. The phenomenon of the Violence of the 1950s was responsible for the restoration of the democratic regime in 1958. Various forms of violence permanently accompanied the evolution of that regime. Violence as a means of political and social protest was combined again and again with the establishment of democratic procedures.

In suggesting such complementarity, I do not mean to follow the example of some writers,[10] who claim that violence is generally inherent to democratic logic itself. In their view, terrorism in Western societies is due to the fact that sovereignty based on majority rule leaves no room for the rights of resistance that existed under the ancien régime. It allows for no court of appeals and thus induces groups of individuals to resort to violence under the pretext of restoring the original thrust to the democracy and of freeing popular will from the deformations imposed on it by representative mechanisms.

We begin with the Colombian experience, which remains halfway in the establishment of political democracy. It certainly recognizes universal suffrage as a means of expressing the political will and the foundation of legitimacy. For a long time, however, it has been a manifestation of the immutable division between the two identities— Liberal and Conservative—around which the social corpus is organized. These identities are not the product of choice but rather links to collective appurtenances dating back to history immemorial. The division, therefore, seems to be inscribed in "the nature of things."

From then on, the democratic regime seemed a series of struggles for the appropriation of power or for divisions of power between the two traditional parties. These struggles or compromises took the place of a political institution of the social order. They were actually only unstable substitutes. Presupposing the reproduction of collective allegiances, the conflicts scarcely refer to individualism or equality of conditions. Consistent with this overriding division, they do not try to make power something that establishes a unified, symbolic representation of the social order; instead, they allow for the possibility of a rupture and therefore a resurgence of political violence.

After more than thirty years of the National Front and considerable transformation of society, it would seem that the traditional division has lost its importance and that there is no longer room for the kind of violence seen in the 1950s. Moreover, contemporary guerrilla movements are obviously outside the sphere of the traditional parties and want to assume responsibility for social mobilization against a set regime. It also can be argued that change has been less than its protagonists believe. The democratic regime undoubtedly relies less on the old division, but it preserves a dissociation between the social and the political orders that feeds a diffuse violence. The guerrilla movements try to absorb this dissociation by invoking a plan of revolutionary change. It is not clear whether they succeed in this endeavor. They do not totally escape the limitations of past violence. The original violence of the 1950s continues as the horizon of all social actors. It has marked the present guerrilla forces in two ways. First, they profit by representing the political and social orders as arenas of violence; and, second, they take advantage of the diffuse social and political violence that has existed since that period as a mode of sociopolitical conflict and as a tactic used by the regime.

The Original Experience: The Violence of the 1950s

One must return to the original event, the Violence of the 1950s, not only to understand the context in which the National Front regime and the first self-defense groups were born but also to interpret what I classify as phenomena of "violence" and what I mean by representations of the social and political orders in terms of violence.[11] Two points are essential. The first is that the Violence of the 1950s is an inextricable mixture of political confrontations and social conflicts, of repression led by Conservatives and fratricidal peasant warfare, of collective strategies and individual actions, of self-defense and large-scale social disorganization, of deliberate acts, and of great fear. Second, the Violence also was a splintered phenomenon that affected some regions and not others. It existed within the framework of the municipality or hamlet and, despite its national repercussions, was never coordinated on a national scale. I will not analyze the reasons for these two characteristics here but will comment briefly on them and suggest their consequences.[12]

The inextricable blend of components in the Violence makes it impossible to reduce it to a partisan war or to a general social confrontation, but these two frameworks are certainly important. Nearly all of the confrontations took place under the banners of the two traditional parties; their geographic distribution partially coincided with that of the great agrarian conflicts of 1930. However, the combination of these themes and of actions deliberate or defensive, individual and collective, blurs the limits between the two. In fact, political massacres, banditry, struggles for land, and a huge rural exodus were just some of the manifestations of the Violence. Two characteristics of the Violence must be stressed: first, the coexistence of an immense destructuring of the old rural fabric and its preexisting peasant organizations with the appearance of rural self-defense groups; and second, the consecration of the gap between the social and political orders. Insofar as the omnipresent element was the power struggle between the two partisan collectivities, the rural masses could make sense of the cataclysm only by appealing to their traditional political identities. From that point on, the two parties emerged from the confrontation with stronger foundations within the population. But the rivalry between the two parties had nothing to do with the social stakes.[13] Under these conditions, the social conflicts were doomed to unfold on another stage, isolated and devoid of political expression. Rural destructuring and dissociation of the political and social orders were the first manifestations of the phenomenon of violence.

To a certain extent, the Violence's sudden explosion depended on the existing precariousness of the Colombian state: its limited influence over a large part of its territory, which was actually no longer under its control; and its precarious authority, for, unlike what happened in Brazil or Mexico, the political, economic, and intellectual elites in Colombia never acceded to the state's role in giving form to the social order. The Violence accentuated this situation, and it ended attempts by the state to regulate social relationships, outlined in 1930 for the urban working classes. It confirmed the atomization of local authority, which was in the hands of an autonomous political personnel. Finally, it left the field open for local and private power relationships to manage local tensions. Fragmentation of social conflicts and acceptance of recourse to force to neutralize them are the two other manifestations of the phenomenon of the Violence.

The Violence thus seems to be a collection of miscellaneous pieces that escapes understanding as a whole. The very term "Violence" suggests a sort of catastrophe without definite actors. Even the peasants who hold to a political/partisan interpretation of these events remain ambivalent. They do not hesitate to accuse their own political leaders who, from the safety of towns, commanded those who actually took part in the fighting. The rural masses, therefore, were pawns to be moved for the profit of those outside their universe. In addition, for years these masses have been unable to transform the pieces into a single episode that would portray them completely as protagonists of movements to modify the political and social structures of Colombia.

Moreover, the Violence simultaneously gave birth to an image of the political and social orders in which violence, as a category, occupies a central place. Claude Lefort wrote of the French Revolution that in order for revolution to take place, it is not enough that the condition of any given category worsen; there must be a vacillation of the common landmarks of a situation, the points of reference (as difficult and conflicting as they may have been) through which this situation formerly was seen as natural, so that other landmarks at least can be glimpsed.[14] The Colombian Violence shook the old landmarks; it did not create new ones. It engendered only ambivalent, redoubled adherence to the traditional references. But it also brought the discovery that at any moment the political order can be expressed as a floating friend-enemy opposition and that the social order, deprived of political formulation, is doomed to allow the power struggles that traverse it to flourish unhindered. In this sense, the Violence, as cataclysm, is not only the basis of a historical memory called upon to stir the masses; it also established a perception of the political and social orders that was to persist no matter what institutional arrangements and electoral legitimacy were claimed by those in power.

Limited Democracy and Violence

The National Front system was worked out in 1958. In addition to the restrictions imposed on demonstrations by the political opposition and the privileges bestowed upon the socioeconomic elite, the system took liberties with everyday regard for democratic rules. It used and abused exceptional measures, such as the establishment of a state of siege, and resorted to various practices of "clientelism" to convince an often indifferent electorate. Abstentionism was certainly a constant of Colombian life. Even in 1946 and 1947, at the height of popular mobilization, it was around 40 percent, but during this period it sometimes exceeded 60 percent. In fact, the National Front cannot be dissociated from the Violence, which, in the form of banditry, continued until 1965. It is one of the systems political scientists call "consociational democracies," in which the participation of the opposition parties seems the only way to maintain the unity of a society split by major politicocultural cleavages.[15]

The National Front democracy owed many other traits to the phenomenon of the Violence. Politically, it benefited from the fact that, by force of circumstances, partisan solidarities were consolidated temporarily. Because of the hatreds engendered by the Violence, for wide sectors of the population, the collective conscience more than ever expressed itself through identification with the two parties. The National Front also endeavored to legitimize itself through self-portrayal as the bulwark against the ever-present possibility of the return of political violence. In every election where the lists of the National Front might not win a large majority, the risk of a new civil war was invoked. The National Front thus was sustained by reference to violence as the essence of the political order.

Socially, the National Front was no less indebted to the Violence. Actually, the National Front represents the restoration of power to the socioeconomic elite. After the Violence the elite was rid of the populist menace, which, from 1945 to 1948 had played a large role in putting the process of violence into gear. It also momentarily was delivered from the dangers that could be caused by the multiplication of agrarian struggles, at that point atomized and isolated, and of urban union organizations, destroyed after 1948 or obliged to place themselves within the direct thrust of the traditional parties. Limited democracy thus has an obvious social connotation. It is above all a *capacitaire* democracy, reserving the essentials of power for the elites.

This quality is made clearer by the fact that the form of the National Front notably weakened the authority of the state. The state's dependency with regard to the various political clans often led to paralysis. The socioeconomic elite, through the intermediary of its various interest groups, gained vital participation in decision making. Moreover, the crisis of the state implied that civil society enjoyed ample autonomy. The Violence contributed to this situation, and the National Front inherited it. Since then, the socioeconomic elite has in many cases been dependent upon its networks of influence within the working classes.

Finally, culturally, the National Front has returned to the Catholic Church a role in guaranteeing social order. In the absence of any possibility of giving substance to the nation-state, the Church plays the role of a unifying institution. Anxious to confer on the political system a normative substructure, the Liberals are just as eager as the Conservatives to sing the Church's praises. As it enters the last third of the twentieth century, Colombia is thus one of the few Latin American countries where the Church still has such an institutional presence.

In all respects this democracy is founded, then, on the effects and the images of the Violence. It has managed nonetheless to gain sizable support. The two traditional parties generally have no difficulty garnering the consent of the vast majority of voters. It matters little that electoral procedures are not always above suspicion and that here and there clientelism, even pure and simple vote buying, is common practice. Even so, the theoretical monopoly enjoyed by the two parties until 1970 does not explain everything. The proof is that after 1974, when this monopoly was abolished—although not in the case of the distribution of government jobs and public offices—the left appeared openly and still never won more than 2 to 4 percent of the vote. The reason for this loyalty cannot be attributed only to the Violence and fears of its eventual resumption. Undoubtedly, partisan allegiances, with their aspect of political subcultures, still have considerable importance.

The question remains, how can such a system, without transforming itself, confront the changes that over the years have affected Colombian society in a variety of ways? For Colombia has experienced the same process of modernization that is affecting neighboring countries: massive displacement of rural populations into the cities, penetration of capitalism into agriculture, industrial development, growth of the service sector, increasing state intervention in economic and social domains, advances in literacy, increased student population, and changing customs.

As limited as the National Front's democracy may be, it is nothing like the authoritarian military regimes that began to take hold elsewhere in Latin America after 1964. The democracy leaves room for social and political differences. Social conflicts manage to express themselves, as do challenges from organizations. Since 1958 independent trade unionism, directed by the Communists and other radical sectors, has tried to regain its strength. The period from 1958 to 1961 saw an increase in serious strikes, and beginning in 1965, radical trade unionism became increasingly important. In 1974 urban movements in turn took off. Under the guise of "civil strikes," they sometimes assumed the aspect of transient insurrections. In 1977 workers and shantytown residents united in a general strike that surprised the government with its violence and resulted in hundreds of deaths. Rural areas were not spared. Of course, there were few peasant movements in the regions marked by the Violence: disorganization was not overcome. But in the departments of the Atlantic Coast, from 1970 to 1974, these movements reached unprecedented heights, as witnessed by the hundreds of invasions of the great estates.[16] Political challenge was expressed, beginning in 1966, by the electoral advances of the National Popular Alliance (ANAPO), a movement formed by Gustavo Rojas Pinilla, which uses a half-conservative, half-populist rhetoric. In the 1970 presidential elections, it was able to compete on an equal footing with the National Front coalition.[17] Revolutionary organizations, notably those incorporating students, began to proliferate from 1965 on.

One must not exaggerate the strength of these social movements. On the whole, the working class has only a limited capacity for action and remains organizationally splintered. Social movements, however intense, have difficulty lasting through time. Numerous factors may account for this relative weakness. One factor—that which concerns us most—is that these movements are caught up in a context where violence, as a mode of action and representation, continues to occupy a central place. In many cases, social relationships are in reality relationships of force calling, in turn, for effective recourse to force. Socioeconomic elites, popular organizations, and political avant-gardes all share, more or less, in this conviction.

The National Front and the socioeconomic elite did not hesitate to use force against the popular sectors. Two elements contributed to this. First, at least in several regions, the weakness of the state and its regulative mechanisms, by confirming the functional autonomy of civil society, led to an unmediated showdown of the social adversaries. Second, in the countryside, many landowners had their own men at arms. In the factories, management and workers often were reluctant to comply with legislation regulating negotiatory procedures. This situation resulted in a vision of the social order profoundly separated from institutional political forms and thus ruled by a still formidable disorder.

Under these conditions, popular organizations too sometimes were moved to define very harsh strategies of resistance or offense. Whether through invasion of lands, or strikes in public services, or even simply through prolonged strikes, these organizations were always outside the law. Their very existence as organizations was often at stake. The strikes of 1958 to 1961, and many others afterward, ran up against intense repression. In 1964–65 army attacks on peasants organized in self-defense at Riochiquito, El Pato, and Marquetalia led to the formal establishment of Communist guerrilla movements under the name of

FARC. The increasing number of political avant-gardes, and the endorsement of armed methods by some of them, brought violence to the forefront. Between 1965 and 1968 the ELN and the EPL were formed. From that time, the problem of guerrilla forces and revolutionary radicalization gave new import to the question of violence. Reference to the previous Violence became insufficient.

Two questions arise. Why did guerrilla forces and revolutionary radicalization take on a chronic character? How are they connected to social movements? These two questions are closely linked.

I shall omit the discussion of the impact of the Cuban or Chinese revolutions. Their influence plays a large role but provides too simple an explanation. I propose another path, which does not exclude others: in the face of changes affecting society, the (relative) immobility of the National Front and its related institutions gave rise to an opposition that, lacking a means of expression, turned toward a plan of radical rupture. The example of the revolutionary priest Camilo Torres symbolizes this course. The Colombian Church is one of those that undertakes no aggiornamento. It simply marginalizes its members seduced by political involvement. By rallying to armed struggle, Camilo Torres seemed to indicate that the system offers to those who would fight it no other choices than marginalization or total breaking away. It was not only the Church that was concerned. In 1969–70 some very conservative organizations suddenly teetered into a revolutionary mode, which was sometimes poorly defined politically but tempted by "immediate action." After 1970 numerous M-19 staff members were drawn from the fairly moderate ANAPO. In addition, looking at the social provenance of many M-19 leaders, one realizes that a large proportion were brought up in traditional families and raised in religious institutions. Generalizations can, with some precaution, be drawn from this. Insofar as the political system is democratic and does include a large part of popular opinion, and despite its refusal of reforms, it is difficult to establish a challenging political opposition.

Moreover, all left-wing dissidences have been defeated quickly. Hence we find the resulting resistance to democratic procedures and the choice of direct conflict. We should consider as well to what extent this choice may also lead to a break with social movements.

The answer to this second question is two sided. Guerrilla movements, of course, often have managed to align themselves with social movements. The FARC must be considered separately, since from the beginning it represented an armed peasant movement. But other organizations have been able to insert themselves into social struggles. It was thus that in 1972–1974, Marxist-Leninist groups, whose military arm was the EPL, momentarily took over the leadership of the Atlantic

Coast peasant movement. Similarly, various militants associated with armed struggle at certain times have won over trade-union leaders and played a considerable role in urban mobilization or general strikes like those in 1977. It is also true that the connection often ended in the splintering of the social movements. By subjecting them to a totally political strategy and involving them in direct confrontations with power, the avant-gardes were often oblivious to the movements' more pressing claims. The Marxist-Leninists of the Atlantic Coast thus wanted to prohibit peasants from growing anything other than the necessities of self-subsistence on the plots of land that they had just acquired and, moreover, to forbid their taking steps to regularize their new owner-ship. Certain urban associations also suffered from this political voluntarism.

The fact is that toward the end of 1977 the revolutionary cause did not seem to be progressing. The ELN had not recovered from the military blows suffered in 1973. The FARC lay low. The EPL barely was surviving and, like the ELN, was especially concerned with set-tling accounts with those who wanted to leave the movement. The peasant movement was in crisis. The working class did not overcome its disarray. Urban actions took place sporadically. The left was not improving its electoral scores. Only the National Front continued un-flinchingly, with its rules relaxed. But in other respects the skepticism, even the rejection, by growing segments of the population of the National Front, brought for many Colombians the certainty that the political order depended on violence.

Why use this term, yet again, when we mention social conflicts, revolutionary guerrilla movements, and immutable partisan solidari-ties? Because, as during the Violence, the juxtaposition of these elements produced simultaneously revolts and disorganization, an increase in confrontations and fragmentation of social movements. Because, out-side the coalition in power, there is still nothing to represent a unity of the social order: violence wells up in the interstices of an invertebrate society where the social order only tangentially touches the political scene.

War and Peace: The Struggle for Democracy

As we have seen, stability began to be threatened again around 1980. Here began a phase when guerrilla forces embarked upon large-scale military operations, occupied new regions, and struggled to win public opinion to their cause. Neither the unconditional amnesty proclaimed by the Betancur government in 1982 nor the cease-fire concluded in

1984 succeeded in restoring peace. Hostilities continued on a considerable scale.

One should not consider this phase as merely the prolongation of the preceding phase. We have just pointed out the defeats suffered, on both the military and social levels, by most vanguard organizations. Awareness of these failures played an important role in deciding the direction armed struggles began to take in 1980. M-19, gestating since the early 1970s, had a major part in this reorientation. Its leaders were the first to want to associate military action with the effort to win the sympathy of wide social sectors in the name of a political program aimed at the establishment of "true democracy"; war thus was placed officially at the service of politics.

To appeal to democracy against the National Front and its restrictive rules was to enunciate to a new urbanized and literate generation that the regime born of the Violence only sustained itself through the exercise of permanent violence. It was also to proclaim the necessity of an "opening" of the political system, which would allow the masses to enter into a "true citizenry." The repercussions of this profession of political faith were due not only to the program's renunciation of *foquista* undertakings or simple rural self-defense. They were just as much a result of the evolving crisis of the National Front and the transformations of a society that the traditional parties proved powerless to control.

Social Changes and the Crisis of the Regime

The crisis of the National Front was manifest by 1977. The hegemony of the socioeconomic and traditional political elites, which had consolidated itself since 1958, was shaken. In 1975 there occurred simultaneously an extraordinary rise in coffee prices, a trend that continued until 1977, and the staggering development of marijuana and cocaine exports, which by 1978 reached the value of coffee earnings. This was a dual challenge for the state, which had to try to neutralize the consequences of the largely clandestine monetary income through austerity measures that adversely affected industrial growth and were also detrimental to agriculture. It was a dual challenge as well for the middle classes, who watched the rise of frenzied financial speculation and the consolidation of an extraordinary complex underground economy and who found themselves competing with owners of rapidly accumulating fortunes. Medellín symbolizes this sudden change: cradle of Colombian industry and the Catholic bourgeoisie, the city became the hub of drug traffic. Corruption and criminality accompanied this sui generis economic miracle. In the context of these unsettling economic changes, the world economic crisis had its own effect, shaking the most powerful financial institutions and condemning industry to a new stagnation.

The old political elite also was affected. As the figures who had dominated the political scene since 1930 disappeared or died, there emerged a new wave of politicians, who substituted for the classic methods of clientelism more cynical and dubious forms. The traditional parties, especially the Liberal party, in which a fraction of the working classes continued to place its hopes, became the theater of factional rivalries. The traditional parties progressively lost their character of subcultures attached to conceptions of the social order anchored in history.

This decomposition of political and economic structures was taking place while the modes of social domination heretofore in force were crumbling. Urbanization brought a weakening of personal dependencies, where they still existed; it especially provoked the attenuation of hierarchical forms peculiar to rural life. Whatever the compartmentalizations of the urban scene and the differentiations within the working classes, there appeared also, in filigree, an awareness of the similarity of conditions. That does not necessarily mean collective solidarities, even less possibilities for organized action. But the inefficiency/indifference of public authorities in rapidly growing working-class neighborhoods, and the lack of influence by the traditional parties in these same areas, found expression, at the very least, in a distancing from the political system and by momentary explosions. In the months following the cease-fire, M-19 managed to gain a foothold in the shantytowns of Cali and Bogotá and to recruit numerous followers there.

Meanwhile, a part of the middle sectors tended to escape completely the influence of the traditional parties. This is especially the case for student environments. Like other Latin American countries, Colombia has seen a rapid growth in the university sector, often formed hastily in mediocre private institutions. Many of the political avantgardes from 1965 to 1975 already had come from the student sector. M-19 would draw from university surroundings many of its staff, militants, and sympathizers. Urban in origin and at first deploying its actions in cities, M-19 would easily garner the political adherence of students, who comprised an important area of public opinion. Attracting the children even of the elite, it captured for a while the goodwill of their families.

Despite this crisis of the National Front and the elite and the transformations of the urban world, the mechanisms of the limited democracy were not jammed entirely. The same proportion of the electorate continued to go to the polls and to vote for the two major parties.

Elected in 1982, Betancur endeavored, through a foreign policy of nonalignment and through negotiations with guerrilla forces, to give the National Front a shot in the arm. He too, successfully at first, tried to win public opinion in the name of peace and democracy.

The confrontation of the guerrillas and the regime was not strictly military. It was political. And politics consists of making one's image of the political order prevail over the adversary's image. The sociopolitical context we have briefly evoked is a backdrop. It has effects only through the interpretation given it. The guerrilla movements were trying to prove that the context caused suppression of democracy, the government that the context was not an obstacle to democratic forms. The war was also a war of representations and images.

The War of Representations and Images

Beginning in 1979–80 the representatives of various guerrilla movements continually asserted that the National Front democracy was only a sham concealing an authoritarian regime in which the military exercised a determining influence. Its equivalency with the military regimes of the Southern Cone thus was affirmed categorically. This analysis certainly had very real justifications. Since 1977 the regime had resorted to an increasingly sophisticated arsenal of exceptional measures, and the armed forces had enjoyed an autonomy reinforced in repressive action. Nevertheless, several comments are in order.

First, the characterization of the regime became political. The left formally denounced the National Front above all as an instrument of the oligarchy. Within the framework of the renewed appeal to armed struggle, the idea was to make armed conflict seem the only means of resistance to a regime surviving only by violence. By again interpreting the political order as a friend-enemy relationship, institutional mediations were, from the outset, insubstantial and negotiating positions at once illegitimate.

Second, the guerrilla forces claimed democratic values for themselves. M-19 distinguished itself in this respect from the other organizations, which all ascribed to a Marxist, or other full-fledged, schema. As the extension of ANAPO, M-19 proclaimed itself only as nationalist and as a partisan of a participatory democracy without further clarifying its social projects. It was also quick to adopt a populist language and to display its respect for religious traditions. In a country where nationalist and populist mobilizations always have come to sudden ends because of the strength of the two political subcultures, M-19 thus reestablished the symbolic link between democracy and national unity.

Finally, the guerrilla movements succeeded through this discourse in reversing at once the fragmentation of the social order and the dissociations between the social and political orders inherited from the Violence. By taking to task the "dictatorial form" of the regime, the guerrilla forces made all opposition social groups avatars of one and the same political subject: the people in revolt against those who had betrayed them. The guerrillas did manage in large measure to have these images confirmed by an element of public opinion. Their success was all the more since the excessive military repression in 1980 allowed them to intervene as well in the name of "human rights."

Nevertheless, the regime was not incapable of responding. By proclaiming an unconditional amnesty—which freed hundreds of guerrillas from prison—and by entering into cease-fire negotiations, Betancur put forth another image of democracy, one that permits conciliation between opposing interests. The composition of the "peace commission" responsible for contacts with the guerrilla movement was a testimony to that image since it granted a place to the "vital forces of the nation" and also to the Communist party and to a pardoned member of M-19. Moreover, Betancur rebuilt an image of democratic authority. It was he who supervised the negotiations without allowing a rather discredited congress to intervene. He also reestablished the link between democratic logic and progress toward social equality. In fact, he attributed the rise of the guerrilla movements to social injustices and did not separate political negotiations from those concerning social reforms. One last element: despite the reluctance of many military leaders about these discussions and various incidents with his ministers of defense, Betancur gave the impression that civil rule was carrying the day.

It was a war of images with public opinion as audience. Clearly, on both sides, the game was to adopt democratic values. It is also evident that beyond these declarations of principle, the adversaries were led to using complex strategies.

The Strategies of the Protagonists

The unconditional amnesty and the opening of negotiations took place in 1982. The cease-fire did not come about until 1984. In the meantime, military operations were even more extensive than before 1982.

M-19 was the first to advance the idea of a negotiation in the form of a great "national dialogue" designed to define the social and political reforms needed to reestablish peace. Throughout 1983 and the beginning of 1984, however, M-19 escalated its military actions, notably in southern Colombia, in Caquetá, and then, in Cauca and Valle del Cauca, leaving a heavy toll of victims. The FARC, for its part, extended its influence into numerous regions. Claiming thirteen fronts in 1982, it established fourteen new fronts over the following months. All the guerrilla movements understood that they must negotiate from a position of strength.

Surprisingly, the FARC was the first definitively to agree to sign a cease-fire in June 1984. M-19 and EPL signed only two months later, with the former standing to lose the political advantage it had won by launching the idea of negotiations. The cease-fire created a delicate situation. On one hand, it challenged the guerrilla forces to become legal political movements and to pursue, through peaceful propaganda, their efforts to insure the support of wide social sectors. On the other hand, the cease-fire left the guerrilla forces' military potential intact since it did not call for a surrender of weapons. There ensued an unstable situation where the keeping of the peace was constantly at stake.

M-19 had always asserted that it wished to become a mass movement if circumstances permitted. In the months that followed, it effectively established itself in working-class areas of various cities. The majority of the political class was fearful of this unwanted presence. The FARC, with the support of the Communist party, got under way with the creation of the political party, the Patriotic Union.

This phase was marked by profound tensions. The army was loath to accept this political legalization of organizations that remained nevertheless on a wartime footing. There were innumerable incidents. Paramilitary groups assassinated a number of M-19 and FARC leaders. M-19 responded with prompt and resounding military operations. Guerrilla organizations sat on commissions charged with putting the finishing touches on "structural reforms." Uncertainty about the guerrillas' underlying intentions and the resistance of the propertied classes gave an unreal aspect to these discussions, all the more so as economic stagnation made prospects for reform largely illusory. The strategic calculations were clear: for the government, it was a matter of demonstrating that it was going as far as possible in its effort to permit the political integration of the guerrilla movements and of shifting the responsibility of a possible breach of the truce to them; for the guerrillas, it meant emphasizing the regime's powerlessness to carry out effective reforms.

The resumption of armed conflict rapidly was becoming a real probability. The killings contributed to a deteriorating mood. In January 1985, in an M-19 bastion near Cali, guerrillas and the army clashed in a three-week battle. All of the guerrilla groups took advantage of the cease-fire to acquire considerable armaments. In June 1985 a day of general strike was called. M-19 detected in this action the possibility of an insurrectionary upheaval, and its militants left the towns to rejoin the ranks of the organization's military groups. The general strike had only limited strength and, in any case, did not give rise to an insurrection. But M-19 still decided to break the cease-fire. War resumed, first between M-19 and the armed forces. All that remained of the peace process was the truce respected by the FARC. Within the framework of the Patriotic Union, the FARC took part in the 1985 election.

In reality, the changes were not negligible. On the armed forces' side as well as on the part of the guerrilla movements, it became obvious that certain groups refused any prospect but war. Public opinion, however, evolved in favor of peace. The operation of taking the Palace of Justice certainly demonstrated the limited prospects of that option. The public watched with surprise as M-19 claimed to use its Supreme Court magistrate hostages to render a public judgment on President Betancur. Simultaneously, the public was stupefied by the fury of the military, which, disregarding government orders, indulged in an indiscriminate massacre.

By participating widely in the 1986 elections and by casting their votes for a moderate Liberal, Virgilio Barco, the people demonstrated their desire for peace, through the National Front system. But throughout the Barco presidency there was every reason to believe that the political powers had limited control of the situation and that violence was the order of the day. No one knew whether FARC too, having passed the stage of its political consolidation, might rally to a return to war.

We have described the protagonists' strategies as if these groups were capable of acting in accordance with definite political plans. The plans did exist. And the strategies were not mere appearances. But the plans were formed on the basis of a situation of social disaggregation, which, in many respects, escaped calculations and plans. Armed struggles and social movements continued to unfold against a gigantic process of disorganization and anomie that spared not even the protagonists of armed conflict. Violence's subterranean toil, and the images inherent in it, continued to be at work.

Guerrilla Warfare and Violence

The guerrilla movements that resumed combat undoubtedly articulated more clearly than before their intention of provoking a revolutionary situation. Reference to "democratic restoration" faded behind "national liberation." Forms of coordination between M-19, ELN, and EPL were outlined. M-19 even tried to give an international character to its struggle, as witnessed by its creation of the America Battalion, which included Ecuadorians and Venezuelans, as well as by its alliance with groups of Peruvian and Ecuadorian guerrillas. Thus the Andes were the theater chosen for realization of the revolution.

These organizations also continued to receive the support of certain urban and rural classes. M-19 attracted the children of the middle class less easily than before, but it had no trouble recruiting among young people in the shantytowns and the countryside. As during the Violence, there were many fourteen- and fifteen-year-old fighters, an indication of the disorganization of the urban and rural social fabrics. The guerrilla movements also remained omnipresent in regions of former or recent colonization, where disputes about land ownership were still quite keen. Caquetá, Meta, and Arauca, those frontier regions where a population from the Andes had settled in the last few decades, were so many more territories on which the state was unable to impose its ascendancy and where guerrilla forces, notably the FARC, obtained considerable support. More and more, guerrilla forces were present as well in economically essential regions, such as the coffee departments, where social tensions created by marginalization of the smallholders favored guerrilla penetration. Even urban unions proved sensitive to the prospects of radical change. The formation then in progress of a trade union central, regrouping all the leftist unions, cannot be separated from the Communist party and other organizations' interpretation of the conjecture as "prerevolutionary." In this sense, social conflicts and armed struggle often converged, indirectly or directly.

In other respects, nevertheless, the guerrilla movements were participating in a situation characterized by many of the traits of the Violence. The convergence of social conflicts and armed struggle was not always the rule. Under fire from two sides, from guerrilla forces and the armed forces, the peasants often tried to escape their roles as victims. In the Cauca region, where some indigenous peoples had been organized for fifteen years and more recently through the armed Quintín Lame front,[18] and where they had succeeded in recovering numerous lands once reserved for them by the Spanish Crown, the peasants had clashed with the FARC, which often refused to recognize their elected authorities. In the Magdalena Medio, which was the scene of especially violent confrontations, many peasants also called into question the methods used by the FARC to strengthen its presence.

In fact, the guerrilla forces' control of many regions was won through methods acceptable during the Violence. To dislodge the great landowners reluctant to pay the "revolutionary levy," kidnappings and ransoms were common practice. These practices were applied in the

cities as well as against industrialists and other "enemies of the people."
The 1984 elections, in which one government condition was an end to
abductions, thus posed financing problems for the guerrillas. But these
practices resulted above all in the strengthening of paramilitary groups
acting on behalf of landowners, hence the chain of violent acts and,
frequently, the difficulty in distinguishing "political" acts from ordinary delinquency.

Beginning in 1983, in regions such as the Magdalena Medio, one
saw the dawn of a multifaceted terror involving the armed forces, the
FARC, and paid assassins, the end product of which was, besides
innumerable killings and kidnappings, the exodus of peasants attempting to find refuge in the cities. The same exodus occurred in Cauca,
where armed forces confronted M-19 and tried to neutralize the FARC.
In this way, the cases multiplied where violence seemed to escape
organizational control and to spread unchecked throughout the entire
social corpus. The assassinations of M-19 leaders during the cease-fire
already have been mentioned. Members of the FARC also continued to
be targets. The armed forces were certainly to blame, as they supported
paramilitary groups, used torture, and caused "disappearances." But
also at fault were numerous gangs acting at the military's command or
on its behalf. Abductions and ransoms afflicted working-class areas as
well, demonstrating that violence cut across all social milieus.

The guerrilla movements did not escape unharmed from this diffusion of violence. Internal accounts were settled. The ELN assassinated
one of its former prestigious leaders, Ricardo Lara, who directed a legal
political group. One outgrowth of the FARC, the Ricardo Franco
group, well known for the capital it had accumulated from kidnappings,
broke away from the FARC and tried to assassinate high-ranking
Communist leaders. After allying itself with M-19, this group finally
self-destructed: its principal leaders, suspecting police infiltration,
executed over eighty of its members. Certain guerrilla organizations
did not hesitate to resort to terrorist methods, including the assassinations of political and military leaders. In addition, many groups lost
nearly all of their experienced staff; such was the case of M-19. Disagreements between the guerrilla groups continued. As we have seen,
the FARC, for the time being, did not resume hostilities. And, in certain
regions, guerrilla movements were led to establish a modus vivendi
with other powerful illegal groups—the drug traffickers.

Military strategies, social struggles, and violent practices thus formed
variable constellations. These elements variously came together or
worked at cross purposes, thereby fostering radicalization and disorganization, conditions that in themselves may join in harmony or in
discord.

Conclusion

At the outset two questions were raised. To what extent does the continuation of limited democracy in Colombia contribute to the ongoing sociopolitical violence? To what extent is the original experience of the Violence still evident in representations of the political and social orders? Many elements suggest a break around 1980. As a consequence of the emergence of a new generation of political leaders and the gravity of the socioeconomic crisis, there seemed to take shape a revolutionary plan aimed at putting an end to the dissociations of the social and political as well as to the separations between the strategy of armed struggle and other political means. But the break remains only half-finished, and regression remains an ever-present eventuality.

By referring to a participatory democracy, the guerrilla movements have tried to impose the image of a National Front that is no more than a military dictatorship. Limited democracy nonetheless maintains its effectiveness. It still guides an important proportion of the population and allows for spaces where social and political oppositions are recognized and contained. Simultaneously nourishing the dissociations between the political and the social, it at least has the ability to marginalize that which, within social conflicts, is too excessive for the system to manage. In so doing, it concurs with the pervasion of violence in the social order and provokes in revolutionary organizations the desire to channel this violence in a definite direction. This does not exclude the possibility, however, that limited democracy might coexist, for better or for worse, with armed struggle, by in turn marginalizing it and exposing it to the dangers of disorganization.

In 1980 the guerrilla movements managed for a time, by still invoking "another democracy," to avoid the traces of the former Violence. In proportion to the new violence's diffusion into the social fabric, the distinction between what was in the service of building a new society and what was a disaggregation of collective ties became unclear. It was the same with the political system. It tried periodically to renew itself. President Barco's regime, for example, tried a different tack at renewal by giving up trying to share the government with the Conservatives. This is a matter of giving substance once again to the old cleavage between the two parties. But heterogeneity and dislocation of the centers of power permit only the illusion of a democracy assuming responsibility for national debates and citizens' rights.

Perhaps one must look beyond this division of powers for a rampart against the outbreak of a generalized armed confrontation, for division works to bring such a confrontation back into its own universe, that of a violence waylaid by degeneration. Perhaps also the democratic illusion is more effective than it seems. Public opinion is deteriorating progressively, and yet Colombians continue in the same proportions as usual, even in a slightly greater proportion, to go to the polls and cast ballots overwhelmingly for the Liberal and Conservative parties. No doubt they have reasons for doing so, for example, the hope of controlling the violence. War and peace, limited democracy and violence; Colombia is far from escaping these prospects.

Notes

1. Since 1972 parties other than the traditional ones have been able to participate in elections. In 1974 the system of presidential alternation between the two traditional parties ended. But an article introduced into the constitution provides for maintaining an equitable distribution of governmental posts and public jobs between the two parties, based on electoral results.

2. The state of siege was used until 1968 not only to deal with "threats to public order" but also to allow the government to act by executive order. After 1968 the government permitted exceptional measures for public order (meetings subject to permission, for example) and assigned to military justice those who threatened public order.

3. Until 1972 all parties had to propose rosters on Liberal or Conservative tickets. Thus the Communist party presented its candidates on the Liberal ticket, and General Rojas Pinilla's populist movement presented its candidates on both the Conservative and Liberal tickets.

4. The ELN in particular lost many of its ranks in the battle of Anori in 1973.

5. M-19 revealed itself in 1974 with the kidnapping and assassination of a union leader noted for his compromises with the right and the U.S. diplomatic and intelligence services; then, in 1979, with a spectacular weapons raid on a barracks near Bogotá; and again in 1980 by taking hostage some twenty ambassadors near the Dominican embassy (following two months of negotiations, M-19 members were allowed to leave for Cuba).

6. Beginning in 1974 there were a growing number of "civil strikes," usually demanding an amelioration of city services, which paralyzed urban activities. Many of these civil strikes were accompanied by violent demonstrations.

7. Each guerrilla group demanded separate negotiations, and M-19 required direct interviews with the president or his representatives. The ELN rejected cease-fire agreements from the outset.

8. Under cover of the cease-fire, M-19 regrouped some of its troops in an Andean village above Cali and tried to introduce itself into certain working-class districts of the town.

9. See Jacobo Arenas, *Cese el Fuego* (Bogotá, 1985). In this book the author, a former FARC official, announces his "eight-year military plan," which, by seizing the right moment in the context of the insurrectional action

of the urban masses, would lead to "proclamation of a provisional revolutionary government."

10. François Furet, Antoine Liniers, and Philippe Raynaud, *Terrorisme et démocratie* (Paris, 1985).

11. I refer to "the Violence" (uppercase) when speaking of the phenomenon of the 1950s (in Spanish, *la Violencia*), and to "violence" (lowercase) when speaking of the modality that political and social conflicts have assumed afterward.

12. See also Daniel Pecaut, *L'Ordre et la Violence* (Paris, 1986).

13. Even if the Liberal party then had the support of the majority of the masses in many big cities, its economic and social orientations seemed no different than those of its rival.

14. *Essais sur le politique* (Paris, 1986), 113.

15. See Arend Lijphart, "Consociational Democracies," *World Politics* 21:2 (1969): 207–25.

16. In 1969 the government set up a peasant organization, the National Peasant Association (ANUC), which after 1970 eluded official control and in 1971–72 launched large campaigns of land invasion.

17. Opponents of the National Front were convinced that only falsification of results prevented an ANAPO victory. Some socialist officials of ANAPO argued from this point that the democratic option was closed and joined in the creation of M-19. In fact, M-19 means Movement of April 19, the date of these elections.

18. From the name of one of the leaders of the peasant-Indian struggles in the 1920s to preserve their communal lands.

11

Public and Private Dimensions of Urban Violence in Cali*

Alvaro Camacho

In this chapter, Alvaro Camacho analyzes the relationship between public and private violence in the particular context of Cali's social structure and the qualities of its ruling elite. The essay is important in a theoretical sense, helping to define the gray area where public and private social roles and violence overlap. As a case study, Cali is of interest in several respects. In terms of size, Cali, with about 1.5 million people, is just slightly smaller than Medellín (Bogotá's population currently is estimated at 6 million). Cali also serves as the base of a powerful drug cartel, which, unlike its counterpart and rival in Medellín, has not openly confronted the Colombian government. In other respects, however, Cali's urban violence is not unlike that of other Colombian cities, and it is this typicality that, in the context of this volume, makes Camacho's contribution so important.

In general, studies of the violence—those in this volume are no exception—tend to concentrate their attention on its public manifestations, especially its political dimensions. These include the roles of the parties and popular protest, the activities and attitudes of the guerrillas, the nature and capabilities of the state, and the relative influence of, and ties between, the military, paramilitary forces, and the drug cartels. Yet if one could calculate the percentage of violent deaths and injuries attributable to the activities of all of these groups, the odds are that it would not be dissimilar to the percentages for public-versus private-sphere violence calculated in Camacho's several tables (roughly 20 to 25 percent public, 75 to 80 percent private). Said differently, all of the

*This essay is part of a joint research project, "Research on the Social Nature of Urban Violence," undertaken with Alvaro Guzmán at the Centro de Investigaciones y Documentación Socioeconómica at the University of Valle, and financed by Colciencias. I wish to take this opportunity to thank Alvaro for his invaluable collaboration and friendship. I also wish to acknowledge the assistance of Alberto Carvajal, Carmen Idalia Campo, and Alonso Arroyo.

casualties from armed confrontations between the guerrilla forces and the army, from terrorist acts of the drug mafia (political assassinations, car bombs, murder of police), and from the terrorist activities aimed at the democratic left by the paramilitary right, pale in magnitude when compared to the everyday private-sphere violence that envelops Colombian society today. Private settling of accounts (involving debt, property, and sexual and marital issues), robberies, barroom brawls, and family violence—acts perpetrated in many cases under the influence of alcohol, a drug whose social effects, unlike those of cocaine, have received comparatively little attention in Colombia as elsewhere— appear to account for three fourths of the casualties from violence in Colombia. This is an extraordinarily high level even by American standards; compared to the level of violence in many European societies, it is astronomical.

Camacho points out ways in which these two spheres overlap and influence each other. This seems to have been the case historically, during the Violence, as well. Part of the license for the violent private settling of grievances comes from the perception that the state and its organs of protection and justice are contested, politicized, arbitrary, or ineffectual. In his important study of the origins of the Violence, *Violence, Conflict, and Politics in Colombia* (New York, 1980), Paul Oquist called this process "the partial collapse of the state." A similar situation seems to be occurring in Colombia today, as the state at times appears about to be overwhelmed by challenges to its authority and legitimacy from the armed left, the paramilitary right, and the drug mafia.

Alvaro Camacho is a sociologist affiliated with the Center for Socioeconomic Documentation at the University of Valle in Cali. He is the author of *Droga y sociedad en Colombia: El poder y el estigma* (Bogotá, 1988).

To better understand the range of expression of contemporary urban violence, the features of its principle forms, and the complementary and contradictory relationships manifested in each form, it is helpful to refer to a dual conception of social reality. In one sense the social comprises the general principles that determine the production and reproduction of a set of recognized and regulated social relations in a population. This sense includes social divisions and conflicts and the way these find expression. But the social also includes the interpersonal relationships through which social groups and their cultural expressions are constituted.

To analyze the social character of contemporary urban violence it is necessary to understand the way it manifests itself in both spheres, examining what might be called a violence of the public sphere and a violence of the private sphere. The private sphere is the social space in which individuals expresss their personalities without their conduct being necessarily determined by the conventional social roles sanctioned by the society in which they live. The public sphere, in contrast, refers to the general social order and to individual behaviors that are open to general scrutiny. It is the space for the expression of social roles that are collectively determined and regulated and that may even be supported and enforced by law.

The public and private spheres, then, involve both the dimensions of the social order as well the behavior expected of individuals. In the first space people are citizens, and in the second they are persons. The difference reflects the old Greek distinction between *domo* and *agora*, *idios* and *demios*, which gave rise to the notions of democracy, political culture, and citizenship. The distinction is less than tidy, however, whenever private behavior occurs in a public space and conversely, when public actions are expressed in the private realm.[1]

We thus can describe a public act of violence by examining 1) the perpetrators, when the act is executed "in the name of" principles of the general social order; 2) the victims, when they are victims because of their reputation, job, or social function; and 3) its form, when the acts reveal evidence that the motivation or objective sought involves the general social order. A private act of violence, on the other hand, is one in which none of these qualities is apparent. In this case, the victims are victims because of the kind of relationship—permanent or casual— they have with the perpetrators, or when the acts can be imputed to the strictly private interests of the actors.

Magnitude and Forms of Violence in the Public and Private Spheres in Medellín and Cali

In its report to the government on urban violence in Colombia, the Commission for the Study of the Violence found that of Colombian cities Medellín and Cali had the highest homicide rates, higher even than Bogotá and much higher than Barranquilla. Yet the number of all crimes in Medellín and Cali was lower than in several other cities with smaller populations. This finding led the commission to classify these two cities as the most violent in the country. Average monthly homicides in 1986 fluctuated between 2.17 and 6.46 per day for Cali and between 5.77 and 9.70 for Medellín (see Table 1).

More detailed examination reveals that violence in the two cities did not result from the same causes and also that, in the context of the different social structures in the two cities, violent acts assumed a different character. From the Medellín statistics, it can be inferred that the violent events that took place there were primarily associated with the private sphere, and that the extent of public violence was in one way or another related to these violent acts, but not determined by them. In fact, all of the available information suggests that Medellín is a center for violence by illegal organizations linked to drug traffic and other forms of organized crime, whose dimensions have turned it into a

Table 1. Average Daily Homicides in Cali and Medellín during 1986

Month	Cali	Medellín
January	3.47	8.87
February	3.33	8.70
March	3.33	9.70
April	3.10	8.86
May	2.17	8.30
June	3.43	8.80
July	3.17	8.10
August	3.43	9.17
September	3.93	5.77
October	2.90	6.57
November	2.36	6.73
December	6.46	7.33

Source: Comisión (1987), Medicina Legal (Cali), and Decypol (Medellín).

genuine problem of public order. This violence is inseparable from a set of strictly private violent actions linked to alcohol consumption, personal vendettas, and ways of obtaining money. Recently, however, groups have appeared that have converted this type of violence into a political problem. These groups execute "undesirable" elements in the population, perform cleanup operations, and commit political homicides. Their objectives are to eliminate defenders of human rights, militants in the parties of the left, union leaders, and other persons who are defined as subversive of the city's social order.

A central fact about homicide in Medellín is that in spite of the many political and law-enforcement measures taken against it, its rate, far from declining, as it seems to be the case in Cali, is accelerating. In 1985, Medellín registered eighty-four homicides for every one hundred thousand inhabitants. The comparative figure for the whole of Germany that year was one per one hundred thousand. In the Americas only strife-torn Guatemala had a higher rate. These data have led observers and analysts to explain the violence of Medellín in terms of a social structure in which the traditional mechanisms of maintaining order are deteriorating rapidly. In Cali the phenomenon seems to have different characteristics, which turns us to consideration of the social structure of the city and the particular forms in which the structure of power is organized. Examination of the kinds of violent acts in Cali reported by the press for the period 1980 to 1986 permits inferences about the power structure in the city and particularly about how a specific urban social order is maintained.

To classify the forms of violence expressed in the public and the private spheres in Cali from 1980 to 1986, I have used a system that combines several variables. First, I have attempted to determine whether the perpetrators were representatives of the state or were private citizens. Second, I have tried to identify the victims to see if they were killed because of their social position, or if they were killed as private citizens in episodes that were also of a private nature. Third, I have tried to determine the context in which the violence took place, and in this way to specify the particular dimensions of the social order affected by the act or acts of violence. Using a methodology described more fully later, it is possible to determine the public or private nature of each act of violence. Fourth, I have attempted to ascertain the origin of each violent act, to see which of the dichotomous poles of the social order gave rise to it. Did it come from the side of the ruling class or from the side of rebellion? Did it arise from the defense of property and privilege or from the actors' need to survive?

An analysis of the violent cases reported in the newspaper *El País* in the sample months of March and October for the years from 1980 to 1984 and of all those registered during the twenty-four months of 1985 and 1986 reveals the following about the perpetrators (see Table 2). Of the 629 (32%) cases for which there is specific information, 78 (about 12%) indicate that the perpetrators were identified as, or at least suspected of being, government officials who had performed the acts of violence in their official roles. Those perpetrators identified as, or suspected of being, private were 551 (roughly 88%).

These data reveal one aspect of public and private violence in the city. They are complemented by the data on the victims. Of the total of 1,300 identified as victims, 291 (about 22%) belonged to the public sphere compared to 1,018 (about 78%) in the private sphere (see Table 3). (Deaths of recognized thugs were included as part of the public sphere, a procedure justified by the fact that such killings were often attributed to the death squads.)

When one examines the scenes of the crimes and classifies them according to whether they belong in the public or the private sphere, the data are fairly congruent with the previous figures. In fact, 141 (about 17%) of the 819 cases for which there is information available occurred in public places, as compared to 678 (almost 83%) in private settings (see Table 4).

Determining the social origin of perpetrators of violence is considerably more complex given the broad overlap possible in the categories available for analysis. One can argue that the 85 (23%) cases classified

Table 2. Perpetrators Identified in Violent Cases in the Public and Private
         Spheres in Cali, 1980–1986

	Public		Private	
	No.	*%*	*No.*	*%*
Identified	76	12.0	280	44.7
Unidentified	2	0.3	271	42.9
Totals	78	12.3	551	87.6

Note: In this table and those that follow, the figures for 1980 to 1984 are based on a
sample; those for 1985 and 1986, on a complete survey.

Table 3. Victims Identified in Violent Cases in the Public and Private
         Spheres in Cali, 1980–1986

Public	*No.*	*%*
Known gangster	57	20.1
Union member	1	0.3
Politician	59	17.7
Justice official	11	3.9
Police	88	31.2
Member, armed services	16	5.6
Prostitute or homosexual	59	20.9
Totals	291	99.7
Private		
Thief	40	3.9
Mafia	1	0.1
Other economic violence	131	12.8
Family violence	30	2.9
Other cases	816	80.1
Totals	1,018	99.8

Table 4. Violent Cases in the Public and Private Spheres in Cali, 1980–1986

Public	No.	%
Armed confrontations	62	43.9
Political cases not involving arms	12	8.5
Mass actions	4	2.8
Cleanup operations	63	44.6
Totals	141	99.8
Private		
Assaults	287	42.3
Kidnappings	3	0.4
Property defense	2	0.3
Drug trade	1	0.1
Settling of accounts	143	21.0
Family	37	5.4
Brawls and alcohol related	193	28.4
Sexual	12	1.7
Totals	678	99.6

Note: The private accounts for 82.7% of the cases. The public accounts for 17.2% of the cases.

as originating from the ruling class or from the rebels are framed fundamentally within the strictly political and, therefore, belong in the public realm, whereas the 284 (77%) cases associated with property and its protection belong in the private sphere (see Table 5). Also, Table 5 shows that a large majority of the cases originate in the ruling pole of the dichotomy, which enables one to see violence as an exercise of domination. This conclusion would tend to point to shortcomings in the exercise of official power, an issue that will be described later. In fact, the ruling pole is more violent than the dominated, which reveals the power relations between the two. These acts supposedly are attempts to punish violations of law and order arising from the rebel pole. This relationship in the public realm shows up especially in violent acts committed in the political sphere (see Table 6).

The foregoing data support the hypothesis that violence in Cali has permeated both spheres of social life. Although violence is expressed more vigorously in the private sphere, public violence has a specific weight that cannot be ignored.

Table 5. Origin of Violent Aggression in the Public and Private Spheres in Cali by Social Position, 1980–1986

	Public		Private	
	No.	*%*	*No.*	*%*
Ruling	50	58.8	250	88.0
Ruled	35	41.1	34	11.9
Totals	85	99.9	284	99.9

Note: The public accounts for 23% of the cases and the private for 76.9% of the cases. Those cases that might be either public or private have been excluded.

Table 6. Number of Deaths and Injuries in Violent Cases in the Public and Private Spheres in Cali, 1980–1986

	Public		Private	
Number of Deaths and Injuries	*No.*	*%*	*No.*	*%*
1 death	52	42.6	389	57.9
2 to 5 deaths	27	22.1	30	4.4
6 to 10 deaths	0	0.0	0	0.0
Injured only	31	25.4	201	29.9
1 dead plus injured	5	4.1	47	7.0
2 or more dead plus injured	7	5.7	4	0.5
Totals	122	99.9	671	99.7

Note: The public accounts for 13.8% of the cases, the private for 84.6%.

Social Structure, Philanthropic Control, and Social Order

The three phenomena described for Cali—the high degree of homicide, its reduction in the mid-1980s, and the importance of violence in the public sphere—have a close relation to the nature of the local social structure and the ways in which social and political control in the city is maintained by the ruling class. The social structure of Cali and its hinterland is described concisely by U.S. sociologist John Walton:

The rural sector is dominated by large landowning elites that employ the bulk of the population as agricultural workers (for example, on sugar plantations and dairy farms). The smallholder or middle peasant class is quite reduced. A marginal urban proletariat has grown substantially in recent years and is partially absorbed in the tertiary sector, though still greatly underemployed. Manufacturing controlled by local or foreign elites is of recent origin and tends to be capital-intensive, creating a small labor bourgeoisie in the midst of a much larger unskilled and migrant labor force. An urban middle sector exists in commerce, artisan industry, and various services including the public bureaucracies, but its numerical importance is small in contract to the lower classes. In short, the pattern of social stratification is distinctly inegalitarian.[2]

This inequality was confirmed later by the Colombian economist Miguel Urrutia, who stresses how in the 1970s

income was redistributed towards the top and the bottom. In fact, per capita income both in poor families and rich ones increased at a higher annual rate than national per capita income. Likewise, head of household income increased for those groups in a period during which real wages of workers in manufacturing grew very slowly. . . . Combining data from several sources on income in Cali, the impression is that during the seventies there was a decrease in poverty, and that the gap between the formal and informal sectors grew smaller; however, this happened in large part to the detriment of the middle class. Although the income of the poor increased more rapidly than per capita income, the gap was also closed because real income in the middle class grew very little or not at all.

With a strange premonitory sense, he concludes his prognosis for Cali by stating that "the decline of the relative position of the middle class has profound political implications. It will be interesting to keep this phenomenon in mind when analyzing the tendency towards a diminution of citizen participation in elections, in the creation of political movements that do not reject violent tactics, and a certain discontent among intellectuals (who represent the middle class) with the economic and political institutions of the country."[3]

The nature of the ruling class in Cali is presented in Walton's study of the power structures in four Latin American cities, Guadalajara, Monterrey, Medellín, and Cali. His study shows that elites in Medellín enjoy less prestige than those in Cali, in spite of the fact that Medellín has a more liberal ruling elite, a more egalitarian distribution of socioeconomic status, greater upward mobility, and more professionalism in the management of government affairs. Cali's elite, even though considered more conservative, less egalitarian, more rigid, and less professional, enjoys higher prestige than the elite in the other three cities.[4] In another study the same author found that the Cali elite was small and tightly knit: "It seems to represent most key institutions, such as government, commerce, industry, services, education, and their interest-group affiliates. [Moreover,] beneath the surface, influence is often concentrated by multiple position holding and the tendency of high-status people to circulate among top posts irrespective of any special expertise."[5]

After reviewing the power structures and discussing three separate research projects on the subject in Cali, Walton concludes that the three studies show substantial agreement on the existence of a closely knit economic elite. The elite's wealth, which originally came from large agrarian properties, had been invested recently in local industry. In this way the political power base of the traditional classes was expanded.[6]

Charles Collins's study on the local press also casts light on the city's power structure. Examining the history of the press, Collins found substantial change. Traditionally, journalism was an informal, almost quixotic, activity practiced by a few local reporters. Recently, however, the press has come to be controlled by two large organizations belonging to two powerful capitalist families, whose wealth came from industrial, commercial, and agricultural interests. In addition, both families figure prominently in political party leadership.[7]

Under such conditions of strong concentration of wealth and power and of obvious inequality in the distribution of both, one must ask what kind of political and cultural system could manage to keep the institutional order functioning, in spite of the high levels of violence. To explain this phenomenon one must understand how the exercise of control operates through a set of extremely efficient mechanisms. Outstanding among these mechanisms is the philanthropy extended by the ruling classes. Cali is a city in which good works are so widespread that there are some 526 community service institutions, 400 of these are private agencies that do not operate for profit. These institutions are concerned with recreation, education and training, care of infants and the aged, health, rehabilitation, construction, community participation, and community development.

Cali is also one of the cities that stands out on the national scene for the public work of its leaders in promoting economic activity and small businesses. And it is the city whose business associations and entrepreneurs most have influenced public opinion on the subject of the social responsibility of business and have shown the most concern about the welfare of the poorest citizens.

Besides the charitable and developmental activities of Cali's purely private business community, there is in the city a very particular kind of interchange of positions between the public sphere and business sectors. The existence of what have been called "polyvalents"—that is, prominent citizens who easily switch back and forth between important positions in the public and private sectors—ensures a degree of continuity and congruence between the two sectors. In these interchanges and in the politics of philanthropy one can detect the actions of a true local bourgeoisie. It is a bourgeoisie not only in the purely classificatory sense of its position as owner of the means of production but also in the sense of a strong force that takes the city as its field of action, tries to model the city into an organic entity conducive to its class interests, and seeks to exercise its power through participation in the search for a solution to local problems.

The policy of philanthropy and local development is not merely an outgrowth of rational calculation in the search for social legitimacy. It forms part of the very character of the ruling class, which conforms to an ideology that systematically supports and motivates civic responsibility as well as love for the city and stresses the obligations of leaders and a sense of belonging to the community. In stimulating these values, the elite tries to attenuate structural inequality and at the same time delegitimize attempts at subversion of the existing social order. It also produces a sense of citizen participation, which, with various degrees of efficacy, makes the inhabitants feel that they are part of the processes of social integration.

The exercise of philanthropy and promotion of civic pride by the elite contrast sharply, however, with the wielding of power by some of the representatives of local party politics. Political power is gained through a set of clientelistic relationships akin to bossism. Favoritism and the private-partisan appropriation of the local and departmental bureaucracies go hand in hand in the city. The response of subaltern classes to this form of exercising political power has been either to abstain from voting, a pattern that reveals a low level of acceptance, or to develop independent electoral movements organized precisely around criticism of the system.

The Limits of Hegemony and Violence in the Public Sphere

The hypothesis that public violence is associated with the power of the elite is more complex than was indicated in the previous section, however. In fact, central to the functioning of elite hegemony is some degree of acquiescence on the part of the people. When such acquiescence exists, power and domination do not have to be maintained with brute force and violence. However, it also is necessary for the powerful to produce at least the appearance of resolving the structural problems of the dominated. In the analysis of the types of violence in Cali, these kinds of relations become clear.

A review of newspaper reports and recent history in Cali corroborate the existence of a link between public violence and the vicissitudes of the system of control. According to data (summarized in Table 7) on the perpetrators identified for the whole period from 1980 to 1986, those in the public sphere rose from 20.3% of the total in 1984 to 30.5% in 1985 and then dropped slightly to 28.8% in 1986. In the private sector the figures rose constantly from 12.7% to 18.5% to 20.6% for the same years. A similar tendency can be observed for the victims identified (see Table 8). Those from the public sector rose from 16.2% to 23.2% to 27%, while those in the private sphere increased from 11.3% to 20.8% to 26.8%.

Table 7. Perpetrators Identified in Violent Acts in the Public and Private Spheres in Cali, 1980–1986

Year	Public No.	Public %	Private No.	Private %	Totals No.	Totals %
1980	6	5.1	84	7.4	90	7.2
1981	6	5.1	228	20.2	234	18.7
1982	6	5.1	102	9.0	108	8.6
1983	6	5.1	132	11.6	128	11.0
1984	24	20.3	144	12.7	168	13.4
1985	36	30.5	210	18.5	246	19.6
1986	34	28.8	234	20.6	268	21.6
Totals	118	100.0	1,134	100.0	1,242	100.1

Note: In this and subsequent tables, estimates for the years 1980 to 1984 were constructed by adding the numbers for the months of March and October, multiplying by 12, and dividing by 2. Note that the percentages refer to the portion of the total for the whole period in question, 1980 to 1986.

Table 8. Victims Identified in Violent Cases in the Public and Private Spheres in Cali, 1980–1986

Year	Public No.	Public %	Private No.	Private %	Totals No.	Totals %
1980	30	6.2	192	10.5	222	9.3
1981	66	13.7	240	13.2	306	16.2
1982	54	11.2	174	9.5	228	9.6
1983	12	2.5	144	7.9	156	6.5
1984	78	16.2	204	11.3	282	11.8
1985	112	23.2	378	20.8	490	20.6
1986	130	27.0	488	26.8	618	26.0
Totals	482	100.0	1,820	100.0	2,302	100.0

Cases of violence in the public sphere undergo a sharp change after 1985, as is shown in Table 9. In 1986 the figure rises considerably over those for 1984 and 1985, from 15.7% to 29.4% to 47.1% (24, 45, and 72 cases, respectively). Rises in the private sector were much less sharp. When we observe the tendency relative to social origin, we find that in the public sphere there is an abrupt increase in the period, while in the private sphere the tendency is much less acute (see Table 10). An estimated 8.6% in 1983 increasing to a documented figure of 25.7% in 1984 (an increase of from six to eighteen cases) in the public sphere contrasts with a change in the private sphere of from 6.2% to 11.2% (from thirty to fifty-four cases). In the former case the figure triples, whereas in the latter it does not even double.

These data indicate that beginning in 1985 there was a notable increase in violence in the area of public life in Cali, while the tendency toward violent activity in private life grew in a more even fashion. The existence of this sharp rise in violence in public life means, in part, that the social order presided over by the philanthropic elite met powerful and violent challenges from other social forces.

This relation is evident in the presence of the military guerrilla group M-19 in the region. At first it established its political headquarters in the neighboring *municipio* of Yumbo and then extended its military presence into the city itself. Subsequently, on the eve of the signing of the peace accords in Corinto and El Hobo in 1985, the M-19 took Yumbo. This sparked severe fighting in which citizens of Cali and Yumbo fought side by side. It was the first sign of the ability of this insurgent organization to alter the rhythm of everyday life for the residents of Cali.

Table 9. Number of Violent Cases in the Public and Private Spheres in Cali, 1980–1986

Year	Public No.	Public %	Private No.	Private %	Totals No.	Totals %
1980	0	0.0	132	9.4	132	8.5
1981	0	0.0	246	17.6	246	16.0
1982	0	0.0	204	14.6	204	13.2
1983	12	7.8	102	7.3	114	7.3
1984	24	15.7	186	13.3	210	13.5
1985	45	29.4	217	15.5	262	16.9
1986	72	47.1	310	22.3	382	24.6
Totals	153	100.0	1,397	100.0	1,550	100.0

Table 10. Origin of Violent Aggression in the Public and Private Spheres in Call by Social Position, 1980–1986

Year	Public Ruling No.	%	Ruled No.	%	Private Ruling No.	%	Ruled No.	%	Totals Ruling No.	%	Ruled No.	%
1980	0	0.0	0	0.0	60	12.3	18	19.1	60	10.8	18	12.5
1981	0	0.0	0	0.0	72	14.8	18	19.1	72	12.9	18	12.5
1982	0	0.0	0	0.0	66	13.7	24	25.5	66	11.8	24	16.7
1983	6	8.6	0	0.0	30	6.2	6	6.4	36	6.4	6	4.1
1984	18	25.7	18	36.0	54	11.2	6	6.4	72	13.0	24	16.7
1985	22	31.4	23	46.0	83	17.1	8	8.6	105	19.0	31	21.5
1986	24	34.3	9	18.0	120	24.7	14	14.9	144	26.0	23	16.0
Totals	70	100.0	50	100.0	485	100.0	94	100.0	555	99.9	144	100.0

The phase following the signing of the accords, while it stimulated important reactions of sympathy with as well as rejection of the new urban role of the M-19, did not generate any noticeable increase in violence. Meanwhile, the M-19 established so-called peace camps in several neighborhoods of the city. Independent of the discussion of peace and the civic action by the M-19, the camps in some ways resembled military organizations.

At the end of 1985, when the truce was broken, the M-19 intensified its presence in some neighborhoods of the city. This generated open fear about the insurgent capabilities of the organization on the part of the armed forces and civilian sectors. In December, a few days after the tragic events at the Palace of Justice in Bogotá, the Colombian army, in an unprecedented show of force, launched a fierce attack against the M-19 in the Siloé neighborhood. This bloody offensive marked the beginning of the end of the organization's urban form and left no doubt about the determination of the army and the local power structure to "sweep the city clean" of subversive elements. It was clear to the elite, however, that the M-19 had won the sympathies of some sectors of the population. They felt it was necessary, therefore, to start a strong campaign of reconquest, which would include the use of violence.

The year 1985 was also the one in which the violent cleanup gangs within the city seemed to proliferate. It looked as though the defense of public order was intensifying through a combination of purely official elements (the army, the police, and civic campaigns) with private, paramilitary elements who were on the same side of the issues. This process produced the first great paradox of this situation. In effect, the "overflow" of public violence, while it defended the general order, reinforced legal authorities, and relieved the state of its monopoly on force, nevertheless threatened the government's legitimacy. It was, in a way, the privatization of the public.

Official violence was also a threat, however. It can be assumed that the ferocity displayed in the eradication of the M-19 affected citizens who had nothing to do with the conflict and that many of these individuals saw the government's military actions as threatening rather than protective. Specifically, in Siloé there were dead and wounded who did not belong to the insurgent group. It is unlikely that their friends and families thought that these victims were being defended by the army.

A second paradox emerges from the fact that this substitution for state force translates into a reduction of the public domain. In fact, the cleanup actions heightened the climate of terror and insecurity for citizens. These actions prompted the increased use of private weapons and encouraged the proliferation of the paraphernalia of private protection, such as guards and armored cars. Many civilians left the city for safer places. Cleanup groups that had no clear political base and directed their violent activities at the elimination of undesirable population groups were a public invitation to reduce the sphere of government.

According to the cleanup groups, certain social types were undesirable. The groups killed homosexuals and prostitutes—citizens who publicly proclaimed their differences with official attitudes toward sexual behavior. In a clear demonstration of intolerance, the groups murdered anyone who assumed an identity that contradicted the usual and expected. But they also killed people who did not assume contradictory identities. To kill a prostitute is, in effect, to deny a role socially ascribed to women in public life. To kill a homosexual is to murder a person because he is not manly and virile enough.

A third paradox lies in the double meaning of some of the civic campaigns that were being promoted strongly in the city. When, on the bodies of persons assassinated by the death squads, signs appeared bearing the city's environmental cleanup slogan, "A beautiful Cali is a clean Cali," the double meaning assumed disturbing proportions. Some individuals, among them a contingent of university professors, received threatening notes bearing this slogan. It appears that an effort to present the city as a place of beauty, relaxation, and pleasure had been transformed, offering instead a violent, intimidating image of the city. In fact, the threatening notes asked the professors to leave the city, a macabre way of announcing that there would be a "sweep."

Hegemony, Personal Relations, and Private Violence

While one side of public violence seeks to transform the social order and the other tries to conserve or rescue it, private violence adopts and expands spheres of individual social action. This process generates a new paradox. In public violence the actors work "in the name of" a social order that they define as obsolete, unjust, or antidemocratic and that must, therefore, be changed. Or else, they act to defend and safeguard that order. In both cases they are representatives or agents of general social views that do not involve necessarily the interests and desires of the collectivity in whose names they are acting, thereby expropriating the representation of the collectivity as if they themselves were in charge of guiding society. When it comes to the social forces seeking to transform the prevailing order, they make themselves into representatives of a popular will that supposedly has delegated to them the role of armed vanguard for the collectivity. When they do defend the collectivity, they often must do so clandestinely, which shows that they are acting above and beyond this supposed delegation of power. In either case the public is converted into a place for violent confrontation and arms are elevated to the category of final arbiters, definers of the collectivity's right to exist. Under these conditions the community remains without nonviolent representation in the public sphere and is rendered incapable of defining the public sphere as a space for coexistence and for the creation of a civilization of democratic confrontation.

Private violence, in contrast to public, operates on the basis of the direct personal business of people in their strictly private lives. In this sphere people act in their own name; they neither challenge nor protect any social order. Their own interests are the referents for their violent acts. An examination of the categories of violence in the private sphere clearly shows the areas in which it is expressed: robberies accompanied by death or assault; property protection that goes substantially beyond the common definition of the rights to life and to property; settling of accounts (which represents a high proportion of cases, 143 in the period under examination, or 21 percent of the total acts of private violence, as shown in Table 4); brawls, often accompanied by alcohol consumption; sexual crimes, which paint a picture of the oppression of women; and family violence, as represented by cruelties family members visit upon their weakest members. This last category differs from the others in that it seeks not the elimination of the victim but his subordination through a demonstration of superiority.

In the form of holdups and robberies (Table 4 shows 287 assault cases in the period, equivalent to roughly 42 percent of the total), private violence is a kind of access to property and money and can be based on the need to commit violence to acquire them. In such cases the elimination of the victim may not be the reason for the act but rather an unplanned consequence. On the other hand, violence may be a form of access to wealth, for example, kidnapping for extortion, that has nothing necessarily to do with the poverty of the perpetrator. Kidnapping is a type of violence that usually requires its practitioners to possess ample resources, both material, such as weapons and vehicles, and social, such as an organization. It is not, therefore, a violence of the poor.

Violence in the private sphere also represents an attitude of intolerance, displayed both in the excesses resorted to for the protection of property and in the facility with which a casual opponent is eliminated in a barroom brawl (193 cases, or 28.4 percent of the total in Table 4).

Showing equal intolerance is a person who targets a woman for sexual reasons or a man who persecutes his wife or children in order to assert his superiority.

Although these incidents take place within the orbit of the private lives of the actors, they do reveal weaknesses in the capacity of the controlling elite to generate a collective life in which citizens subscribe to the slogans and values that the elites promulgate. In fact, a substantial part of the elite's good works are directed at improving the home environment, establishing patterns of peaceful relations among citizens, fighting poverty, and reaffirming Cali's image as a beautiful and clean city in which people treat each other with respect for life, honor, and property. On a strictly social level, private violence activates and supports the prevailing order by reinforcing the traditional differences between rich and poor, the weak and the powerful.

Violence, Rights, and Democracy

This whole set of forms of public and private violence has a direct impact on the human and civic rights of Cali's inhabitants. In fact, political violence in Colombia has led to a state of affairs in which the defense of human rights is expressed in the political arena, particularly in the confrontation between the political apparatus of the state and its citizenry. This confrontation has reached such high levels that, often, the remaining violence can be relegated to a secondary plane.

As I have maintained consistently, however, the political regime does not account for the whole society, and political violence does not account for all violence. Both the data presented by the Committee for the Study of the Violence[8] and the statistics in the present study show that although the violence of confrontation between state and citizen today occupies a central place in Colombia, other types of violence— acts that are committed by individuals or groups seeking to protect or restore a social order or by citizens trying to resolve strictly personal conflicts or to assert their positions—occupy a place of equal importance.

Neglect of this finding has led to an overemphasizing of human rights and a downplaying of those dimensions—such as safety—that define the citizenry. It is no coincidence that an astonishing number of urban polls on local problems show that the citizens rank the problem of safety—or lack of it—as their central concern and also that the same citizens, to the extent of their financial abilities, resort to private means to provide themselves with security.

In Cali there are more than 4,500 private policemen registered with local authorities, and the same authorities estimate that there are at least an equal number not registered. The local police force, meanwhile, has about 2,800 men. Thus there are an estimated 11,800 security personnel for the population, not counting members of the army, who in the regular course of their duties perform similar tasks. This means that there is approximately one security officer for every 188 inhabitants of the city and to that must be added the proliferation of arms in the hands of private citizens.

Whereas political protection does not discriminate according to the social or economic position of citizens, private security does depend on the ability to pay for it, leaving individuals with few resources at an obvious disadvantage. Their civil rights—and, one might add, their human rights—are dependent upon the action that government agents take to protect them. Lack of security at times has reached such high levels that on various occasions private citizens have expressed their support for the death squadrons' cleanup activities in the city.

This situation brings us to yet another paradox: while criticism of the death squads is made in the name of theoretical principles of justice and democracy, in reality these expressions of support are based on the felt need for safety. This is understandable if one considers that public violence generates a distinguishable type of social actor whereas private violence does not discriminate among citizens, even if it is directed preferentially against the weakest and least protected.

This form of private violence, when it reaches levels as high as those discussed here, becomes a problem of public order and democracy. It is public to the extent that the citizens themselves define their lack of security as an overriding problem and demand protection from the state. It is also public in the sense that quite apart from the cracks it reveals in the elite hegemony, it tarnishes the image of the city the ruling class tries so hard to maintain. Private violence is a problem of democracy not only in the field of the exercise of civil rights but also to the extent that it makes routine coexistence impossible. There is nothing to guarantee the possibility of a democratic political order if there is no social order of the same nature.

Let us return to the reference of the Greeks. For them the private was the space of noncitizenship, of nondemocracy. It was the space of *idios* (root of the word *idiot*). The distinction indicated the indispensably democratic nature of the public. This ethical principle can be applied today in some of our cities. In fact, it is possible that violence in the public sphere is precipitating a search for protection in the private sphere, a space in which the individual finds just as much violence. What kind of democracy is this?

Notes

1. On these issues, see Joseph Bensman and Robert Lilienfeld, *Between Public and Private* (New York, 1979); Richard Sennett, *The Fall of Public Man* (New York, 1978); and Barrington Moore, *Privacy* (New York, 1984).

2. John Walton, *Elites and Economic Development: Comparative Studies on the Political Economy of Latin American Cities* (Austin, TX, 1977), 64.

3. Miguel Urrutia, *Los de arriba y los de abajo: La distribución del ingreso en Colombia durante las últimas décadas* (Bogotá, 1984).

4. Walton, *Elites and Economic Development*, 141.

5. Alejandro Portes and John Walton, *Urban Latin America: The Political Condition from Above and Below* (Austin, TX, 1976), 178.

6. Ibid., 162.

7. Charles D. Collins, *Prensa y poder público en Colombia* (Cali, 1981).

8. *Colombia: Violencia y democracia* (Bogotá, 1987). See Chapter 12 of this volume for a part of this report.

12

Organized Violence

Commission for the Study of the Violence

What do informed Colombians think about the violent state of affairs in their country? Specifically, how do they understand the relationship between the drug trade, paramilitary groups, and the institution of the hired assassin known as the *sicario*? What, in their opinion, needs to be done to eliminate these forms of organized violence, which threaten the stability of the state and work to destroy the social fabric of the nation?

One answer to these questions comes from the report of a special commission appointed by the Colombian minister of government in 1987. The report, published in book form as *Colombia: Violencia y democracia* (Bogotá, 1987), was prepared by a select group of nine educators and a retired major general in the army (who disagreed with some of the recommendations that grew out of the section presented here). Coordinated by Gonzalo Sánchez, the commission viewed its task very broadly. It considered political violence (that perpetrated through the guerrilla movements) as only one manifestation of a deeper problem of social and economic injustice; others were criminal violence, family violence, and violence against indigenous peoples.

The section reproduced here deals with what the commission calls "organized violence," that is, violence committed by organizations involved in the drug trade, by paramilitary organizations of the right, and by organizations of professional assassins. This selection should be of special interest to U.S. readers because it reveals how many Colombians view the effects of foreign demand for narcotics on their own society, why many Colombians oppose the concept of extradition, and what, concretely, is being proposed by Colombians outside the government to deal effectively with a central aspect of the violence today.

This section describes and analyzes some of the forms of organized violence that exist in Colombia. It clarifies the processes of the structuring, the superimposition, and the territorial transfer of these forms of violence, as well as the involvement of specialized groups in the implementation, administration, planning, and diffusion of violence.

The study addresses the ways in which violent social relations develop around the goal of the acquisition of wealth, whether through the exploitation of natural resources or the illegal production and distribution of certain kinds of merchandise. As will be shown, the exploitation of the emerald mines has been a veritable microcosm of ways in which the multiple forms of violence are articulated. Mining activity has spawned organized groups to ensure territorial control, often through "cleanup" operations. Similar phenomena cluster around the cultivation of coca, in a different geographical region but with an undeniable continuity of social actors. It seems as if the economy has turned violent as an extension of these forms of social relationships.

Both in areas where emeralds are mined and in those where coca is cultivated, groups specializing in killing are used as a means of shoring up criminal activities and exercising territorial control. However, these groups, in the form of *sicarios* or of death squads, are not confined to one region. Rather, they circulate throughout the country claiming their victims. Their purpose may be to protect property and business, to serve political causes, or to sustain a local social order or replace it with another, depending on the interests of those who organize and finance the groups.

The Continuity and Superimposition of Violence: The Case of the Emerald Mines

This section describes a representative, but not unique, case of the complex relationships that can be established among the various manifestations of violence, all of which are increasingly stimulated by a form of organized violence. The Minero River basin, especially the zones of Muzo and Coscuez, in the western part of the department of Boyacá, where 80 percent of the national production of emeralds takes place, is a microcosm in which various kinds of violence converge, both in time and space. Throughout the twentieth century, the zone has been the setting for considerable partisan violence. This was true early on, at the beginning of the thirties, in the context of what some call the first violence. It was true in the forties, in such characteristic forms as the *chulavitas*, whose activities covered the whole Andean region of the country. And it was true in the last phase of the violence, that of the political banditry of the sixties.

Most important, however, each of these forms of violence created the conditions for its reproduction and its superimposition on subsequent forms. In fact, the permanent presence of armed bands has been one of the most notable characteristics of the region for the last fifty years. Thus we have the first sequence: the bands of Angel María

Colmenares and Héctor Muñoz, among others, in the thirties; those of José María Sosa, "Cucacho," in the forties; and those of the Conservative Efraín González and the Liberal Carlos Bernal in the sixties.

The bridge between this first type of band and the ones formed later in the emerald-mining area was built by Efraín González, who, through the so-called war of the emeralds, established what was practically a regional empire to control the black market, aided by his two brothers, who went to work as employees of the Coscuez and Peñas Blancas mines. When Efraín González died in June 1965, internal rivalries resurfaced, often involving sectors of the army and the police. These rivalries ceased only with the reestablishment of the authority of the "Ganzo" (Swan), Humberto Ariza.

Since the end of the 1970s a new process has been under way: the transfer of money made in emeralds to the cultivation, processing, and sale of coca, keeping intact the structure that came from the emerald economy and taking advantage of a subculture of illegal activity whose characteristics are quite similar in both industries. In addition, the presence of several guerrilla groups on the periphery of the region was added to the picture. The most important were the eleventh and twenty-second fronts of the Fuerzas Armadas Revolucionarias Colombianas (FARC).

The mobility of violence must be understood in the context of these complex circumstances. For example, the "Medellín cartel," made up of important drug kingpins, has established close ties in the zone. In this way, rivalries originating in emerald mining are transferred to other areas, among them the distant colonization territories of the Guaviare in the east, where people formerly associated with the emerald business now make their fortunes in coca and establish conflictive relations with the guerrillas who are based in the region. Internal relations in these situations are complicated by the fact that the norms that rule the different organizations are very strict and demand very definite adherences and loyalties whose transgression may be punished by death.

The Modes of Practicing Violence

The convergence of these types of violence implies, furthermore, a confluence of the ways that it is practiced. These ways include the organization of private armies for the protection of the highest-ranking persons linked to the exploitation and trafficking in emeralds and drugs or for the maintenance of political control of a region; the settling of accounts among competitors for the control of resources; the liquidation of spies and informers; the consolidation of a market in arms and specialized services, such as those provided by bodyguards as well as by individuals who carry out dirtier jobs requiring more anonymity; the mounting of motorized operations with modern weapons in urban and rural actions whose targets range from cattle rustlers to political or union activists thought to be connected with guerrilla groups; the rise of armed self-defense groups; the organization of cleanup operations against juvenile delinquents and petty criminals; and the use of intimidation, such as bombs or machine-gun fire directed at the residences or places of business of rivals, as a pressure mechanism to collect business debts, resolve affairs of passion, or, more generally, deal with interpersonal and family disputes.

In this context, the state has not acted as an arbiter of the different economic and political interests at play. It is thus not possible for these interests to express themselves thoroughly through legal channels. The state, in its various manifestations, has seemed rather to be an institutional entity of very low legitimacy, beside which, or in relation with which, organized groups operate, taking over state functions (such as providing security and justice). A social world thus is erected where multiple systems of law and justice reign, a world where official institutional government and the noninstitutional coexist. The profound crisis of the Colombian state appears clearly in this context, and it stimulates a variety of forms of organized violence that permeate a region without God and without law.

Drug Traffic and Violence

The production and distribution of prohibited mind-altering substances has been an extremely important source of recent violence in the country. In spite of the fact that it is difficult to isolate its effects from the whole picture of violence in Colombia, its magnitude, possibly exaggerated, has been highly significant for a variety of reasons. It has been intimately associated with the violent deaths of persons connected to the government, the courts, and the press, that is, with crimes that palpably affect the public order and arouse the emotions of the nation. To this must be added the climate of fear and anxiety it fosters, which hinders the functioning of the judicial system, the ethical conduct and objectivity of the press, and the free investigation of the myriad facets of the drug phenomenon.

The drug traffic also has been associated with a deterioration of the country's image in the view of third parties, which has had serious effects on international relations. This deteriorated image is especially true of the way in which Colombians are viewed, and view themselves, abroad and even on native soil. The Colombian government also has been placed in the uncomfortable position of having to take measures against drug production and traffic, measures that have not necessarily emanated from a broad national debate but rather have been a response to foreign demands.

In the field of politics, drug activity has become a new form of power that challenges the position of elected officials. At the same time, it consolidates itself as a private power parallel to that of the state yet penetrating the state's power in various ways. Along another dimension, the penetration of drugs into the activity of the guerrilla groups has hampered state efforts to come to terms with such groups by distorting their image and imputing motives and actions to them that are not consistent with their stated political ends. In addition, the drug traffic has been associated with a noticeable increase in official corruption, which reaches into high levels of decision making, and this also contributes to the demoralization of citizens and honest government officials alike.

Drugs also have penetrated into several areas of social organization. The coincidence of this phenomenon with a period of rapid social and economic change, in which new groups are exerting pressure to move up in the hierarchies of power and privilege, has created a situation where those who traditionally occupied these positions resist change and confuse legal and legitimate upward social mobility with criminal, illicit behavior.

In the economic sphere, the drug traffic has translated into significant distortions in prices not only of basic necessities, because of the substitution of coca for staple crops, but also of other goods as well. The latter results from a rise in conspicuous consumption and the need to legalize the money spent in such activities. It has also meant changes in the national economy associated with the availability and price of foreign currency and the export of capital, among other factors. As for production, its phases of expansion and recession have meant drastic changes in the agricultural activities on large expanses of land through the accelerated replacement of food crops by the raw material for the production of narcotics and the consequent transformation of the life styles of entire populations. This transformation, however, does not constitute a real improvement but rather a decline in the quality of life, including even the cultural identity of indigenous communities.

Finally, as we have already seen, the drug trade has stimulated the proliferation of armed groups, which rain violence and terror on the cities, meting out death as a form of justice, a way of settling accounts, or simply a means of intimidation. The drug traffic, then, has become the central element, not only in the violence in Colombia but also in the conditions of Colombian life.

It is important to stress that the solutions that have been formulated to combat the drug trade have not been the most appropriate ones. It must even be said that they have been dominated by an attitude that frequently implies unacceptable levels of violence. In fact, repression has been elevated to priority status, subordinating programs that are aimed at reintegrating those who are involved in the drug traffic into a peaceful way of life after paying the legal penalties as stipulated as well as programs that respect the cultural identity of those groups who consume hallucinogens as part of an ancestral culture.

The practice of coca crop eradication by spraying fields with highly toxic chemicals may destroy the crop in the short run, but in middle- and long-range terms its efficacy is questionable. It is an act whose consequences are damaging to the natural environment and to the living conditions of peasants and the indigenous poor. At the same time, by creating a shortage of coca in the marketplace, it pushes prices up, producing fatter profits and creating stronger temptations to get into the business. In contrast, the practice of raiding and seizing laboratories, when it does not involve excessive violence, conveys a firm, deliberate commitment and demonstrates a wish to behave calmly while indicating to the drug traffickers that their activities will not succeed and must be abandoned.

A sane government policy on the matter should begin with the recognition that not everyone involved in the drug trade is in the same condition or has the same degree of responsibility. On the one hand, there are small producers and distributors, and on the other, large drug dealers. The state should treat each group with special methods, operating on the criterion that measures should be directed at eliminating the persons involved in the traffic. Such measures must be, furthermore, institutional, integral, democratic, and autonomous.

Another major consideration should also inspire government action. Resorting to violence against the drug traffic not only aggravates the conflict, but it also stimulates more violence and has encouraged private persons to use force, mainly to eliminate small dealers, who are only one of the weakest links in the chain. In the area of consumption the rehabilitative action proposed by the government and some advisory institutions has been stigmatized and condemned by the contrary behavior of certain sectors of the population, in clear defiance of the constructive remedies.

In the face of the violence unleashed by the big dealers and major commercial agents in the drug trade, the government's policy must be to strengthen its own criminal investigation apparatus, judicial institutions, and mechanisms to make penal legislation effective. It does not seem right for the Colombian government, in light of the ineffectiveness of its own institutions, to turn away from tackling the problem and delegate the authority to impose punishments on its nationals to other states. The government thereby converts other countries into intermediaries between Colombian nationals and foreign courts, which, furthermore, operate according to judicial traditions and legal norms that are alien to us.

This renunciation is even less advisable when the response of other governments to the efforts of the Colombian executive branch is neither reciprocal nor entirely unequivocal. President Virgilio Barco's insistence that it is impossible to eradicate production when measures to reduce drug use in the consumer countries are inadequate not only is true but also serves as a basis to redefine a new attitude on the part of the Colombian government vis-à-vis the society of nations.

In this area our government has an ample field of action, and it could provide the initiative in promoting the organization of the producing countries so that they could present the consumer countries with a united demand to make efforts to curb consumption reciprocal with efforts to eradicate commercial cultivation. Such an association of producing countries at the same time, could pose the possibility of suspending the international treaties relating to drug traffic as long as there is any doubt about whether the official entities of the consumer countries are using the activity for political ends that are contrary to the treaties and are linked to efforts to destabilize governments with whom the Latin American nations, in particular, maintain diplomatic relations and friendly ties. Simply for reasons of national honor, the Treaty of Extradition should be suspended until the relevant U.S. Senate committee clarifies U.S. intervention in illicit activities against the government of Nicaragua.

When it comes to small- or medium-size producers of raw material, the Colombian government should not continue the practice of indiscriminate fumigation in the production zones, at least not until other countries take similar action and it is demonstrated, with no room for doubt, that this measure works and there are no side effects harmful either to the health of humans or to the environment. It is no secret that such practices have been prohibited in countries where the crops have become important, precisely because of these side effects, and a government scarcely can risk taking actions over that which it does not have effective and unequivocal control in response to overbearing pressures from other governments.

A policy against production must concentrate its efforts in line with the overall policy against drugs, which is to make sowing and cultivation less attractive. In order to do this it is necessary to draw up and implement programs for the substitution of crops through subsidized loans, technical assistance, transportation and marketing facilities, and other measures tending to consolidate an agriculture economy that suits the needs of the Colombian people and that respects and encourages the cultural identity of the communities that have been victims of the drug traffic.

These kinds of measures, aimed at discouraging the drug trade and at integrating the Colombians presently involved in it into the legal economy, are a substitute for today's violence. They are also a demonstration that the government, utilizing its army and its institutions, really can confront a problem that at the present time is central to life in Colombia.

The Violence of the Death Squads

Death squads, which arise and develop as either a replacement or an extension, through arms and violence, of the government entities in charge of administering justice and maintaining public order, share features with similar groups in other Latin American countries. These bands direct their acts of extermination against political movements and parties, opposition leaders, union members, and sectors presumed sympathetic to the guerrillas. They also target the marginal sectors of society, which supposedly breed forms of delinquency that the squads try to eradicate with cleanup operations in the large cities.

The appearance of the death squad Muerte a Secuestradores (MAS, or Death to Kidnappers), whose sponsorship by drug groups has not been denied, fueled this criminal mode of action, and now there are countless groups specializing in crime. The groups are organized either by private groups or by individual military or police officers, in a patent abuse of their positions and direct defiance of clear official orders and existing laws. The existence of this kind of activity, which announced the advance of the so-called dirty war in our country, was fostered by provisions of Law 48 of 1968 on national defense. This law permitted the military to organize and provide arms to groups of civilians called "self-defense" units, so that they could fight back against organized delinquents and also against armed groups operating in certain peasant regions. The squads also may be a response to feelings of impotence in the face of the ineffectiveness of government justice, which spurs civilians to replace it with violent methods. Death squads are, at the same time, the product and continuation of intolerance against persons or actions that do not conform to what they consider the ideal socio-cultural pattern, and who supposedly are a threat to them. In any case, this type of violence, protected by an imprudent law allowing citizens to bear arms sponsored by the Ministry of Defense, led to a weakening of the order it was supposed to defend and to a growing privatization of the government's prerogative to dispense justice.

After the killing of more than three hundred activists from the political party Unión Patriótica and dozens of amnestied people from other groups, it is clear that the death squads have shifted considerably from their initial objectives and have become instruments of revenge, reprisal, and intimidation against groups and sectors linked, affectively and ideologically, to guerrilla activity or to delinquency. Apparently, the squads now seek to liquidate the Unión Patriótica or at least to prevent it from expanding and from launching new political activities outside the two-party system.

With their cleanup campaigns in the cities and the provinces—in a clear and damaging attempt to associate their activities with the legal political struggle against crime—the squads also attempt to eradicate anyone who protests against injustice, anyone who supports the consumption of drugs, anyone who has committed any crime. Although these groups supposedly are organized to defend the economic, political, and cultural order, their actions translate into the destruction of that very order.

The possible connection between elements of the police and the armed forces with these bands is not a matter to be treated lightly, nor can it be easily proven. For a variety of reasons, however, the public is anxious about the matter, and it therefore behooves the government to make every effort to clarify the situation if it wants to avoid the definitive failure of the process of pacification, with all that this would mean for the generalization of a dirty war with incalculable consequences.

At the same time, it is essential to emphasize the repeated condemnations of these activities that have been made by leaders in the military and police forces and to recognize that, although there may have been some case of excesses, which cannot be imputed to official policy, these acts are not tolerated by the military establishment. Yet the solidarity demonstrated by the high military command with fifty-nine officers and enlisted men from the army and police accused by the Procuraduria General of the nation of being involved in MAS activities did not contribute to a good image of the military. This ill-advised solidarity prevented full clarification of the behavior of these men.

As long as these groups of killers are not disbanded, the Colombian government lacks the necessary legitimacy to demand a faster return of those bearing arms to the legal struggle, since it cannot effectively guarantee them respect for their lives and for their new political activism within the legal framework. The commission believes that the strengthening of the institutions of justice is fundamental today, but this is not enough to contain the wave of violence that infects the country. To achieve this, it recommends two complementary measures:

1. The creation of a judicial panel to investigate—on the political, not the judicial plane—the present wave of assassinations that might be imputed to criminal groups, particularly those of a political nature that threaten peace and national reconciliation. We cannot wait, as Argentina did, for thirty thousand people to be tortured to death before we act. Argentina's Tribunal Sábato showed the value of listening to public opinion, which was unanimously organized around the goals of a return to peace and the cessation of violence. The creation of that tribunal prevented a further outpouring of violence and started a process of solutions through political channels in which the law declared itself against those who were trying to destroy the country. Today, before the rate of political crime reaches the terrible levels of Argentina in the seventies, it is possible to stop the criminal hand of these groups who are committed to crimes against humanity. We can do this if we act swiftly and energetically.

It is assumed that, in accordance with the measures proposed throughout this document, the state will use every means to secure the rehabilitation of those individuals and their reintegration into normal society.

2. In the text of the decree that created the special court, that entity was not given jurisdiction to judge members of the armed forces or the police, who are still covered by a special set of judicial procedures, the *fuero castrense*. We consider this to be an error. Crimes against the person, which by their nature go against military honor (torture, "disappearing" people, killing outside of combat), should be judged by a civil court that strictly applies the full weight of the law. We have arrived at this recommendation for three reasons. First, it is unthinkable, in the words of General Fernando Landazábal Reyes, for members of the armed forces or the police to commit these crimes while on active duty or in the name of the service. Second, the military institution cannot afford damage to its prestige because of crimes against humanity committed by its members as individuals. Finally, in light of the wave of indignation sweeping across the country, and the perhaps hasty accusation that official entities are solely responsible for such crimes, it behooves these organizations to forego their special *fuero* in favor of other judicial procedures, so as to dispel any doubts about their participation in these lamentable events.

In any case, it must be emphasized that military penal justice should apply only to those criminal acts committed during active military service or in the name of the military but not to common crimes, as is established unequivocally in Article 170 of the constitution, which has prevailed uninterruptedly and without modification since 1886. Therefore, the Special Court, if it is declared constitutional, or some other court, must bring under its jurisdiction, both for investigation and judgment, all those persons implicated in the crimes committed by the already mentioned groups, without granting them any privileged status whatever. Only in this way can the influence of esprit de corps, which on previous occasions has revealed itself as a factor contributing to military impunity, be avoided, along with loss of credibility concerning official promises to pursue peace.

The Violence of Hired Assassins

The phenomenon of *sicarios* (hired assassins) is just as alarming as any of the other forms of violence described earlier. The hired assassin is a gunman at the service of the highest bidder. He has no loyalty or adherence to any of the organized groups, he is indifferent to his victims, and his activity takes the form of a contract to kill in exchange for remuneration. Unlike the death squads or the violent gangs of organized crime associated with illegal trade, the *sicario* is hired to kill for indiscriminate ends. It might be to settle accounts in matters of money, family, or honor. It might be an act of private justice against a violator of promises, contracts, orders, or private codes. It might be aimed at a representative of the state or the media. No one is safe from the *sicario*.

Recently, the *sicario*'s presence has become more widespread, to the point where the job has begun to look attractive. This has led to a process of growing organization, in which entrepreneurs hire gunmen and assign them to missions contracted for by third parties. This process reflects, in a way, the absence of ethical limits on the possible ways of acquiring wealth that has become generalized in Colombia. It also reflects the ease with which conflicts are resolved violently, showing that institutional justice can be supplanted easily.

Three central actors, then, participate in this activity: the contractor, who may be an individual or organized group; the entrepreneur, who organizes the "job"; and the practitioner, the last link in the chain of death. The *sicario*, in spite of the fact that he might be formally independent, could not survive without this organizational structure to support him. This means he is more an effect than a cause, and any policy must consider these relationships.

The contractor might resort to this method because of a need to settle accounts, when he feels that this is the most effective way in light of the inefficacy of the official justice system. Or he might do it in order to eliminate witnesses to criminal acts. Or, government officials, acting as individuals, might hire a *sicario* to eliminate persons who are presumably guilty of altering the public order or overstepping cultural boundaries. In this case the activity becomes an extension of the dirty war in Colombia, which does not regard either the nature of encouraging such entrepreneurship or the conversion of Colombians into assassins for pay as hindrances.

The entrepreneur, in turn, profits from a form of organization that responds to the foregoing criteria. He becomes an intermediary who centralizes the activity and makes it viable and efficient. Like other intermediaries, his business is to make candidates into practitioners. He assesses them, equips them, and very probably tries to convince them that there is justification for the act they are going to commit, arguing that their fee is remuneration for a job. He profits, thus, from unemployment, poverty, and the cultural uprootedness of certain sectors of our youth.

The *sicario*, in turn, runs the risks of his actions, since any mistake can result in death, either at the hands of the victim in self-defense or by an act of those who hired him, if they consider him ineffective or dangerous. In this regard, success in the commission of the crime and the possible prestige it might bring are a function of his capacity to kill. Paradoxically, success can also spell the *sicario*'s death because now he "knows too much." Thus the chain is temporarily broken, simultaneously obstructing the workings of a judicial system whose central premise is the testimony of witnesses. The accomplishment of his goals implies that the *sicario* has been prepared properly. Unfortunately, on occasion the military organizations of the state have contributed to these successes, paradoxically subsidizing the killings by supplying well-trained unemployed former soldiers willing to engage in such activities.

This brief description of the organization of *sicario* activity emphasizes fundamental points with respect to the attitude that should be adopted with respect to it. To understand this phenomenon it is necessary to see it in all its complexity, without isolating the *sicario* as the only guilty party. To understand it also implies recognizing that in this activity, as in drug trafficking, without demand there is no supply.

13

The Crisis of the Current Political Regime and Its Possible Outcomes

Luís Alberto Restrepo

In this essay, Luís Alberto Restrepo succinctly delineates the multiple causes of the contemporary crisis facing Colombia and eloquently argues that the only viable solution to it is construction of a broad national movement for democratic reform. His analysis spares no one. He indicts the leadership of the traditional political parties, the legacy of the National Front, the Catholic Church, the military, the drug cartels and the paramilitary right, the guerrillas and the leftist intellectuals who still sympathize with them, the Communist party, and the consuming nations, particularly the government of the United States. In doing so, Restrepo summarizes not only this third section but also, in a general sense, this volume as a whole.

This essay was written in 1988, before the escalation of conflict between the government and the drug cartels that was precipitated by the assassination of the popular reformist Liberal presidential candidate Luís Carlos Galán in August 1989. That event led President Virgilio Barco to intensify the war on drug operations and to implement extradition procedures against important figures in the mafia. The "extraditables," as they call themselves, responded viciously. Car bombings aimed at government officials, police stations, the headquarters of political parties, banks, and even supermarkets wreaked havoc in Colombia's major cities, killing scores of innocent bystanders and wounding hundreds. Two additional presidential candidates, both representing the left, Bernardo Jaramillo Ossa of the Unión Patriótica and Carlos Pizarro of the M-19, were assassinated by *sicarios* on suicide missions just weeks before the election in May 1990.

However ominous this recent turn of events, it is possible to see in the outcome of the election certain encouraging signs. The president-elect, the Liberal Julio César Gaviria, inherited the followers of the slain reformist Galán and pledged to continue the policy of peace negotiations with the guerrillas advanced by President Barco and successfully completed with the

M-19 during 1989–90. (Gaviria also endorsed the necessity of extradition in the context of the ineffectiveness of the Colombian judicial system.) Although the Unión Patriótica abstained, the M-19 candidate, Antonio Navarro Wolf, won a surprising percentage of the vote (some 12 percent, or almost eight hundred thousand votes), more than double the share ever won by the left in a presidential election. Meanwhile, the Conservative party split, its official candidate far outpolled by longtime presidential aspirant Alvaro Gómez (son of the former president); the party's combined share of the vote (about 33 percent, compared to Gaviria's 47 percent) confirmed its decided minority status and continuing decline. Finally, Colombians voted in favor of a constituent assembly, a measure placed on the ballot due in part to a novel groundswell of democratic student activism.

Restrepo's discussion can aid in interpreting each of these developments, including the potential—and dangers—of the constituent assembly. It is a measure of the lucidity of his analysis that in virtually all respects, the terms of the contemporary crisis presented in this essay seem as valid today as they were in 1988.

Luís Alberto Restrepo is a philosopher affiliated with the Institute of Political Studies and International Relations at the National University in Bogotá. He is the author of *Actores en conflicto por la paz: El proceso de paz durante el gobierno de Belisario Betancur* (Bogotá, 1988).

The narrowness of the bipartisan regime inherited from the National Front, with the consequent absence of political alternatives that would provide channels for social protest, is still the country's fundamental political problem. The distance between the *país político* and the *país nacional** has reached enormous proportions. On the one hand, this state of affairs has forced social nonconformists to find expression in civic strikes and peasant marches. On the other, it has led to the bureaucratization of the traditional parties, which are more concerned with control of the government apparatus than with popular needs and demands. Although it cannot be said that the distance between the state and the subordinate classes is the cause of the armed struggle, neither can it be ignored that the state has offered no alternatives.

The military confrontation between the guerrillas and the state shows signs of disorganization on both sides. It has degenerated into terrorist acts from the left and the right, if these political terms have any meaning when applied to such acts. Extortion, kidnapping, and "settling of accounts" have been practiced for a long time, to one degree or another, by all Colombian guerrillas. These forms of action have been supplemented more recently by the economic terrorism of the Ejército

---

*The terms are Jorge Eliécer Gaitán's. The first refers to the small, oligarchical political elite, the second to the rest of the nation.

de Liberación Nacional (ELN). The repression exerted by the Establishment now invests the situation with the character of a "dirty war." The principal victims of the persecution are not the guerrillas themselves, however, but rather legal popular organizations and their activists, democratic leaders, independent thought, and culture—that is, the victims are all of the social and political forces that attempt to transcend the closed bipartisan scheme left by the National Front.

The lack of political alternatives has led to a whirlwind of colliding violences. When we add the violence among rival drug mafias, the violence the mafias direct against the government, and the violence that seems to be directed at the drug bosses by as yet unknown forces, we might say that the country is in the eye of the hurricane.

This essay analyzes the five principal areas in which the crisis of the regime manifests itself today. Four of these are internal to Colombian society; a fifth, the result of the drug trade, has its origins outside it. However, it is important to begin with some considerations about the historical roots of the present situation as a reminder of the fundamental features of our political culture.

The government of Virgilio Barco has sought to bring about a political solution to the crisis in two ways: first, through the stimulation of a loyal opposition program, and second, through the popular election of mayors, a reform begun under the previous administration. Proposals, not yet enacted, for a plebiscite and a constituent assembly have now been added to these. While the government-opposition dialectic is trying to break through the confines of the National Front and work toward the revitalization of the parties and the congress, the popular election of mayors opens a space for the emergence of new political forces and thus stimulates the renovation of the traditional parties.

In the arena of armed confrontation one also finds evidence of the deterioration of the regime and of the desperate attempts to overcome it. Superimposed on the futile confrontation between insurgent organizations and the armed forces is a campaign of intimidation and annihilation systematically levied against various democratic sectors.

Retaliation by the drug barons against the political class adds still another ingredient to the crisis. To a certain extent this element is external to the crisis insofar as it does not represent a threat to the Establishment. But it does bring to light deep ambiguities and internal contradictions in the ruling classes and the regime itself, which are fundamental to the current process of capitalist accumulation. To better comprehend the depth and orientation of the disintegration of the Colombian political regime, it is necessary to recall its origins.

The Heritage of the National Front

The intense periods of the Violence (1948–1953) and the National Front (1958–1974) were the result of a long Colombian tradition, two of whose characteristics are worth highlighting because they still weigh decisively in our political culture. Until the bipartisan agreement was reached, the Liberal and Conservative leaders based their monopoly on a singular and passionate dialectic of bitter confrontations and transitory national reconciliations. Beginning in the nineteenth century they nourished the sentiment of party loyalty among the subordinate classes, feeding prejudices and mutual hatred. Party leaders launched the people into cycles of civil war that ended in pacts of national reconciliation arranged by the same leaders. The parties were at the same time the source of division and of national unity, of annihilation and of salvation. They managed in this way to maintain broad-based party loyalties, drawn more from hereditary hatreds than from the parties' capacities to represent and channel the economic and social aspirations of the subordinate majority.

The emotional and violent character of the political debate had a religious nucleus that gave it particular virulence. To a largely rural population, the fundamental difference between the parties, at least since the era of the Regeneration (ca. 1886–1900), lay in their different relations with the Catholic Church. The Conservatives were Catholics, while the Liberals were considered to be anticlerical and, later, to be Masons or Communists. From the pulpit and in the schools, the Church played a determining role in party affiliation for Colombians. In this way, violent political passions acquired the pseudoreligious dimension of a sectarian confrontation between Good and Evil.

This political culture reached its consummation during the Violence and the National Front, "consummation" in a double sense of the word. The Violence was the political culture's highest expression and imposed the necessity for its permanent abolition. The National Front abolished it with the sacred rite of reconciliation.

For the most traditional sector of the ruling class, the National Front civilized our political customs. In fact, the bipartisan pact put an end to one hundred years of Colombian history. It extinguished the dialectic of war and peace between the two parties and took away its traditional religious basis. The Catholic Church thus lost its political referent and politics became secular by decree. In this way, the bipartisan agreement destroyed the emotional point of confrontation between Colombians. Never again—not even with the government-opposition program—would it be possible to revive sectarian affiliation with the traditional parties.

The national pact above all civilized the customs of the historical parties because from that time on their leaders closed ranks against the growing pressures of social protest and armed insurrection as well as against any eventual political alternative that might threaten their monopoly of government jobs. Precisely for this reason, the National Front did not allow any institutional expression of the social conflicts that were besetting the country. It did not, then, civilize our customs but rather contributed to the displacement of the axis of the old barbaric ways. Deprived of the pseudoreligious pretexts of the past, the defenders of the regime and some of their radical opponents of today nevertheless are heirs to the same dogmatic, intransigent, and sectarian attitudes. They consider themselves defenders of the only salvation from the evil that is sweeping the nation.

With the National Front, the Church lost the central place it traditionally had occupied in the Colombian political order. As a catalyst to partisan affiliation, its role had been decisive. When it lost this function, social conflicts were revealed for all to see. Religious emotions could no longer divert attention from them. Today we are witnessing the tortuous gestation of a new political order, which must mediate between all the conflicting social sectors. The disappearance of the Church's role generated a loss of legitimacy for the parties that still exists and that gradually has been replaced by military coercion. The present regime depends more and more on force.

In light of the ecclesiastical hierarchy's current efforts to rebuild its lost leadership, a brief review of the Church's political evolution since the National Front is in order. In 1958 the Church moved the line between Good and Evil: it abandoned its exclusive loyalty to the Conservative party and its old condemnation of the Liberals to become a stalwart defender of the recently created bipartisan "democratic institutions," which stood in opposition to "Marxist, totalitarian, and atheist subversion." Since this time, Colombian bishops have viewed nearly all forms of protest through this prism.

However, the Church's new position did not attract the same support as previously, and it even contributed to the generation of internal divisions. In fact, the formation of the National Front, the process of urbanization, the expansion of the education system, and the growth of the communications media have secularized political activity in Colombia to a large extent. In addition, the ecclesiastical hierarchy has had to assume a particularly uncomfortable and imprecise position since the nominal end of the National Front in 1974. While the Church has maintained its support for the nation's democratic institutions, it finds it necessary to formulate ever sharper moral critiques of the ruling classes and the parties. Thus, it defends institutions in the name of no one. It floats in a political vacuum without precise reference points. Instead of exercising decisive influence in national events, as it had in the past, the Church finds the parties' identity crisis reflected internally, leading to the emergence of a progressive political differentiation among the clergy, which has generated considerable tension and conflict. An important segment of the Church has abandoned its traditional oligarchical nexus and has started to build new links with subaltern classes.

In the mid-1980s, however, the Colombian bishops—under the leadership of Cardinal López Trujillo—have tried to recover their earlier important place in national political life. Once a rigid element in the conflict between the Establishment and "subversives," the bishops now offer to mediate between the two camps, a role that might place the Church on the political stage again. In return, the Church's offer implies tacit pressure against any modifications to the treaty that regulates relations between the Vatican and the Colombian state and that might limit ecclesiastical privileges. Paradoxically, as a result of their efforts the clergy has won the enthusiastic support of the Communist party and the Unión Patriótica party. Because of the secularization already noted, however, it is unlikely that the Church will be able to recapture a position as influential as the one that it had in the past. The traditional political order will never return. The regime's fulcrum of support has moved toward the pole of force, at least for as long as no real alternative to the government exists for the great majority.

After the National Front

In 1974 the alternation of Liberals and Conservatives in the presidency came to an end. The ensuing executives, Alfonso López Michelsen (1974–1978) and Julio Cesar Turbay Ayala (1978–1982), could not nip the crisis in the bud. López Michelsen tried an initial response with the "little constituent assembly," but, foreseeing failure in congress, it was a limited reform in terms of its social scope. His administration frustrated the hopes that important majorities had placed in him as heir to his father's revolution (1934–1938) and as the former leader of the Liberal Revolutionary Movement, a faction of dissident reformist Liberals who split from the main party in the early 1970s. The civic strike of September 1977 was an index of popular disenchantment and the consequent aggravation of the political crisis.

Turbay Ayala did not create a real solution either. His formula was to finish what the National Front had begun. The mutual agreement already had transformed the traditional parties into electoral enterprises and had entrusted social conflict to the power of the siege and of military repression. Turbay Ayala took this line to its ultimate consequences. He rose to political office through inside connections, governed with the backing of the political machine, and dealt with social nonconformity and armed insurgence through the traditional expedient of repression. The result was exactly the opposite of what he had hoped for. At the end of his term the M-19 guerrilla group was becoming stronger, while the national and international unpopularity of the armed forces and the government itself had swelled considerably. The logic of the National Front exhausted itself with Turbay Ayala. War had failed as a solution to the political crisis of the country.

The next two presidents, Belisario Betancur (1982–1986) and Barco (1986–1990), were obliged to deal with the grave deterioration of the regime in a serious manner. Both men attempted to revive the political dialectic, each in his own way. Betancur tried to make room for radical opposition forces, outside the bipartisan establishment, hoping even to include guerrillas who wanted to pursue a process of peace. Barco could not retreat from this effort, but he sought national repoliticization within the narrower framework of the two traditional parties while at the same time trying to inject social content into the Liberal party programs.

Betancur failed because he did not accompany his program with social reforms, because he did not dare to organize his own independent backing, and because he became bogged down in the failure of political will on the part of the opposition groups. His program against the conflictive logic of the National Front collapsed. Betancur's failure was also, in a way, the failure of peace.

Barco has inherited and embodies the uncertainty of the ruling classes. He has tried to find a solution based on prior experience. Initially, he retained the formalities of the peace initiatives while allowing the dirty war to continue. Barco has tried to undermine the insurgency by introducing social programs, and he has tried, in vain, to redirect the vastness of social nonconformity into the exhausted channels of the Liberal-Conservative confrontation.

Whereas Betancur's peace process addressed, above all, the "subjective causes" of subversion, Barco's "social economy" claimed to attack its "objective causes" and restore a reformist profile to the Liberal party. It was, without question, a noble attempt. But the Barco government's two pet projects—agrarian reform and urban reform—bogged down in congress. The National Rehabilitation Plan and the Plan to Eradicate Absolute Poverty were praiseworthy efforts at redistribution implemented through public spending. However, the attempted redistribution was not financed through the most direct and expeditious route, taxation. Tax reform was made in favor of capital, and social spending has a meager budget compared to other categories, such as security or energy.

Under Turbay Ayala, war failed. Under Betancur, peace appeared to fail. Under Barco, the process of peace nominally is maintained while the informal war prospers. The country still has not found the political strength it needs to carry out serious reforms, negotiate peace, and open up the democratic process to all.

The Settings of the Crisis at This Juncture

As was pointed out earlier, the crisis of the regime is occurring today on four different internal fronts, two of them political and two of them armed. The political scenarios are the government-opposition scheme and the popular election of mayors. The armed fronts are the guerrilla struggle and the dirty war.

The Government-opposition Scheme

Since the start of his administration, President Barco has been committed to the establishment of a government-opposition scheme as a primary element of the dialectic that must provide a channel for the expression of accumulated nonconformist political views. In line with his desire to revive political polarization around the Liberal-Conservative axis, Barco has tried to create a reformist image for the Liberal party.

This scheme is pondered in the lofty reaches of the *país político*, far above the day-to-day concerns of the *país nacional*. Nevertheless, its success would mean a decisive advance: the dialectic of political alternatives is vital to any dynamic regime. In Colombia, moreover, it would put an end to the National Front and lead either to the revitalization of the traditional parties or to their gradual extinction. They would find themselves face to face with the task of reconciling the state with the popular majority.

In practice, the scheme has stimulated a needed moral watchdog over the government, through the vehicle of the Conservative party, but until now it has shown itself unable to generate real alternatives to the government's power, at least in the short run. In fact, the effort has been limited to give and take between the two traditional parties, both of which retain oligarchical roots that have never been eradicated and both of which, by tradition and social makeup, lack any reformist vocation. Furthermore, the surviving nucleus of the National Front opposes the establishment of the government-opposition scheme, just as it opposed the peace process, and carries on an underground effort to restore the bipartisan regime. It should be noted that the recent worsening of violence and rising political instability have accelerated the reorganization of the National Front and have dampened executive persistence on this central project of the regime. The greatest limitation, however, derives perhaps from the lack of political direction by the president himself, the absence of a government party, and the absence of a strong party presenting real political opposition.

Without a real government, it is difficult to have a government party. At the beginning of Barco's term, sectors of the ruling classes reproached the president for his lack of leadership. It is worth recalling, though, that Barco was chosen as a presidential candidate precisely because of his low political profile. In the eyes of the public, he represented neither peace (like his predecessor) nor war (like his opponent). To the Liberal barons, he looked like a "no-man's-land," easily taken by the first to arrive. His image as an expert served to shield the party from the moral criticisms of dissidents such as Galán. Barco was the perfect expression of the uncertainty of the ruling classes.

Once elected president, having received more votes than were won by his Liberal machine electors, Barco distanced himself from his party; for more than one year he took refuge in a kitchen cabinet made up of his friends and private advisers. He delegated his public duties to representative figures from the Liberal party and surrounded himself with technical ministers and advisers. His administration became a high-level management system of public works. Political leadership of the country fell to second place. The government had to face the crisis, therefore, without clear presidential guidance, at least until the beginning of 1988.

Meanwhile, the government-opposition scheme has continued to progress without a government party. The Liberal machine has not overcome the crisis that it entered after Turbay Ayala's term. The party appears to be an association fragmented by personal rivalries that go deeper than the political differences separating it from the Conservative party. The situation has reached the point where the Liberal party itself has become the opposition. The way that the president has treated the regional leaders of the party has led to a Liberal "political class" playing the part of the opposition in congress. Abstention on and the blocking of executive proposals have been the party's weapons. Just as there is no government party, there is also no strong opposition. The Conservative party is equally affected by erosive tendencies. The distance between the followers of former president Misael Pastrana Borrero (1970–1974) and those of Alvaro Gómez (the son of Laureano Gómez, president of Colombia from 1950 to 1953) keeps growing.

It is not easy for either of the traditional Colombian parties to survive outside the bureaucracy and to act as the opposition. Both parties lack the experience, social base, and, above all, the political will to do so. The Conservative party has been able to play this role only to a small extent. During the first months the party exerted pressure on all sides for a return to the bipartisan regime of the National Front. Later, at the stubborn insistence of the president, it took on the role of a moral opposition party. But as yet the party has not come forth as an alternative government, and it will not be easy for it to do so. Given the new situation created by the drug traffic and by guerrilla attacks on oil pipelines, the party's leadership seems inclined to support the executive as a gesture of disinterested patriotism.

The only political opposition to bipartisanship is expressed by the Communist party and the Unión Patriótica. Yet they have not succeeded in becoming a popular alternative. Of course, the restrictive policies of the regime have made their task difficult. To Barco's administration, the Unión Patriótica has been a second-class political force. In addition, its leaders and activists are being annihilated systematically in an atmosphere of impotent indifference on the part of the government. The Unión Patriótica's hundreds of dead members embody the narrowness of the regime. Limitations on these parties, however, are not imposed only from without. The Communist party and the Unión Patriótica do not appeal to the majority. Because of its rigidity, dogmatism, and authoritarian hierarchy, the Colombian Communist party as yet has not achieved *perestroika*. It still displays the pseudoreligious character of the political context in which it was formed. The Unión Patriótica, inspired by the Communist party and established by the Fuerzas Armadas Revolucionarias Colombianas (FARC), finds itself in a difficult and contradictory process of becoming integrated into democratic life, into a life that, furthermore, the extreme right is trying to stifle. Perhaps the country is waiting for a popular alternative that is fully committed to democracy.

The crisis of the parties is expressed in congress. What should have been the scene for the nation's renovation has been rather the theater for its decline. The Liberal party launched "operation turtle" in congress against its own president, and the Conservative party practiced an opposition aimed more at partisan revenge than at the creation of alternatives for the country. Agrarian reform, fundamentally watered down, was approved belatedly, due to the secret transfer of votes in exchange for favors from the Liberal senators. The reform was approved in spite of the cheating during the voting that the whole country could see on television. Urban reform still is stalled even though the program has been subjected to severe mutilation already. These now habitual practices in the legislature constitute a "subversion from above" that is more destructive than the "subversion from below" whose best justification arises from the former.

With the inability of the parties and congress to interpret and channel the great national emergencies, President Barco also has resorted—as Betancur did—to a "parallel institutionalization" of the state. Presidential advisers and commissions proliferate in a replication of the inefficient institutional government structure. The process does not lack ambiguity. These pocket institutions seem to testify to the executive's good will, but at the same time they embody and conceal the general lack of political will.

This ambiguity is also the case with respect to human rights. The problem of the dirty war and terrorism, central to any democracy, is diverted from congress and the parties to a presidential adviser, which does not mean that his appointment lacks importance. The adviser can play a useful role if he confronts the fundamental threats against the integrity of the state not only from insurgent forces but also from the state's own security forces and important sectors of the ruling classes, without whose cooperation the dirty war would not be possible. But the adviser's role can prove frankly detrimental if he approaches the problem with measures that, although good in themselves, are superficial and innocuous. In all, the advisers are painful testimony to the parties' inability to face the basic challenges of a democracy.

In a similar vein, the president has proposed a plebiscite calling for a constituent assembly.* This mechanism embodies the president's critical distance from the government's institutional structure. Aside from its undeniable potential, the plebiscite signifies a self-imposed coup d'état carried out at the highest levels of government. Because of the way in which it has been proposed, however, without promises by the executive as to the composition and content of the eventual constitutional assembly, the plebiscite is at this point a blank check handed to the people who support the president. Both sides of public opinion have embraced the official proposal in a gesture of desperate hope and confidence in the magic of the mechanism of the constitutional primary. But the plebiscite is still no answer to the crisis, which will become evident in its full force when it is time to determine the rules governing the assembly. Inept management of the proceedings could deepen national polarization even further. It is necessary to realize that

---

*As noted at the beginning of this chapter, the plebiscite was held and the constituent assembly approved in the presidential election of May 1990.

the pervasive nonconformity of the subordinate classes does not have enough sufficient means of social and political representation.

The Popular Election of Mayors

The election of mayors is the second front of the national political crisis. It is the only significant achievement that survives from the "democratic aperture" fostered by Betancur at the beginning of his administration. The importance assumed by this reform is out of proportion because of the narrowness of the current regime and the stingy antireformist impulses of the ruling classes. The magnified importance of this reform has generated disproportionate expectations and, in fact, has endowed municipal reform with greater significance than it would have achieved by itself. Electoral contests for mayors, more than just government-opposition exercises, have revitalized political activity.

Events in Bogotá and Medellín related to recent mayoral elections are good indications of the crisis of the traditional parties and their attempts to resolve it. Personal conflicts within and between the parties have led to complex alliances among Liberal and Conservative factions that seek vengeance on their own party through the opposing party. It is possible, however, that these squabbles are opening a path for new ideological tendencies separated by the axis of the regime's crisis, a path for peace and progress toward a real democratic opposition. There is a tacit convergence of the parties' right wings on the one side and their center-left sectors on the other. A realignment of this sort might clarify national politics and give more meaning to a government-opposition scheme.

The mayoral campaign shows that the political class is conscious of the deterioration of its own image. The parties look for shortcuts to overcome this deterioration not in an in-depth political and ideological restructuring but through recourse to a changing of the generational guard. The major candidates are young, and youth is presented as an implicit synonym for modernization.

The traditional parties also want to project a civic image for their candidates, rather than a partisan one. *Civic* involves a semantic problem here. It is an attempt to relate to the civic movement that has swept the country in recent years. However, although *civic* is synonymous with *popular* for the social movement, for the political parties the word refers to the leaders of business associations or the directors of powerful communications media organizations. These men represent civic society but only that society that is expressed through the business elite, not the society that takes part in strikes.

The Guerrilla Struggle

The government-opposition plan and the election of mayors are the two areas where attempts are being made to overcome the political crisis and achieve modification of the bipartisan regime through institutional channels. The confrontation between the armed forces and the guerrilla movement is both the actual materialization of the crisis as well as a desperate effort to overcome it.

As is well known, the guerrilla movement arose in Latin America inspired by the triumph of the Cuban Revolution. But the tradition of sectarianism and political violence implanted by the traditional parties and the profundity of the social crisis gave the guerrilla movement in Colombia its own peculiar stamp. The narrow bipartisan regime offered no alternative institutional channels and did not permit their formation.

The traditional parties, once installed in government, became accustomed to responding to social protest through repression, ignoring its political threat and reducing it to the status of a problem of public order. The nearly permanent recourse to a state of siege demonstrates this response. In this way, the Liberal-Conservative agreement has contributed decisively to the militarization of the political terrain in Colombia. Moreover, the bipartisan monopoly has impeded the rise of a political opposition separate from the two-party system that might offer an alternative to armed insurgency. The blocking of the political left thus continually has reinforced the armed movement. If the current social protest movement does not find channels of political expression, it will continue to push progressively in the direction of insurgent fighting.

At the same time, the role played by the guerrilla movement during Turbay Ayala's administration contributed to the breakup of many fledgling legal organizations on the left. It took over their political space. In the same manner, the current dirty war led by the Establishment against Unión Patriótica and other social movements outside the two-party system produces results contrary to those intended. The conflict eliminates political alternatives, and this works in favor of armed rebellion.

Even after twenty-five years of fighting, the revolutionary guerrilla movement in Colombia is far from becoming an alternative power. In the current proliferation of violence, it has not distinguished its own political profile for the majority of Colombians. Its now prolonged frustration inclines it today toward desperate forms of military action. The movement thus has become a factor not of revolutionary unity but of the chronic instability that contributes to constriction of the space for the popular democratic struggle.

From the 1960s until 1974, the guerrilla movement was confined to the countryside and made military and political progress with difficulty. In the 1970s the M-19 burst onto the scene and a new era began. That group's public relations triumphs and the clumsy repression exercised by Turbay Ayala's administration made it into a powerful force with which the government had to reckon. The M-19 won increasing sympathy among the popular, middle-class, and intellectual sectors of the population. As the peace process later would demonstrate, it was playing a role far more important than its political leadership was able to handle. As a result, during Betancur's administration, the M-19 lost the legitimacy that it had won; finally, it committed political suicide at the Palace of Justice. Peace had been its downfall. Thus concluded the second phase of the Colombian guerrilla movement.

The new phase of the guerrilla movement was capitalized on by the ELN, an organization that had remained on the sidelines during the failed peace process. This phase is characterized by the contradiction between the guerrilla movement's military growth and its political impoverishment. The misguided management of the peace process disconnected the armed movement, in large part, from intellectuals and from volatile public opinion. It has increased its recruitment of militants in marginal sectors, from among people without intellectual background who are desperate because of the acute social crisis. As the depoliticization of its membership increases, the movement's military activity becomes more acute. Kidnapping and assault proliferate. For the common man in Colombia it is difficult today to distinguish the violence of guerrilla activity from that of drug trafficking or common crime.

The guerrilla group FARC is, like the present government, suspended between peace and war. From the beginning the text of the truce was confusing. The armed forces have demonstrated their definite opposition to the agreement, while the FARC has continued to strengthen its military capabilities.

The surprising formation in 1987 of an umbrella organization designed to coordinate the efforts of the leftist guerrilla groups, the Simón Bolívar Coordinadora, was not the product of a conception shared by the different armed organizations but rather the result of a "no way out" policy that set before the groups the need to make an impression on the government. The undeniable military power, without any clear political orientation, of the guerrillas foreshadows a process of disintegration in the near future. The payment of wages to many guerrilla militants does not guarantee the development of their political consciousness; instead, it encourages a mercenary mentality that could lead to their criminalization.

The Dirty War

The dirty war is the terrorism of the Establishment. Colombia today is witnessing the systematic extermination of its popular democratic leaders. In the military dictatorships of the Southern Cone and Central America the dirty war was conducted by high-ranking government officials. In our country, it functions outside the executive but with a certain degree of tolerance from it. In classic form, it seems to be mimicked by and entangled in the jumble of confused violence. This deliberate muddling by the ruling classes is a form of legitimization and covering up, and it is, therefore, futile to hope for judicial clarification. It is necessary to go to the war's political sources.

The immediate genesis of the dirty war is clear. It arose from the failure of both the guerrilla war and its repression, on the one hand, and of the peace process attempted during the governments of Turbay Ayala and Betancur, on the other hand. Barco has maintained the formalities of the peace process, but it is eroded by the dirty war, which is abetted by people who are committed to reestablishing the tranquil monopoly of the National Front. Even during Betancur's administration, the repression had begun to be transformed into an informal paramilitary war. But with Barco's government, the dirty war has become the basic style of repression, encouraged or tolerated by the ruling classes, and aided—in some regions—by drug traffickers whose interests are threatened.

The dirty war in Colombia was long in preparation. During the last forty years a gradual *"coup d'état* of civil society" has been in the making, which has made a classic coup d'état unnecessary, at least for now. Until the coup of 1953, the military forces were the armed branch of the state, not of the parties. Today the relation is reversed. Many civilian leaders are the political branch of the armed forces. With the defection of the political class that accompanied the National Front, and in the context of the growing social conflict, military men almost obligatorily have become the ideologues of the dominant classes of civilian society. And, as is logical, they have impressed their own professional perspective on society: a vision of order and national security. In this manner, decisions on war and peace and on basic social problems—the axes of all policy—have become first and foremost military problems. Force has become a fundamental part of the present political order.

The emancipation of the armed forces from civilian rule is the result of a long process. The coup that the traditional parties directed against themselves, under the leadership of General Gustavo Rojas Pinilla, stripped the parties of their credibility and authority in the eyes of the military and nourished messianic sentiments in the general.

Later, the facile resort of different governments to a state of siege gave the military growing responsibility and independence in the management of the central political problem of public order. Today the army high command knows the reality of the country better than most of the political leaders do. Simultaneously, military training has become more and more independent of the knowledge and control of civilian power. Officers take specialized courses abroad, and civilian officials know nothing of the content or of the interests to which they respond. The armed forces have created their own university, thereby contributing to the distance from society that their profession always generates. Thus the process of military education encourages the development of a unilateral perspective on the country.

From independence from civilian rule, the military has progressed to a growing position of superiority vis-à-vis civilians on questions of public order. Unique institutions have emerged. For fifteen years military training has been offered to civilian leaders: professionals, businessmen, politicians, journalists, priests, and others are trained as reserve officers. Apart from this training, the military gives frequent courses and seminars to these same sectors on the situation in the country. A solid alliance between business associations and the armed forces has been forged. In the military academies, of which there are many, run by either retired or active officers, students are trained in military skills. More recently, some officers have abetted peasant self-defense groups. Finally, in recent years the military has sold innumerable weapons to civilians.

The whole process of the militarization of civilian society is ruled by the idea of self-defense. A parallel army has been formed in Colombia; it was not provided for in the constitution, and it is not subject to the president or to any other clearly defined authority. This army's existence carries with it the implicit assumption that every person can defend his own interests with arms. It presupposes the abdication and helps to erode the authority of the state. It furthers the coup of civilian society that is sought by economically powerful classes that are, however, incapable of leading the country.

The dirty war of today is not, therefore, unexpected. It emerged from a society with a history of militarization. It operates in either centralized or autonomous form. The ruling classes in general, and the traditional parties in particular, bear responsibility for it. This war is not directed against the guerrillas but rather is the result of the frustration produced by the impossibility of eradicating them. It is a war of intimidation and extermination fought against independent thinking, democracy, and culture, against all of the forces that might broaden the narrow bipartisan regime and transform armed struggle into political struggle. This informal war is the best justification for guerrilla activity; it makes achieving peace impossible although it does not further military victory for the Establishment either.

Until Betancur, the country's political challenge consisted of building a new social pact among warring factions—the guerrillas and the state—and opening a wide political channel for the opposition. Today the problem is different. It is not possible to negotiate with a guerrilla force that has not been militarily defeated unless the paramilitary entities are dismantled first and the dirty war is stopped. But it is not possible to negotiate with the promoters of the dirty war either because they will not show their faces. What is necessary, then, is the political elimination of all violence as an indispensable condition for future negotiation. Betancur negotiated with a politically triumphant guerrilla movement that did not believe in peace except as a means to war. The new peace dialogue requires, as a precondition, a national pact against the use of violence as a method of political struggle.

The Drug Traffic and Disorganization

Without North American pressure the drug traffic in Colombia would not have acquired the acute destabilizing influence that it has today. The drug mafia is part of the Establishment, and it is not interested in destroying either the state or the political regime. It is, in fact, among the regime's most ardent defenders. It protects private property with blood and fire against either subversion or popular movements. Its struggle is directed exclusively toward tacit acceptance of the drug trade and the elimination of the Treaty of Extradition. To this end, the mafia has neutralized the power of the justice system and subordinated an important part of the nation's legislative power and the political class. If the drug mafia runs afoul of the law along the way, violence is exacerbated, and the disorganization of society and the state is deepened. However, the mafia has no program for creating a society that is different from the existing one.

For their part, the ruling classes argue over two contradictory goals: the need to accumulate capital and the need for legitimization. Internally divided over these two objectives, the ruling classes have maintained a deliberately ambiguous stance toward the drug traffic. They have invested their capital pragmatically in the national economy in order to guarantee the process of accumulation, sporadically erasing the traces of certain especially scandalous crimes. This game has given rise to a singular paradox: business is going well, but the country is going badly. However, needing legitimacy, the ruling classes refuse to recognize the close link between these two phenomena caused by the drug traffic.

Illegal money has been integrated officially into the national economy through the tax amnesty of 1987, the "sinister window" of the Bank of the Republic, and the laundering of dollars. These mechanisms have helped the Colombian bourgeoisie to surmount the difficult Latin American economic situation with relative ease. The unprecedented bonanza for builders, industrialists, and merchants was due, in large measure, to this "nontraditional export." But from time to time—when notorious crimes are perpetrated by the mafia, when the drug lords try to challenge the political control of traditional political bosses, or, especially, when North American pressure becomes severe—broad sectors of the traditional party leadership express their indignant rejection of the drug traffic and make a fleeting attempt to prosecute it.

The only essential contradiction between drug traffickers and the traditional ruling classes—that is, their relation with the United States— has become an explosive issue. The drug dealers reject the Treaty of Extradition and assert national independence from North American justice. On this point they are anti-North American not for political reasons but for motives of personal safety. The Colombian oligarchy, in contrast, needs the backing of the United States in order to maintain its model of economic development and its political control, especially under present conditions in the country. It may be said in passing that the North American government pursues the drug trade more out of commercial than ethical motives; otherwise, it would have to launch an effective campaign against consumption and not simply against importation of narcotics. Some observers contend that marijuana is today the second most valuable agricultural product of the United States.

Economic pressure from the United States, which hangs over Colombia like the sword of Damocles, presents the Colombian bourgeoisie and government with a difficult dilemma. Should the nation seriously pursue the great mafia kingpins and face reprisals, or should it continue its tacit alliance with the mafia and absorb the sanctions from North America? In order to block any attempt to reestablish the extradition treaty, drug traffickers have initiated a fierce war against the state. Their initial attacks were directed, for the first time, against the political class, which suddenly seems to have realized that a grave national crisis exists.

The dilemma between accumulation and legitimacy with relation to the drug traffic momentarily destabilizes the Colombian state more effectively than could armed insurrection or social protest. The government's response to the mafia's declared war will mark a very important line on this road. In any case, the precedents set by the drug traffickers at this time—especially their assassination of the attorney general—have made the situation extremely difficult. Those individuals responsible for these events may recover economic tolerance, but they will have to contend with deep-seated social rejection.

The most serious aspect of the situation is that the ruling classes insist on ignoring the true nature of the drug lords. Hounded by the need for legitimacy at home and abroad, they cling to the North American hypothesis of the narco-guerrilla and in this way try to divert national indignation and government repression toward guerrilla organizations and popular movements. It seems clear that the guerrilla groups have had or do have incidental contact with the drug traffic, such as commercial involvement in the Guaviare, and arms contraband. But in principle there is an irreconcilable antagonism between the drug traffickers, who defend their immense, forcibly acquired fortunes by any and all means, and revolutionary guerrillas, who at least question the present distribution of wealth. Many drug chiefs are now large landowners, and they respond to guerrilla pressures by paying hired assassins. It is obvious too, on the other hand, that elements of the ruling classes have cast their lot with the economic resources provided by the drug trade, that more than a few members of the controlling sphere are in the drug business, and that important concessions from the parties, the state, and the security forces have been bought with drug money. The refusal to recognize this situation has launched the ruling classes, at least for now, into a contradictory and sterile policy.

The Current State of Affairs

Looking at the national evolution as a whole, one sees a predominance of forms of armed confrontation over civilized, political forms of interaction. This armed confrontation has advanced the process of national disintegration and fostered the steady deterioration of the narrow confines of Colombian democracy. Three dissimilar, even contradictory, forces are moving the nation in this direction today: the guerrilla movement, the drug traffic, and the dirty war. Under these conditions the rejuvenating accomplishment of the popular election of mayors is weakened substantially, at least in the short run. The government-opposition scheme has tended to be supplanted by a version modified by the old assumptions of the National Front. The risk of resorting to force for a solution is growing (the Statute for the Defense of Democracy seems to point in that direction). However, if the eventual constituent assembly includes authentic representation of the subordinate classes, if its agenda permits discussion of social and political problems in depth, if the ruling classes understand the needs of the moment and are flexible, and if the government exercises adequate leadership in the process, it could open a decisive course toward the civilization of the conflict.

Colombia is neither in a prerevolutionary phase nor on the eve of civil war. The clash of contradictory violences generates only confusion, revulsion, and general repudiation. It does not stimulate a process of organization and confrontation between classes. There is no consensus in any sector, neither in the ruling classes nor in the subordinate classes, on what road the country should take. No one dares to predict what the final results of various alternatives might be. Even the military establishment seems to be unclear about an eventual coup d'état. The situation borders on anarchy. In addition, the proliferation of violence nourishes the desire for order at any price. If the option taken is to be the explicit application of force, the repression could be just as violent as its results are unpredictable, and it will not fall on the drug bosses, with whom the ruling classes and the state have multiple ties, but on the popular democratic movement as a whole.

In the face of this ever more generalized, anarchical, and futile confrontation, a broad-based national movement definitely is needed now. It could take one of two forms. The first would be the restoration of the National Front, organized and motivated from above, by the government and the parties, to impose order through repression. The second would be a citizen movement driven from below, from all entities in society, and with the free participation of individuals from all political parties. This movement would allow for the political destruction of the diverse forms of violence and would put pressure on the state and the parties to address urgent political and social reform issues. The first formula, the most probable, would mean the repetition and entrenchment of the crisis of the bipartisan regime left by the National Front.

It is hard to see how the traditional parties, who are the fundamental engineers of and actors in the crisis, could be the moving force behind its resolution. What the country needs is a broad-based democratic movement. This is the great challenge of the present day. Every effort to ignore or repress this political imperative, such as by tolerating or supporting the dirty war, can make things only worse.

14

Conclusion: Surveying the Literature on the Violence

Ricardo Peñaranda

As this bibliographical essay makes clear, part of the phenomenon of the Violence is the process of cultural understanding through which Colombians (and others) have tried to make sense of it. These efforts began with partisan justifications or rationalizations, include eyewitness accounts by victims and participants, and, today, emphasize theoretical and analytical attempts at explanation. Ricardo Peñaranda shows that as this intellectual process has developed since the beginning of the Violence in the late 1940s to the present day, it has moved from emotional and polemical description toward more sober, reasoned analysis. At the same time, scholars have expanded the domain of study from an original focus on the Violence proper to include, on the one hand, its antecedents in the nineteenth and early twentieth centuries and, on the other hand, its projection into the contemporary period. Finally, Peñaranda demonstrates that since the early 1960s academic studies of violence have been closely tied to a political project: to banish violence by understanding it. In the contemporary period this tendency has carried scholarship out of the narrow realm of the academy into the center of public debate on the current crisis.

Each of these developments in the literature on violence, whose contemporary features are well represented by the chapters included in this volume, must be seen as eminently positive. Current scholarship on violence is one bright spot in what often appears as a frightening and uncontrolled crisis with limited prospects of peaceful, democratic resolution. In concluding this volume, Peñaranda makes explicit our intellectual and political intent in putting these essays together. Collectively, they constitute a body of analysis and a platform for democratic action that we believe holds great promise for the resolution of the crisis facing Colombia today.

Ricardo Peñaranda teaches history at the Universidad Javeriana in Bogotá. He coedited the collection *Pasado y presente de la Violencia en Colombia* (Bogotá, 1986).

The Violence is the term that Colombians have adopted to describe the complex political and social phenomenon—a mixture of official terror, partisan confrontation, political banditry, pillage, and peasant uprising—that the country endured for nearly twenty years between the 1940s and the 1960s. *Passionate, enigmatic,* and *savage* are the adjectives usually used in referring to this period that, even today, we continue to call the Violence. Written with a capital *V* to denote this specific phenomenon, the Violence has become not only the historical agent that brutally transformed Colombian society but also the subject for study by many researchers, who, in the last twenty-five years, have produced the most voluminous set of studies on a single subject ever seen in Colombian historiography.[1] The goal of these studies has been, unfortunately, elusive: to destroy the Violence by understanding it.

Colombia today is considered to be a unique case in the Latin American context. Colombia combines a state of law, apparently solid—which formally embodies high levels of civil liberty and democratic process—with a persistent, generalized situation of violence that makes it one of the most convulsed societies in the world. A country that prides itself on having the most consistent civic and democratic tradition in Latin America is the very same country that has the most persistent and prolonged guerrilla history in the hemisphere. In Colombia, democracy and violence have coexisted for a long time, until the two phenomena have become, paradoxically, two faces of the same coin.

Officially the Violence ended in 1957, the year in which the leaders of the traditional Liberal and Conservative parties declared that their differences were over and reached an agreement known as the National Front, which functioned for nearly thirty years. By the terms of this agreement, the parties promised to alternate government control and share the state bureaucracy equally between the two political conglomerations. From this moment on they tried to cast a cloak of silence and forgetfulness over the Violence, intending to erase those terrible years from Colombian memory, to silence the voices of the victims, and to distort the political reality of the country. The very word used to name the conflict repeatedly has been called—and with just cause—elusive, ambiguous, aseptic. It is aimed at hiding the class character of the conflict and the responsibility of those who promoted it. But in fact the term *the Violence* acknowledges, above all, the irrational, savage, and destructive aspects of the conflict, which make it into something uncontrollable and almost supernatural, a phenomenon that overpowers its victims and destroys them but for which nobody is responsible.

To the ambiguity of the word used to label this phenomenon must be added the difficulty of fixing the phenomenon in time. The term, originally employed to refer to the fiercest period of confrontation between the two traditional parties (1949–1953), has widened its frame of reference to encompass earlier and later years. On the one hand, the search for immediate and even remote antecedents has necessitated looking back as far as the agrarian conflicts of the 1920s and 1930s. It even has meant looking further back into the past at the sharp partisan confrontations of the last century, which included eight general civil wars and fourteen local ones, when the bipartisan tradition in Colombia was born. On the other hand, in trying to identify the consequences or the possible evolution of the phenomenon, it has become obvious that the Violence has projected itself into the present, and not only in the political sphere, through the National Front. In practice it traverses every area of Colombian society and constitutes the matrix of the present social and political conflicts in our country.

Under these circumstances the questions of when the Violence began and when it ended—if it has ended—lack entirely satisfactory answers. This uncertainty has led, understandably, to the idea of a society in a state of "permanent war," an idea that nourishes a recent hypothesis that violence may be a constituent element of the current Colombian political regime or even a cultural element in our democracy. One analyst of the conflict has called attention to the caution with which this possible continuity must be handled. For Gonzalo Sánchez this "nearly permanent" war, although it contains meaningful common features, presents at least three clearly distinguishable phases.[2] The first phase, the civil wars, is characterized as a confrontation between routinely warring factions of the ruling class for power. The second phase, the one we usually know as the Violence, is fundamentally, in spite of the ideological control maintained by the ruling classes, a peasant war that slowly abandoned its initial character of partisan confrontation to become a class conflict. The third stage, which currently besets the country, has its roots in the latter part of the previous stage and manifests itself as open class conflict, led by guerrillas who are in some degree Marxists and whose goal is to abolish the present political regime.

Works on the Violence, not only in history and the social sciences but also in the arts and literature, have followed a tortuous path closely tied to the political situation in the country. In an attempt to erase what has happened, successive governments and the information media decided that the best thing would be not to talk about it. Therefore, they treated expressions of growing social discontent in a marginal and diffuse way. Between 1964 and 1982, Colombia was "officially" a country at peace. Insurgent groups did not exist officially and the country lived in a democracy with full freedoms for all, only occasionally disturbed by the intrusions of "foreign" ideologies. In this happy Arcadia, the Violence was considered a tragedy fortunately overcome, like a bad memory that should be forgotten insofar as possible. For these reasons, for many years research on the Violence was restricted to academic circles and its diffusion was limited; those scholars conducting such research were accused of being antipatriotic and even subversive. Threats against them reached such levels that at various points during these years some of them were forced to live in exile.

Reality finally asserted itself, however. In the late 1970s the worsening of the crisis in government, coupled with the expansion of the guerrilla movements and growing popular discontent, obliged the government to acknowledge the existence of an armed confrontation between subversive forces and the state and to initiate a long and tortuous process toward peace. Once peace became the center of national attention, it became necessary to mention the war and talk about its origins in the Violence, the tragic backdrop of present-day Colombia. This renewed interest in the Violence found answers in the research that, as just noted, had begun in 1960 and that, taken as a whole, constitutes the greatest effort in Colombian historiography. As a result, perceptions of the Violence slowly have recovered their complexity and diversity, and little by little the Violence has lost the omnipresent, irrational character that stood in the way of its comprehension.

Antecedents

Almost simultaneously with the development of the Violence, between 1948 and 1964, a great deal of literature was produced on the topic. In general it consists of disparate works in terms of quality, and the main motivation of many authors was to defend their own political party and blame the opposition. Absent was any desire to contribute to the clarification of the situation or at least to present the central themes of the period. This literature produced a Manichean image of victims and victimizers in which the Violence was always the result of the evil doings of "the other side." In spite of their problems, these works are a valuable collection of information on the political parties' views of themselves and their opponents, and for this reason they have been used again in some of the more recent studies.

The literature produced from the Conservative point of view emphasized the Liberal party's responsibility for the social and political disorder, primarily its inept management of the country during the so-called Liberal Republic (1930–1946). For the Conservatives, the Liberal party was also responsible for having limited the civilizing activities of the Catholic Church and having lowered its guard against international communism, which many Conservatives considered the origin of the Colombian crisis. Among the books written from this point of view, mention should be made of Francisco Fandiño Silva's *La penetración soviética en América Latina y el 9 de abril* (Bogotá, 1949); Joaquín Estrada Monsalve's *Así fué la revolución* (Bogotá, 1950); José María Nieto Rojas's *La batalla contra el comunismo en Colombia* (Bogotá, 1956); and Rafael Azula Barrera's *De la revolución al orden nuevo* (Bogotá, 1956).

The Liberals, in turn, tried to prove the antidemocratic and fraudulent origins of the Conservative governments and wanted to attract the attention of international public opinion by denouncing the obvious sympathies held by Conservative leaders for the European fascist regimes. They unanimously declared themselves faithful defenders of the constitution and the law, and they painted themselves as victims of the brutality practiced by government security forces. Some of the works written in this vein are Carlos Lleras Restrepo's *De la república a la dictadura* (Bogotá, 1955); Abelardo Forero Benavides's *Un testimonio contra la barbarie política* (Bogotá, 1953); and Germán Arciniegas's *The State of Latin America* (New York, 1952).

Also part of these antecedents to the modern literature on the Violence are numerous eyewitness accounts written by persons who saw the Violence from different angles and who wanted to write the story, often autobiographical, of how they lived and suffered during the conflict. Since these authors were immersed in the process that they were trying to describe, these works often lack a general perspective. They almost always focus attention on specific aspects adopted by the conflict in certain regions and localities, but this characteristic does not diminish their importance or their testimonial value.

In this genre the best-known work is probably the account of guerrilla commander Eduardo Franco Isaza, *La guerrilla de los llanos* (Bogotá, 1959), which contains valuable information about the logistic and organizational aspects of the Liberal guerrilla movement that took control of the extensive plains of eastern Colombia. The book attempts an analysis of the causes that led to the dissolution of the movement and its cooptation by the military government in 1953. Also about this same region, this time from the opposite camp, is Colonel Gustavo Sierra's memoir, *Las guerrillas de los Llanos Orientales* (Manizales, 1954), which evaluates the movement with a view to formulating proposals for its dismantling and control. On the Antioquia region there is an unusual memoir by the priest Fidel Blandón Berrío, who wrote, under the pseudonym Ernesto León Herrera, *Lo que el cielo no perdona* (Bogotá, 1954). This work emphasizes the degree of barbarity the confrontation reached in this zone of the country, mixing the author's own testimony as a priest who visited several localities with that of the commander of the Liberal guerrilla movement in the region. The central zone of the country also has a valuable account in Jaime Vásquez's historical novel, *Guerrilleros buenos días* (Bogotá, 1954). The book tells the story of the evolution of the Liberal guerrilla movement, from its genesis until its dissolution, in the region of Yacopí and the central Magdalena River valley.

Chronologically grouped with these antecedents, but entirely outside the two genres just described, is a book by Vernon Lee Fluharty, *Dance of the Millions* (Pittsburgh, 1957), which was widely read in North America. As a member of the U.S. embassy staff in Colombia, Fluharty had an opportunity to observe—from a position outside party prejudices—the conflict the country went through between the assassination of Jorge Eliécer Gaitán and the fall of the Conservative regime in 1953. Perhaps that circumstance and the fact that he was deeply influenced by a book by the distinguished socialist intellectual Antonio García, *Gaitán y el problema de la revolución colombiana* (Bogotá, 1955), allowed him to perceive, early on, the antidemocratic character of Colombian society and the class conflict that lay behind the party confrontation. This work also includes valuable information on the first years of the military regime of General Gustavo Rojas Pinilla and the evolution of the Violence during this phase. Covering Rojas's period there is another work of testimonial character, the compilation of speeches and documents that are part of the trial of the general in the Colombian Senate in 1959. It was published under the title *Rojas Pinilla ante el Senado* (Bogotá, 1959).

Modern Studies on the Violence

In the early 1960s the priest Germán Guzmán, the sociologist Orlando Fals Borda, and the lawyer Eduardo Umaña Luna began a new phase of studies on the Violence. Their work started a research trend that has developed without interruption for the last quarter century. The study done by these three pioneers, *La Violencia en Colombia* (Bogotá, 1962, 1964), breaks with the "traditional" literature that had been produced until then, a literature characterized in most cases, as we have seen, by heavy doses of sectarianism and low levels of analysis. As its principal author recalled in 1984,[3] the purpose of *La Violencia en Colombia* was to encourage Colombians to think about the Violence, in hopes of reaching a consensus that would put an end to the conflict and, at the same time, begin the work of scientific study of the phenomenon.

La Violencia en Colombia had its origin in the experiences and documentation compiled by the Commission to Investigate the Causes and Present Circumstances of the Violence, created by government Decree 0942 of 1958. Germán Guzmán, at that time the parish priest of violence-torn El Líbano in the department of Tolima, was a member of the commission. Also deeply involved in the commission's work were members of the recently created sociology department of the National University in Bogotá, among them Orlando Fals Borda and Camilo Torres. The initial undertaking of the new department was to aid the commission in its investigation. These two facts help to explain the painstaking descriptive treatment that characterizes the book, a quality that, given the book's analytical weakness, constitutes its principal limitation. At the same time this descriptive detail is its principal asset. Practically speaking, until the mid-1970s, the voluminous primary information compiled in this book served as almost the exclusive source for the different interpretations that appeared on the Violence.

In addition to being the first attempt at descriptive generalization on the Violence, this work was the first to present the discussion about its origins along the two main lines that would preoccupy subsequent investigators: the one favoring class conflict, the other assigning more importance to party antagonism. At the same time it covered the national dimensions of the phenomenon without neglecting its regional expressions, and it included study of the historical antecedents of the Violence. The publication of the book stimulated an angry debate in which Liberals and Conservatives began with mutual accusations and ended, together with the Church, by discrediting the authors and raising all sorts of suspicions about them. For the new generation of social scientists, however, the work was the first milestone of academic research on the Violence. Because of it, the topic was brought to the center of Colombian historical and sociological research. This was unquestionably the work's greatest contribution.

The appearance of Guzmán's book opened the door to a series of studies that in large measure were supported by the empirical evidence contained in this first synthesis. These works tried, in general, to go beyond the descriptive level and offer hypotheses. To one degree or another they were attempts to discover an explanatory framework for the evidence gathered by Guzmán and his collaborators. All accepted the description of the evidence as "la Violencia." But how could it be explained? What was its specific nature? To what causal order could it be attributed? What were its consequences? These were the questions addressed by most of the work produced until the mid-1970s. Taken together these works constitute the first great analytical effort to explain the phenomenon.

For Camilo Torres the Violence created the most important socio-cultural change in the peasant areas since the conquest.[4] His hypothesis held that in a society whose channels of social mobilization were blocked totally, the Violence served as a means to incorporate rural communities into a process that implied great transformations in their mentality, their socialization, and the division of labor itself. These changes were effected through channels not provided for in the prevailing structure. The principle behind the changes was the armed mobilization of the peasantry, which led to the development of a rural subculture that could assimilate a revolutionary class consciousness. Camilo, then, posed the possibility of seeing the phenomenon as an agent of transformation and not exclusively as an agent of destruction.

The hypotheses of the sociologist Orlando Fals Borda, developed in several essays written during this period,[5] are oriented along these same lines. For him the Violence was a political response—irrational but effective—to the effort to preserve the essential aspects of the same old sacred order. One thus could see the confrontation as a desire to transform—and in some cases to destroy—an immovable social structure.

The English historian Eric Hobsbawm called attention to the importance of the Violence in the study of the rural protest movements, stating that the Violence was the greatest armed peasant mobilization in the recent history of the western hemisphere. According to Hobsbawm, the Violence was the result of a frustrated social revolution, the fruit of the failed attempt to channel revolutionary social tensions through institutional means.[6]

The consequences of the Violence, particularly in the rural economy, were another topic of discussion. On this subject two divergent positions flourished. For Francisco Posada, the Violence represented "a reinforcement of the factors favorable to underdevelopment and therefore a genuine regression." According to this logic he had no reservations about classifying it as a process of "refeudalization."[7] This hypothesis contrasts with the view of those who saw the Violence as the expression of capitalist development in the countryside, which brought with it as a consequence the forcible expropriation of thousands of peasants and the acceleration of the process of capitalist accumulation. This position was expressed forcefully in the work of the economist Salomón Kalmanovitz.[8]

In a somewhat similar vein are two works by Pierre Gilhodés. While they give proper emphasis to its complexity and regional diversity, both books see the Violence as a "brutal purge" destined to liquidate the relations of precapitalist production, leaving the field free for the subsequent development of modern agriculture. Gilhodés is probably the first to situate the Violence within the framework of peasant movements, calling attention to the connections between it and the appearance of the peasant organizations after 1967.[9]

Lamentably, in spite of its enormous importance, this debate has not continued to develop. This failure to extend the debate is due in part to the difficulty of finding reliable sources that take account of the impact of the Violence on the structure of agrarian property.

Daniel Pecaut, in an essay that includes some of the hypotheses that he would amplify in later works,[10] thought the Violence had to be seen as part of a very broad process of social struggle in the twentieth century. In the stage prior to the generalization of the conflict, this process includes the annihilation of the popular urban organizations, a development that led to the dual urban-rural nature of the Violence. Pecaut also points out that the Violence arose from a disparity between the weight of the state apparatus and the actual power of the state, which was not the result of the conflict between the two traditional parties, but, in his view, the effect of the accentuated economic liberalism imposed by the ruling classes since 1944.

Finally, we must include Sánchez's essay, "La Violencia y sus efectos sobre el sistema político colombiano,"[11] in which he isolates the particulars of the phenomenon of the Violence. In his opinion, the Violence combines three types of peasant movements: political banditry, reformist agrarianism, and revolutionary agrarianism. This combination of features makes the Violence a unique case in the context of Latin American social movements. In another conclusion in this essay, he emphasizes the class character of the Violence, which he considers its "predominant tendency." Class conflict led to a rearrangement of relations between the two parties that culminated in the National Front, an arrangement aimed at preserving the traditional class structure.

This first great interpretative effort closed with a new attempt at synthesis, Paul Oquist's book, *Violencia, conflicto y política en Colombia* (Bogotá, 1978), in which he tried to construct an integrated theory that would account for the many variables in the conflict. Oquist argued that, given its multifaceted character, the Violence could not be considered as a unitary phenomenon, explicable by a single set of factors for the whole country. He proposed a "structural regionalism" for the Violence that combined geographical aspects with the types of conflict that developed in each region. The other hypothesis put forth in this book is his controversial idea of the "partial collapse of the state," through which he attempts to address the question of the temporal simultaneity of different "regional" processes. For Oquist, contrary to what happened during the nineteenth century, the growing power acquired by the state throughout the twentieth century was accompanied by the dissolution of the mechanisms of social control. This process magnified the importance of the state and drove the two partisan elites into a dispute for the exclusive control of power. That process, in turn, led to a partial collapse of the state, which was manifested in the erosion of political institutions, conflict within the military establishment, loss of the government's legitimacy, and, in some regions, its actual physical absence.

This attempt at generalization was quickly superseded, since the bulk of academic research on the Violence was published in subsequent years. These new studies broadened both the research horizon and the appreciation of the complexity of the phenomenon, making the need for a synthesis ever more urgent.

The New Phase of Studies on the Violence

Since the end of the 1970s, research on the Violence has reached a notable level of development not only in terms of volume but also in terms of refinement. The advances along this line of historical research can be explained by the convergence of several circumstances. One of these is the result of an enormous academic effort, carried out by a new generation of well-trained scholars who have enriched the discussion with new questions and new theoretical and methodological tools. Another factor is that this academic effort coincided with the worsening of the crisis of the Colombian state, the accelerated deterioration of the situation of public order, and the beginning of the uncertain peace process in which we find ourselves today. These circumstances produced a diversion of attention toward recent history in a search for answers to the present crisis, and this trend has been accompanied by growing expectations on the part of the public for the discussion to extend beyond the limits of academic discourse. Today the study of the violence has become practically a political debate, as is shown by the massive attendance at different forums and seminars held in recent years and the growing number of publications on the subject.

This research effort, as Pecaut points out, coincides with the end of the era of grand causal explanations. It takes place in a context of general concern about the relevance of insisting on the global character of the phenomenon or, on the contrary, of emphasizing its diversity. This preoccupation is expressed in the proposals to abandon the concept of "the Violence" in favor of the concept of "phenomena of violence." While this debate has not been resolved yet, there is no question that the majority of recent works have centered their attention on the study of specific facets of the global phenomenon. This implies, perhaps, an attempt to discover the unity of the conflict by first exploring its diversity.

In spite of their enormous variety, it is possible to group the research projects of recent years into three large categories. The first includes studies of a regional character, a quite positive aspect in the development of the literature in the last few years. Among the regions that have received particular attention is the coffee zone. This was the subject of an early and carefully researched book by Jaime Arocha, *La Violencia en el Quindío* (Bogotá, 1979), that sought to establish the characteristics of the conflict, its stages and persistence, through analysis of juridical, economic, and ecological factors. Arocha's study was followed by one by Carlos Miguel Ortiz Sarmiento, *Estado y subversión en Colombia* (Bogotá, 1985), that attempted to situate the Violence in this same region in the broad context of the colonization process that began in the nineteenth century. It also explores the links with bossism that guaranteed the continuity and expansion of coffee production.[12] Also on the coffee region, this time focused on the department of Caldas, is the study by the Canadian Keith Christie, *Oligarcas, campesinos y política en Colombia* (Bogotá, 1986), which departs somewhat from the relation between local agrarian structures and the Violence in order to concentrate on bossism, the electoral struggle, and religious conflict.

On Tolima, we have the work of the anthropologist Darío Fajardo, *Violencia y desarrollo* (Bogotá, 1979). Fajardo examines the processes of geographical redistribution of the population and the capitalistic development of agriculture, phenomena that were influenced greatly in this department by the Violence. Also on this region is James Henderson's book, *Cuando Colombia se desangró* (Bogotá, 1984), which analyzes the Violence from a local perspective by studying its manifestations in the *municipio* of Santa Isabel, in the north of the department of Tolima. Henderson sees in this phenomenon the expression of a conservative force produced by defective institutional functioning rather than a kind of popular protest.

Other regions also have attracted the attention of students of the Violence. The department of the Valle del Cauca was studied by the architect Jacques Aprile. His book, *Urbanización y violencia en el Valle* (Bogotá, 1980), which he published under the pseudonym Urbano Campo, attempts to present the Violence as an expression of the Cold War, a perspective that at times misrepresents the regional profile he intends to portray. Curiously, two regions in which there were important Liberal resistance movements that, moreover, were topics for early and well-documented eyewitness accounts, have received scant attention by researchers. I refer to the eastern plains and the northwest part of the department of Antioquia. Nevertheless, the first region is the subject of a monographic study by Justo Casas, *La Violencia en el occidente del Casanare* (Bogotá, 1986), which focuses its attention on one of the commands that made up the insurgent movement on the plains. Most of the general studies allude to this movement, but it still remains practically uninvestigated. The second region, northwest Antioquia, is treated in an as yet unpublished monograph of descriptive character by the sociologist Wilson Granados.

A second category is comprised of works that approach the Violence from a specific thematic perspective. This group includes the book by Gonzalo Sánchez and Donny Meertens, *Bandoleros, gamonales y campesinos* (Bogotá, 1983), on the relations that were established among the principal social agents in the coffee zone in the central part of the country. This study is the most important contribution to date on the last and most obscure phase of the Violence (1958–1965), which was played out during the first years of the National Front. A knowledge of this period is indispensable to the understanding of the evolution of the insurgent peasant movement toward social and political banditry. This evolution in some cases merged with the first forms of revolutionary insurgency, which, in turn, were linked to the birth of the contemporary Colombian guerrilla movement.

Another topic that has attracted ample attention is Gaitán's movement and the 9th of April uprising known abroad as the *Bogotazo*. The studies that have been written on this subject have contributed to a revival of the image of Gaitanismo as a channeling of popular protest and also emphasize its influence at the national level at the beginning of the Violence. These studies have permitted recognition of the revolutionary potential of the 9th of April uprising and suggest the possible relation between the government's repression of the rebels and the birth of the first Liberal guerrilla groups. The best study of Gaitanismo and its relation to the traditional parties is unquestionably Herbert Braun's *The Assassination of Gaitán: Public Life and Urban Violence in Colombia* (Madison, 1985). Braun provides a detailed analysis of Gaitán's political development and the way in which he led people onto the national political scene, slowly penetrating an area that until then had been reserved for the great leaders of the traditional parties. This process came to a head with the assassination of Gaitán and the ensuing popular uprising, in the midst of which the traditional social order dissolved. Other works on the 9th of April are the volume of eyewitness accounts of the Bogotá uprising and its antecedents compiled by Arturo Alape, *El Bogotazo: Memorias del olvido* (Bogotá, 1983); the study by Carlos Eduardo Jaramillo, *Ibagué: Conflictos políticos de 1930 al 9 de abril* (Bogotá, 1983), on the way in which events developed in the capital of the department of Tolima; and Jacques Aprile's *El impacto del 9 de abril sobre el centro de Bogotá* (Bogotá, 1983), which describes the impact the event had on the infrastructure of the capital. Gonzalo Sánchez's *Los días de la revolución: Gaitanismo y 9 de abril en provincia* (Bogotá, 1983) reconstructs the national dimensions of the uprising and brings together valuable information on the organizational styles and the sometimes openly revolutionary character the movement assumed in the Colombian provinces.

Another thematic approach that has gained great importance focuses on the relation between the Violence and the state. Even though the subject is touched upon in several research studies completed in recent years, it is worth pointing out two works in particular. The first is Francisco Leal's *Estado y política en Colombia* (Bogotá, 1984), a collection of several articles about two principle concerns: the genesis, development, and crisis of the Colombian two-party system; and the low level of military intervention and the subordination of the army to the political parties.

The second notable work, although its scope goes beyond the state-Violence relationship, is Daniel Pecaut's *Orden y violencia: Colombia, 1930–1954* (Bogotá, 1987). This unique book, which is unquestionably one of the most ambitious projects ever undertaken on contemporary Colombian history, sweeps through the nineteenth and twentieth centuries in an effort to understand how to reach a definition of "the social" in that country. Pecaut concludes that the state has never been wholly recognized as the legitimate agent of societal unification and that, in Colombia, the "social" is subject to the "political." In consequence, for Pecaut, Colombian democracy is the expression of a division of the social, which maintains the marginal status of the unassimilated popular sectors. The violence takes place on the borderline of this division. Therefore Pecaut does not find the coexistence of violence with Colombia's restricted model of democracy paradoxical. For him, violence is consistent with the exercise of a democracy which, far from being based on the homogeneity of its citizens, rests on the preservation of their natural differences, collective loyalties, and private networks of social control. Rather than trying to institutionalize the relations of force that rule the society, Colombian democracy makes them into the mechanism of its continuity.

As for the Violence proper, it must be mentioned that for Pecaut it is first and foremost a juxtaposition of "irreducible violences." Their unity can be analyzed only in reference to the political, which makes the party rivalry for power the only context in which the Violence can be deciphered. That is, the Violence is the measure of the extent to which the popular masses were stripped of any principle of citizen identity other than that which the traditional parties offered them. The process concludes, logically enough, with the installation of a new political order, the National Front, which retained, apparently unchanged, the same social and party structures and the same precariousness of the state. The National Front, for Pecaut, "cannot be dissociated from violence." After having played a part in stabilizing the Violence, violence has never been entirely absent from its functioning.

The third tendency apparent in the works of this new phase of research projects is characterized by the broadening of the temporal frame in which the Violence is cast. In fact, one of the topics that has attracted the most interest in recent years is the question of the continuities or discontinuities that can be established between the Violence and the historical processes that preceded or followed it. The discussion goes beyond an attempt to define a succession of causes and consequences, since it assumes the possibility of establishing the presence of structural phenomena that exercised prolonged influence on Colombian society.

Among the works that can be grouped into this category is David Bushnell's study (see Chapter 2 of this volume), which stresses the precocity of political development with respect to overall development, which took place at a much slower pace. This early development was accompanied by the early entrenchment of a partisan mystique, a product of the characteristic electoral zeal in Colombian politics. This circumstance has led some scholars to pose the possibility that the bipartisan division of the Colombian people does not have a political character, properly speaking, but a "cultural" one. Another work in this category is that of Carlos Eduardo Jaramillo,[13] who writes about guerrilla organization during the last civil war of the nineteenth century and its possible relation, in terms of styles, tactics, and zones of operation, to the guerrillas of the era of the Violence. On the relation between the Violence and the agrarian conflicts spawned in the process of the colonization and expansion of the agricultural frontier in the nineteenth and twentieth centuries, there is Catherine LeGrand's *Frontier Expansion and Peasant Protest in Colombia, 1850–1936* (Albuquerque, 1986), some of whose ideas are presented in Chapter 3 of this volume. Also in the area of antecedents are Charles Bergquist's *Labor in Latin America* (Stanford, 1986) and his Chapter 4 of this volume, both of which link the repression directed against the labor movement during the Violence with its dismantling and disorganization during the years preceding it. This process, in Bergquist's opinion, is intimately tied to the fate that befell the most important sector of the Colombian labor force during the first half of the century, the workers in the coffee sector. On the relationship between the Violence and the development of the social movements of the last few decades, we must include Medófilo Medina's work on the peasant resistance movement in the south of the department of Tolima and its evolution toward new forms of guerrilla organization through the Fuerzas Armadas Revolucionarias Colombianas (FARC).[14] On the creation of the contemporary Colombian guerrilla movement and its relation to the Violence, we also must include the work of Eduardo Pizarro (see Chapter 8 of this volume).

In conclusion, I wish to point out that this phase of the research has been characterized principally by the broadening of the topic of study and the heterogeneity of the research projects. This does not mean that the unity of the Violence has been ruptured, but the situation does demand, for purposes of explication, more refined attempts at synthesis. Examples of these new efforts can be found in Pecaut's work just cited and in Sánchez's essay in Chapter 5 of this volume.

The Violence after "The Violence"

One research problem that has attracted a great deal of attention in recent years is the possibility of studying the "new stage of the war," that is, the insurrectionary violence of the 1970s and 1980s as it relates to the previous stage, the Violence proper. The topic is uniquely important because, when it comes to armed insurrectionary movements, the current situation in Colombia is unusual compared to the rest of the continent. This is true not only with regard to its scope—it is exceeded only by guerrilla activity in Central America—but also and most particularly with regard to its origins and duration. Colombia's is the oldest guerrilla movement in Latin America, and unlike those of other countries in the area, it already had a long history of experience by the time the example of the Cuban Revolution promoted the creation of insurgent groups in the rest of Latin America.

In recent years a relationship between the Violence and the various types of popular insurgency has been suggested constantly. In fact, more than fifteen years of the Violence left ineradicable consequences that in many cases have nourished the conflicts that characterize later stages. The "historical memory" of the Violence constitutes an accumulated experience for the new guerrilla organizations, which even count among their members former Liberal fighters from the 1950s. On the whole, the most substantial bridge that can be established between the Violence and today's insurgent movements is found in the political field, because the mechanism created to put an end to the bipartisan confrontation of the 1950s—the National Front—installed a model of limited democracy, monopolized by the two traditional parties, that denied legal political action to other social forces. These forces found their efforts declared illegal and encountered repression whenever they tried to become active outside the bipartisan system, leading many to take up the alternative of arms.

The differences between one period and the other, nevertheless, are notable. The main distinction between the two can be found in the overt class dimensions of the present conflict. In addition, there has been a transformation of the actual character of the struggle. The guerrilla movements of the present day want to destroy the present political system, not be included in it as they did in the 1950s. Moreover, in the country's current situation, the violence of the guerrillas coexists with other kinds of violence, notably those exercised by the paramilitary groups and the drug traffickers. This makes the situation even more complicated, to the point where some consider that the country is now passing through several wars superimposed on one another and that their development implies not an insurrectionary perspective but an anarchical one.

The studies produced about this new phase of violence focus their attention on the action of the different guerrilla groups and, with important exceptions, replace analysis with the testimony of persons who have been involved with the guerrillas. These studies, in most cases, can be classified as a kind of "historical journalism" that recalls, to some extent, the testimonial treatment of the Violence of the 1950s. Although these works doubtless will constitute an invaluable source for future analysis, until now—despite or perhaps because of their quantity and enormous diversity—they have not contributed in all cases to the clarification of the present situation.

The first works produced along these lines appeared in the early 1970s and recorded the testimony of Communist combatants. They focus on the organization and evolution of their commands during the era of the Violence proper and end with the creation of the FARC in 1964. These works are *Cuadernos de campaña* (Bogotá, 1973), by Manuel Marulanda Vélez (present commander of the FARC), and *Ciro: Páginas de su vida* (Bogotá, 1974), an autobiographical account by Ciro Trujillo, one of the founders of the FARC, compiled by José Modesto Campos. At the end of the 1970s, when the M-19 was at its peak, the journalist Patricia Lara wrote *Siembra vientos y recogerás tempestades* (Barcelona, 1982). Her book was based on interviews with the principal leaders of the movement and emphasizes the continuity between the bipartisan nature of the Violence and the struggle of the new guerrilla organizations. It was the first important written account of this group.

In 1982, with the process under way that led to negotiations and the temporary truce with nearly all the guerrilla groups, there was the boom of the so-called Literature of the Process of Peace. During this period more than forty books were published of the most diverse kinds. These range from detailed descriptions of guerrilla action related by commanders of such actions—the best-known example being Rosemberg Pabón's account of the seizure of the Dominican embassy in Bogotá[15]— to luxurious editions that document milestones of the peace process, such as the national march for peace in which thousands of white doves were painted on the walls of Colombian cities.[16] For purposes of future analysis, the most important of these books are probably those that deal with the history of the various guerrilla groups. Notable among these are *FARC: Veinte años de Marquetalia a la Uribe* (Bogotá, 1984), by Carlos Arango, and *EPL: Diez hombres, un ejército, una historia* (Bogotá, 1985), by Fabiola Calvo. Perhaps the best of the books in this genre is that by Olga Behar, *Las guerras de la paz* (Bogotá, 1985). On the position of the guerrillas with regard to the peace process two works stand out, that of the political commander of the FARC, Jacobo Arenas, *Cese el fuego* (Bogotá, 1985), and Ramón Jimeno's interview of the highest chief of the M-19, Jaime Bateman, which was published under the title *Oiga hermano* (Bogotá, 1984). On this same aspect, but written from an entirely different perspective, is former Minister of Defense General Fernando Landazábal's *El precio de la paz*, a synthesis of army thinking on the peace process.

Although the topic scarcely has begun to be developed, quite systematic treatment has been given to the recent process of land colonization and its links to the guerrilla movement. The books that have been published in this field have revealed the multiple relations and the almost complementary character that exist between these two movements. Isolated not only geographically but also legally, the areas of colonization encourage the development of a type of social and economic relation in which the Colombian state does not participate even in symbolic form. Important in this group of works is a suggestive article by William Ramírez, "La guerrilla rural en Colombia, una vía hacia la colonización armada," *Estudios rurales Latinoamericanos* 4:2 (1986), and a collection of stories on colonization in Caquetá, *Selva adentro* (Bogotá, 1987), by Alfredo Molano. Of special note is *Colonización, coca y guerrilla* (Bogotá, 1986), prepared by an interdisciplinary team of professors from the National University made up of Jaime Jaramillo, Leonidas Mora, and Fernando Cubides. These researchers carried out fieldwork, with the participation of the colonizers, in the extensive forest region of Caquetá. Their study attempts to establish the dimensions and characteristics of the colonizing process and the kind of relations established between colonizers and guerrillas through the development of coca production, a crop which, because of its illegality and high profits, is adapted perfectly to the natural and social conditions of the region.

The impact of the drug trade on Colombian society, although it has been the subject of numerous newspaper and magazine articles, has begun only recently to be studied through systematic research. In addition to the already mentioned *Colonización, coca y guerrilla*, attention should be called to the first book published on this subject, *Narcotráfico: Imperio de la cocaína*, by Mario Arango and Jorge Child (Medellín, 1984), and Arango's study, *Impacto del narcotráfico en Antioquia* (Medellín, 1988). The latter book, based on an investigation of twenty drug leaders, poses several hypotheses on the habits and motivations of the drug kingpins that suggest a degree of continuity between the Antioquian spirit of enterprise and the activities of the "new contraband drug business." Also worthy of mention is Alvaro Camacho's *Droga y sociedad en Colombia* (Bogotá, 1988), the most detailed attempt to date to analyze the social and economic impact of drugs and the disruptive effects of the drug trade on the Colombian political system. In addition to these works, there are several books of a journalistic nature, such as Fabio Castillo's *Los jinetes de la cocaína* (Bogotá, 1987), which abound in sensationalistic revelations about the eccentricities of the drug lords and the immense fortunes and enormous power they have amassed. These studies generally do not rise above the level of the anecdotal and in most cases only contribute to nourishing the myths that have grown up around the drug bosses.

Finally, a work that merits special mention is the report of the Comisión de Estudios sobre la Violencia, *Colombia: Violencia y democracia* (Bogotá, 1987), a portion of which is included as Chapter 12 of this volume. The most profound and rigorous assessment of the present situation in the country, it was undertaken by an interdisciplinary commission composed of ten specialists on the subject, a kind of collective research effort practically unknown in Colombia. In addition to presenting a diagnosis of the nature of the complex situation of violence affecting the country, the report contains a set of recommendations designed to overcome the problems highlighted in it.

In general terms the report concludes that Colombia is today the scene of multiple violences that overlap and are superimposed on one another in such a way as to lead to a chaotic situation that runs a high risk of becoming general anarchy. For the authors, the major characteristic of the contemporary violence is precisely its multiple expressions, which "do not exclude, but do overwhelm, the political dimension." The study establishes a typology of the current violence, including political violence, which encompasses the confrontation between the state and various guerrilla groups; urban violence, which includes a wide gamut of crimes against life and the person and is a product of social and moral marginality and disintegration; organized violence, which in general is exercised by powerful groups nourished, for the most part, by the illegal economies of the drug trade and emeralds, and which includes the death squads and the gangs of paid assassins; violence against ethnic minorities, which is exercised by nearly all social and economic groups against the surviving indigenous communities; violence and the communications media; and finally, family violence.

Although these different types of violence are expressed in different ways and require particular solutions in each case, they all have their origins in a common matrix: the limitations of a democracy that does not recognize the plurality of the society it claims to represent and that thereby impedes the free exercise of the rights of all citizens and foments inequality among them. Because of this, on the whole, the commission's recommendations stress a common proposal: "In a word, the extension of civilization, democracy, and equality to all areas of collective life."

Research Perspectives

A tentative assessment of the research written on the subject of the Violence suggests at least two general conclusions. First, the effort to broaden the thematic and chronological parameters of the Violence has extended the topic beyond the individual research capabilities of any one person. The subject now demands collective research efforts of an interdisciplinary nature. The second conclusion is that the debate on the Violence, given its implications for the current situation, overflows the strictly academic realm and has become, in fact, a problem of deep political repercussions.

Assessing the whole body of published works, it is also possible to discern the areas where the research has placed major emphasis and those that have received scant attention. Among the latter, a significantly neglected area is the study of the economic effects of the Violence, a subject emphasized in this collection of essays (see, in particular, Chapters 6 and 7) and one that deserves much more work. Also neglected has been the study of the role played during the Violence by such important institutions as the Catholic Church and the army,[17] subjects explored, for the contemporary period, in Chapter 13 of this volume. The possibility of studying other dimensions of the phenomenon, such as messianism and religiosity, hardly has been touched on. On another front, it is noteworthy that in spite of the importance attributed to the Violence in the geographical redistribution of the population, there have been no systematic studies concerning its influence on the accelerated process of urbanization in recent decades.

Another area that demands more attention is artistic production on the theme of the Violence. In fact, while a good part of literary, film, theater, and pictorial arts in recent times has revolved inevitably around this phenomenon, the scarcity of analytic studies or even compilations of work representing the Violence in Colombian art is noteworthy.[18]

Finally, another important area that needs development is what has come to be called "the culture of violence," by which is meant the fabric of interpersonal day-to-day relationships that make up the ambiance in which the Violence developed and in many cases reproduced itself. This area of study, which calls on the participation of psychologists, anthropologists, and sociologists, is perhaps one of the most promising avenues that might provide interpretations that have until now been missing in academic work on the subject. Additionally, through this approach it is probable that studies will be done on phenomena as troubling as the traumatic transformation of the ethical and social values of the Colombian people, who to a large extent are now abetting the sometimes invisible "daily" and "underground" types of violence that lie at the root of the pervasive attitude of aggression so foreign to democratic coexistence.

Turning to research currently in progress, one can highlight the work of several interdisciplinary teams working in the country's major cities. One ambitious program that brings an overall outlook to the Violence and its current political projection is being carried out in Bogotá by a group of eleven researchers who intend to cover a broad thematic spectrum, including four investigations on the regional level: Boyacá, Valle, Sumapaz, and Llanos Orientales. The group also envisions projects on the effects of the Violence on agrarian structures, the projection of the Violence into recent decades, and the literature of the Violence.[19] Another project is being carried out in the cities of Medellín and Cali by two research groups that are studying the present manifestations of urban violence.[20] This research includes the activities of paramilitary groups who attack public figures, crimes committed by hired assassins, crimes committed by gangs of drug traffickers, and the activities of groups in charge of "cleaning up" the city of undesirable elements. When we add to these projects those being conducted by government organizations in charge of rehabilitation programs in zones of violence, plus a large number of monographs and theses in preparation, we can say that in the coming years the topic of the Violence will continue to occupy a central place in the concerns of Colombian researchers, who are engaged in a dramatic effort to elucidate a phenomenon that exerts decisive influence on our society.

Notes

1. In spite of being long out of date, Russell Ramsey's bibliography is still useful: "Critical Bibliography on la Violencia in Colombia," *Latin American Research Review* 8:1 (1973): 3–44. A more current overview of studies on the subject is Gonzalo Sánchez, "La Violencia in Colombia: New Research, New Questions," *Hispanic American Historical Review* 65:4 (1985): 789–807. This essay establishes the basic classification scheme that is used in the present essay. Finally, there is the recently published bibliography compiled by Guillermo Cardona, *Para un estudio sobre la Violencia en Colombia* (Bogotá, 1989).

2. Gonzalo Sánchez, "Raíces históricas de la amnistía o las etapas de la guerra," in his *Ensayos de historia social y política del siglo XX* (Bogotá, 1985).

3. Germán Guzmán Campos, *Reflexión crítica sobre el libro La Violencia en Colombia*, in *Pasado y presente de la Violencia en Colombia*, ed. Gonzalo Sánchez and Ricardo Peñaranda (Bogotá, 1986).

4. Camilo Torres R., *La Violencia y los cambios socio-culturales en las áreas rurales colombianas* (Bogotá, 1963).

5. See, for example, Orlando Fals Borda, *Lo sacro y lo violento: Aspectos problemáticos del desarrollo en Colombia* (Bogotá, 1965).

6. Eric Hobsbawm, "The Anatomy of the Violence in Colombia," in his *Primitive Rebels* (New York, 1959).

7. Francisco Posada, *Colombia: Violencia y subdesarrollo* (Bogotá, 1969).

8. See especially his *Desarrollo de la agricultura en Colombia* (Bogotá, 1978).

9. Pierre Gilhodés, *La Violence en Colombie: Bandisme et guerre sociale* (Paris, 1976).

10. Daniel Pecaut, "Reflexiones acerca del fenómeno de la Violencia," *Ideología y Sociedad* 19 (1976).

11. *Cuadernos Colombianos* 9 (Bogotá, 1976), 3–44.

12. For a synthesis of Ortiz Sarmiento's ideas concerning the relationship between the coffee economy and the Violence, see Chapter 6 of this volume.

13. "La Guerra de los Mil Días: Aspectos estructurales de la organización guerrillera," in *Pasado y presente de la Violencia en Colombia*, ed. Gonzalo Sánchez and Ricardo Peñaranda (Bogotá, 1986).

14. "La resistencia campesina en el sur del Tolima," in *Pasado y presente de la Violencia en Colombia*, ed. Gonzalo Sánchez and Ricardo Peñaranda (Bogotá, 1986).

15. *Así nos tomamos la Embajada* (Bogotá, 1985).

16. *Los artistas por la paz* (Bogotá, 1985).

17. On the role of the army, see Russell Ramsey, *Guerrilleros y soldados* (Bogotá, 1981), and the articles by Eduardo Pizarro, "La profesionalización militar en Colombia," in nos. 1 and 2 of *Análisis Político* (1987). On the Catholic Church, see Rodolfo de Poux, *Una iglesia en estado de alerta* (Bogotá, 1983).

18. A complete picture of the literary production on the theme can be found in Lucila Inés Mena, "Bibliografía anotada sobre el ciclo de la Violencia

en Colombia," *Latin American Research Review* 14:3 (1978). An overview of film production is offered in Isabel Sánchez's compilation, *Cine de la Violencia* (Bogotá, 1987), which brings together the six best screenplays, some of them still not produced, that have been written on the subject. On literature the best analysis is still, in the eyes of many, Laura Restrepo's "Niveles de realidad en la literatura de la Violencia colombiana," *Ideología y Sociedad* 17 and 18 (1976). Also important is a book by Manuel Antonio Arango, *Gabriel García Márquez y la novela de la Violencia en Colombia* (Mexico, 1985). Essays by North American scholars on the subject are collected in Jonathan Titler, ed., *Violencia y literatura en Colombia* (Madrid, 1989). On the plastic arts, the only work published to date is an essay by Germán Rubiano, "El arte de la Violencia," *Arte en Colombia* 25 (1985).

19. "Actores, regiones y periodización de la Violencia," research project, Instituto de Estudios Políticos, Universidad Nacional, coordinated by Gonzalo Sánchez G.

20. The Cali research group is coordinated by Alvaro Camacho and Alvaro Guzmán. An example of this work appears as Chapter 11 of this volume. The Medellín group is based at the Department of Sociology at the University of Antioquia.

Glossary

ANAPO
: Alianza Nacional Popular (National Popular Alliance). Political party formed in the 1960s by followers of deposed president/dictator General Gustavo Rojas Pinilla. Initially composed primarily of Conservatives disaffected with the National Front, the party eventually attracted a wide spectrum of followers, including socialists. Partisans of ANAPO, especially those from within its socialist wing, later would join with disaffected Communists to found the guerrilla group M-19.

ANUC
: Asociación Nacional de Usuarios Campesinos (National Peasant Association). Organization of rural workers and smallholders promoted by the government of Carlos Lleras Restrepo in the late 1960s. It fostered radical agrarian mobilization in the early 1970s; it declined rapidly thereafter as guerrilla groups and urban reformists attempted to capture its leadership and the government withdrew its support.

baldíos
: Public domain lands. Since the nineteenth century, law has regulated their privatization through occupation and productive use. Often initially settled by land-hungry rural families, the bulk of *baldío* lands have been adjudicated to large landowners, merchants, and professionals. From the 1880s to the midtwentieth century this dynamic was particularly pronounced along parts of the coffee frontier. In subsequent decades it has characterized areas of recent settlement in the river

valleys and coastal lowlands of western Colombia and in the plains of the east.

Bogotazo   Term used primarily outside of Colombia to refer to the destruction of downtown Bogotá by crowds following the assassination of the popular Liberal leader Jorge Eliécer Gaitán on April 9, 1948. In Colombia the event is referred to more commonly as the *Nueve de abril* and its participants as *nueveabrileños*.

boleteo   Form of extortion. The term derives from the means—the short, anonymous, often handwritten notes, or *boletas*—used to convey threats and terms to victims, usually rural property owners. Widespread during the Violence, the *boleteo* is once again common in many rural areas.

cacique   Local political boss. Taken from the Spanish word for Indian chief, cacique is used interchangeably with *gamonal*, or local strongman.

caudillo   Political strongman or political boss, usually of national stature.

Chispas   The bandit leader Teófilo Rojas, who was active in the 1950s and 1960s.

chulavitas   Conservative police involved in the repression of Liberals during the Violence. The name derives from Chulavita, the *municipio* in the department of Boyacá where many were recruited.

colonos   Usually, settlers on lands in the public domain who are eligible under Colombian law for adjudication as a freehold of the land that they improve.

CTC   Confederación de Trabajadores Colombianos (Confederation of Colombian Workers). National labor federation formed under Liberal and Communist party auspices in the 1930s. Its influence declined under the increasingly antilabor governments after 1945. Eventually, it was displaced as the country's leading labor organization by the Conservative-supported rival federation, the UTC.

CUT
: Central Unitaria de Trabajadores (Unitary Federation of Workers). Labor federation founded in the mid-1980s. It united Liberal-, Conservative-, and Communist-dominated unions as well as independent ones.

department
: Administrative unit of Colombia, roughly equivalent to a state in the United States.

ELN
: Ejército de Liberación Nacional (Army for National Liberation). Revolutionary guerrilla group founded in Colombia in the early 1960s. Inspired by the Cuban example, and drawing early recruits from among university students, it consolidated itself in the Magdalena Medio, especially around the oil enclave at Barrancabermeja, Santander. During the 1980s it specialized in the sabotage of oil pipelines and the kidnapping of executives of and technicians working for foreign oil companies operating in Colombia. Unlike other major guerrilla organizations (the FARC, and the M-19), the ELN has proved unreceptive to government peace initiatives; its tactics of economic sabotage are criticized even within organizations of the revolutionary left.

EPL
: Ejército Popular de Liberación (Popular Army of Liberation). Maoist-inspired guerrilla group linked to the pro-Chinese Communist party in Colombia, the Partido Comunista Marxista-Leninista (PCML).

FARC
: Fuerzas Armadas Revolucionarias Colombianas (Revolutionary Colombian Armed Forces). The largest and most powerful of the guerrilla groups in Colombia. Unlike other early Marxist guerrilla groups formed in the 1960s, the FARC was not inspired by the Cuban Revolution. Rather, it evolved in response to the offensive in the mid-1950s launched by the military government of Gustavo Rojas Pinilla against the Communist-led rural

enclaves of smallholders that had developed out of the struggle for land in the 1920s and 1930s. By the 1980s the FARC had more than a score of armed "fronts" operating in the country, most of them in peripheral areas and including zones deeply involved in the cultivation, processing, and commercialization of coca.

FEDENAL
Magdalena River Transport Workers Union. Its members labored as stevedores and ships' crewmen on the river that was historically Colombia's most important link with the outside world. Led by Communists and leftist Liberals, FEDENAL was, in the early 1940s, the most powerful affiliate of the CTC labor federation. In 1945, following a long period of declining river traffic, the union launched a major strike in order to avoid layoffs and share available work among all its members. The strike was crushed by the transitional Liberal government of Alberto Lleras Camargo, signaling growing repression of leftist labor and the decline of the Liberal-dominated CTC in the postwar era.

Frente Nacional
National Front. Bipartisan governmental arrangement (1958–1974) in which Colombia's two major political parties, the Conservatives and the Liberals, sought to end the Violence by agreeing to alternate control of the presidency and to divide governmental positions equally between themselves.

Gaitanista
Follower of Jorge Eliécer Gaitán, the charismatic Liberal leader assassinated in Bogotá on April 9, 1948.

gamonal
See cacique.

Guaviare
Region of recent settlement and coca production in eastern Colombia.

latifundios
Large landed estates. In Colombia they are commonly devoted to cattle raising, although they are not uncommon in other forms of agriculture, including coffee production. Owners of such estates are called *latifundistas*.

Laureanista   Partisan of Laureano Gómez, Conservative leader
                     and president of Colombia from 1950 to 1953.

ligas campesinas   Organizations formed by rural workers, *colonos*,
                     sharecroppers, and smallholders during the struggle
                     for land and improved conditions of labor in the
                     1920s and 1930s.

llanos   Plains of eastern Colombia. *Llaneros* (cowboys)
                     from this cattle-raising region played an important
                     role in Simón Bolívar's campaign to dislodge the
                     Spaniards from highland Colombia; joined the
                     Liberal revolutionary Rafael Uribe Uribe in
                     threatening Bogotá during the War of the Thousand
                     Days (1899–1902); and formed the largest, most
                     radically reformist, and most successful of the
                     Liberal guerrilla groups during the Violence. Today,
                     this is an area of expanding agricultural settlement,
                     widening social conflict, and guerrilla activity; it
                     includes important zones of coca production,
                     processing, and trade.

Magdalena Medio   Central Magdalena River valley, encompassing
                     low-lying parts of the departments of
                     Cundinamarca, Boyacá, and Santander to the east,
                     and Tolima and Antioquia to the west. It borders
                     on the emerald zone of western Boyacá, whose
                     long-established organizations of contrabandists
                     moved easily into the illegal drug trade, and it
                     includes the petroleum complex around the port of
                     Barrancabermeja, where militant leftist labor unions
                     have existed since the 1920s. It is the scene of
                     much recent agricultural development, by
                     smallholders and squatters as well as by large-
                     scale commercial farmers and cattle ranchers. In
                     the 1980s the area became a major theater of
                     violence in which leftist guerrillas, the paramilitary
                     right, the drug mafia, and the Colombian army
                     were all involved.

M-19   Movement of April 19. A revolutionary group
                     formed in 1972 following the defeat of the populist
                     candidate General Gustavo Rojas Pinilla in the
                     presidential election of April 19, 1970. Many

observers, not just the M-19, suspect that Rojas Pinilla received more votes than the National Front candidate, Misael Pastrana Borrero, who was declared the winner. An eclectic group of middle-class populist Conservatives and leftists, the M-19 evolved into one of the most powerful guerrilla groups in the country. It declined following its abortive attack on the Palace of Justice in 1985, and in 1990, after protracted negotiations, it signed a peace agreement with the government of Virgilio Barco. In the elections of 1990, the M-19's first presidential candidate, Carlos Pizarro, was assassinated; its second, Antonio Navarro Wolf, won a sizable share of the vote.

municipio   Administrative unit of Colombia, roughly equivalent to a county in the United States. The name of a *municipio* refers both to its largest town, or county seat, and to the county as a whole.

Nueve de abril   See *Bogotazo*.

Ospinista   Follower of the Conservative leader and Colombian President Mariano Ospina Pérez (1946–1950).

Quindío   Region encompassing primarily the present-day departments of Risaralda and Quindío and part of the department of Caldas in the central Andean range. The last to develop and the most productive of Colombia's major coffee-growing regions, it is also the one where small- and medium-size family farms are most prevalent. Although among the areas hardest hit by the Violence of the midtwentieth century, the region has proved resistant to leftist guerrilla activity in recent decades.

sicario   Hired assassin. Typically, a teenage male recruited from the poor peripheral neighborhoods of Medellín and trained (in some cases by foreign, including U.S. and Israeli, mercenaries) in the use of automatic weapons and explosives in schools financed by the drug mafia. Generally devoid of ideological conviction, the *sicario* sees the successful completion of his "job" as proving his manliness and professionalism. The suicidal nature of many *sicario* attacks frustrates even the most careful attempts to protect their potential targets. Victims of *sicarios* range far beyond the three presidential candidates whose assassinations received much international attention during the 1989–90 election campaign; in recent years victims have included members of rival drug organizations, leftist and union leaders, judicial officials and police officers, and prominent figures in the media. Victims also include ordinary citizens who might have angered a relative or an associate or been in the path of a stray bullet or in the destructive radius of a car bomb.

UP   Unión Patriótica (Patriotic Union). Leftist party formed in 1985 to participate in electoral politics. It has close ties to the Communist party and the FARC. Since its founding, the UP has had significant local electoral success. However, hundreds of its activists, including its presidential candidates in 1986, Jaime Pardo Leal, and in 1990, Bernardo Jaramillo Ossa, have been murdered at the hands of right-wing paramilitary groups.

Urabá   Major banana-producing region on the Atlantic Coast in northern Antioquia. During the 1980s the site of violent contention between powerful Communist-led unions, management-supported goon squads, leftist guerrilla groups, and the Colombian army.

UTC   Unión de Trabajadores Colombianos (Union of Colombian Workers). National labor federation formed in the late 1940s with the support of the Conservative party, the Catholic Church, and U.S. labor organizations. From the 1950s through the 1970s it was Colombia's most important labor federation.

Index

Marighella, Carlos: Brazilian guerrilla
    leader, 171
Marín Ospina, Alfredo, 177
Marino Ospina, Iván, 175, 182
Marique, Ramón: author, 90
Marquelita, 181, 188; guerrilla
    movements and, 226–27
Marquetalia, 198
Márquez, José Ignacio de, 13;
    Bolivarianos and, 23
Marroquín, José Manuel, 14; comes to
    power, 16
Marshall, George C.: Pan-American
    Congress and, 81
Martz, John, 111
Marulanda Vélez, Manuel, 93; author,
    308
Marxism: guerrillas and, 3; labor
    system and, 53–55
Marxist-Leninist League, 179
Marxist-Leninist Tendency, 179
Marxist-Leninists, 228
Masseti, Jorge Ricardo: Argentine
    guerrilla leader, 171
Maximilian, Archduke Ferdinand, 28
Mayorga, Silvio: Nicaraguan guerrilla
    leader, 171
Mayorías newspaper, 183
Mayors: election of, 284
McCarthyism, 88
McGreevey, William Paul: on
    casualties in Colombian civil
    wars, 15
Medellín, 131, 135; drug trafficking
    in, 229–30, 263; homicide rate in,
    1–2, 243–44; mayoral elections
    in, 284; power structure in, 249–
    50; research on the Violence in,
    312
Medellín del Ariari: guerrilla activity
    in, 206
Medina, Medófilo, 5, 195, 307; author,
    155; on agrarian issues, 92
Medina Morón, Victor, 177
Meertens, Donny: author, 75, 120, 304
Mejoras (improvements of land), 34,
    65
Melo, José María, 13–14, 16, 26; coup
    attempt against, 17, 24
Meta: EPL in, 210; land colonization
    in, 200, 208

Mexican Revolution (1910), 52;
    compared to the Violence, 91
Ministerials: alternate name for
    Conservatives, 25
Modesto Campos, José, 308
Molano, Alfredo, 3, 6, 164; author,
    196, 309
Molina, Gerardo, 82
Monagas, José Tadeo, 17
Montalvo, José Antonio, 80
Montenegro, 133, 147
Monterrey: power structure in, 249–50
Mora, Leonidas: author, 309
Mora Toro, Libardo, 179
Morales, Carlos Alberto, 179
Morillo, Pablo, 89
Mosquera, Joaquín, 13
Mosquera, Tomás C., 13, 23; comes to
    power, 16; coup against, 18
Mosquera family, 21
Movimiento 26 de Julio: in Cuba, 183
Movimiento Anticomunista
    Colombiano (Colombian
    Anticommunist Movement):
    guerrilla group, 190
Movimiento de Izquierda
    Revolucionaria (MIR): Peruvian
    guerrilla organization, 171
Movimiento de Liberación Nacional
    (MLN), 182
Movimiento Obrero Estudiantil
    Campesino (MOEC), 171, 173–
    74, 176–78
Movimiento Obrero Independiente
    Revolucionario (MOIR), 173, 177
"Movimiento Pan y Libertad":
    guerrilla organization, 188
Movimiento Revolucionario Liberal
    (MRL): guerrilla organization,
    175
Movimientos Políticos Regionales,
    187
Muerte a Abigeos (Death to Rustlers),
    189
Muerte a Invasores, Colaboradores y
    Patrocinadores (Death to Land
    Invaders, Their Collaborators and
    Supporters), 190
Muerte a Secuestradores (Death to
    Kidnappers): death squad, 268–69
Muñoz, Héctor, 263

Varela, Juan de la Cruz: Gaitanista
 leader, 92, 104, 113, 119, 198
Vargas, Hermógenes: guerrilla leader,
 93
Vargas, José María, 17
Vásquez, Jaime: author, 298
Vásquez Castaño, Fabio: guerrilla
 leader, 175, 177
Vásquez Rendón, Pedro, 179
Veintimilla, Ignacio, 26
Velásquez, Eliseo: occupation of
 Puerto López and, 87
Vélez: election fraud in, 26
Venezuela: American Battalion and,
 235; governmental transitions in,
 17
Vereda (districts), 96
Viejo Caldas, 85, 90, 120; declining
 population in, 106
Viento seco (Caicedo), 90
Villarica: Communist activity in, 173;
 guerrilla conflict in,
 180–81
The Violence, 3–7, 14, 42; basic
 components of, 123; death toll
 during, 218; eruption of, 70–71;
 guerrilla activity in, 91–100;
 historiography of, 293–312; in
 Cali, 241–59; in Quindío, 125–
 51; interpretations of, 75–123;
 labor movement and, 51–72;
 nature of research on, 311–12

*Violence, Conflict, and Politics in
 Colombia* (Oquist), 242, 301
Violencia y desarrollo (Fajardo),
 303
Viotá: Communist party in, 67–68,
 104, 180
Voting fraud: in 19th-century
 Colombia, 26–27

Walton, John: on social structure in
 Cali, 248–50
War of the Supremes, 13, 16
War of the Thousand Days, 12–13, 16,
 29, 57; Bergquist on, 14–15;
 casualties of, 14
War of Villarica, 198–99, 208
Worker-Student-Peasant Movement
 (MOEC), 122

Yacopí: destruction of, 89;
 reconstruction of, 107
Yon Sosa, Antonio: Guatemalan
 guerrilla leader, 171
Yopal: guerrilla activity in, 103
Yosa, Isauro: guerrilla leader, 93,
 198
Youth of the Revolutionary Liberal
 Movement (JMRL), 177
Yumbo: M-19 and, 253

Zabala, Vladimir, 186
Zalamea, Jorge, 82

Latin American Silhouettes
Studies in History and Culture

William H. Beezley and
Judith Ewell
Editors

Volumes Published

William H. Beezley and Judith Ewell, eds., *The Human Tradition in Latin America: The Twentieth Century* (1987). Cloth ISBN 0-8420-2283-X Paper ISBN 0-8420-2284-8

Judith Ewell and William H. Beezley, eds., *The Human Tradition in Latin America: The Nineteenth Century* (1989). Cloth ISBN 0-8420-2331-3 Paper ISBN 0-8420-2332-1

David G. LaFrance, *The Mexican Revolution in Puebla, 1908–1913: The Maderista Movement and the Failure of Liberal Reform* (1989). ISBN 0-8420-2293-7

Mark A. Burkholder, *Politics of a Colonial Career: José Baquíjano and the Audiencia of Lima* (1990). Cloth ISBN 0-8420-2353-4 Paper ISBN 0-8420-2352-6

Kenneth M. Coleman and George C. Herring, eds. (with Foreword by Daniel Oduber), *Understanding the Central American Crisis: Sources of Conflict, U.S. Policy, and Options for Peace* (1991). Cloth ISBN 0-8420-2382-8   Paper ISBN 0-8420-2383-6

Carlos B. Gil, ed., *Hope and Frustration: Interviews with Leaders of Mexico's Political Opposition* (1991). Cloth ISBN 0-8420-2395-X Paper ISBN 0-8420-2396-8

Charles Bergquist, Gonzalo Sánchez, and Ricardo Peñaranda, eds., *Violence in Colombia: The Contemporary Crisis in Historical Perspective* (1991). Cloth ISBN 0-8420-2369-0   Paper ISBN 0-8420-2376-3

Heidi Zogbaum, *B. Traven: A Vision of Mexico* (1992). ISBN 0-8420-2392-5